*Academy
and
Community*

Academy and Community

The Foundation
of the
French Historical Profession

William R. Keylor

Harvard University Press
Cambridge, Massachusetts
1975

© Copyright 1975 by the President and Fellows of Harvard College
All rights reserved
Library of Congress Catalog Card Number 74-81867
ISBN 0-674-00255-5
Printed in the United States of America
Publication of this book has been aided by a grant from the Andrew W. Mellon Foundation

*To my mother
and
the memory of my father
with deepest gratitude*

Acknowledgments

This study grew out of a doctoral dissertation which I completed under the supervision of Professor Jacques Barzun of Columbia University, who sponsored the project, and Professor Robert O. Paxton of the same institution, who served as second reader. In addition to their many other kindnesses, both furnished me with instructive comments and criticisms, for which I am deeply grateful. Professors Rudolph Binion, Arthur Danto, Georg G. Iggers, Bert M.-P. Leefmans, Fritz K. Ringer, Nancy Lyman Roelker, and Fritz Stern read the entire manuscript at various stages of its progress and offered useful suggestions for revision. I also owe a special debt to my colleagues Sidney A. Burrell and John G. Gagliardo, whose encouragement and counsel were of great help, as well as to my friends Hilah Thomas and Martin Siegel, with whom I discussed certain questions of fact and interpretation. I profited from the opportunity to test many of the ideas contained in this book before a number of attentive and helpful audiences, including the history departments of the University of Illinois at Urbana and Brown University, the Brandeis University-Boston University Program on Social Thought and Context, and the New England Historical Association.

My thanks also go to the Fulbright-Hays Commission of the United States government for providing me with an Advanced Teaching Fellowship which enabled me to spend a year consulting pertinent source material in various archives and libraries in Paris; to the Woodrow Wilson Foundation, which facilitated the completion of the manuscript with a dissertation fellowship; to the American Council of Learned Societies, the Research Council of Rutgers University, and the Graduate School of Boston University for furnishing supplementary financial assistance. I also wish to express my appreciation to the staffs of the following libraries for their unfailing courtesy and advice: the New York Public Library; the Boston Public Library; Widener Library of Harvard University; Butler Library of Columbia University; La Bibliothèque Nationale; Les Archives Nationales; La Bibliothèque de la Préfecture de Police, Département de la Seine; La Bibliothèque Sainte-Geneviève; La Bibliothèque Mazarine; La Bibliothèque Jacques Doucet; La Bibliothèque de l'Arsenal; and the Library of the British Museum.

It is a pleasure to record my debts to Marie Allen for her assistance in typing the manuscript in its original form; to Virginia Xanthos for her assistance during the early stages of its preparation; to Mark Dyer for his help in compiling the bibliography; to William Gum, formerly of Harvard University Press, whose efficiency in handling the manuscript from submission to acceptance demonstrated once again why he is held in such high regard by members of the historical profession; and to Gordon Wright and Bryce Lyon, for forcing me to rethink certain of my conclusions.

In conclusion, there are three people without whose encouragement this study would never have been conceived, let alone completed. The author would never have embarked on a career in modern French history had it not been for the inspiration of Professor Gordon Wright of Stanford University. The generosity of my mother, Thelma Keylor, in typing preliminary drafts of the manuscript was merely the most recent expression of a lifelong commitment to easing the burdens of those who have had the good fortune to know and love her. I know of no way to record an adequate acknowledgment of the contribution made to this book by my wife, Rheta Grenoble Keylor. By mentioning her innumerable suggestions for improvement of both style and substance, her successful efforts to clarify particularly elusive questions of interpretation, and her admirable skill in counteracting pessimism about the possibility of meeting various deadlines, I do not begin to do justice to the many ways in which she has left her imprint on this work.

Contents

Prologue 1

Part One The Era of Hopes and Accomplishments
1 Prelude to Reform, 1866–1870 19
2 History's Role in the Regeneration of the Fatherland 36
3 The Institutionalization of Historical Study in the New Sorbonne 55
4 In Search of La Méthode Historique 75
5 History as Civic Instruction: The Conflict of Science and Patriotism 90
6 The Record of Scholarly Achievement, 1876–1900 101

Part Two Interdisciplinary Conflicts and Revised Objectives
7 The Challenge of the Science of Society 111
8 Henri Berr and the "Terrible Craving for Synthesis" 125
9 The Dissolution of the Republican Consensus 141
10 Social Science and the Restoration of the Republican Synthesis 163

Epilogue 208
Appendices
A Number of students enrolled in each faculty, University of Paris, 1901–1910 218
B Teaching positions in history, French and German universities, 1904–1905 219
  Increase in number of teaching positions in history, French and German universities, 1895–1896 to 1904–1905 219
C Teaching positions (professeur, professeur adjoint, maître de conférences, chargé de cours) in nonscientific disciplines, French universities, 1895–1896 220
D Teaching positions in nonscientific disciplines, German universities, 1895–1896 222
E Number of chairs in Paris and provincial faculties, Ecole Normale Supérieure, Collège de France, 1865–1966 224
F Theses submitted for the diploma of advanced studies (diplôme d'études supérieures), faculties of letters of French universities, 1907–1909 225
  Inaugural dissertations submitted for the doctor of philosophy degree, faculties of philosophy of German universities, 1906–1908 226
G Foreign students enrolled in the Faculty of Letters of Paris, 1902–1910 227
  Foreign students enrolled in all faculties, University of Paris, 1901–1910 227
  Students (French and foreign) enrolled in all faculties, University of Paris, 1901–1910 228
H Course offerings in history departments of selected Parisian institutions of higher learning, 1914 229

Notes 231
Works Cited 266
Index 279

Academy and Community

Prologue

Few students of recent historiography would dispute the conclusion arrived at independently by two distinguished historians, one American and the other English, that France has paced all other European nations, both quantitatively and qualitatively, in the production of historical scholarship since the end of the First World War.[1] A cursory exposure to the works of such celebrated historians as Henri Berr, Albert Mathiez, Ernest Labrousse, Marc Bloch, Lucien Febvre, Georges Lefebvre, Fernand Braudel, Albert Soboul, and Pierre Goubert, not to speak of the dozens of less renowned contributions to monographic historical scholarship that have appeared in the *Annales*, the *Revue de synthèse historique*, the *Revue historique*, the *Revue d'histoire moderne et contemporaine*, and *La Révolution française*, would surely elicit from even the most hardened of Gallophobes the grudging admission that if the foundation of modern historical scholarship in the nineteenth century was a German accomplishment, its continuation and enrichment in the twentieth century must be attributed in large part to the labors of the French.

To anyone familiar with the general development of historical studies in the modern world, it may seem hardly worth pausing to remark that the site of the revival of historical studies in twentieth century France was that nation's university system. It was the German academic tradition, after all, that developed and disseminated during the preceding century what came to be known as the methods of modern historical scholarship, and by the First World War most historical research of a serious nature was being conducted in institutions of higher learning. But to make the ahistorical assumption that such was always the case would be to accept as given what in fact was the consequence of a long and complicated process. Indeed, the monumental achievement of the handful of scholars who managed, in the face of formidable obstacles, to prepare the groundwork for an academic historical profession in France is a development that deserves, and has yet to receive, sufficient scholarly attention.

This book is an attempt to fill in that lacuna in our knowledge. It has two dominant themes that are interrelated both topically and chronologically. The first is the establishment of history as an academic discipline in the French university system between 1870 and 1914, and the second is the formation of the "scientific" school of history during the same period and in the same institutional framework. It will presently become clear that these two dates were selected not arbitrarily, but because it was during those four decades, between the Franco-Prussian War and World War I, that the French historical profession was organized, furnished with a set of professional goals, and provided with the theoretical and institutional means of achieving them. A new generation of French historians succeeded in transforming the craft of history, which had formerly been an avocation of journalists, politicians, men of letters, and amateurs from other walks of life, into a scholarly discipline pursued by specialists who had been trained in and were subsequently employed by the state university system. It was this new group of specialists in the study and writing of history that was responsible for severing the umbilical cord that had tied history to its two parent disciplines, literature and philosophy, thereby enabling it to hitch its wagon to the advancing juggernaut of science.

But it would be misleading to represent this as a monographic examination of the birth and growth of a single academic profession. For the historians treated in this book harbored ambitions for their craft that far exceeded those entertained by the members of other scholarly professions. They intended to establish history not merely as a reputable academic discipline, but as the veritable *science maîtresse* of the entire university system. Though this ambition was never fully realized, the French historical profession did play a predominant role in the educational reform movement that created the modern French university system during the last quarter of the nineteenth century, and its most illustrious members proceeded to occupy prominent positions within the revised structure of higher education. The profession spawned a number of public-spirited scholars and pedagogues who dominated the ministerial councils that revised the educational curricula and filled key posts in educational administration, textbook production, pedagogical journalism, and the management of public archives. These multifarious activities earned for them an authority and influence far out of proportion to their numbers and ensured the widest possible circulation of their ideas in French academic circles.

Nor was their influence limited to the higher echelons of the educational system. The monolithic character of the French *Université*, an untranslatable term denoting a vast pyramid of instruction with the primary schools at the base, the secondary schools at the center, and the universities and the Ministry of Public Instruction at the apex, ensured a rapid and thorough diffusion throughout the entire system of the guiding principles formulated at the top. The historians installed at the summit of the educational hierarchy enjoyed the privilege of seeing their ideas filter down to the *lycée* and primary school level through the instructors they had trained, the textbooks they had written, and the curricula they had devised. Their influence extended not only to history classes proper, but also to the various courses organized under the rubric of "civic instruction," which had been introduced after the defeat of 1870 for the purpose of instilling patriotic sentiments in the nation's youth. The French historians regarded themselves as more than merely recorders and communicators of their nation's heritage. They were also molders of opinion who had been entrusted with the task of employing the lessons of history to restore a sense of national pride among the citizens of a recently humiliated fatherland in search of regeneration and revenge. Hence, we will have occasion to examine the sources and consequences of the patriotic uses of history.

On another level, this book must be regarded as an essay on the political uses of history. As the nineteenth century drew to a close, the historians of the French universities, who had served for the better part of two decades as the principal agents of France's patriotic revival, were invited to assume an additional burden that further broadened the scope and purpose of historical education in France. The appearance of extremist political movements at both ends of the political spectrum in the wake of the Dreyfus Affair constituted the first serious challenge to the political legitimacy of the Third Republic. As functionaries of the republican state and messengers bearing the republican catechism, the academic historians, in conjunction with their colleagues in other branches of the university, placed their scholarly and pedagogical talents at the disposal of the harried regime with the intention of repairing the republican consensus that had been disrupted by the political turmoil of the *fin de siècle*. The promoters of the eclectic ideal of patriotism that permeated the French educational system in the waning years of the nineteenth century became the exponents of a specific political creed, the ideology of the Radical Republic, in the early years of the twentieth.

No one, least of all the historian, needs to be reminded that historical scholarship has frequently been used for partisan political purposes. In Western European historiography, the writings of Guizot, Treitschke, and Macaulay are representative examples of history conceived as a political apologetic, the first for constitutional monarchism, the second for authoritarian German nationalism, and the last for English Whiggery. But all three were products of an age in which history functioned as a branch of literature and literature as a servant of politics. During the last quarter of the nineteenth century, a new school of French historians, intoxicated with the newly-acquired scientific pretensions of their discipline, began to herald the approaching demise of the polemical period of historical writing. Historical scholarship, the argument ran, was on the verge of developing an objective approach to its subject matter that would liberate it from its role as a handmaiden of politics and establish it as a science immunized against the influences of ideology. Yet the mounting political involvement of the very historians in France who were announcing the advent of *la science historique* was, as we shall see, itself dramatic testimony to the persistence of the traditional connection between history and politics.

It may be instructive to preface this study with a cursory comparison of the academic historical professions in France and the United States during the period to be covered. Since this book is addressed primarily to an American public, such a comparison may serve the reader who possesses a general familiarity with the institutional framework of the American academic professions but is unaware of the special characteristics peculiar to their French counterparts. It seems to me unlikely that a book of this nature could have been written about the academic historical profession in the United States in view of the palpable dissimilarities between the educational systems and scholarly professions of the two countries. The decentralized institutional structure of American education has engendered a degree of diversity, pluralism, and heterogeneity that contrasts sharply with the highly centralized, monolithic, homogeneous educational system of France. At the level of higher education, the proliferation of state universities and privately endowed colleges, not to speak of the numerous schools with religious affiliations, created an institutional barrier to the comprehensive nationwide programs of academic innovation that serve as the subject of this study. Moreover, the decentralized system of decision-making in American higher education has, at least until rather recently, enabled the American university to avoid the complicated political entanglements and ideological controversies at the national level that proved to be an inevitable consequence of direct control of education in France by the central government.

The pluralistic character of American higher education was reproduced in the individual scholarly professions, and the American historical profession was no exception to this rule. Herein lies another striking contrast between the French and American situations. A major portion of this study is devoted to describing the emergence of a unitary school of academic history in late nineteenth century France. The foundation of such a school was made possible by the fact that the most prominent historians in France at that time shared a common fund of formative experiences that fostered a collective spirit of collegiality and professionalism. With few exceptions, all of these men studied at the same academic training ground (the exclusive Ecole Normale Supérieure), served their apprenticeships at the most coveted teaching posts in secondary or higher education, returned to the Latin Quarter to accept appointments at one or more of the institutions that collectively comprised the nerve center of historical study in France (the Ecole Normale, the Ecole Pratique des Hautes Etudes, and the Sorbonne), became either editors or regular contributors to the growing number of professional periodicals, and enlisted in the post-1870 campaign to revitalize and reorganize the French educational system. This institutional network of intradisciplinary relationships eventually produced a system of professional standards and regulations, which, in turn, enhanced the development of an *esprit de corps* among French academic historians that their counterparts in other nations, trained in less uniform circumstances and scattered more widely throughout their respective countries, could never hope to equal. The absence of such a pattern of common educational influences among American historians precluded the appearance of any such American school of history. The closest that one could come to such a designation would be to identify a set of relatively homogeneous subgroups of historians within a broader, heterogeneous collectivity. One can point to the emergence of a Columbia school of history during the decade prior to the First World War, for example, without being accused of succumbing to the temptation of excessive schematization, provided that one is careful to specify that the New History of Harry Elmer Barnes, James Harvey Robinson, and their colleagues on Morningside Heights represented merely one of several competing factions vying for predominance in the American historical profession. Even when analyzing the more homogeneous historical profession of nineteenth century Germany, one must be careful to distinguish the Berlin school from the Göttingen school from the South German school, and so forth in order accurately to capture the relatively pluralistic character of German higher learning. But to speak of a Parisian school of French history during this period would be to indulge in excessive and misleading scrupulosity, roughly analogous to discussing the Bayreuth school of Wagnerian opera.

Perhaps the most striking difference between the American and French professions appears in their respective attitudes toward the problems of historical methodology. American historians have displayed an egregious lack of interest in the methodological controversies that have long occupied the attention of European historians and which dominated the writings of the French historians between 1870 and the turn of the century.[2] The reasons for this disparity have no bearing on the subject of investigation here and therefore will not be explored. I mention it only in anticipation of a question that is likely to occur to the reader whose familiarity with continental European historiography is minimal: why is so much attention devoted in this book to abstruse disputations concerning historical methodology? The answer is a simple one: because methodological issues dominated the discussions and debates among historians in the formative decades of the French historical profession. The most perplexing and elusive problem with which they had to grapple was that of formulating a universally acceptable definition of the historical method that would justify the institutionalization of history as an autonomous academic discipline. They encountered little difficulty in vindicating history's claim to pedagogical utility in a nation renowned for its intense historical consciousness, particularly in a period when public officials themselves recognized the potential uses of historical instruction in elementary schools as a generator of patriotism and "good citizenship." But their desire to advance history's claim to the status of a separate academic discipline also required persuasive proof that the historical profession possessed a distinctive epistemology appropriate to the study of man and society, an established assortment of methodological tools sufficiently different from those employed by the existing branches of humanistic scholarship to justify its claims to an independent status.[3]

The French historians succeeded in carving out a preeminent niche for themselves in the hierarchical system of French education by convincingly demonstrating that the study of history represented a unique enterprise that distinguished it from the two dominant humanistic disciplines in the universities: philosophy and literature. They dismissed the latter two endeavors as obsolete remnants of a bygone age when man and society were studied by ill-equipped amateurs trained in the inappropriate arts of metaphysics, rhetoric, and belles-lettres, and proposed that they be supplanted by the new discipline of history, whose practitioners were prepared to apply the spirit and methods of the natural sciences to the study of social phenomena. They expected history, the empirical science *par excellence,* to liberate French social thought from the straitjacket of formal philosophy and classical literature that had retarded its development during the nineteenth century, while Germanic and Anglo-Saxon civilization was experiencing an enviable vitality. During the very years that confidence in the applicability of scientific methods to the study of human behavior was beginning to dissipate in other European countries,[4] the French historians capitalized on the persistence of that faith in their own society to advertise their discipline as the principal custodian of the scientific spirit in the French university.

But once they had succeeded in institutionalizing the study of history in the university system and had added the term *la science historique* to the academic lexicon, their efforts to develop and refine an acceptable definition of the scientific historical method plunged them into a morass of ambiguities, inconsistencies, and convoluted explanations. These difficulties were in large part due to the fact that all of the leading proponents of scientific history in France were products of a conventional education which emphasized such traditional subjects as classical languages, French literature, rhetoric, and philosophy. Having had little or no exposure to scientific studies, a defect in their intellectual formation which they bitterly regretted in later life, they tended to romanticize and idealize the scientific method without ever having acquired a precise notion of what it comprised. Their resentment at the inadequacy of their own educational experience led many of them to adopt a simplistic conception of the scientific method which embodied many of the very virtues that they themselves had sorely missed. Whereas philosophy had taught them to reason in a theoretical, deductive, a priori manner, science would alert the next generation to the superiority of practical, experimental, empirical thought; whereas rhetoric had instructed them in the arts of verbal eloquence and formal declamation, science would confine them and their charges to a Spartan regimen of patient observation and analysis; whereas classical languages and literature had shaped them into cultured dilettantes imbued with reverence for the superficial elegance of "general ideas," science would orient French civilization in the future toward the particular, the factual, the concrete; and the fruit of this intellectual transformation was to be a science of history that would address itself to the "crude facts" of historical reality contained in the archival documents, waiting to be disclosed. The French historians' exaggerated confidence in the efficacy of the scientific method and its applicability to historical scholarship can thus partially be explained as a compensatory reaction against the formalistic, speculative, deductive variety of social theory that had long been associated with the French intellectual tradition.

This tendency was reinforced by their largely inaccurate understanding of the historical method that had been developed in the German universities by Leopold von Ranke and his disciples, who had contributed greatly to the vitality of German higher education in the nineteenth century and, it was widely believed, had inspired the national revival that culminated in the war of 1870. Following France's disastrous military defeat, the French academic historians tended to adopt uncritically the dichotomous conception of Germanic erudition and profundity (thought to characterize serious scholars who confined themselves to investigations of the "facts" of historical "reality") and Latin speculativeness and superficiality (thought to characterize frivolous dilettantes who delighted in fashioning intellectual arabesques that were bereft of substance and unrelated to concrete developments in the phenomenal world).

Such distortions of the German theory of historicism were common throughout most of Western Europe during the nineteenth century and have only recently been subjected to the type of scholarly criticism that they deserve. In his English edition of major selections from Leopold von Ranke's collected works, Georg G. Iggers has made the important observation that Ranke's oft-quoted admonition to historians about the necessity of reconstructing history "as it really was" has been misunderstood by disciples and critics alike. He has shown that Ranke's conception of *Historismus* did not imply, as so many historians have believed, a "purely factual recreation of the past." Iggers remarks that this misconception, which fails to recognize that Ranke's historiography "rested on certain assumptions regarding the nature of history and politics," has often led to a "soulless fact-oriented positivism which Ranke rejected, but with which he was often wrongly identified."[5] The present study purports to demonstrate, among other things, that such misinterpretations of German historicist doctrine were particularly widespread in French academic circles after the debacle of 1870.

Professor Iggers's reference to a "soulless fact-oriented positivism" brings to mind a rather annoying problem of semantics that has recurred throughout the preparation of this study and which requires some elaboration here. Both the defenders and detractors of the methodological approach adopted by the French academic historians between 1870 and 1914 frequently designated it as "positivism" in precisely the same sense that Iggers has given to the term, namely, the belief that the facts of history are essentially self-explanatory and do not require the mediation of preliminary hypotheses, interpretative theories, or operational definitions. From this epistemological assumption it follows that the historian's principal function is to locate, accumulate, collocate, and authenticate historical documents, and that such procedures constitute a scientific approach to the study of history. But the catch-all term "positivism" also surfaced from time to time in the writings of theorists who used it to denote a quite different conception of scientific history. In this second sense positivism assumed a more general denotation, that is, the conviction that history could develop analogues of the organic or mechanistic models employed in the natural and physical sciences and apply them to the study of human behavior. To increase even further the imprecision of this overworked term, the author of a recent work on the subject entreats us to reserve its use for specific reference to the philosophical system of Auguste Comte, who first popularized it.[6]

Several other terms have appeared in the historiographical literature of late to designate one or the other of the first two concepts.[7] In a forthcoming work on the development of historical thought in modern Europe, Iggers himself has adopted a new descriptive term, "hermeneutic historicism," in reference to the event-oriented, exegetical approach to historical study.[8] Norman Cantor and Richard Schneider have coined the adjective "scientific-nominalist" to designate the "new breed of academic historians" of the late nineteenth century who emphasized the importance of textual criticism and who were "hostile to any general and meaningful interpretation" of the historical events described in the documents.[9] Fritz K. Ringer has suggested that the term "hyper-empiricism" might supply a more precise rendering of the meaning of the same concept. The somewhat confusing and virtually untranslatable term *histoire historisante*, coined by Henri Berr and kept in circulation by Lucien Febvre, has recently reappeared in a French treatise on historical methodology as a label for the French branch of this school of history.[10] The word "scientism," frequently used as a synonym for positivism, suffers from the same imprecision that afflicts the latter term; that is, it has been employed both in the limited sense to designate an antitheoretical empiricism as well as in the more general sense to signify the belief in the applicability of the methods of the natural sciences to the study of human society.

Confronted with these multifarious semantic difficulties, I have decided to avoid using any single term to characterize the school of French history treated in this study. I have chosen instead to present a detailed description of the methodological and epistemological assumptions that formed the basis of this school, of the way in which the study of history was institutionalized in the French university system, and of the sociopolitical context within which that institutionalization occurred. If the term positivism has crept into my prose from time to time, it is only because it was that term, rather than "scientism," "hyper-empiricism," "scientific-nominalism," *histoire historisante*, "hermeneutic historicism," or any other term of relatively recent vintage, that was most frequently employed during the period under consideration. This final warning to the reader that the word is used here in the fact-oriented sense, rather than in any of the other senses described above, should be sufficient to preclude further confusion on the subject.

A related semantic controversy surrounds the precise meaning that the founders of the French historical profession gave to the term *la science*. Like the German *die Wissenschaft*, the French *la science* contains a double entendre that enables it to be rendered in English as either "science" or "scholarship." It is necessary to resolve this ambiguity at the outset of this study not merely in the interest of accurate translation, but also because the French historians' use of the term implied certain important commitments of an epistemological and methodological nature. Fritz Ringer has remarked that the German historians after 1890 used the term *die Wissenschaft* to support their contention that the type of historical scholarship in which they were engaged was a humanistic and philosophical branch of learning rather than a scientific type of investigation (an enterprise for which they reserved the specific terms *naturwissenschaftlich* and *positivistisch*).[11] The French historians employed the term *la science* for precisely the opposite purpose, that is, in such a way as to establish a distinction between their scholarly discipline and the humanistic tradition and to identify it with the tradition of the natural sciences. When they intended to refer to scholarship in the English sense, they resorted to the term *l'érudition*. But when describing the nature of their scholarship, its methodological assumptions, its procedures, or the results obtained, they invariably employed the terms *la science* or *la science historique*.

The second section of this study traces the growing disenchantment with the nature of historical scholarship in France on the part of critics both inside and outside the profession and treats the historians' response to these multifaceted criticisms. The most serious challenge to the methodological assumptions of the scientific historical school emerged from the ranks of the sociologists, who had begun to achieve academic recognition of their own discipline in the French university system by the turn of the century. Like the leading academic historians, Emile Durkheim and most of his colleagues had received their intellectual training in philosophy. But they had never experienced the fervent feeling of revulsion at the inadequacies of their education that had prompted the historians to repudiate the philosophical tradition and attempt to erect a scientific scaffolding for their discipline. Most French sociologists pointed with pride to the philosophical roots of their science, chided the historians for their narrow conception of the scientific method, and proposed a bold program of social research to be carried out under the auspices of academic sociology.

Similar rumblings of discontent with scientific history began to appear on the periphery of the historical profession itself by the turn of the century. A small but vocal band of scholars loosely associated with Henri Berr and his *Revue de synthèse historique* began to voice serious misgivings about the direction that academic history was taking, particularly the trend toward specialization and the emphasis on factual documentation. Inspired by the vitalist philosophy of Emile Boutroux, this group inveighed against what it described as the arid, esoteric approach of scientific history for overemphasizing the importance of the past for its own sake at the expense of the more urgent concerns of the present. They resolved to breath new life into the scientific study of the past by expanding its horizons to embrace the totality of human experience. They urged historians to adopt a broader, more synthetic, more philosophical posture by incorporating the concepts and methods of the theoretical social sciences, an outlook which they hoped would impel the scholar to identify laws, trends, and general tendencies in the past rather than merely to accumulate a meaningless collection of unique, isolated facts.

The French historians' subsequent modification of their original attitudes toward the nature of their calling was less a direct response to these probing critiques from the sociologists and dissident, philosophically-oriented historians than an indirect consequence of their participation in the political turmoil that convulsed French society at the turn of the century. Their decision to join the sociologists and the bulk of the academic intelligentsia in defending the political institutions of the Third Republic against the ideological onslaughts that issued from the revolutionary left and the counterrevolutionary right signified the acquisition of a renewed confidence in the relevance of history to the problems of the present. This descent into the political arena helped to blunt the criticism that had previously been directed at academic history in France for its excessive specialization and its preoccupation with antiquarian minutiae, and to establish it as an integral component of the tradition of social science in the French university.

Since questions of historical methodology will recur throughout these pages, it seems appropriate at this juncture to furnish an explicit formulation of the methodological assumptions underlying the study itself. I must first record my suspicion that its methodological posture is unlikely to meet the particular specifications of the intellectual historian, who may feel somewhat uncomfortable with two aspects of it. First, he may object to the seemingly inordinate attention devoted to intellectuals of the second order, minor thinkers whose methodological and scholarly writings were hardly lasting contributions to French thought. He may make the legitimate observation that the work of a Gabriel Monod or a Charles Seignobos has not survived the test of time, whereas the historical scholarship of a Fustel de Coulanges, an Albert Sorel, or a Hippolyte Taine has continued to serve as the subject of spirited discussion among specialists in their respective fields. The same criticism has been directed at Julien Benda for having focused on the treacherous activities of minor "clerks" in his famous study of the French intelligentsia, *The Betrayal of the Intellectuals*.

My response to such a charge would be simply to point out that while the select group of historians whose thoughts and activities dominate the following story were neither the finest historical minds nor the authors of the most memorable contributions to historical scholarship of their generation, it was nevertheless through their efforts, rather than through those of their more illustrious colleagues, that the scientific historical tradition was firmly implanted in the French university system. Sorel, Taine, and Fustel de Coulanges, perhaps the three most renowned French historians of the last half of the nineteenth century, did not play prominent roles in the campaign to create an academic historical profession after 1870. The first two were largely free-lance scholars who participated only peripherally in academic life after the Franco-Prussian War in the privately-endowed Ecole Libre des Sciences Politiques, an institution which had no formal ties to the *Université*. The celebrated Fustel de Coulanges, though an influential member of the university system at the Ecole Normale and the Sorbonne, was not a member of the inner circle of historians who formed the modern school of French history. Indeed, all three of these eminent scholars were to come under attack from the leading members of the historical profession for the alleged deficiencies of their approach to historical scholarship.[12]

It is also possible that the historian of ideas will complain that I have not always defined the doctrines of the French academic historians with sufficient precision. This shortcoming, if indeed it is one, resulted from my concern for faithfully rendering the substance of these men's historical thought. In many cases their own explanations of these conceptions were muddled, confused, and ambiguous. The single theme that held together the tenuous threads of their methodological writings was their faith in the applicability of the scientific method to historical research, but even the expression of that conviction suffered from the imprecisions discussed above.

I would also not be surprised if this study were to disappoint certain practitioners of the social sciences, specifically those researchers who are committed to alternative means of studying elite groups in society. The empirical-minded social scientist may regret that I have confined my investigation to the dozen or so historians at the top of the professional hierarchy, rather than, say, employing quantitative methods to determine the social origins, political preferences, and career patterns of the entire profession. Or perhaps the more theoretically-inclined social scientist may fault my study for the absence of theoretical models or "ideal types" of the institutionalization of academic innovations similar to those employed by social scientists such as Terry N. Clark and Joseph Ben-David.[13]

I have no desire to disparage or dismiss any of these alternative ways of addressing the subject of my study, for I consider them all to be legitimate and worthwhile exercises in historical analysis. The history of ideas, notwithstanding the criticism that it has recently received, continues to be a viable and important branch of history. It will always be useful to have scholars who are adept at elucidating the seminal works of exceptional intellects and evaluating them according to the criteria of internal consistency, logical rigor, and verisimilitude. Nor do I intend to denigrate the techniques of quantitative history, an approach to the past which I consider valuable so long as its limitations are recognized and acknowledged. Though it is obvious that quantification is a much less useful tool for determining the social functions of ideas than for identifying recurrent patterns of human behavior, I could certainly conceive of the possibility of a statistical analysis of the personnel that comprised the French historical profession during the period covered by this book. I need hardly mention that an investigation of this type would, by its very nature, pose different questions and produce different conclusions from those to be found herein.

Similarly, it would be useful for historians to have at their disposal heuristic models of the institutionalization of academic innovations that could be applied to the historical profession in France. I have myself refrained from explicitly formulating such hypothetical constructs, though I am fully aware that my mind has implicitly organized, selected, and discarded data, and that unstated and in some cases unrecognized assumptions have shaped the material that follows. I prefer to conceive of the present study as being located at the point of intersection of intellectual history and institutional history. The ideas that were articulated by the historians treated in this book, however inchoate, crude, and contradictory they may appear in retrospect to the fastidious student of historiography, were rapidly transformed into social facts of interest to the institutional historian once they began to be introduced into the French educational system (and thereby transmitted to the educated elite of the nation) by the disciples these historians had trained, the textbooks they had written, and the curricula they had devised. My method of unraveling the tangled sequences of causation that eventually left France with a historical profession dominated by a particular school of history is that of a historian seeking to interpret a series of developments which I believe to have exercised an enduring influence on modern French culture. I have striven to relate the following developments not as they "really were," nor as I interpret them through the perspective of heuristic models or operational hypotheses, but rather as I have been able to reconstruct them in spite of, or perhaps more accurately, with the assistance of, my own prejudices, presuppositions, and preferences.

Having disclaimed any a priori, conceptual framework for my study, however, I must hasten to add that in the final stages of my writing I happened upon a theoretical treatise which postulated a model of the behavior of "scientific communities" that resembled in many respects my own conception of the "community of scholars" that created the historical profession in France. Thomas Kuhn's *The Structure of Scientific Revolutions* was already a decade old when I first noticed a passing reference to its author as "an imaginative historian of science . . . from whom historians in every field have much to learn."[14] Though allusions to Kuhn's work continued to crop up in my reading,[15] I remained unappreciative of its relevance to my own research until my *American Historical Review* arrived containing an article by David A. Hollinger entitled "T. H. Kuhn's Theory of Science and Its Implications for History."[16] In this piece Hollinger presented a brief summation of Kuhn's thesis regarding the emergence of schools of scientific thought and the ways in which they manage to achieve universal acceptance of their "shared paradigms," or commonly-held epistemological assumptions, and then proceeded to construct a "Kuhnian" model of the historical profession which, to my surprise and delight, seemed to fit the description of the historical fraternity treated in my study.

My subsequent reading of Kuhn's work itself, to which I had been drawn by such a circuitous route, furnished numerous instances in which his conceptualization of the behavior of scientific communities described rather accurately the actual behavior of that group of French historians who tried so desperately at the end of the nineteenth century to achieve for their guild the status of a scientific profession. His theoretical analysis of the relation between scientific tradition and innovation, his notion of a scientific consensus which is enforced by an intricate reward system administered by the professional elite, and his appreciation of the relationship between political transformations and alterations of scientific world-views, are but a few of the points on which his theory tended to reinforce the conclusions that I had reached a posteriori.[17]

My discovery of Kuhn forced me to reexamine with greater care the writings of Ben-David, Clark, and other social scientists, which I had previously read with great interest but which my historian's prejudices had impelled me to discount as abstract exercises in sociological theorizing of little relevance to the historian and the concrete reality that he seeks to understand. Largely as a result of this reexamination I have acquired a grudging respect for the type of model-building that social scientists engage in with such alacrity. It goes without saying that many of the conclusions that I have drawn after what I hope has been a thorough and judicious consideration of the historical evidence on which this study is based fail to conform neatly to the theoretical models of academic innovations proposed by these and other social scientists. I continue to believe that the nominalist criticism that historians customarily direct at social scientists represents a necessary corrective to theoretical flights of fancy that too often sacrifice historical accuracy in the interests of conceptual harmony. But the profit that I have derived from testing my historical interpretations against the relevant heuristic hypotheses of sociology[18] has led me to the very same conclusion that the French historians reached in the early years of the twentieth century: to wit, that both disciplines are bound to achieve mutual enrichment through cooperation and intellectual interchange.

Part One
The Era of Hopes and Accomplishments

1
Prelude to Reform, 1866–1870

"The vast majority of writings on the historical method of investigation and on the art of writing history in France . . . are superficial, insipid, and unreadable."[1] This sweeping, ungenerous evaluation, recorded as the nineteenth century drew to a close, was the synoptic reflection of the co-directors of the new historiography course at the University of Paris as they surveyed the unimpressive record of historical scholarship in France from the Revolution to the Franco-Prussian War. Such critical estimates of the achievements of their professional forebears were quite prevalent among the generation of French historians who began their careers in the shadow of the military humiliation of 1870. The widely held belief that the discipline of history in France was defective for lack of a universally accepted set of methodological principles caused many of these young scholars to turn their backs on that tradition and seek ways of endowing their ancient craft with a professional orientation, an achievement which, they had come to realize, necessitated the transformation of history into a respectable academic discipline. In the last quarter of the nineteenth century, the energy and idealism of an entire generation of historians was harnessed to a single, overriding purpose: the foundation of a historical profession in the French university system.

Though this movement owed its major impetus to the military debacle, it originated in the last decade of the Second Empire. It was during that period that the pioneers of professional history in France first became aware of the seemingly insuperable obstacles to their professional plans posed by the deteriorating condition of French higher education and began to devise means of transforming the French universities into suitable sites for the revival of historical studies. The decrepitude of the educational system that had once been the envy of the Western world first came to public attention during the tenure at the Ministry of Public Instruction of Victor Duruy, a respected historian of antiquity whom the Emperor had installed at the rue de Grenelle in 1863. It was through the efforts of his ministry that the groundwork was laid for the creation of an academic historical profession in France.

Long before his ministerial appointment, Duruy had discovered and begun to bemoan the inadequacies of historical instruction in French schools. His original inclination was to hold the authors of history textbooks responsible for this unhappy situation. In his diary he complained that most of the history primers employed in French secondary education were "lacking in criticism and style, and produce boredom in the students."[2] With the intention of remedying these defects, he recruited thirty historians in 1849 to collaborate on a projected sixty volume survey of the history of man. This collection, which included textbooks on the history of literature, the arts, and science, was eventually brought out under the title *Universal History Published by a Society of Professors and Learned Men under the Direction of M. Duruy*.[3] It represented the first major attempt in France to centralize the production and improve the quality of history manuals destined for use in the public schools.

Upon his accession to the leadership of the educational bureaucracy in 1863, Duruy initiated a series of policies aimed at strengthening the position of historical instruction in the public school curriculum. Under the *ancien régime* history had been taught only to the sons of monarchs and notables, in order to prepare them for their future political responsibilities. Historical instruction on a broader scale began to appear in the nineteenth century, but only as a subsidiary subject which was not taught as a special course.[4] Duruy intended that historical instruction augment (and ultimately replace) the religious training that he hoped would be an early casualty of the Second Empire's increasingly liberal posture. As a dedicated French patriot, Duruy regarded history as the ideal instrument for instilling patriotic sentiments in the nation's youth. "The greatness of France is my religion," he once declared, and he remained convinced throughout his tenure that familiarity with the national heritage was infinitely preferable to religious piety as the foundation of civic virtue, *amor patriae*, and social cohesion.[5]

Besides promoting the study of history and encouraging the production of improved textbooks for classroom use, the enterprising minister proceeded to tackle what proved to be the most vexing pedagogical problem of all: the decline in the quality of instruction in all areas of French education. Eager to determine the extent of educational decadence in France, Duruy commissioned an exhaustive inquiry into that subject while concurrently instructing French ambassadors and consuls to report to him on the progress of higher education in other major European countries for purposes of comparison.[6]

The results of the former inquiry confirmed the minister's most pessimistic suspicions about the deterioration of French higher learning during the past half-century. They conclusively demonstrated the type of education offered at the degree granting faculties of the Napoleonic *Université* to be haphazard, disorganized, and lacking in purpose. Professors hired more for their eloquence than for their scholarly abilities were permitted to discharge their professorial obligations in weekly lectures to enormous audiences of curiosity seekers (including a large proportion of society ladies and pensioners in search of effortless edification) who were admitted to the vast university amphitheaters without regard to academic qualification. In the words of the Belgian historian Paul Frédéricq, a periodic visitor to the major academic centers of historical education in France and Germany, the Duruy ministry found itself presiding over university faculties that "hardly deserved to be considered true institutions of higher education; the public lessons, [though] brilliant and oratorical, were intended not for students—there weren't any of them—but rather for an audience that was continually replenished by intelligent *rentiers*, women, and idle characters of every category."[7] Even the few *universitaires* who could legitimately lay claim to the title of scholar displayed little interest in forging and strengthening professional ties with colleagues or sharing their expertise with students.

This dismal situation prevented French historians from establishing the type of self-perpetuating professional tradition which enabled their counterparts in Germany to replenish their ranks with competent successors and thereby guaranteed the continuation of their influence. The few genuine students who managed to crowd into the large lecture halls amidst the hundreds of unregistered auditors were condemned to vegetate "without any precise direction, specific counsel, or support."[8] Even the revered Sorbonne constituted a mere "administrative entity" rather than a community of scholars, as the educational reformer Louis Liard later observed. Its sole function was to provide public entertainment for bored bourgeois, to prepare students for the state examination, and to confer degrees. The faculty had little interpersonal contact except on examination boards. Each professor remained isolated in his private world, and there was "no common goal, no coordination of efforts, no community of interests, no collaboration. Only individual isolation and egotism."[9]

The impersonal nature of the lecture system and the lopsided student-faculty ratio also discouraged the formation of extensive personal ties between lecturer and student. By failing to attract and inspire a group of "assiduous students," Duruy observed, the great masters, despite their illustrious reputations and spellbinding performances at the lectern, were in effect making no contribution to the advancement of their profession. The French universities were dominated by "eloquent professors who attract listeners by the hundreds," but who refuse to train disciples capable of carrying on their teaching and of exposing the lacunas, errors, and deficiencies of previous scholarship in their respective fields. As a result, he warned, the professorial chairs occupied by these eminent men were running the risk of remaining unoccupied in the future, because of the dearth of specialists in each field who could qualify as successors.[10]

The disrepair of French higher education was reason enough for the ambitious educational reformer Duruy to despair. But the comparison to the educational institutions of other nations compounded his sense of urgency. The reports from the embassies and consulates that crossed his desk were replete with praise for the universities of the other major European nations. Germany and England furnished particularly conspicuous examples of sweeping reforms that had vastly improved the quality of scholarship and teaching in their institutions of higher learning. Duruy's memorandum to the Emperor summarizing the results of his investigations underscored the manifest inferiority of French universities vis-à-vis their English and German counterparts. He complained that all previous efforts to establish a scholarly tradition in French higher education had been "blunted and weakened" on account of the Gallic tendency to combine a preference for "pure letters, general truths, the portrayal of characteristics and passions, the analysis of the human heart, and the brilliant style of facile reading" with a disturbing predisposition to "disdain scholarship."[11]

An anticipatory fear of the very type of political and social instability that was soon to become a reality in the winter and spring of 1871 was one of Duruy's principal reasons for recommending remedial measures to modernize French higher education. A loyal spokesman for the conservative middle classes, Duruy was troubled by the faint rumblings of democratic sentiment that occasionally disturbed the tranquility of the Second Empire. He believed that educational institutions should be reshaped in such a way as to enable them more effectively to preserve the privileged position of the propertied classes upon which the Empire depended for its political survival. In a revealing letter to the Emperor written in the first year of his ministry, Duruy had specified his conception of the social function of education. "Since France is the true moral center of the world," he declared,

> let us assure the children of the well-to-do classes, those who dominate the liberal professions, those who, by birth or personal wealth are called upon to march in the first rank of society, let us assure them the broadest and most fertile cultivation of the mind by means of Letters and Sciences, Philosophy and History, in order to fortify the aristocracy of the intelligence . . . in order to create a legitimate counterweight to that democracy that is overflowing everywhere.[12]

To Duruy's dismay, his vision of the university as the seedbed of the intellectual elite of the nation collided with the evidence of educational decadence that his office was receiving. He therefore set out to identify the institutional defects of the French educational system and to develop means of remedying them.

It did not take the inquisitive minister long to discover that the principal source of the native hostility to the tradition of academic scholarship was the Faculty of Letters of Paris. In the beginning, Duruy entertained the idea of initiating a direct assault on the antiquated pedagogical and scholarly practices of the Sorbonne, but eventually decided to circumvent it in order to avoid the explosive confrontation with the entrenched defenders of that ancient temple of the intellect that such a policy would inevitably entail.[13] Temporarily resigned to the necessity of leaving the Faculty of Letters intact with all its egregious imperfections, he turned his attention to the three "special schools" attached to the national university system, only to discover that each was similarly unqualified, for a variety of reasons, to sponsor the educational reforms that he envisaged, particularly with regard to historical instruction.

The Ecole Normale Supérieure, a creature of the First Empire whose principal function was a pedagogical one—it served as a recruiting station and training ground for candidates for the most coveted teaching posts in secondary education—lacked the resources and personnel to provide adequate instruction in the modern methods of historical scholarship. Moreover, its traditionalist curriculum was altogether ill-suited to the requirements of such technical training. Dominated by such subjects as Greek, Latin, rhetoric, and philosophy, it was designed to acquaint prospective schoolmasters with the principles that were deemed conducive to lucidity of thought and clarity of expression. Of the twelve professorial chairs allotted to the Letters section of the Ecole Normale, only two were earmarked for history. The remainder belonged to Greek literature, Latin literature, French literature, and philosophy (two each) and comparative grammar and geography (one each).[14] The faculty of the Ecole Normale yielded to none in its hostility to the "Teutonic" methods of historical scholarship.[15]

The Collège de France, a hallowed remnant of the *ancien régime* that had originated as a center for scholarly research,[16] had long since become even more firmly wedded to the oratorical tradition than had its neighbor across the rue Saint Jacques. Indeed, in the absence of statutory authority to enroll students, the Collège de France found its sole *raison d'être* in weekly public lectures delivered by the select group of professors who had been elected to it. A nomination to occupy one of its prestigious chairs traditionally came at the end of a distinguished academic career. It represented a reward for past greatness rather than an obligation to assume the type of tutorial responsibilities that would accompany membership in an institution devoted to the development of a scholarly tradition.[17]

The Ecole des Chartes, the only division of the university that deserved to be designated as a research institution, represented the most plausible candidate to become the center of historical scholarship in France. Founded by royal ordinance in 1821 to prepare scholars for careers in archival administration and paleography, it offered a three-year program in the various auxiliary sciences of historical study, such as paleography, diplomatics, bibliography, and source criticism. But it was disqualified because of its small enrollment and limited size, and the specialized nature of its curriculum. It normally admitted only twenty students annually, most of whom planned to become archivists or librarians rather than historians. Their three years of study were spent analyzing and criticizing primary source materials drawn exclusively from the medieval period. No effort was made to connect this preliminary stage of documentary analysis to the process of generalization and synthesis that is appropriate to historical scholarship, and the concentration on archives of the distant past excluded the last four centuries from serious scholarly attention.[18]

Hence, Duruy's quest for a site for the revival of historical studies in the existing academic structure had led him into a cul-de-sac. The Ecole Normale produced pedagogues imbued with *la culture générale*, the Ecole des Chartes trained archivists and librarians to collect historical evidence from the medieval past, and the Collège de France joined the Sorbonne in staging historical orations for the purposes of public amusement. But no segment of the *Université* was engaged in producing historians or in imparting the principles of historical scholarship to an organized student body, and none seemed likely to undertake such tasks in the near future.

Duruy had no cause for embarrassment at the inability of a highly regarded minister of an authoritarian empire to surmount the institutional roadblocks to educational reform. He had only to recall the earlier tribulations of a French ruler who had even fewer excuses for impotence, Francis I, whose failure to persuade the Sorbonne scholastics to provide institutional support for Renaissance studies compelled him to establish the autonomous institution that eventually became the Collège de France. Like his royal predecessor, the enterprising minister of Napoleon III was forced to attempt innovation once renovation had proved to be impossible.[19] Armed with the irrefutable evidence of educational atrophy in France, he induced the *Corps Législatif* to finance the creation of a special center for scientific scholarship outside the existing system, hoping that it might set an example that the remaining branches of the university would follow at some future date. On July 31, 1868, with the enthusiastic endorsement of the amateur historian who sat on the imperial throne, the Ecole Pratique des Hautes Etudes was born.

Duruy's instructions accompanying the decree that established this new institution summarized the minister's long-range plans for his educational brain child. He unabashedly acknowledged the inspiration of the foreign model, expressing the hope that French professors would soon recognize the wisdom of training "veritable disciples, like their counterparts in German universities" and of devoting more time to "the labor of literary and historical scholarship, which is so much in evidence on the other side of the Rhine, [but] which is so sadly lacking among us."[20] The new school was aptly dubbed *pratique*, for it was designed to provide practical experience in the use of the methods of historical criticism rather than theoretical instruction in substantive topics, an obligation that was adequately discharged by the crowd pleasers who dispensed instant culture at the faculties. The overriding purpose was to create a community of scholars imbued with a "common spirit" that would produce a "continuity of tendency and inspiration" among students and faculty alike.[21] By encouraging emulation of the German universities, where groups of distinguished specialists had long been engaged in elaborate projects of historical research, Duruy was, in effect, challenging French public opinion to accept the novel notion that specialized instruction in research techniques, rather than the traditional exposure to "general culture," was the appropriate mode of preparation for a career in historical scholarship.[22] In keeping with this conception, the metaphor of the medieval guild rapidly became the most fashionable method of describing the new type of technical training that was available at the Ecole Pratique. Louis Liard later characterized it as a "sort of workshop in which the students are apprentices and the teachers, masters."[23]

These broad, theoretical objectives were translated into educational policy by means of several innovations in the structure, curriculum, and teaching personnel of the Ecole Pratique. It was subdivided into four autonomous sections in order to foster a greater coordination of effort and unity of function within each specialized discipline than had obtained in the more loosely organized structure of the regular faculties. One section was devoted exclusively to the historical and philological sciences, a novelty which reflected the minister's belief in the increasing importance of historical research, in the philological underpinnings of historical methodology, and in the legitimacy of history's claim to the title of science.

Since the new institution lacked a physical plant of its own owing to legislative parsimony, the history section was lodged in the few available rooms of the Sorbonne library that Duruy was able to requisition without provoking undue complaint. The abominable overcrowding that resulted from this arrangement moved one frequent visitor to remark that "one could neither raise one's eyes nor make a movement without seeing books."[24] Notwithstanding such irksome physical handicaps, enthusiasm ran high and much groundbreaking work was begun. The inclusion in the curriculum of such technical subjects as paleography, epigraphy, comparative philology, diplomatics, and source criticism introduced scores of prospective historians to techniques of research and documentary analysis that had formerly remained in the exclusive possession of archivists and librarians. But the most important innovation of all was the establishment of a system of *conférences*, or small seminars, in which a select group of students were to be assigned certain documents relating to a particular period to analyze and authenticate under the watchful supervision of a *répétiteur*, or seminar leader.[25]

These structural and curricular innovations would have constituted little more than empty forms of intellectual progress had Duruy been unable to recruit a cadre of gifted instructors schooled in the modern techniques of historical erudition and devoted to their dissemination. The dearth of such candidates in the regular university system might well have brought about that unfortunate result had the perspicacious minister not taken the necessary precautions. But for several years he had made a practice of encouraging the most promising *agrégés* of French universities to spend time in Germany acquiring the scholarly expertise that was not obtainable at home.[26] This provident policy began to bear fruit in the late 1860s. The dozens of young French scholars returning from the German universities constituted an available reservoir of talent upon which he was able to draw to form the nucleus of a highly qualified faculty for the Ecole Pratique. Gaston Paris, who had studied philology at Bonn and Göttingen and paleography at the Ecole des Chartes, became a professor of Romance philogy in 1868.[27] In the same year a select group of young historians who were steeped in the German methods of historical scholarship received appointments as *répétiteurs* at the new school. On a very modest scale, these young *érudits* began to introduce the modern conception of historical study into French higher education.

Duruy's failure to locate receptive allies within the existing academic structure for his program of historical reform was largely due to certain peculiarities of the French historical tradition. To begin with, in contrast to its increasingly professional character in the other major European countries, history writing in mid-nineteenth century France remained an avocation of amateurs—politicians, lawyers, journalists, clerics, and other free lance *littérateurs* and armchair philosophes who had neither received formal instruction in the methods of historical scholarship nor displayed the least inclination to employ such methods in their work. Nowhere in the France of this period was there to be found the conception of history that had already taken hold in Germany: that of a full-time vocation of technical specialists assembled in the universities for the purpose of conducting scholarly research and training successors to perpetuate the practices of the discipline. Even the few noted historians who held university positions tended to regard their professorial chairs primarily as sources of a steady income and resting places for pedagogues weary of secondary education rather than as the apex of the academic hierarchy to which all ambitious scholars should aspire. Their university positions added nothing to their notoriety as men of learning. On the contrary, it was they who, by virtue of the reputation that they had acquired from their published works, lent prestige to the schools in which they taught.[28]

The French conception of historical writing as a pastime of dilettantes was a bequest of the eighteenth century. What passed for the historical tradition of France during the Enlightenment was the work of Montesquieu, Raynal, Mably, Voltaire, and other men of letters who drew upon their abundant literary talents to produce elegant histories whose popularity rested more on their indisputable stylistic excellence and polemical force than on their more dubious scholarly merits.[29] This "literary" tradition of historical writing endured and prospered because it conferred advantages upon both writer and reader. By emphasizing style over content, speculative imagination over patient research, and political efficacy over scholarly objectivity, it assured the historian a greater influence over the reading public while furnishing the emergent middle class with entertainment, leisurely instruction, and, not infrequently, ideological ammunition for its incipient campaign against the institutions of the *ancien régime*.

The sole example of a tradition of historical scholarship worthy of the name in eighteenth century France was to be found in the Académie des Inscriptions et Belles-Lettres, where a small band of Benedictine monks had begun to collect and edit the historical documents retrieved from the dispersed archives of the medieval era. But the laborious efforts of these anonymous *érudits* attracted little attention outside the restricted circle of the monasteries and scholarly academies. The reading public's thirst for popular history was dutifully quenched by the merchants of belletristic prose in the world of letters, while the absence of a tradition of historical scholarship in the university prevented the ascetic scholar-monks from gaining an academic audience. By the end of the *ancien régime*, two separate and identifiable schools of history had crystallized outside the French university: the one, conceiving of history as a literary genre and engaged in the remunerative practice of writing general works for public consumption; the other, devoted to the less rewarding task of accumulating and authenticating the original documents that contained the material evidence of the nation's past.[30]

Following the suppression of the religious orders and the scholarly academies during the Revolution, this dichotomy of the "literary" and "scholarly" traditions of historical study reappeared in the national university system that had been established by Napoleon to serve as the center of French higher learning. By the advent of the Bourbon Restoration, the unattached philosophes and *littérateurs* who wrote popular histories during the Enlightenment had been succeeded by a new group of writers who transported the literary historical tradition to the faculties of letters of the *Université*. They discovered enthusiastic allies in the world of letters and public life during the Romantic period, when the idealized past of France supplied a continuous stream of themes for literary and political works. "Everything takes the form of history today," Chateaubriand observed in 1831, "polemics, theater, the novel, poetry."[31]

Guizot, Thiers, Lamartine, Thierry, Mignet, Quinet, Michelet and other contributors to this period of prolific historical production who straddled the worlds of politics, journalism, and higher learning could hardly be described as professional historians. Attracted to a variety of callings, these successful authors of general histories were understandably ill-suited to the time-consuming drudgery of archival organization, textual criticism, and monographic scholarship. Nor were they interested in recruiting and training a school of disciples. Such an obligation was regarded as an improper intrusion on the intellectual territory of great minds, since genius could not be shared with one's own contemporaries, let alone be transmitted across the generations. It was the vitality and persistence of this conception of history writing as the prerogative of gifted men of letters that constituted the most serious impediment to the transformation of history into a scholarly profession in France.[32]

The task of preserving the single tenuous thread of that tradition of historical scholarship after 1815 was once again consigned to an obscure corner of French intellectual life. The Ecole des Chartes had taken up the standard of historical scholarship that had been borne by the Benedictines of the Académie des Inscriptions et Belles-Lettres under the *ancien régime*.[33] As before, the literary and scholarly approaches to historical study continued to diverge until by midcentury "the world of the *chartistes* did not mix with that of the *universitaires* any more than the world of the eighteenth century scholars [at the Académie] mixed with that of the philosopher-historians."[34]

Because of its isolation from the mainstream of the academic world during the first half of the nineteenth century, the Ecole des Chartes remained a relatively inconspicuous, insignificant island of historical erudition amidst the vast ocean of historical vulgarization that set the tone of historical writing until the closing years of the Second Empire, when it was joined by the Ecole Pratique. Thenceforth both institutions represented what one noted French historian later called "the only centers for initiation into historical research" of any importance in a period when history in France languished in "a miserable state."[35]

Two years prior to the establishment of the Ecole Pratique, two related innovations in the world of historical journalism had helped to accelerate the irreversible trend toward the establishment of a veritable historical profession in France. We have seen how the absence of the research seminar in the university system precluded the transmission of cumulative methodological knowledge from the professorial to the student generation, thereby impeding the development of history as an academic discipline. Of equal concern to the champions of professional history was the absence of a periodical literature devoted to historical questions, a deficiency which delayed the promulgation of professional standards of scholarship and the creation of institutional means of enforcing them. But since neither official approval nor government financing was required to remedy this problem, the foundation of a professional historical periodical was accomplished almost unnoticed by all but specialists in the discipline. At the beginning of 1866 a small group of university-trained historians, inspired by the example of the *Historische Zeitschrift* in Germany and dismayed by the absence of a reputable analogue in France, founded the *Revue critique d'histoire et de littérature*.

Though modest in format—it did not solicit scholarly articles and rarely exceeded twenty pages in length—the new journal adopted the unprecedented practice of publishing evaluations of recent works of historical scholarship that were written by specialists in the particular area treated by the work under review. Moreover, the editorial board was composed of young scholars nurtured on German historical methods who took a dim view of the methodological assumptions held by the reigning historians in France.[36] One of the editors, Charles Morel, armed with a recently acquired doctorate from the University of Bonn, launched a devastating exposé of the absence of critical standards and the "preconceived notion of truth" that impaired the progress of historical studies in France.[37] He singled out for special criticism on this score no less a luminary than Fustel de Coulanges, whose *Cité antique*, a monumental study of the political system of ancient Greece, had earned for its author universal critical acclaim and a prize from the *Académie Française*. After attributing the book's success among the "lettered public" to its agreeable style, its "simple and clear method" of exposition, and the "cleverness and eloquence" of its author, Morel proceeded to explain why it should not be taken seriously by scholars. He brazenly denounced it as a hodge-podge of facile generalizations and undocumented conclusions which demonstrated little except the author's disregard for the stringent requirements of careful scholarship. Fustel's notorious *esprit de système* predisposed him to select out only those historical events which conformed to his preconceived plan, Morel announced. "Solely preoccupied with proving his theory," he made no effort to conduct a "serious examination of facts and details," and was therefore able to reach conclusions which "can only elicit a smile." Consequently his book has failed, as will all books whose authors attempt "to construct history a priori."[38]

The permissive attitude toward historical scholarship that prevailed throughout the first half of the nineteenth century had effectively immunized historians against such professional criticism, thereby enabling a flood of mediocre and in some cases inaccurate works of popular history to masquerade unchallenged as the fruits of erudition. Authors of historical works were obliged to satisfy only the conditions imposed by the reading public, which judged a book on the basis of its capacity to entertain, and those imposed by the literary intelligentsia at the *Revue des deux mondes*, the *Journal des débats*, and the other organs of higher culture in Parisian journalism, which required that it satisfy the criterion of literary merit. This resulted in the dispensation of "undeserved rewards" to the authors of numerous works which rested on the shaky foundation of second-rate scholarship.[39]

The effect of Morel's bold broadside, and of subsequent pieces of a similar nature, was to put all French historians on notice, regardless of reputation, that they would henceforth be held to account for the legitimacy of their conclusions and the authenticity of their evidence by the reviewers of the *Revue critique*. The nature of historical writing in France was never to be quite the same again. Ernest Lavisse later recalled how the *Revue critique* "policed the publishing trade" with a vengeance unprecedented in French culture. Its "pitiless denunciations" of the methodological deficiencies that marred so much historical scholarship of the period compelled historians to toe the line of scholarly scrupulosity for "fear of the lash."[40] The "public correctives" that it issued to the purveyors of illegitimate scholarship appeared to Charles Seignobos, who was later to become the leading authority on the historical method at the Sorbonne, as a sort of "justice through terror" in the realm of historical studies. By the end of the Second Empire, a French historian could ill afford to publish a work without having taken precautions to ensure that it was beyond reproach on methodological grounds, lest it run the risk of becoming the target of one of the frequent "police operations" conducted by the editors of the *Revue*.[41]

The frantic rejoinders of those unfortunate writers who saw their works subjected to professional ridicule merely helped to confirm the journal's reputation as an arbiter of historical scholarship that could not be ignored. Unable to dispute the hawk-eyed reviewers' exposure of the numerous factual inaccuracies contained in their works, the beleaguered authors retreated to a second line of defense. By choosing to rebut the journal's complaints about the absence of sufficient documentation in their writings, they laid hold of an issue that enabled them to tap the wellsprings of French cultural pride. "I live pretty close to the Rhine, sir, but at least on the left bank," a furious Fustel de Coulanges wrote from Strasbourg in response to Morel's diatribe. "I wanted to write in the French manner, that is to say, simply and clearly; I was satisfied to indicate my sources at the bottom of pages, and I did not insist that the footnotes be longer than the pages . . . I love erudition, but I do not like superfluous window-dressing."[42] A subsequent victim of the *Revue critique*'s campaign against works that violated its standards of historical criticism adopted the same tactic, proudly declaring himself a member of the French school of historical writing and denouncing his detractors for applying German standards to French writing.[43] But the review always had the last word. The editors frequently noted with pride that the most prevalent criticism that was raised against it from disinterested parties was the allegation that it was excessively severe on those whom it regarded as errant scholars. They steadfastly defended their right to expose the methodological deficiencies of even the most celebrated works of history and reaffirmed their goal of demolishing all those methodologically defective studies that "encumber the terrain of science."[44]

In the same year a group of Catholic historians founded a rival periodical of historical scholarship, the *Revue des questions historiques*, whose programmatic statement closely resembled the agenda of the *Revue critique*. According to its founders, the *Revue des questions historiques* had been established for the express purpose of relieving ecceliastical history of the stigma that identified it as a polemical genre of questionable scholarly legitimacy. The editorial board of the Catholic periodical joined the founders of the *Revue critique* in endorsing the methods of critical historical scholarship perfected in the German universities and urged French historians to launch an operation of "historical revision" to discredit the exaggerated and inaccurate interpretations of much recent historical scholarship in France, particularly that dealing with ecclesiastical subjects.[45]

The appearance within the French Catholic tradition of a school of history committed to the principles of scholarly objectivity was not nearly as paradoxical as it might appear at first blush. There were concrete historical and ideological reasons for such a development. The precedents established by their coreligionists at the Académie des Inscriptions et Belles-Lettres before the Revolution furnished the clerical coterie that launched the *Revue des questions historiques* with sufficient grounds for representing themselves as the modern custodians of the venerable tradition of historical scholarship that had originated in the bosom of the church. While the editors of the Catholic journal could trace its roots to purely French soil, those of the *Revue critique* were obliged to invoke the authority of German learning to justify their novel approach to historical study, a circumstance that was to pose difficulties for the founders of the French historical profession in the poisonous atmosphere of Germanophobia that pervaded French intellectual circles after the turn of the century.

But this effort to defend the doctrines of Catholicism with the modern methods of historical scholarship was favored by ideological conditions as well. Both the *Revue critique* and the *Revue des questions historiques* had been formed to combat the tendency among nineteenth century French historians to utilize their craft for partisan purposes. But whereas the academic scholars at the *Revue critique* directed the brunt of their criticism at writers such as Fustel de

Coulanges, whose works they condemned as apolegetics for organized religion,[46] the Catholic review railed against what it described as the "long conspiracy against truth" represented by a much more prevalent and influential tradition: the school of liberal, anticlerical historians who charmed the French reading public during the first half of the nineteenth century with their "clever exposition" and the "magic of their style."[47] Convinced that the undocumented accusations against church and king contained in the historical writing of this school[48] were responsible for the universally negative evaluation of the institutions of the *ancien régime*, the editors of the *Revue des questions historiques* proclaimed their intention to redress the balance by subjecting these works to the rigorous standards of modern historical criticism.[49]

These heirs to the Benedictine tradition realized that as the modern practitioners of the "conscientious and austere science" of historical scholarship, they had no more hope of competing with the didactic, *pittoresque* historical melodramas which romanticized the eternal conflict between the common man and the oppressive forces of autocracy and obscurantism than had their predecessors in the *ancien régime*. "How can we [hope to] rehabilitate ourselves in the eyes of the masses, and conquer their sympathies?" was their plaintive question. "We are engaged in the dispassionate analysis of issues, having no ideological axe to grind, with the sole desire of seeking the truth and telling it, . . . aided by original sources that have been carefully researched through the use of scrupulously studied texts and rigidly controlled evidence."[50] That their profession of scholarly impartiality was patently exaggerated and misleading did not detract from the significance of their urgent appeal for a new type of historical writing that would be liberated from ideological constraints. It represented yet another contribution to the cacophony of criticism directed at the unprofessional, impressionistic nature of history writing in France.

The confluence of these developments produced the first faint glimmering of a historical profession worthy of the name in France by the end of the 1860s. The history section of the Ecole Pratique constituted a modest but instructive example of a training ground for professional historians that the regular degree-granting faculties might subsequently be induced to follow. Duruy's expression of interest in the pedagogical function of history reflected the growing conviction that French schoolchildren should be exposed at an early age to the drama of their nation's past. The two new professional journals provided a public forum for the dissemination of information on scholarly subjects, the publication of the fruits of recent historical research, and the ostracism of historical works that the editors deemed unworthy of consideration by historical scholars.

The potential advantages of such a professional orientation were readily apparent to those who had been active in pressing for its adoption. As the charter members of the nascent profession, the professors at the Ecole Pratique and the scholars at the *Revue critique* understandably expected to fill the key posts within the professional hierarchy of the established university system as they became vacant. Once entrenched in the regular faculties, they would be in a position to launch the campaign to reorganize the university system on the German model.[51] They would acquire the right to supervise the intellectual formation of future members of the discipline, the formulation and enforcement of professional standards of historical scholarship, the publication of the results of that scholarship, and the production of primary and secondary school textbooks that would disseminate established historical truths to the young generation. Only by achieving such positions of influence in the *Université* could they begin to weed out the persistent remnants of the amateurish literary and philosophical school of history and replace it with the scholarly or scientific approach to historical study. Writing to a German friend to announce the foundation of the *Revue critique*, Gaston Paris voiced the hope that the progress of the scientific historical tradition would help to remedy the ignorance that pervaded French society while securing for the historians a recognized social function as the principal bearers of that illumination.[52]

But, as was the case with so many of the highly touted reforms of the Liberal Empire, the attempts to create a historical profession in France produced little more than window dressing that preserved the entrenched system essentially intact. Duruy once described the Ecole Pratique to Gabriel Monod as "a germ that I am depositing in the cracked walls of the old Sorbonne" which will one day "make them collapse."[53] But for the duration of the Bonapartist Empire, the walls of the university gave no indication of losing their solidity. The centers of power in the academic hierarchy remained in the control of the traditionalist historians, who were prepared neither to be summarily dislodged by these upstart innovators nor to preside over the supersession of their methods of instruction and scholarship without spirited defiance. Moreover, notwithstanding its popularity with a restricted clientele of research scholars, the *Revue critique* failed to live up to its promise to become the French version of the *Historische Zeitschrift*. Gaston Paris himself publicly acknowledged the shortcomings of his review less than a year after its appearance and called for the creation of a French historical journal patterned more closely after Sybel's groundbreaking periodical.[54]

Before the movement of historical reform could gain momentum, an unhappy train of events compelled the postponement of its ambitious projects. Duruy was dismissed by Napoleon in a cabinet reshuffle in July of 1869, and a year later the Prussian army and its German allies put an abrupt end to France's myopic vision of a return to imperial glory. The promising young historians who had shared in the brief flurry of excitement engendered by the Duruy reforms emerged from the doldrums of national humiliation not in despair about the future of their profession, but with even greater determination to complete the task.

2
History's Role in the Regeneration of the Fatherland

The two leading spokesmen for the historical reform movement in postwar France had both been deeply affected by the intellectual ferment that appeared within the ranks of French historians in the final decade of the Second Empire. Gabriel Monod, a brilliant graduate of the Ecole Normale (class of 1865), had first encountered the modern methods of historical scholarship at the University of Berlin, where he spent the year following his graduation attending the seminar of the historian Philipp Jaffé, one of Leopold von Ranke's most brilliant pupils.[1] In 1867 he enrolled at the University of Göttingen to pursue medieval studies with Georg Waitz, whose seminar was reputed to be the most celebrated gathering of historical specialists after Ranke's own. Dissatisfied with the superficial preparation that he had received at the rue d'Ulm, Monod had succumbed to the allure of German erudition. As was the case with so many scholars of his generation, he was to receive what he later called his "scientific baptism" across the Rhine.[2]

The young *normalien* was introduced to a tradition of higher learning that contrasted sharply with that of the Ecole Normale, where he had majored in literary studies and taken the traditional courses in the classical curriculum. A charter member of the German historicist school, which strove to reconstruct the past *wie es eigentlich gewesen* through the resurrection of the surviving documentary evidence,[3]

Waitz emphasized the importance of sticking to the primary sources and cautioned his students against the temptation to employ "a priori constructions" and "subjective theories" of historical interpretation, which frequently reflect the "religious or political biases" of the writer. Continually urging his disciples to scrutinize the documents with the utmost care, to limit severely the scope of their scholarly investigations, and to confine themselves to empirically verifiable conclusions, he was fond of repeating the dictum that "every generalization is nothing but a grouping of facts."[4] Even more striking than this new epistemological doctrine was the method by which it was imparted. The esteemed mentor gathered together his best students once a week to review the progress of their studies on an individual basis, to subject them to constructive criticism, and to offer advice.[5]

Monod left the Waitz seminar convinced that he had acquired not only "clearer ideas and a well-ordered mind," but also a heightened "love and respect for truth and science."[6] The opportunity to consult with the master in a weekly tête-à-tête and to work in common on collective research projects with a select group of scholarly apprentices left him with a lasting impression of Germany as a "vast historical laboratory" in which historical research was "concentrated and coordinated" and where "no effort was wasted."[7] In a phrase that was to return to haunt him in later years, when relations between the two nations were no longer so cordial, he saluted France's powerful neighbor as "the second fatherland of those who study and think."[8]

Intent on putting into practice the ideas that he had absorbed at Berlin and Göttingen, Monod began to make discreet inquiries upon his return to Paris in the spring of 1868 about the possibility of a university position. He quickly secured an audience with Victor Duruy with the help of two former classmates at the Ecole Normale who had the minister's ear—his son Albert and his personal secretary, Ernest Lavisse.[9] The educational reformer summarized his plans to establish a new research institute on the periphery of the *Université* that would incorporate many of the educational innovations introduced in Germany, and proceeded to offer Monod a post as *répétiteur* in the history section.

Upon receiving official notification of his nomination in the fall of 1868, Monod waxed lyrical in his journal about his dreams of establishing *"conférences* of historical criticism" in this recent addition to the French university system.[10] By the opening of classes in January of the following year, his mind was fairly bursting with projects for establishing in France "a university life analogous to that of Germany," by which he meant the spirit of intimate scholarly collaboration that he had witnessed in Prussia and Hanover.[11] By dint of circumstance, the intimacy between teacher and student at the Ecole

Pratique proved to be even greater than Monod had anticipated. So inadequate were the facilities of the new school in its early years that the young instructor, who was scarcely older than his students, was frequently obliged to conduct his classes in early medieval history and historical bibliography in the drawing room of his own apartment.[12] Notwithstanding such inconveniences, he set to work assigning a specific research project to each student and organizing joint meetings in which methodological matters of mutual interest could be discussed in common.[13] This novel method of historical instruction was also employed by two other members of the history and philology section of the Ecole Pratique. Alfred Rambaud, another classmate of Monod's at the Ecole Normale (class of 1864), was named as a *répétiteur* in modern history in the same year and conducted *conférences* on that subject while completing work on his doctorate.[14] Gaston Paris proceeded to apply in his philological seminars the methodological principles that he had learned as a disciple of the eminent German philologist Friedrich Diez at the University of Bonn.[15] The contrast between these small groups of specialists engaged in common projects of scholarly research and the public lectures that were still in vogue at the university faculties could not have been more blatant.[16]

Before Paris, Rambaud, and Monod had begun to lay the foundations of the French historical profession at the Ecole Pratique, another alumnus of the Ecole Normale's class of 1865 had already begun a long and distinguished teaching career that was to become inextricably intertwined with the development of history as an academic discipline in France. Like his classmate and friend Monod, Ernest Lavisse had left the rue d'Ulm thoroughly disenchanted with his recent educational experience. He complained of having received "vague and obscure learning" which had "no definite objective," and which left him with "no idea of where I am heading in this chaos of bits and pieces [of information]."[17] He later recalled being led through a course which covered a thousand years of history without ever coming into contact with a single historical document, and remembered the experience of a classmate who composed a treatise on the Germanic legal system without having read a single law. Nor did the weekly lectures at the Sorbonne, which he and Monod occasionally attended on the side, offer an acceptable alternative to the superficiality of historical education at the Ecole Normale. The two young scholars-to-be were submerged in a throng of auditors who applauded the professor at his entrance and exit as though he were a performer rather than an instructor. "It seemed that the master could have summoned us to his lectern and spoken to us, but it wasn't the custom," he later observed with unconcealed bitterness. "It was almost as though the teacher and the students didn't have the right to get to know each other."[18]

Whereas Monod's principal passion was historical scholarship, Lavisse's distasteful memories of his own deficient training had left him with a special interest in the pedagogical function of history. Instead of pursuing his classmate across the Rhine for a postgraduate course in the methods of German erudition, he accepted a post in secondary education in the hope of breathing new life into what he had come to view as a moribund enterprise. But after an exasperating three-year stint grappling with the outmoded practices and curricula of a succession of *lycées*, he was driven to seek temporary refuge from the source of his malaise. Fortunately, like Monod, he was blessed with personal connections with the centers of academic and political power in the Second Empire which greased the path of upward social mobility. Though his unfamiliarity with German scholarship ruled out a nomination to the Ecole Pratique, his friendship with Duruy's son landed him a position as personal secretary to the Education Minister in early 1868.[19] A few months later, owing to the elder Duruy's timely intervention at the Tuileries, Lavisse was awarded the coveted post of preceptor to the Prince Imperial, which he retained until his hapless pupil was forced into exile after Sedan.[20]

As the last decade of the Second Empire approached its end, Lavisse became increasingly apprehensive about the future implications of France's educational deficiencies, particularly after perusing the officially-commissioned descriptions of the German universities. The reports submitted by the vice-consul in Königsberg, which commended the Prussian efficiency of that city's university, had such an unsettling effect on him that he reread it ten times. "I understood for the first time that schools could produce moral states and invincible moral forces," he later recalled, "and Germany frightened me." Recognizing the analogous role that historical education, which had become a required course of study, could play in France, he considered it only logical that steps be taken to devise more effective methods of instruction and to renew the campaign that Duruy had launched to improve the quality of history textbooks.[21] But whereas Monod, Rambaud, and Paris enjoyed greater freedom to innovate at the Ecole Pratique (an experimental institution grafted onto the regular university structure whose faculty were given free rein to introduce the pedagogical and scholarly methods developed in Germany),[22] Lavisse was continually hampered by the stubborn resistance to reform that pervaded the secondary schools in which he taught. After failing to discover enthusiasm for innovation among the teaching personnel of the *lycées*, he bided his time at the imperial palace, awaiting a more opportune moment to renew his proposals for educational modernization.

By the end of the 1860s, these four precocious historians—each had yet to reach his thirtieth year—had already compiled a dossier of professional credentials that ensured them positions of prominence in the academic world. Gaston Paris had obtained a doctorate at age twenty-six, an editorial post at the journal of the nascent historical profession at twenty-seven, and at twenty-nine a professorship of philology at the only institution in France devoted exclusively to scholarly research. Monod and Rambaud had become the dominant influences on the development of historical training at that institution at twenty-four and twenty-six, respectively. And Ernest Lavisse, though a temporary drop-out from the teaching profession, had gained entree to the inner sanctum of the Education Ministry and, at age twenty-six, of the Imperial palace itself.

But their budding careers and ambitious plans for the future were abruptly interrupted by the unanticipated outbreak of war between the French Empire and the allied states of Germany. The cries of "*A Berlin!*" that echoed through the streets of Paris in mid-July 1870 came no longer from those Frenchmen who longed to learn history and philology from Ranke and Diez, but from those who wished to teach a lesson in military prowess to Bismarck and Moltke. Instead of speedy victory, however, the young historians witnessed the humiliation of the French military forces and observed with disbelief the abrupt collapse of the political regime under whose aegis they had so quickly established their reputations. The grandiose hopes for national renewal that had been fostered by Napoleon III during the past decade (and which the historical reformers all shared) were dashed in two months of confrontation with the Prussian needle-gun and an aftermath of domestic agony in the besieged and, later, insurgent French capital.

In such periods of total national degradation defeated peoples have frequently reacted by trimming their sails and turning inward in search of spiritual consolation. This agonized quest has often assumed the form of a heightened degree of historical consciousness, which impels the intellectual leaders of the chastened nation to dredge up past evidence of national glory to help compensate for the present sentiment of national humiliation.[23] Appropriately, historians have often played a major role in such reassertions of national pride, and the French historians who resumed their careers after the disaster of 1870 were no exception.

The sentiment of despair and disillusionment that pervaded French society after Sedan weighed particularly heavily on the young historians who began their careers in the last years of the Second Empire. The downfall of the regime momentarily dampened Lavisse's personal ambition, which had been fueled by the uninterrupted string of successes that had catapulted him from the rue d'Ulm to the rue de Grenelle to the Tuileries in less than three years. The dim prospects for the tutor of the Bonapartist pretender dashed whatever hopes for personal advancement that the twenty-six year old historian might have harbored, so he decided to retreat across the Rhine to complete his doctoral research. His letter to the education ministry requesting a leave of absence conveyed a combined sense of anguish at his nation's humiliation and his personal misfortune as well as a resolution to heal those painful wounds. "No one has felt more deeply than I [these] adversities for which I will never be able to console myself," he lamented, "and no one is more determined than I to work . . . for reparation."[24]

To Gabriel Monod, the most alarming consequence of the defeat was not the resulting political, social, and economic dislocation, as bad as that was, but rather the threat to the "intellectual and moral unity of the nation."[25] In a similar vein, Lavisse somberly observed that the self-confidence and pride of a once great nation had been gravely impaired. France had permitted the Germans to "invade our national domain and install themselves as masters," he declared, referring not to the temporary military occupation but to what he feared was the permanent damage to French cultural pride.[26] Defeated and humiliated, the French understandably turned in large numbers to history for explanations of their present plight and compensatory, reassuring references to France's historic grandeur.

The new generation of French historians was only too happy to oblige. Many of them were determined to employ the tools of their trade to help deliver France from her national inferiority complex and heal the psychological wounds inflicted by the invader. "The study of France's past, which will be the principal part of our task, has a national importance at this moment," wrote Gabriel Monod. "Through it we can provide our country with the moral unity and vigor that it needs, enabling it both to become familiar with its historical traditions and to comprehend the transformations that it has undergone."[27] This confidence in the restorative power of history remained with Monod throughout the period of national mourning. His lectures at the Ecole Alsacienne (which was founded after the war to keep alive the memory of the lost province) were replete with patriotic themes spiced with evocative historical references. "The future is in your hands." he informed his students. "Prove yourselves worthy, my deal children, of the France of Saint Louis and Joan of Arc, of Rocroy and Valmy."[28] In the funeral procession for Léon Gambetta, the leader of the French resistance during the war of 1870, Monod carried a banner on which was inscribed what he regarded as the most memorable phrase to emanate from the lips of that departed patron of national regeneration: "History is the master science."[29]

Lavisse also assigned to history the function of reviving patriotic pride in the minds of French youth by acquainting them with past glories of the fatherland and producing "the feeling of what we have been and what we are in the world."[30] Both he and Monod recalled the precedent established by the German historians who had contributed to the spiritual regeneration of Prussia after the Battle of Jena. Lavisse remarked that "nowhere has that patriotic uprising been praised more highly than in France, for ours is the privilege reserved to generous peoples of being capable of admiring our enemies."[31] His early career was marked by an obsession for discovering the historical sources of Germany's national power. His doctoral dissertation, *La Marche de Brandenbourg sous la dynastie ascanienne: études sur l'une des origines de la monarchie prussienne*,[32] was an attempt to explain how the migration of the various nationalities that sought refuge in Brandenburg-Prussia following the turmoil of the Thirty Years War strengthened the monarchical institution that was to become the federator of the Germanies.[33]

It is a historical truism that defeated nations frequently choose to adopt those domestic institutions of their conquerors which they regard as having played a decisive role in the military outcome. This willingness to import foreign institutions to replace indigenous ones is rooted in the conviction that diplomatic and military success is ultimately dependent upon domestic vitality. France's international hegemony during the seventeenth and first half of the eighteenth centuries, for example, caused many of the political units of central Europe to exchange several of their native traditions and institutions for French ones. As the motherland of classical culture, France radiated her influence far beyond the areas that fell within the shadow of her military might. Several German intellectuals who saw their fatherland divided and dominated by the Gallic invaders during and after the Thirty Years War came to believe that their only hope for the attainment of "civilization" lay in the abandonment of their native customs and the adoption of the manners, styles, and traditions that were being cultivated at Versailles.

Many of the most promising young historians in France reacted in a similar fashion after the Franco-Prussian War. They attributed Germany's speedy success on the battlefield to the fact that she possessed a fighting faith, an inspirational ideology of patriotism that had been successfully communicated to the masses through her superior educational system. As Claude Digeon has aptly remarked, many Frenchmen were convinced, whether rightly or wrongly, that Germany had "materially triumphed" because she was "better armed spiritually" than France.[34] Though repelled by the authoritarian, irrationalist content of the Germanic ideology, Monod could not help but marvel at its hold on the populace: "God, Fatherland, and Family is the triple inspiration that created the unity of the German army and the German nation," he declared, and despite its obvious shortcomings, it has contributed something "noble and poetic" to the German mind.[35]

Furthermore, Monod suspected that the source of this inspiration was an intense historical consciousness, which produced a serene sense of confidence in the historical destiny of the Germanic spirit as it unfolded through the progressive victories of its earthly embodiment, the German nation. The catalysts of this new trend of historical thinking were the great historians of the German universities whose writings had contributed to the reawakening of German national consciousness: Niebuhr, Sybel, Treitschke, and others. "Never before," Georg Iggers has written, "had German historians played such an active part in the course of German events as in the decisive years between 1830 and 1871 which saw the struggle for national unification. The history of Germany . . . cannot be written without devoting considerable space to the central role played by the historians."[36] It was to these men that many French historians of the postwar period turned for inspiration, hoping to play an analogous role in the spiritual reawakening of the French nation by implanting in the French people a sense of their historical destiny.[37]

This eagerness to profit from the experience of a foreign nation, especially one that continued to be regarded as a hereditary enemy, was a sentiment that had few precedents in France. For over two centuries she had been exporting her own cultural traditions to the newly emerging nations of the Western (and in some cases, the non-Western) world, and had remained relatively unreceptive to reciprocal influences. But the blatant contrast between her decaying educational system and the thriving German schools that was heightened by the calamity of 1870 produced a sense of consternation that helped to break this cultural isolationism.[38] The historians of France realized that they would have to bring to a successful conclusion the reforms proposed earlier by Duruy and the editorial staffs of the new professional periodicals if they were to match the achievements of their German counterparts and assume the leadership of the patriotic revival in France. What had begun as a reform movement of modest proportions in the Second Empire blossomed into a major campaign to modernize the procedures and methods of French historical scholarship and teaching after 1870. The new generation of historians recognized that if their discipline were to serve as the catalyst of a national renaissance in postwar France, their immediate obligation was twofold: to redouble their efforts to implant a tradition of scientific historical scholarship in France, and to establish the discipline of history on a truly professional footing by extending the pedagogical innovations introduced at the Ecole Pratique to the entire system of French higher education.

The chastening effects of the military debacle produced an air of stridency in their criticisms of the historical tradition of France. The relatively mild dissatisfaction with the state of the profession that had prompted the moderate reforms of the Liberal Empire was superseded by an angry mood of recrimination in the early years of the Third Republic. Its two chief targets were first, the historians ensconced in the principal centers of higher learning who had succeeded in compelling Duruy to postpone his plans to introduce modern methods of scholarship; and second, the amateur historians outside the universities who had played such an important role in perpetuating the literary tradition of historical writing that was under attack.

This renewed critique of the French historical tradition echoed many of the complaints of the prewar reformers. The reform-minded historians revived the familiar indictment of the unscientific nature of French historical scholarship. They attributed this defect to history's traditional identification with the disciplines of literature and philosophy. The literary influences on historical scholarship, they charged, resulted in an overemphasis on the importance of style at the expense of factual documentation. Monod complained about "the important role that form plays in the work of our savants." By "form" he meant not only "style" but also "the art of exposition, the ingenious and original arrangement of [logical] demonstrations," qualities which are "entirely personal" and therefore "cannot be taught."[39] He compared the impressive record of historical production in Germany to the meager French output and concluded that the contrast in performance of the two nations was due to their conflicting attitudes toward scholarship. Noting that German historians had made the "greatest contribution to the historical labor of our century," he attributed Germany's superiority in that field to "its particular genius," which is "essentially appropriate to patient scholarly research."[40]

Monod was careful to defend German historical scholarship against the oft-repeated accusation that it fostered the qualities of pedantry, slavish fact-gathering, and a marked incapacity for formulating meaningful conclusions and general ideas. German scholarship does produce generalizations, Monod insisted, but in contrast to the hastily-formulated generalizations that abound in much French historical writing, "they are not literary fantasies, invented in a capricious moment for the charm of the imagination." Instead of spinning out "systems and theories destined to please by their beautiful appearance and their artistic structure" the great German historians "slowly and rigorously" formulate hypothetical generalizations designed to explain "already established facts" and encourage the "exploration of facts [that are] still obscure."[41]

Monod denounced the peculiarly French propensity for formulating general ideas that are unsubstantiated by the empirical evidence as an oppressive legacy of Cartesian philosophy. He also identified the Gallic obsession with literary form and style as a bitter fruit of the French classical tradition. He complained that the French manner of thinking is more spontaneous, more capricious, more "prone to the seductions of the imagination and art" than is that of the more "toughminded" Germans.[42] Despite the patient efforts of the Benedictines at the Académie des Inscriptions et Belles-Lettres and their secular successors at the Ecole de Chartes to forge a scientific tradition of historical scholarship, the old tradition of literary and philosophical vulgarization, which considered careful research in primary sources as a drudgery beneath its dignity, has retained its stranglehold on the intellectual life of nineteenth century France.[43] It was becoming increasingly clear to the new generation of historians that the rebirth of historical studies in France would require them to repudiate and eventually rid themselves of the twin albatrosses of Cartesian philosophy and classical literature.

From the harshness of these attacks, one might easily be led to the conclusion that no history worthy of the name had been written in France during the first half of the nineteenth century. Yet the names of Guizot, Thierry, Mignet, Quinet, Michelet, and many others conjure up the composite image of a fecund era of historical production. Indeed, the prolificacy of the French historians during this period caused Monod himself to designate the first half of the nineteenth century as the golden age of historical writing in France.[44] Furthermore, since the current interest in history had been prompted by the growing recognition of its potential value as a source of patriotic instruction, the modern reformers' wholesale condemnation of the earlier period implied that they saw little evidence that history had discharged this obligation during the first half of the century. Yet the indisputable popularity of the historical narratives that flowed from the pens of the historians of this period, during which France was recovering from an earlier military setback, indicates that history had indeed played a significant role in the national recovery after 1815. What was it that prevented these old masters, whose historical writings had helped rescue the French spirit from the despair caused by Waterloo, from serving as models for the historians who were hoping to heal the wounds of Sedan?

The answer to this question emerges from an examination of the different nature of the nationalist movements of the two epochs. The nationalist revival that inspired the historical writing of the first half of the century was closely identified with the Romantic movement in French culture. Most of the historians who wrote during the Romantic period shared the dominant values and beliefs of their contemporaries in the world of letters. They placed a premium on the qualities of personal inspiration, subjective imagination, and evocative self-expression. They regarded their historical writing as the fruit of artistic creativity, the achievement of gifted, idiosyncratic geniuses, a lasting monument to the miraculous process of the human consciousness confronting the variegated reality of the past. The historians of the post-1870 era, by contrast, were striving to construct a sturdy institutional edifice upon which they could establish a tradition of historical scholarship that would nurture a school of practitioners capable of preserving and augmenting the body of cumulative knowledge that they had begun to amass.

The nationalist movement of the 1870s, in which the historians played an important role, severed its ties with the Romantic nationalism of the earlier era. The new nationalism had been captured by the scientific spirit of the modern age, and the historical movement of the postwar generation was profoundly influenced by this new mood. By mid-century the scientific method had assumed a measure of prestige that rendered it virtually immune to criticism until the antipositivist revolt of the *fin de siècle*. The German victory of 1870 enhanced its reputation even further, since it was generally assumed that the Teutonic monopoly on modern scientific knowledge had been instrumental in the French defeat. And since scientific procedures were characterized by the spirit of collaboration, teamwork, and self-effacement on the part of those engaged in empirical research (as compared to the type of singular creativity displayed by the philosophe, *littérateur*, or artist), they were thought likely to flourish only within a highly-organized, institutionalized framework of laboratories, seminars, and workshops. It was precisely this type of organizational discipline that Monod, Lavisse, Rambaud, Paris, and their associates were seeking to establish in France on a broader scale.

But the official inquiries of Duruy had conclusively demonstrated that the institutions conducive to the creation of such a tradition of historical scholarship were virtually nonexistent in France, and the subsequent innovations initiated under his ministry had only scratched the surface of the old system. The type of specialized technical preparation that was considered necessary for the intelligent exploitation of documentary material was still confined to the poorly-financed seminars of the Ecole Pratique, an institution which continued to be regarded as an "adjunct school" and was therefore denied the authority to enroll students of its own or grant degrees. The Ecole d'Athènes, founded in 1846 but insignificant as a center of historical research until the 1870s, and the Ecole de Rome, founded in 1873, were also considered complements to existing institutions, and confined their scholarly activities largely to archeological studies of classical antiquity. The Ecole des Chartes continued to provide only a highly-specialized type of training in medieval studies and to grant degrees in archival management.[45]

Moreover, the proliferation of professional historical journals in Germany put the French output of such periodical literature to shame. The scholar who wished to publish the preliminary results of his research had only the Catholic *Revue des questions historiques* to turn to. The *Revue critique*, on which historians were totally dependent as a forum for the evaluation of scholarly works, temporarily ceased publication in 1871. In short, it had become evident that a sustained, concerted effort would have to be mounted before the hope of establishing a historical discipline in France could be fulfilled.

The French historians recognized that the success of their ambitious designs for their profession would depend in part on their success in soliciting the support of the political elite that had recently replaced the discredited Bonapartists. Duruy had succeeded in translating his proposed reforms into law largely because he enjoyed the confidence of His Imperial Majesty and his court. Though most of the young historians who achieved positions of influence in the immediate postwar period had won their spurs as loyal servants of the Second Empire, they hastened to make their peace with the newly established republican regime.[46] For their part, the republican politicians who gained the upper hand in the struggle with the royalists and Bonapartists for political control of postwar France in the 1870s welcomed the support of the French intelligentsia. It was this social group, after all, that had traditionally furnished the ideological justification for the regnant political system in France.

Historians in particular have often exercised a considerable influence on the formulation of political ideologies in modern societies.[47] In some cases they have used the resources of their craft to bestow the imprimatur of a favorable historical judgment upon an established political regime in order to help legitimize it in the eyes of the public. In other cases they have furnished ideological ammunition to counter-revolutionary movements by using historical arguments to discredit the present system and demonstrate the necessity of restoring the status quo ante. In still other cases, historians have served the cause of revolutionary forces by criticizing the existing order as a temporary impediment to the predetermined process of historical evolution.

Historical writing readily lends itself to all three of these purposes. In cases where history has served as an ideological apologia for the existing political regime, it is employed to portray that particular system as the ineluctable product of centuries of historical evolution, the highest stage in the nation's political development.[48] Such a doctrine presupposes, of course, belief in the inevitability of progress in history. The multitudinous political evils associated with past epochs are contrasted with the improved political conditions of the present, and the agency of progress is traditionally attributed to the regime in power. In cases where history has served as the handmaiden of counterrevolution, the converse method has obtained. It has been used to indict the present governing elite by presenting an unflattering comparison of the prosaic present and the preferable situation that obtained in some glorious era of the past.[49] The underlying assumption of this second type of ideological history is a conception of historical retrogression or decadence. A vision that idealizes a long-lost Golden Age is juxtaposed against the critical interpretation of contemporary reality, and the present political system is held responsible for abandoning the successful ideals of the past.[50] Similarly, historians and philosophers of history who have functioned as the ideological champions of revolution have sought to uncover objective laws of history that purportedly demonstrate the ineluctable evolution of certain historical forces tending toward a total transformation of the existing order.[51]

The writings of Guizot furnish an instructive model of historical sermonizing, in both its Utopian and conservative manifestations. His works of Restoration vintage, which were thinly veiled indictments of monarchical absolutism and vigorous defenses of the English tradition of constitutional monarchy, eventually resulted in the suppression of his history courses between 1822 and 1828.[52] After his rise to ministerial power under the July Monarchy, he became the ideological apologist of the new political order, and did not hesitate to invoke the authority of history to buttress his political doctrines. He presented the Orléanist regime as the legitimate heir of the French Revolution and its principles of measured liberty.

Augustin Thierry, like Guizot, transformed history into what a subsequent observer has called "a weapon of combat." His vituperative attacks on the Bourbons that filled the pages of *Le Censeur européen* between 1817 and 1820, later collected and published as *Dix Ans d'études historiques,* were typical examples of the new variety of liberal history that was beginning to gain popularity in France. To Thierry, as to Guizot, the formula for the political use of history was to rediscover in the past "the foundation of all the liberties that people were seeking" and then to demonstrate how the disappearance of these liberties in the present was caused by the "brutal conquests of an aristocracy" which had imposed "an odious yoke on the people."[53] A later work, entitled *L'Histoire de Jacques Bonhomme,* bristled with appeals for the liberation of the "oppressed nation," from the Bourbon yoke, and portrayed the average Frenchman as a miserable, maltreated victim of royal repression and clerical superstition. Thus both Thierry and Guizot, whose moderately liberal political views colored their historical writing, "searched a bit naively in the past centuries for the starting points of the political evolution that was to culminate, according to them, in the constitutional monarchy of Louis Philippe."[54]

Jules Michelet was to become the most prominent French historian to place his talents at the service of a political cause. His passionate invocation of the revolutionary mystique and the ideals of humanitarian nationalism that he regarded as its most precious legacy played a role in subsequent regimes analogous to that played by the historical criticism of the Bourbons. By subjecting the drab, uninspired character of the July Monarchy's foreign and domestic undertakings to a historical comparison with the adventuresome policies of the Revolutionary period, his works constituted a perpetual embarrassment to the Orléanist regime.[55] Whether serving a critical or supportive function, history had demonstrated by mid-century that it was ideally suited to serve a political purpose.[56]

Neither the historians who rose to prominence in the aftermath of the national disaster at Sedan, nor the republican statesmen who shepherded the new regime through the first decade of its existence, could have avoided envisaging the mutual advantages that might flow from a *mariage de convenance* of politics and history under the Third Republic. The republicans remained in a precarious political position throughout the balance of the 1870s. Monarchist majorities controlled the National Assembly in the years following the defeat, and the proponents of a parliamentary republic were able to gain legislative approval of their constitutional laws in 1875 by the margin of a single vote. After this rather inglorious accession, the republicans were compelled to reckon with influential, well-financed circles of Bonapartists, Orléanists, and Legitimists, which had begun to employ modern techniques of political propaganda to arouse public opinion against the fledgling regime. The shaky foundations of their political position compelled the defenders of the Republic to search for means of forging a political consensus that would enable them to tighten their grip on the reins of power. The young French historians who constituted what I have called the "scholarly" school of historical study, on the other hand, were eager to receive official blessing (and monetary support) for their plans to renew the projects to establish an academic historical profession that had been interrupted by the war. The objective conditions for a mutually beneficial alliance between republican politicians and historical reformers persisted for the remainder of the nineteenth century. By providing historical apologetics for the revolutionary republican tradition in France, and by portraying the Third Republic as its legitimate heir, the historians could help to establish the consensus that the new regime was so desperately seeking. In return, the republican government, by supporting and financing the professional and educational reforms proposed by the historians, could contribute to the revival of historical studies in the French universities.

This is not to suggest that any official bargain was ever struck between these two parties. Indeed, the leading spokesmen for the nascent academic historical profession in France issued periodic declarations of political neutrality and vigorously defended the ancient conception of the university as a refuge from political influence. But in spite of these frequent protestations, the last quarter of the nineteenth century was characterized by a de facto collaboration, based on mutual advantage, between the republican political leadership and the promoters of the historical revival.[57]

Once this tacit alliance had solidified, each party was quick to recognize that the common vehicle through which its future objectives could be realized was the state-controlled educational system. The political regime was led to expect that the establishment of an academic historical profession in the French universities would ultimately produce an army of scholars whose teaching and writing would help to rekindle public enthusiasm for the French revolutionary tradition (and thereby recruit new converts to the republican cause). The historians likewise stood to gain a multitude of benefits from such a policy. The centralization of historical scholarship in the academy would set the stage for the establishment and enforcement of the professional regulations and standards that Duruy had been unable to impose on the prewar university. The voluminous historical archives of France, which were languishing in dismal condition due to centuries of neglect, could be assembled and catalogued in a systematic fashion. Bibliographical material could be organized and made available to the historian to orient him in his research. Perhaps most important of all, the system of seminars and *répétiteurs* (seminar leaders), which had met with such success within the limited confines of the Ecole Pratique, could finally be introduced in the university system at large.

The first significant indication that the prewar campaign to organize a historical profession in France had been revived appeared in the middle of the 1870s with the foundation of a professional journal devoted to establishing and enforcing standards of historical scholarship. The *Revue critique* had ceased publication during the war and, except for an abbreviated series of postwar issues, was not to reappear, in a totally revamped form, until 1876.[58] But by the time of its reappearance it had already been superseded by a new periodical which rapidly achieved recognition as the official organ of historical opinion in France. In January of 1876, exactly one year after the Wallon amendment to the constitutional laws enacted by the National Assembly had established the de jure existence of the Third Republic, Monod and Gustave Fagniez, a paleographer trained at the Ecole des Chartes, launched the *Revue historique*.

In the preface to the first number, Monod took the occasion to review the progress of historical studies in France during the past century. He noted that history had flourished in the intellectually exciting atmosphere of the Enlightenment, chiefly at the hands of writers who used their pens for partisan political purposes. He singled out Mably as having originated the practice of "searching in history for arguments supporting the nascent democratic ideas" that eventually triumphed in 1793.[59] He remarked that the political leaders of the Revolution and the Empire had almost totally suppressed the study of history owing to their "blind aversion for all institutions of the past." By destroying the religious orders and the academies they succeeded in bringing all scholarly work in the field of history to a standstill.[60] He then grudgingly paid tribute to the Restoration for restoring to France the consciousness of her past that had been suppressed during the previous quarter century. The efforts to revive the traditions of the ancient monarchy, which he scorned, were nevertheless accompanied by an admirable desire "to draw nearer to and understand the past."[61]

But unlike Duruy before him, Monod did not shrink from expressing feelings of intense disappointment regarding the woeful state of historical studies in the *Université* in general, and particularly in the Sorbonne. He noted sadly that the only important instances of progress in historical scholarship in France were to be found outside the university system, in the scholarly activity of the clergy and the academies. What a striking contrast to Germany! There the tradition of historical scholarship has been preserved in the centers of higher learning, where "the exploration of the diverse domains of history follows a regular and systematic progression" and is facilitated by the combined efforts of the university professors and their disciples.[62] "No country has contributed more than Germany," he observed, to providing historical studies with a "rigorously scientific character."

The free lance tradition of historical writing in France, on the other hand, had inhibited the growth of "any general scientific discipline, any directing authority," as well as the respect for "methodological rules" and "habits of collective labor" that only a university education fosters.[63]

Monod blamed the *malaise* of the French historical studies on the traditional antagonism between "literature" and "scholarship." He reiterated Duruy's complaint that many *lettrés,* both within and without the university, harbored a deep-seated distrust of scholarly research. For them, "imagination, good sense, a certain dose of the philosophical spirit, and style" were sufficient preconditions for historical writing.[64] The *érudits* at the Ecole des Chartes commit the opposite sin of cultivating an excessive disdain for hypotheses, theories, and general ideas, which they regard as mere superfluous exercises of the undisciplined imagination, and take refuge in minutiae and factual details that are often without interest to anyone but specialists.[65] Once again, in the manner of Duruy, he blamed this bifurcation of the French historical tradition on the haphazard organization of the national system of higher education. The scholars of the Ecole des Chartes receive an overly specialized and technical type of instruction while the educated gentlemen at the Ecole Normale and the Sorbonne are subjected to a vague, superficial mish-mash of useless generalities. Even his beloved Ecole Pratique, despite the efforts of its distinguished young faculty, had as yet failed to create an effective bridge between these two contradictory methods of historical instruction.[66]

Monod believed that a remedy for this deficiency in the French historical tradition would be forthcoming once scholars had agreed upon a common purpose that could unite historians engaged in diverse types of research. He was confident that the preconditions for such a professional orientation existed in France, but he impatiently complained that the spirit of professionalism suffered from stunted growth. He remarked that though the small group of historians who had adopted the latest techniques of historical scholarship were hard at work on various specialized projects, they did not yet regard themselves as researchers united in a common commitment to extend the boundaries of historical scholarship and received little institutional support. He was convinced that the ideal site for such a coordination of scholarly activities was "a well-organized system of higher education." Pending the creation of such an academic historical profession, he hoped that the *Revue historique* would serve not only to dispense valuable information about historical subjects, but also to encourage young men who intend to enter the career of history to adopt the methods of scientific scholarship.[67]

To protect the new journal from accusations of political partisanship, Monod took great pains to establish its credibility as a thoroughly independent organ. Ridiculing the Catholic *Revue des questions historiques* as an example of a historical periodical which continually violates the principle of "disinterested and scientific research" in order to further the cause of certain political or religious ideas, he promised that the *Revue historique* would remain independent of all ideological movements or parties. The scientific approach to the past, which was to be required of all its contributors, would ensure scholarly objectivity and guard against a revival of the partisanship that had typified previous French historical writing. "We will therefore take up no banner," he announced. "We will profess no dogmatic creed; we will put ourselves at the disposal of no party . . . Our strictly scientific point of view will suffice to provide the unity of tone and character to our journal."[68] This explicit pledge of impartiality was borne out in the list of contributors to the maiden issue, which comprised the leading representatives of the French historical profession, regardless of political persuasion.[69] In no instance did Monod seek to identify the new professional periodical with the political ideology of the regime under which it was launched, nor did he rule out the possibility of publishing historical works that might conflict with the republican orthodoxy. Indeed, during the first two decades of the review's existence one is hard put to discover any concrete evidence of political bias in the selection of contributors or reviewers.

This nonpartisan spirit was a natural outgrowth of the relatively quiescent nature of French political life during the last quarter of the nineteenth century. Aside from periodic spasms of counterrevolutionary activity by the dispersed forces of the right (such as the abortive adventure in presidential authoritarianism of Marshal MacMahon in 1877 and the royalist and Bonapartist machinations on behalf of General Boulanger a decade later), challenges to the existing political system were the exception rather than the rule during the twenty years following the foundation of the *Revue historique*. The Republic had apparently achieved widespread acceptance after a slow, painful birth in the wake of military defeat, and did not yet need to be defended from hostile domestic critics. In these early years it represented, as its first chief executive accurately described it, the regime that divided France the least. The primary objective of the republican ruling elite, once its right to govern had been secured after 1875, was to recover the sense of national pride that had been temporarily lost in 1870, and to this cause the editors of the *Revue historique*, like all good Frenchmen, were committed. It was not until the Dreyfus Affair at the end of the century that the Third Republic faced a serious domestic challenge. Only then did the unabashed republican sympathies of the directors of the *Revue historique* shine through the façade of scientific impartiality that Monod had so carefully erected.

Having innoculated his new review against possible allegations of republican bias, Monod felt obliged to take precautions against the potentially more damaging accusation that he and his colleagues were bent on abandoning the French tradition of logical consistency and literary excellence in favor of the erudite, pedantic approach of German scholarship. He conceded that the editors would demand of all contributors "strictly scientific methods of exposition," with each generalization or conclusion accompanied "by proof, by source references, and by quotations," and reaffirmed his intention to exclude from consideration works that contain "vague generalities and rhetoric." But he was careful to commit the new journal to the preservation of "that literary quality that scholars as well as French readers justly value so highly."[70] Moreover, the review was not to be regarded solely as a professional medium catering to an exclusive elite of specialists, but rather was intended for any literate citizen who has a general interest in history.[71]

The foundation of the *Revue historique* had an electric effect on the French historical profession. It set an example of professional excellence and scholarly objectivity that was soon emulated by a plethora of scholarly journals and professional societies, all of which in turn helped to establish a network of collegial ties among historians and to foster a sense of professional obligation among them that had never existed in France.[72] Monod vigorously defended this novel conception of professional unity as a *sine qua non* of truly scientific historical scholarship. He deplored the tendency of French historians to regard their works as definitive, an assumption which frequently caused them to republish them at twenty-year intervals without changing a word.[73] He believed that the new professional organizations and periodicals would help to create a fund of historical scholarship that would enable the individual historian, whatever his claim to genius, to improve the quality of his future scholarship and to update the material in his works already published by drawing on the cumulative research of others in his field. The historical profession would thereby serve to put the people of France in contact with a scientifically accurate reconstruction of the past grandeur of their fatherland. And like their German counterparts after the defeat at Jena, the French historians would use the lessons of history to revive the flagging spirits of a vanquished people.

3
The Institutionalization of Historical Study in the New Sorbonne

After the foundation of the *Revue historique,* the first item on the agenda of the historical reformers was the enterprise that had proved too challenging for Duruy: the establishment of history as an academic discipline in the regular university system. Because of its pre-eminent position in French higher learning, the reformers looked to the Sorbonne as the ideal site for the transformation of historical study from a haphazard enterprise into an organized activity. It was hoped that the shining example of scholarly activity furnished by the Ecole Pratique, together with the nascent historical profession's demonstrable contribution to France's national recovery—two arguments that had not been available to Duruy—would attract sufficient support for the creation of a historical discipline in the very heart of the university. The transformation of the Sorbonne into an organized center of historical scholarship can be divided roughly into two phases. The first, covering the years from the military defeat to 1885, was the period of preparation, marked by several important reforms coupled with increasing agitation on behalf of more fundamental innovations. The second, from 1885 to 1905, saw the realization of the historical reformers' projects in a totally reconstituted system of higher education.

The educational atmosphere at the University of Paris in the decade of the 1870s had changed little since the prewar period. The public courses still more closely resembled the street schools of ancient Athens than the celebrated centers of academic scholarship across the Rhine. The absence of attendance controls, the spaciousness of the amphitheaters, and the reputation that many professors cultivated as entertaining lecturers, all served to attract what Ernest Lavisse derisively labeled the *public de passage* and to discourage serious students, who preferred to prepare for their examinations at home or in cafés. Since the only academic function of the faculty was to administer examinations for the *baccalauréat* and *licence* degrees, the number of professorial chairs seldom exceeded the number of questioners that were needed to constitute an examination jury. Consequently, until 1878 the Sorbonne had only two chairs in history (compared to eight each at Berlin and Leipzig) and no counterparts of the *Privatdozenten* (junior faculty members below the professorial rank) who assisted the regular faculty of the German universities.[1]

The reformers realized that they had little hope of establishing a tradition of historical scholarship in the Sorbonne until they could succeed in uprooting the obsolete tradition of the public lecture. Remarking that the deterioration of French higher education was due to the absence of "serious students," Gabriel Monod, from the vantage point of an outsider at the Ecole Pratique, suggested that the large amphitheaters be replaced by small seminar rooms patterned after those already in operation at his institution. He urged that these "intimate meetings" be reserved exclusively for scholarly researchers who would be assigned specific seats. "The idle and frivolous public," he declared, "will soon be, if not formally excluded, at least diverted from these courses by the very nature of the lessons, which will be accessible only to assiduous and hard-working students." If curious amateurs insist on their right to attend, and if the educational authorities feel that "the door must be left open to them," he asserted, they should be "relegated to the back of the room, if space is still available."[2]

But once the classrooms had been cleared of *les curieux,* a way would have to be found to attract dedicated students to replace them. Financial inducements in the form of state scholarships, improved classroom facilities, a dramatic increase in the number of qualified faculty members, and a host of other innovations were called for before the Sorbonne could hope to divert talented students from the advanced research institutes such as the Ecole des Chartes and the Ecole Pratique with the promise of a genuine scholarly education. In the same year that he launched the *Revue historique,* Monod expressed the hope that the University of Paris would one day absorb all the scattered, autonomous branches of higher learning in the capital to form one centrally-directed educational complex. The specter of a "truly encyclopedic school" in the city that had once been the intellectual center of the Western world filled him with anticipations of renewed grandeur. "Could any other university in Europe be compared to it?" The very universality of such a *Université,* he predicted, would rapidly erase "the divergences of philosophical and religious prejudices" that had long plagued French society and replace them with "the superior idea of science."[3]

The increasing frequency with which the term "science" appeared in the lexicon of the historical reformers was indicative of their growing realization that their proposals for academic innovations were more likely to receive sympathetic consideration if they were clothed in scientific garb. They did not fail to take account of the mounting prestige of the scientific method in the eyes of the French public, a development that reflected popular recognition of the pioneering discoveries of Pasteur and Claude Bernard in medicine, Charcot in psychopathology, Berthelot in chemistry, and the Curies and the Becquerels in physics. These and other laboratory investigators in the natural sciences had begun to restore France to its former position as a major center of scientific research, a field in which it had been overtaken and surpassed by Germany since the middle of the century. But more important, the practical uses to which their discoveries had been put lent credence to the claim that scientific research deserved public support because of the tangible benefits that it conferred on the common man and the contributions that it made to national strength.[4]

Furthermore, by some curious twist of logic, a necessary affiliation between science and democratic political institutions became a cardinal faith of the intellectual apologists of the Third Republic. Few Frenchmen in the late nineteenth century would have taken issue with Emile Durkheim's assertions that "a democracy would be unfaithful to its principle if it did not have a faith in science" and that scientific progress was more likely to occur under democratic auspices freed from the constraints of autocracy and superstition.[5] The fact that French scientific achievement reached its apex in the first three decades of the nineteenth century under the aegis of an authoritarian empire and a reactionary monarchy, or again that German science prospered under the Hohenzollern autocracy,[6] was conveniently ignored for obvious ideological reasons.

No one deserves more credit for popularizing this conception of science as a natural ally of democracy in the early years of the Third Republic than the neopositivist philosopher Emile Littré. After discarding the authoritarian, hierarchical, antidemocratic elements of Auguste Comte's original formulation of positivist doctrine that had served as a perpetual source of embarrassment to the liberal devotees of social science, Littré succeeded in recasting positivism in a democratic mold that rendered it more congenial to the political atmosphere of France after 1870. From the writings of Littré and his disciples emerged the image of science as the effective tool with which the people, meaning the sober bourgeoisie, could construct a new social order unencumbered by the constraints of the past.[7] The technological breakthroughs that resulted from research in the natural sciences appeared to confirm the assumption that the citizen in a democracy and the scientist in his laboratory were destined to derive mutual benefit from a policy of cooperation with each other, the citizen authorizing his elected representatives to furnish political and financial support for scientific enterprise in return for the expectation of enjoying the fruits it was likely to yield.

In view of the rising popularity of science, the educational reformers of the late nineteenth century did not think it unreasonable to expect that the citizens of the Third Republic would willingly support, for reasons of self-interest, a rational scheme of education innovation that promised to improve the scientific quality of higher learning in France. But if public support for scientific education was anticipated with certainty, popular sympathy for the creation of an elaborate program of historical study in the university was much more problematical. For while the more advanced members of the historical profession may have convinced themselves of the scientific character of their calling, they could hardly expect the average citizen, who was likely to be blissfully unaware of the recent developments in the profession, to regard history as anything other than what it had been considered for centuries: a branch of the humanities.

What troubled the historical reformers most about this lag in public awareness was the fact that French letters had traditionally flourished under the benign patronage of those leisured elites whose political power rested on a firm base of wealth and privilege. Who could predict with certainty whether this willingness to subsidize and encourage "higher culture" would be maintained by the newly enfranchised citizens, most of whom had not been able to enrich themselves before becoming electors? What distinguished the sciences from the humanities in the mind of the average citizen was the potential "relevance" of even the most esoteric variety of scientific research to his daily struggle for existence. "Of what importance to democracy," asked an astute observer of French higher education, "is the deciphering of a palimpsest or the corrections that can be made in the chronology of Manetho? Each person can feel the need for the serums of the *Institut Pasteur,* but no one except the egyptologists is concerned about the Pharaohs."[8] The historian Ferdinand Lot complained that the pervasion of the "utilitarian" spirit in French democracy placed the historian and philologist at a distinct disadvantage vis-à-vis the scientist in the annual scramble for public funds to support research and endow new academic chairs. The citizen can easily understand "the necessity for professors of chemistry and botany" because their research produces immediate and tangible benefits to society, he noted, but the historian or philologist could make no such claim to social usefulness.[9]

The founders of the French historical profession were painfully aware of the need to demonstrate the usefulness of history to the general public before they could hope to gain widespread support for their plans to institutionalize historical research in the university system. As they began to confront the task of convincing the political elite and the citizenry of the Third Republic of the worthiness of their cause, they could not help but recall that the First Republic and its successive ruling cliques had been uniformly hostile to the elitist nature of higher education. Upon returning from his postwar sojourn across the Rhine, Lavisse compared the sumptuous classrooms and lavishly stocked libraries of imperial Germany to the academic desert that greeted him in republican France, and asked himself whether there might exist a "democratic prejudice against higher education."[10] Charles Seignobos continued to agonize over the incompatibility of the old conception of the university as a training ground for the intellectual elite and "the conditions of contemporary France, that is to say, of a liberal democracy." He wondered whether a democratic society could be counted on to tolerate the existence of an elitist system of higher education "that would appear to have no [practical] use," such as a faculty of letters.[11] An acerbic comment by Pierre Leguay, a contemporary observer of the campaign to renovate the Sorbonne, suggests one possible explanation of how the reformers of that institution sought to justify their radical schemes in the eyes of the recently enfranchised citizens of the Third Republic. "If the sciences and democracy go hand in hand," he declared, it is obvious that "the humanities, in order also to adapt to democracy, will have to model themselves on the sciences." With sarcastic candor, he noted that "while the 'barbarians' have no love for the humanities, they have a superstitious respect for science. Hence, in order to save themselves, the humanities will have to be disguised or transformed into sciences."[12]

Since the itemized budget of the Ministry of Public Instruction required the approval of the Chamber of Deputies, all academic innovations that included expenditures of money had to be justified in political as well as educational terms. The record of unwavering legislative support for the succession of educational reforms that revolutionized the structure and function of the Sorbonne between 1880 and 1914 indicated that the French public, speaking through its elected representatives, had either suspended its traditional hostility to the impractical, "irrelevant" type of higher learning associated with the faculty of letters, or had been beguiled by humanistic education's scientific disguise.[13] Moreover, the records of student enrollment at the University of Paris indicate a steady rate of increase for the Faculty of Letters that exceeded that of the Faculties of Science, Medicine, and Pharmacy (see Appendix A). From the standpoint of governmental patronage and student clientage, the Sorbonne experienced an unparalleled period of prosperity and popularity between 1880 and 1900.

The most revealing index of governmental support for higher education was the creation of new professorial chairs, a process which also required the approval of the Minister of Public Instruction and a financial appropriation from the legislature. The statistics on the number of new teaching positions, both in Paris and in the provinces, furnish conclusive testimony to the hegemony of the historical profession in French higher education. In the last two decades of the nineteenth century the rate at which professorial chairs in history were created in the French university system far exceeded that of the German universities (See Appendix B). By the turn of the century the number of chairs in history exceeded the number of chairs created in each of the other nonscientific disciplines, with the exception of classical philology (see Appendix C), though this relative superiority in the French universities compared unfavorably with history's relative position in Germany (see Appendix D). The two disciplines that had predominated in the unreformed faculties of letters in France throughout the nineteenth century, literature and philosophy, were overtaken and surpassed by the discipline of history in the reformed *Université* with regard to the number of new professorial chairs (see Appendix E) as well as to student interest (see Appendix F).

The signal success of the historical reformers in achieving their professional objectives was made possible by their ability to secure appointments to an inordinate number of key administrative and advisory positions in the French educational bureaucracy. The earliest institutional vehicle through which the academic historians began to exercise their influence on the government was a quasi-official pressure group dedicated to the promotion of educational innovation at the university level, the Société de l'Enseignement Supérieur, founded in 1880 by Lavisse, Monod, and others, the former of whom served as perpetual secretary general.[14] The principal function of the society was the publication of the *Revue internationale de l'enseignement,* which rapidly became the official mouthpiece of the reformers and was widely read in political and educational circles. The review probed, examined, and criticized every aspect of French higher education. It published the annual budget of the Ministry of Public Instruction, commissioned comparative studies of the faculties of letters in the French universities and their counterparts in Germany, and provided a forum for those educational innovators who were bent on upgrading the system of higher learning in France. Virtually every reform introduced during the last two decades of the nineteenth century was first proposed in the pages of this important organ.

The political influence that the historical reformers enjoyed by virtue of their domination of the Société de l'Enseignement Supérieur was strengthened by more formal connections with the center of academic power in Paris. Although legal authority for all important decisions regarding the French university system rested with the Minister of Public Instruction, a substantial amount of power was delegated to several academic organizations composed of leading *universitaires*. Foremost among these was the Conseil Supérieur de l'Instruction Publique, a blue ribbon advisory panel of which Lavisse was a perennial member, which advised the minister on a wide range of educational matters affecting the entire structure of the *Université*.[15] Scarcely less influential were the various Conseils de l'Université, the governing body of each of the fifteen universities, which had the power to administer the funds appropriated by the legislative body, to organize new courses, and to advise the minister on such matters as the preparation of the next year's budget, the creation of new professorial chairs, and the abolition of existing ones. As was the case with the Conseil Supérieur de l'Enseignement Publique, the Conseil of the University of Paris contained an inordinate representation of historians, in either an ex officio or an elected capacity.[16]

This intricate network of institutional ties brought the leaders of the historical reform movement into close and regular contact with the political leadership of the Third Republic, particularly that segment of it specializing in educational matters. One important benefit that the historical reformers reaped from this increasingly intimate relationship, in addition to political support for the establishment of an elaborate program of historical studies in the French universities, was the privilege of holding the reins of administrative power in the reformed university system of Paris. When the Sorbonne and the Ecole Normale were finally transformed into modern centers of academic scholarship in the last years of the nineteenth century and the early years of the twentieth, two historians who had spearheaded the reform movement, Alfred Croiset and Ernest Lavisse, were appropriately designated to preside over those two renovated institutions.[17]

If domination of informal pressure groups for educational reform such as the Société de l'Enseignement Supérieur, membership in advisory bodies such as the Conseil Supérieur de l'Instruction Publique and the Conseil de l'Université de Paris, and administrative power at the Sorbonne and the Ecole Normale were insufficient to guarantee the implementation of the historical profession's program for the reform of French higher education, its eventual success was ensured by the fortuitous presence of well-placed members of the profession in the Ministry of Public Instruction itself. As in the days of Guizot, Thiers, and Duruy, when French historians combined careers in scholarship and government, the historical profession in the early years of the Third Republic produced a number of men who entered politics and rose to positions of power in the burgeoning educational bureaucracy. It was this entree to republican politics, perhaps more than any other advantage, that enabled the historical reformers to secure the requisite political support for their proposed innovations in education and scholarship.

The first wave of reform began in 1877, under the leadership of Minister of Public Instruction William Waddington, a philologist, numismatist, and republican politician who had served with Monod and Rambaud in the original faculty of the fourth section of the Ecole Pratique des Hautes Etudes as professor of Greek philology.[18] The three major educational innovations dating from this period were all designed to dilute the power of the entrenched professoriate of the Sorbonne and the other degree-granting faculties, to break the monopoly of the notorious public course, and to establish a tradition of faculty-student intimacy and cooperation. Three hundred university scholarships *(bourses d'études)* were created to attract the most qualified candidates for the *licence*[19] to the faculties. This financial support was intended to enable these students not only to prepare for the state examination but also to pursue an organized course of study under the direction of qualified instructors. A limited number of seminar-like classes with restricted enrollments *(cours fermés)* were instituted to permit students and teachers to work together on projects of a technical nature that could not be dealt with in the public lectures.[20] To accommodate the anticipated influx of students the new position of *maître de conférences* was established to provide a temporary niche in the faculties for the most promising instructors from the *lycées*. Resembling in many respects the post of *Privatdozent* in the German university system, the new position carried a one-year appointment which was normally renewed until the incumbent became eligible for a regular post with the completion of his doctorate.[21] This important innovation was designed to fortify the faculties, and particularly the Sorbonne, with aspiring scholars trained in the methods of critical scholarship who were capable of providing students with the type of technical preparation that had previously been unavailable. That the nomination of each *maître* was to come directly from the minister increased the likelihood that prospective *érudits* untainted by the obsolete scholarly practices of the faculties would fill these critical posts.

The second stage of university reform began at the instance of Alfred Rambaud, who interrupted his scholarly career at the end of the 1870s to join the government as private secretary and special adviser to the education minister, Jules Ferry. Rambaud's intimate collaboration with the great educational reformer from 1879 to 1881 resulted in several policies that directly benefited the nascent academic historical profession, of which he continued to be an active member throughout his political career.[22] The Ferry ministry earmarked two hundred additional fellowships for candidates for the *agrégation*[23] to supplement those previously made available to students preparing for the *licence*, thereby enhancing the attractiveness of the Sorbonne and the other faculties in the eyes of prospective students. These measures were followed by the creation of several new professorial chairs, including a number in history, and it came to be understood that these new posts would no longer be awarded to *lycée* professors who had achieved prominence on the basis of their rhetorical abilities and encyclopedic knowledge, but rather would be reserved for young scholars who had demonstrated in their doctoral dissertations a capacity for distinguished original research. In addition, a vast construction project at the Sorbonne was begun for the purpose of providing the new students and faculty with adequate facilities for teaching and research. Old buildings were remodeled and new ones constructed to create seminar rooms, specialized libraries, and faculty offices where students and teachers could meet on an intimate and informal basis.[24]

Perhaps the most important reform sponsored by Ferry and Rambaud from the standpoint of the historical profession was the modification of the antiquated examination system. Before 1880 the student who aspired to a teaching position in the secondary school system was required to pass a comprehensive examination for the *licence* which required a thorough knowledge of classical literature (still regarded as the best source of *culture générale*), but which tested neither the candidate's aptitude for more specialized subjects nor his capacity to engage in independent scholarly research. Ferry instituted the *licence spéciale* and the *agrégation* in history, which were designed to permit moderate specialization and to test the student's knowledge in his field of concentration in addition to his general comprehension. The effect of this modification in degree requirements was to generate the need for an organized body of courses in history that would prepare the student for the specialized section of his examination. There gradually developed a four-year program in history, with the first two years devoted to preparation for the *licence* and the latter two for the *agrégation*.[25] In a ministerial circular dated August 5, 1881, Ferry decreed that the preparatory courses for the *licence* should provide "general instruction in history and geography," while candidates for the *agrégation* must be made to acquire not only general knowledge but also an "aptitude for personal work and scholarly research."[26] The creation of these specialized degree programs enabled the regular faculties to divert students who planned to pursue professional careers in history from the Ecole Pratique (where no degree was granted), the Ecole des Chartes (where the only degree awarded was an archivist's certificate), and the Ecole Normale (where training in scholarly techniques was subordinated to pedagogical preparation).

These extensive structural innovations were followed by a full-scale administrative reorganization of higher education in France which vastly strengthened the position of the degree-granting faculties. A governmental decree in 1885 bestowed a "civil personality" on each faculty and created a governing body composed of all permanent members which was to advise the Ministry of Public Instruction on matters such as new appointments and curricular changes. A financial law of 1889 provided each faculty with a separate budget; a law of 1893 unified the various faculties under the jurisdiction of a single administrative body, the *corps des facultés,* and finally, on July 10, 1896, with Alfred Rambaud at the helm of the Ministry of Public Instruction, the term *corps des facultés* was replaced by the term *Université*.[27]

This series of reorganization statutes revolutionized French higher education. Ever since 1808, when Napoleon I had created a system of separate faculties to replace the universities that had been abolished during the Revolution, France had been without universities in the strict sense of the term. The various faculties—law, medicine, pharmacy, letters, and science—had no real connection with each other. The first three functioned as professional schools and the latter two largely as training grounds for secondary school teachers. The reorganization statute of 1896 drew together most of the faculties and transformed them into universities. The principal beneficiary of this transformation was the illustrious Faculty of Letters of Paris. Both the Ecole des Chartes and the Ecole Pratique were deprived of their autonomy and linked to the Sorbonne by the end of the century. All that remained was the absorption of the Ecole Normale—and that was to come in 1903—before Gabriel Monod's dream of a vast unified educational complex in the Latin Quarter would be realized. Meanwhile, the success of the Sorbonne in recruiting a distinguished faculty and an outstanding group of students during the last two decades of the nineteenth century, together with its newly acquired status at the apex of the reformed university system, established it as a major center of scholarly activity in the Western world. It was entirely fitting that William Waddington and Alfred Rambaud, whom Victor Duruy had recruited in 1868 to teach in the history and philology section of the Ecole Pratique after deciding against an attempt to reform the Old Sorbonne, were to preside over the creation of the New Sorbonne during the last quarter of the nineteenth century.

Between 1880 and the turn of the century, during the period when history was attaining the status of an academic discipline in the reconstructed university system of France, the first generation of historians to embrace what I have designated as the "positivist" paradigm of historical scholarship gradually began to achieve positions of preeminence in the major centers of academic power in Paris. They gained access to the Sorbonne and the Ecole Normale, the two bastions of academic conservatism in France, either by filling vacancies created by retirement or by securing appointment to the new professorial chairs that were gradually created by the education ministry after 1877. They entered the university intent on proselytizing for their particular conception of historical study and on creating an institutional environment within which it could be practiced. They formed what Terry Clark has called a "cluster": "an association of perhaps a dozen persons who shared a minimum core of beliefs about their work and who were prepared to collaborate to advance research in a given area."[28] By the end of the century these historians had risen to the top of the academic hierarchy, each having sired a subcluster of disciples specializing in a particular area of the discipline which served to perpetuate the master's influence.

The four scholars who had begun their careers in the last years of the Second Empire under the watchful eye of Victor Duruy resumed their rapid pace of advancement in the early years of the Third Republic. Gaston Paris, who had temporarily replaced his father as professor of French Literature of the Middle Ages at the Collège de France in the late 1860s, received the chair in 1872 at the tender age, academically speaking, of thirty-three. He continued to divide his time between lecturing at the Collège de France, which he called his "great church," and supervising scholarly research at the Ecole Pratique, which he called his "little chapel," until his premature death in 1903.[29] In both capacities he formed a veritable army of disciples who spread his theories of Romance philology throughout the entire continent of Europe.[30] It was largely through his influence that the philological approach to the study of the past continued to dominate the French academic historians' conception of scientific historical scholarship. When Ernest Lavisse informed the history students at the Sorbonne that "the veritable historian is a philologist, in the broadest sense of that word" and urged them to concentrate on their "lessons in criticism, the reading of texts, philology and paleography," he was conveying to them the notion of historical study that had first been popularized by France's most eminent philologist.[31]

Alfred Rambaud had secured professorial appointments at the faculties of letters of Caen and Nancy, respectively, during the early years of the Republic, and produced a number of distinguished scholarly works on the history of Germany and Russia before being summoned to governmental service by Jules Ferry in 1879. Five years later, he accepted an appointment to the newly created chair in Modern and Contemporary History at the Sorbonne. For the remainder of the century he pursued a joint career in scholarship and politics, achieving renown in both callings.[32] He is remember less as an inspiring teacher than as an effective statesman-administrator, who helped to secure for the historical profession the political and financial assistance that it required. He cannot be said to have founded a school, but he must be credited with having played an important role in the foundation of a university.

After completing his doctorate in 1875, Ernest Lavisse was named *maître de conférences* at the Ecole Normale, and in 1880 was summoned to substitute for Fustel de Coulanges in the chair of medieval history at the Sorbonne when the latter was named director at the rue d'Ulm. Three years later he became assistant professor and was selected by the Minister of Public Instruction (at the suggestion of Ferry's former private secretary and Lavisse's colleague Alfred Rambaud) to become the first director of historical studies at the Sorbonne, a position which enabled him to become the personal adviser of hundreds of future historians trained at the Sorbonne during the next three decades.[33] In 1888 he succeeded Henri Wallon, another historian who dabbled in politics and educational administration,[34] in the chair in modern history. It was from this post that he produced his celebrated works on the history of Germany, edited the collective history of France, co-edited with Rambaud the collective history of the Western world, and produced the numerous textbooks for use in the primary and secondary schools, for which he is perhaps best known.[35] "How many students have entered that Sorbonne office where he greeted them with such cordiality" exclaimed a former student in an effort to do justice to Lavisse's pervasive influence. "How many professors and historians were not marked with his imprint? How many thousands of Frenchmen have acquired the only knowledge they have ever had or ever will have of history from those admirable little books of less than a hundred pages" that Lavisse produced for the schoolchildren of France.[36]

Gabriel Monod pursued a similar path of advancement at the Ecole Normale, where he was called to replace Lavisse in 1880 after his old classmate had intervened on his behalf with the new director, Fustel de Coulanges. In 1888, the same year that Lavisse graduated to the chair in modern history at the Sorbonne, Monod received a full professorship in medieval history at the rue d'Ulm, thereby completing the game of academic musical chairs that had brought the two founding fathers of the historical reform movement to the center of academic power in Paris. He retained his position at the Ecole Pratique, where he succeeded Gaston Paris as president of the historical and philological section in 1895, and continued to edit the *Revue historique* until his death in 1912. Though he produced few memorable works of historical scholarship himself, he trained an entire generation of *érudits* who proceeded to extend the boundaries of medieval studies in France.[37] His tireless efforts to place his protégés in academic posts and arrange for the publication of their scholarly work represent his most lasting legacy. He once confided to a friend that while he regretted that his multifarious tutorial activities had prevented him from producing great works that would endure after his death, "when I see my students write such good books, I tell myself that they are realizing my own literary and scholarly dreams better than I would have been able to myself, and that in giving myself entirely to them, I am thereby writing the best books."[38]

To ensure that the field of ancient history was adequately covered, Alfred Croiset, a young Hellenist, was appointed *maître de conférences* at the Sorbonne in 1877. A specialist in the politics and literature of ancient Greece, Croiset advanced rapidly up the academic ladder. In 1883 he became *chargé de cours* (deputy lecturer) and *directeur d'études* (faculty adviser) in letters and philology, the same post created for Lavisse in history. Three years later he became a full professor. But like so many of the leading members of his profession, his love of scholarship had to make room for his passion for academic politics. In 1898, during the Dreyfus Affair, he was named dean of the Sorbonne, and from this influential post he spearheaded the campaign waged in the early years of the new century to reform the curriculum of the secondary schools along lines determined by the university professoriate and to abolish the autonomy of the Ecole Normale and link it to the University of Paris.

With the accession of Paris, Rambaud, Lavisse, Monod, and Croiset, the reorganized university system, particularly in the capital, began to provide adequate coverage of the principal chronological categories of Western history—ancient, medieval, modern, and contemporary. Since students who were enrolled in any one of the several branches of the Parisian university complex could cross register or take courses in the others, virtually any course of study that a student of history wished to pursue was available to him. One subject that had received scant attention in the early years of the Republic was the one which, it was feared, would arouse the greatest controversy: the Revolution itself.[39] But this initial hesitancy to open the ideological Pandora's box represented by this important period dissipated once the Republic had secured itself by the end of the 1870s, and the Revolution became, in the hands of the new republican leadership, the supreme historical symbol of national grandeur. The extent of this transformation is reflected in the extensive use of the "principles of '89" in the civic instruction programs of the primary schools following the educational reforms of Jules Ferry.[40] But equally symptomatic of the republican regime's passion for retracing France's revolutionary origins was the central position that the study of the Revolution came to occupy in the historical curriculum of the reformed university. The first important manifestation of this trend appeared at the end of 1885, when the municipal government of Paris appropriated funds for the endowment of a permanent chair in the History of the French Revolution at the Sorbonne

The Revolution had already inspired a plethora of laudatory historical works from the pens of several literary and political figures of nineteenth century France—Michelet, Thierry, Lamartine, Blanc, and others. But most of these earlier attempts at historical explanation were flawed by the same egregious defect. They had been written without benefit of full access to the documents relating to the revolutionary period, most of which lay scattered in total disarray throughout the entire country. The first occupant of the new chair of revolutionary history, Alphonse Aulard, estimated in his inaugural lecture of March 12, 1886, that less than a third of these documents had ever been catalogued.[41] He later complained that even those historians who had gained access to important archival materials, such as Taine and Albert Sorel,[42] had produced works based on incomplete documentation in which "historical truth" was sacrificed to the "necessities of art," a deficiency which, he was convinced, had rendered their conclusions "almost useless to history."[43] It was Aulard's ambition to establish a truly objective, scientific approach to the study of the Revolution and to encourage a more careful utilization of the available documents relating to that event.[44]

The man who was to occupy the chair of the History of the Revolution at the Sorbonne from 1886 to 1922 was an unlikely candidate to engage in, or even to sponsor, the production of scientific historical scholarship. A graduate of the Ecole Normale in 1871, he had served as a professor of humanities at various provincial *lycées* before receiving his doctorate in literature in 1877 for a dissertation on the Italian poet Leopardi.[45] From 1878 to 1884 he taught French literature at faculties of letters in Aix-en-Provence, Montpellier, Dijon, and Poitiers, and at the time of his accession to the Sorbonne was teaching rhetoric at the *lycée* Janson-de-Sailly. With no formal training in the methods of scientific history, no past experience as a teacher of that subject, and a less than distinguished record of historical scholarship,[46] this *littérateur* and rhetorician seemed to personify the very tradition of literary history that the Sorbonne *érudits* were endeavoring to supplant.

Indeed, Aulard's attitude toward the French Revolution, as evidenced in his written and spoken words on the subject, recalled the spirit of a Quinet or a Michelet rather than foreshadowing the modern type of scientific scholarship that was gradually being introduced at the Sorbonne. He had been drawn to the subject of his life's work not by the disinterested curiosity of a scientist, but by a dedicated French patriot's conviction that a deeper understanding of the Revolution would help to restore a sense of pride in his nation's heritage. As a consequence of what a colleague dubbed his faith in the "therapeutic" uses of history,[47] and of what a distinguished successor called his quest for "the psychological compensation of contemplating more glorious days,"[48] Aulard's lectures and writings were marked by an accent of passionate commitment rather than dispassionate analysis. "He who does not sympathize with the Revolution sees only the surface," he announced in his inaugural lecture at the Sorbonne. "In order to understand it, it is necessary to love it."[49]

But the labor of love that occupied Aulard for the remainder of the nineteenth century proved to be much more significant than the singular oblation of a nostalgic devotee of the revolutionary mystique. Indeed, it constituted nothing less than the institutionalization of the historiography of the French Revolution as an autonomous field of study in the French university system. By the beginning of the twentieth century Aulard had become the universally acknowledged authority on the political history of the Revolution,[50] the founder of an entire school of scientific history dealing with the revolutionary period, and the beloved mentor of dozens of scholarly disciples who were actively engaged in research on various aspects of the central event in modern French history.[51] That such eminent twentieth century historians as Pierre Caron, Philippe Sagnac, Albert Mathiez, and Georges Lefebvre have differed with Aulard on scholarly particulars and diverged from his interpretations of the Revolution at several points in no way detracts from his reputation as the father of modern French Revolutionary historiography. On the contrary, the fact that these and other disciples of Aulard have deemed it necessary to record their differences with the master is perhaps the most conclusive proof of his enduring influence.

The intellectual qualities that Aulard, Monod, Lavisse, and the other historians searched for in the prospective student were those that one might expect of an apprentice in a craft. In order to fulfill Duruy's old dream of creating an academic climate that would produce "an ensemble of ideas, customs, taste, and principles that are transmitted from the fathers to the sons,"[52] they set out to imbue their disciples with professional reverence for the shared consensus of the guild. Speaking to the first group of students that chose to concentrate in history under the new guidelines of 1881, Lavisse advised them to adopt a "corporative spirit" and praised those among them whom he knew to possess the one important quality that would contribute to their academic success: "deference toward their masters."[53] The vehicle for the promulgation and enforcement of the scholarly standards required by the new profession was to be the "restricted course" (*cours fermé*) wherein professors and *maîtres de conférences* could supervise the scholarly work of a select group of student apprentices, thereby guaranteeing the perpetuation of their influence. "We are forming a veritable intellectual community," Lavisse announced in his inaugural lecture to the first year history students in 1883, "the masters giving to the students the example of their lives dedicated to labor and communicating to them the fruits of their research, that is to say, their method and their knowledge, the students responding to this solicitude through their zeal, busy enriching their mind through knowledge and disciplining it with a method, thereby preparing to inherit our legacy, to work as we do, and as a fortunate consequence of our own efforts, better than we do." He noted with pride that the Sorbonne had already farmed out several of its most promising *agrégés* to teach in secondary education, and predicted that within a decade hundreds of Sorbonne students, trained in the modern methods of historical scholarship, will have been placed throughout the French educational system.[54]

The traditional French conception of higher learning as an informal, unstructured association of lecturer and auditor was the first sacrifice on the altar of scientific scholarship. The closed courses served as both recruiting stations for future members of the profession and laboratories equipped to provide practical experience in the use of scholarly techniques, such as the authentication of documents and the deciphering of texts. In the larger lectures, the unregistered auditors were soon joined by regular students who, in the words of Lavisse, intended to "constitute and remain *un corps savant.*"[55] A strict control of identification cards was instituted, and everyone was required to sign a registration book upon entrance.[56] The historians in particular required strict adherence to the new academic regulations. Lavisse locked the classroom door before each lecture "to discourage idle curiousity," required special permission for nonstudents to attend, and reserved the first rows for the regular students.[57]

This new spirit of professionalism in academic history was variously characterized as military, monastic, and commercial in spirit. Monod preferred to regard the new relationship between faculty and students as analogous to that between a general staff and an army of soldiers.[58] Other historians modified the metaphor, describing the reorganized university as a monastery or a workshop.[59] But whether they thought of themselves as generals leading an army of soldier-scholars in pursuit of the Golden Fleece of historical truth, as monks engaged in historical research after the fashion of the Benedictines, or as artisans laboring in their *ateliers*, the implication was the same. These were no longer the free-floating *littérateurs* who wrote history to entertain the educated gentlemen of the world beyond the walls of academe. These were serious scholars attached to and sustained by the state university system, an institution that was dedicated to the discovery and dissemination of the higher truths of science. The principal objective of the newly reconstituted history department of the Sorbonne, according to its eminent director, was to teach students the importance of "deriving your knowledge from the original sources and of being totally penetrated by the historical and critical spirit." The instruction dispensed there was entirely founded on "the historical, philological, and critical study of texts, on the methodical science of facts."[60]

In his address at the inaugural ceremony of the reconstructed university in the autumn of 1897, Lavisse took note of the revolutionary innovations that had transformed French higher education during the past two decades. He recalled how students in the Old Sorbonne had traditionally lived in isolation, attending impersonal lectures in enormous amphitheaters and spending countless hours in cafés. They prepared for examinations, took degrees, and entered professions without ever having acquired the sense of belonging to a community of scholars. The New University, he proclaimed, had returned to the medieval conception of a university as an autonomous social entity, with its own unique laws, regulations, and customs.[61]

This exclusive, tightly-knit fraternity, confident of the worthiness of its scholarly endeavors and disdainful of the public's philistinism, strove to establish its reputation as the undisputed authority on all matters relating to France's past.

The successful campaign to dilute the oratorical tradition of the public courses provoked few objections compared with the bitter campaigns that were being waged in the primary schools between the defenders of clerical control and the promoters of a secular system. Some ripples of discontent did reach the surface after the first unregistered auditors were turned away from the university classrooms. A few republican newspapers and journals complained about the undemocratic implications of an educational policy which catered to a scholarly elite pursuing a highly specialized course of study.[62] One recalcitrant Sorbonne professor of the old school hit upon a point that was later to assume major significance in the educational polemics that began to fill the pages of Parisian journalism after the turn of the century. The institution of a "private course" in which attendance is both limited and obligatory, he argued, was likely to create a situation in which the instructor would no longer feel obligated to develop means of communicating the fruits of his specialized scholarship to the average literate citizen. The general public rendered an important service to the professor by obliging him to be interesting as well as erudite. He reminded his readers that the people are sovereign in a democratic state and predicted that if the faculties become indifferent to the desires and concerns of the public, they will be suppressed at some future date.[63] But such defenses of the public lecture system in the name of democracy were isolated, retrograde expressions of resistance to what had become an irreversible trend by the beginning of the 1890s. The absence of a sustained public opposition to the university reforms introduced between 1876 and 1896 signified a willingness on the part of the French populace to support the new elite institution of higher learning, with its specialized courses and arcane subjects. By the turn of the century the Sorbonne had reestablished its reputation as a major center of higher learning, and no group within it was more celebrated than its corps of historians.

The rising reputation of the French academic historical profession is perhaps best reflected in the observations of three foreign visitors who attended courses in the Latin Quarter during the years when history was acquiring the status of an academic discipline. In 1882, with 125 students enrolled in the newly instituted courses leading to the *licence* and *agrégation* for history, the Belgian historian Paul Frédéricq spent two months sitting in on the lectures and *conférences* of Monod, Rambaud, Lavisse, Paris, Gabriel Hanotaux (who was teaching at the Ecole Pratique), and the other leading French historians. He was astounded by the superior quality of historical instruction that he had observed not only in the Ecole des Chartes, but at the Ecole Pratique, the Ecole Normale, and the Sorbonne as well. Expecting to encounter the notorious public lecture system for which the French universities had long been infamous, he discovered instead small groups of eminent professors and selected students poring over facsimiles of historical documents and discussing scholarly problems together. He left Paris convinced that a "brilliant school of historians [would] emerge from this fruitful movement" that would bring great credit to the French system of higher education.

These observations were all the more striking because their author had recently returned from an extended visit to the major centers of historical scholarship across the Rhine. "None of the great German universities can boast of so many historical courses as are to be found scattered through the various institutions for advanced study in Paris," he remarked with surprise. In the 1881–1882 academic year Berlin had listed twenty-six courses in history, Leipzig twenty-one, Breslau sixteen, Bonn fourteen, and Göttingen fourteen. A year later, he counted at least fifty in the great educational complex in Paris.[64] The centers of historical erudition in Germany, which had reigned unchallenged throughout most of the nineteenth century, were apparently being bypassed by the new French universities, which had been reformed by men who had learned their trade at Berlin, Bonn, and Göttingen.[65]

Further confirmation of the revolution in historical studies that was occurring in the French universities was forthcoming a decade later. Henry Wickham Steed, a correspondant for the London *Times* who spent several months in the Latin Quarter during the 1893–1894 academic year after studying at the University of Berlin, was similarly struck by the high quality of scholarly work that was carried on in the Parisian universities. He audited the courses of Lavisse and his pupil Charles Seignobos, expecting to witness the "shallowness" that French historians were known to display when dealing with the "grave and ponderous problems" that their German counterparts handled with such skill and profundity. But he discovered to his surprise that this reputed superficiality was like "the play of ripples on the surface of clear deep waters" and that "in comparison with this pellucid air, the air of a German university was heavy and dense." He concluded from this experience that if the rest of French society is as vigorous as the Sorbonne historians, "foreign estimates of French resilience might be woefully wrong."[66]

Similar sentiments were forthcoming in 1896 from a Harvard professor who noted a "reaction in America against the German methods [of historical scholarship] that have been too closely followed up to now." One sixth of the professors teaching in American graduate schools in 1896 had received a German doctorate (155 out of 850) while none boasted a French *doctorat ès lettres*. But the young generation of American scholars, he claimed, is beginning to revolt against the German methods, which "frequently appear not to distinguish the wheat from the chaff, which give the same importance to all facts, provided they are new, and which take no account of the need to present these facts in a clear and attractive manner." He observed that many American students are beginning to turn toward the French universities to help them to combat the nefarious influences of German learning, now that "a true system of higher education has been established" in Paris.[67] These personal testimonies to the growing international reputation of the University of Paris and its affiliated institutions as a center of humanistic scholarship are borne out in the statistics for the number of foreign students enrolled in the university in general and the Sorbonne in particular during the first decade of the twentieth century, which reveal a dramatic increase (See Appendix G).

That the historians of France had succeeded in firmly establishing their craft as a preeminent academic discipline by the mid-1890s is indisputable. But that success was marred by a frustrating failure that continued to hinder their successive efforts to establish the scientific credentials of their discipline. Their quest for a universally acknowledged definition of the scientific historical method, which they heralded as the key that could unlock the hidden secrets of France's past, encountered a variety of unexpected obstacles. The combined effect of their own inability to agree upon a satisfactory definition of the historical method and the increasing encroachments on their scholarly domain by the incipient discipline of sociology posed a serious threat to the self-confidence that had originally characterized the prophets of the new historical school in France. By the opening decade of the new century, as we shall presently see, they found themselves riddled with self-doubts and subjected to increasing animadversion from critics both inside and outside the profession.

4
In Search of La Méthode Historique

The first and most celebrated member of the new generation of *universitaires* to propose a definition of the scientific historical method was Charles Seignobos. Born in 1854 to a Protestant, republican family, he became one of the first protégés of Lavisse at the Ecole Normale, from which he received his *agrégation* with highest honors in 1877. After embarking on the German expedition that had become the initiation rite of prospective historians,[1] he returned in 1879 to receive an appointment as a *maître de conférences* at the Faculty of Letters of the University of Dijon.[2] Since there were as yet few bonafide students in the unreformed university to place claims on his time and attention, he spent his spare moments researching his doctoral dissertation in the private archives of the Burgundian aristocracy. He received his *doctorat ès lettres* in 1882 with a thesis entitled *Le Regime féodal en Bourgogne* and, after a long leave, received a *maîtrise de conférences* in 1890 at the Sorbonne with Lavisse's assistance. His professional advancement was swift, and by the mid-1890s he had become a leading exponent of the modern approach to historical study in France. The future development of historiographical thought in the Third Republic bears the indelible imprint of his teachings.[3]

Two years after his return from Germany, the young *normalien* contributed an article to the *Revue internationale de l'enseignement,* the organ of the educational reformers edited by Lavisse, Monod, and others, in which he summarized the impressions of the nature of modern historical scholarship that he had gathered across the Rhine.[4] He noted that in the German academic tradition "philology dominates history, furnishes its methods, directs its research, and imposes its very goal." He criticized the German universities for producing cataloguers, collectors, and philologists instead of historians, in the broadest sense of the term. By concentrating on paleography, source criticism, and the analysis of obscure historical documents, the Germans tended to neglect the final and most important stage of historical scholarship, which he called "scientific synthesis." He warned that the classification and authentication of the sources was no substitute for the synthetic reconstruction of the past. The former approach yielded results of dubious value and fostered a sense of purposelessness and futility among young scholars in Germany. He suspected that many of them had "lost sight of the goal of history" and had begun to "search for an intrinsic value in the [historical] materials themselves. They have become experts in the criticism of texts, but they have lost in the solidity of the intellect what they have gained in technical skill." He hastened to concede, however, that the German historians deserved credit for having expelled rhetoric and superficial generalizations from historical writing and for having insisted that the historian return to the original documents, two innovations which their French counterparts would do well to emulate.[5]

Seignobos was hesitant at such an early stage in his professional career to suggest a solution to what he regarded as the incompleteness of the approach to historical scholarship that he had observed in Germany. He did refer in passing to the "analogical method" as a possible organizational principle that might assist the historian in completing the task of historical reconstruction, though it was several years before he refined his definition of this concept. In subsequent numbers of the same review and in other professional forums, he spelled out in broader detail what he believed to be the function of the historian's creative imagination in the process of rendering intelligible and meaningful the multitude of isolated facts that he encounters in his research. He reminded his readers that historical periods do not constitute "realities" in themselves, but rather represent "imaginary divisions" which the historian employs as a means of simplifying the complexity of the past. "The laws of the mind are not the same as the laws of reality," he observed. "Reality is continuous; the mind grasps only fragments. When one wishes to make the mind deal with realities, one must adapt reality to [the needs of] the mind."[6] He later defended this sketchily defined method as a *via media* between the "oratorical and superficial procedures" of the French historical tradition, which sins on the side of unsubstantiated generalization and unrestrained imagination, and the "heavy and confused system of the Germans," which devotes excessive attention to the surviving documents and the facts they record. He was hopeful that by adopting a scholarly posture that was "simultaneously precise and general" the historian might avoid the twin pitfalls of Latin dilettantism and Germanic pedantry.[7]

These inchoate attempts to propose a new method for dealing with the problem of historical synthesis did not appreciably affect the development of French historical thought during this early part of Seignobos's career. The young scholar had not yet secured an influential position in the academic hierarchy, and his preliminary musings on the historical method lay buried in the pages of professional periodicals. But as he advanced up the academic ladder in the 1880s, he began to achieve notoriety as an articulate spokesman for a uniquely French approach to the problem of historical knowledge. As was the case with his master Lavisse, it was Seignobos's reputation as an inspiring teacher and author of textbooks and general works of synthesis, rather than his contributions to the growing body of monographic scholarship, that was responsible for the broad dissemination of his ideas.[8]

As early as 1883 Seignobos had proposed a complex program of study for the select group of history students who were being attracted to the Sorbonne in larger numbers by the lure of the newly endowed scholarships and the prepossessing prospect of participating in the foundation of a new discipline. He planned to test his novel conception of the historical method on his disciples by convincing them to apply it to their dissertation research. After working with his own students to develop and perfect these techniques for several years, Seignobos finally gained access to a wider audience. In the academic year 1896–1897, he and the medievalist Charles Victor Langlois inaugurated the first historiography course at the Sorbonne. The methodological doctrines that he had been promoting in professional journals were henceforth communicated to the succeeding generations of history students that enrolled in this enormously popular course. The lectures delivered by these two historians (the most important of which were subsequently brought out in book form and translated into several languages) gave substance to the skeletal proposals for a new historical method that Seignobos had launched a decade earlier.

The two Sorbonne historiographers prefaced their opening lectures with the startling observation that "most of those who are engaged in the career of history are, in effect, in it without knowing why, without ever having been asked if they are well suited to historical labor, the nature of which they often know nothing about." In order to rectify this unfortunate situation, which they attributed to centuries of neglect, Seignobos and Langlois purposely designed their lectures to inform the new students at the Sorbonne "what historical studies are and what they should be."[9] They hoped to acquaint their charges with the precise nature of the historical method, to differentiate it from the methods employed by other disciplines, and to convince them of its universal applicability to the study of the human past.

In subsequent lectures and writings Seignobos reformulated several of the tentative notions regarding the historical method that he had broached during his early days as an obscure instructor. He labored to distinguish his own from previous attempts to establish a methodology of historical study for use in the French universities. He expressed grave reservations about the fashionable belief that the historian is obligated to suppress his own personality and let the facts speak for themselves. Seignobos believed that the scholar who conceives of his function as one of fact-gathering and documentary analysis is operating under a serious delusion caused by an inability to recognize that a historical document is not a fact in the true sense of the term. The historian who immerses himself in the primary sources is not, as is often supposed, in the presence of a surviving component of the past reality that he is seeking to comprehend. The only "material reality" that the historian has at his disposal is the written document, which he interrogates in order to identify "the particular historical facts of which the document is the trace."[10] But from this preliminary stage he must proceed to assemble these indirectly inferred facts "in a systematic construction in order to discover the connections between them."[11] It is this second crucial step in the process of historical understanding that Seignobos accused the Germans and their servile French imitators of tending to neglect. "There is no historical characteristic inherent in the facts," he declared. A historical account represents an effort not to resurrect, but to understand, the variegated reality of the past. "History is not a science," he concluded, "it is only a process of knowledge."[12] The natural scientist is capable of apprehending the object of investigation directly, but the historian is barred from such direct observation, since the historical evidence is an indirect trace, a mere reflection, of past events.

Since the historical documents themselves are indirect, fragmentary reflections of times past, and are therefore incapable of yielding information sufficient to permit one to reconstruct those bygone times in their entirety, the historian must develop supplementary means of filling in the lacunae. Seignobos concluded that only the mind and the imagination of the investigator can provide these essential linkages. "Instead of directly observing facts," he asserted, the historian must operate indirectly by "subjecting the documents to rational analysis *(raisonnement sur les documents)*."[13] Historical understanding is general and indirect when it seeks to make sense out of the heterogeneous mass of facts it encounters in the archives. History, therefore, is "essentially a science of reasoning."[14] Seignobos recognized that the historian's imprisonment in his own historical situation implied that his reasoning about past events would necessarily reflect the influences of his personal experience in the present. But he saw a hidden advantage in this apparent limitation to historical objectivity. The scholar's direct observation of events in his own time and place furnishes him with a variety of ready-made and useful models of present reality to which he can compare his indirect observations of historical phenomena. "We do not observe past reality," he declared. "We know it only by its resemblance to present reality."[15] The historian can employ "rational conclusions drawn from observable facts *(raisonnements à partir des faits connus)*" to fill in the gaps in the documentary evidence of the past.[16]

Seignobos was careful to distinguish this approach from the methods employed in the natural sciences. In the sciences of "direct observation," he remarked, "when a fact is missing in a series, one searches for it by a new observation." The historian, on the other hand, cannot rely on direct observation, and therefore must strive to increase his knowledge through the use of rational analysis. He must venture beyond the evidence presented in the documents "to infer new facts. If the reasoning is correct, this process of knowledge is legitimate."[17] Unfortunately, the degree of certitude is much smaller in the historical sciences than in the sciences of nature. The theoretical speculation of the historian, no matter how convincing it may appear, produces only a presumption of truth. But when several presumptions are grouped together, "they confirm each other and end up producing certitude." History is thus able to fill in many of the gaps in the documentary evidence "through an accumulation of reasonings *(raisonnements).*"[18]

Yet Seignobos regarded the collection of facts and reasonings as merely the penultimate stage in the operation of historical reconstruction, yielding a "mass of facts juxtaposed in *cadres*," which have no significance in themselves. He was well aware that the operation of historical synthesis, which leads to "the final conclusions of history," was both the most difficult and the most crucial, for it furnishes the ultimate justification for considering the study of history a genuinely scientific enterprise. Seignobos used the term "science" in the sense of "an economy of time and effort obtained by a process that quickly renders the facts understandable and intelligible." It consists of "slowly gathering a quantity of detailed facts," and then of condensing them into a series of "uncontestable formulations."

Seignobos therefore defined the final step of historical synthesis as the attempt to "isolate the general characteristics" of the facts and to discover their interconnections. Only after the performance of this essential task will historical study yield a deeper understanding of the past. The function served by these generalizations is similar to that served by the formulations employed in the natural sciences. History shares the obligation common to all sciences to "rise above the simple verification of facts in order to *explain* them by their *causes*" (italics original). While conceding that history had yet to arrive at a scientific system of classification, he voiced the hope that further refinement of the historical method would eventually enable its practitioners to grasp the elusive "soul of society" that the historians and social theorists had vainly pursued for decades.[19]

This doctrine, considered in its entirety, might easily be taken as a retreat from the positivist spirit of historical understanding that had been fostered by the historical reforms of postwar France. Seignobos's suggestion that the historian employ his mental processes to rethink the past by referring to his own perceptions of present reality resembled in many respects the doctrines of neo-idealism that had begun to infiltrate the universities of Italy and Germany in the last years of the nineteenth century. His claim that this method was "particularly suited to the French mind," his frequent references to the crucial role of reason in historical analysis, and his sweeping indictment of Germanic "fact-grubbing," might also be taken as evidence of an atavistic regression to the deductive, a priori spirit of the philosophical school of French history that had predominated in the earlier part of the century.

But Seignobos's misgivings about the event-oriented, return-to-the-documents approach and his appreciation of the organizing power of the historian's mind in the rational comprehension of historical processes did not impel him to renounce the doctrine of scientific history and to adopt a competing paradigm of historical knowledge such as that represented by the philosophical school.[20] Indeed, he took pains to disassociate himself from the "theory of the rational character of history," which holds that history "conforms to an intelligible general plan."[21] He indicted the Hegelian tradition (and its French pastiche represented by the theories of Cousin, Michelet, and others) for poisoning French historiography with the unscientific methods of philosophy. What most disturbed Seignobos about the contemporary practitioners of the philosophy of history in Germany was that, though posing as "advocates of factualism," they tended to abandon themselves to "their natural penchant for the exposition of general questions . . . They take sides; they blame; they praise; they color; they embellish."[22] The French popularizers of this doctrine have flooded the historical profession with works replete with "puerile generalizations" and "the most erroneous and contestable opinions," all of which are presented with "a tone of tranquil authority."[23]

He was no more charitable to the school of literary or artistic history that had seduced generations of Frenchmen with its wit, charm, and grace of style. It irritated him that the "intellectual confusion, ignorance, and negligence" displayed in the writings of this group were often effectively camouflaged behind a brilliant literary façade. The untutored public, "whose education is greatly lacking in these matters," was usually incapable of spotting these defects of scholarship because of the typically French notion that "form determines content" in historical writing, which it continued to regard as an art.[24] The amateurish practitioners of literary history in France had achieved widespread recognition and popularity because they were willing to undertake the task of synthesis that many qualified scholars had dismissed as a form of unsubstantiated generalization unworthy of their effort. The works of these historical popularizers appealed (some would say pandered) to "the vulgar, superficial general public," in whom scholarly criticism inspires nothing but disdain.[25]

He found both the *érudits* and the popularizers guilty of the sin of excess. The dedicated research scholars at the Ecole Pratique and the Ecole des Chartes were often "attracted by the difficulty of the [historical] problems rather than by their intrinsic importance," and behaved as though "scholarship had had an end in itself." While they had reduced to a scientific form the analytical aspect of historical investigation—that is, the authentication of sources and texts—their conception of the synthetic stage of historical understanding remained haphazard.[26] The historical vulgarizers, on the other hand, acted as though they were capable of "reconstituting past reality through the sole force of reflection and art applied to questionable documents that were in the public domain."[27]

What particularly alarmed Seignobos about the success of these historical popularizers was the example that they set for the younger generation of historians that the Sorbonne professoriate was hoping to win over to the modern methods of scientific scholarship. He feared that these incompetent writers who scorn the methodological guidelines established by the profession and court public favor with their entertaining works of historical exposition might set back the cause of the historical reform movement by demonstrating to prospective scholars that fame and fortune awaited those willing to engage in historical vulgarization.[28] He and his colleagues in the university had already begun to notice with growing apprehension that many young people entering the profession were "animated by a spirit that is more commercial than scientific." Seignobos remarked that these academic *arrivistes* dream of achieving worldly success instead of patiently devoting themselves to serious scholarship (a vocation which, they realized, was likely to bring them neither substantial financial rewards nor public acclaim).[29]

Seignobos was confident that a remedy for this discouraging situation was to be found in the newly-established history departments of the revamped universities (especially that of the Sorbonne). He believed the impressive array of talented historians who had been pirated from the special schools to be ideally suited to bridge the gap that separated the worlds of monographic scholarship and synthetic generalization. By establishing a division of labor in which specific tasks of monographic scholarship could be parceled out to trained specialists, the university historians would be able to replace aimless intellectual inquiry with a planned, controlled policy of applied science. Once these teams of historical investigators began to address scholarly problems "whose solutions are important" in the opinion of the master planners, provided that their work is properly "disciplined and directed from above," the results were much more likely to be fruitful.[30] This, in turn, would free the generalists from the drudgery of grubbing in the primary sources, thereby giving them "more freedom to proceed to works of higher criticism, combination and construction." In historical studies, as in industry, he observed, "the effects of the division of labor are the same, and are very favorable: a production that is more abundant, more successful, and better regulated."[31]

Though no other French historian during this period produced such a detailed methodological defense of the new discipline of history to equal that of Seignobos, a number of other *universitaires* contributed valuable services to the cause. Seignobos's colleague Charles Victor Langlois brought a somewhat different spirit to bear on the problem of historical knowledge. While Lavisse, Rambaud, Monod, Seignobos, and the other leading members of the modern historical school were products of the Ecole Normale and its literary tradition of historical scholarship, Langlois had received his professional training at the Ecole des Chartes, where he had studied with the German-trained former editor of the *Revue critique,* Paul Meyer. He then studied with Lavisse at the Sorbonne, receiving the highest grade for the *agrégation* in 1884 and a *doctorat ès lettres* three years later. Langlois joined the Sorbonne professoriate in 1888 at the early age of twenty-eight after leap-frogging over secondary education to serve brief stints at faculties of letters in the provinces. Once in Paris he was appointed professor of paleography and bibliography, and took charge of the course in the "auxiliary sciences of history" that all history majors were required to take.[32] While the *normalien* Seignobos continually expressed reservations about the Germanic conception of historical scholarship, the young *chartiste* Langlois never wavered in his determination to implant the tradition of critical scholarship in the regular university system that Germain-trained *chartistes* such as Gaston Paris had established in the Ecole Pratique. It was largely through his efforts that this special conception of scientific history gained a foothold in the Sorbonne.[33]

Langlois was chiefly responsible for popularizing the new image of the Faculty of Letters as a laboratory of historical erudition. In his introductory lecture to new students in the 1897–1898 academic year, he praised the new conception of *La Faculté comme atelier* and hailed the recent innovations as delivering "the death blow to the Sorbonne of Richelieu." He characterized the new spirit animating the university as "the pure scientific spirit," by which he meant the widespread acceptance of a variety of postulates regarding the methods and objectives of respectable scholarship.[34] He proudly announced that the resurrection of the French universities had produced institutions in which a new respect for the critical method was finally being taught on a regular basis and in which scientific equipment was finally being made available to the students.[35] He boasted that the earliest results of this transformation had fulfilled the fondest expectations of those who were seeking to breathe new life into France's tottering system of higher learning. The universities had already begun to turn out teams of "investigators and writers prepared for very diverse specialities" who were expanding and increasing everywhere the level of production of historical scholarship.[36]

For all their passionate tributes to scholarship, Monod and Lavisse remained wedded to the literary tradition of the Ecole Normale that they had imbibed in the 1860s. Their most durable contributions were in the fields of historical popularization, educational reform, textbook production, professional journalism, and public service, rather than in erudition and monographic scholarship. Even their fellow *normalien* Seignobos, whose analyses of French political developments in the nineteenth century and the history of modern Europe were solid, well-documented works of historical erudition, exercised his greatest influence through more discursive writings: primers on historical methodology, program guides for historical curricula in the primary and secondary schools and historical essays of a general nature. But Langlois was virtually unique among his more renowned colleagues in that he practiced in all of his scholarly work what he preached in the classroom and in his methodological writings. He put to good use at the Sorbonne the technical training that he had received at the Ecole des Chartes, and his own scholarly achievements served as exemplary models for the young historians under his tutelage. He not only produced a number of valuable monographs on medieval history, but also supervised the collection and publication of several primary source documents that had formerly lain buried in the anonymity of French and Vatican archives.[37] Unlike his master Lavisse and his colleague Seignobos, Langlois stubbornly resisted the temptation to stray from the circumscribed domain of monograpic, analytical history.

This passion for monographic specialization became, for Langlois, a general principle that strongly influenced his views on educational reform. He blamed the classical curriculum of French secondary education and its notorious sanction, the comprehensive *baccalauréat* examination, for encouraging the student to concentrate on acquiring a superficial knowledge of a vast panorama of subjects at the expense of developing expertise in a special field. At the urging of Langlois and other *universitaires*, the examination system was modified to give greater weight to technical preparation. The new diploma of advanced studies *(diplôme d'études supérieures)*, a necessary credential of all candidates for both the *agrégation* and the doctorate, was awarded only to those students who demonstrated a comprehension of "the principles of the investigative method, the instruments and procedures of scientific labor, and the means of using them."[38] He was confident that this new emphasis on practical, technical training would reap even greater benefits in the future for the new university.

> As soon as our students are invited . . . to the apprenticeship that will enable them, if they are willing and able, to become the scientific workers of the future, there is no reason why we cannot obtain from them what was obtained from their masters at the Ecole des Hautes Etudes and the Ecole des Chartes, that is to say, a great deal of honest labor and a few examples of very distinguished labor that will result in finished works of scholarship.[39]

He noted with pride that the dramatic increase in the number of doctoral dissertations had already helped to reestablish the Sorbonne's reputation as a leading center of higher learning in the world.[40]

Langlois's Spartan commitment to monographic, analytical history implied a renunciation of all ties to the literary historical tradition that had long dominated French historical writing. The impressionistic, literary tradition that had flourished for the past three quarters of a century had begun to decay, he announced, because the "perfecting of historical 'science' cannot help being fatal in the long run to the 'art' of historians."[41] A product of the Ecole des Chartes, Langlois was virtually immune to the nagging self-doubts about the scientific nature of the historical method that were beginning to plague some of his *normalien* colleagues. It is entirely possible to imagine, he claimed, "because they really exist, books of historical exposition that are entirely objective and impersonal, to such an extent that there is so to speak only one manner of writing them at a given moment."[42] He asserted that the teams of monographic researchers that were being assembled in the universities and provided with specific assignments of a highly-specialized nature deserved the utmost respect of the profession as well as the general public. It was their arduous researches in the primary sources, after all, which furnished the historical synthesizers with the empirical data that enabled them to construct general works that could legitimately lay claim to the adjective "scientific."

Perhaps more than any of the other leading *universitaires,* Langlois brooded over the dilemma that confronted the scholarly specialist who was expected to tailor his work to the popular tastes of a mass democracy. He never achieved the widespread public acclaim that greeted Lavisse, Monod, Seignobos, Aulard, and others. Confined by prior training to the Middle Ages and by propensity to the monograph, he resented the public indifference to the scientific procedures of analytical historical scholarship that he had helped to transfer from the Ecole des Chartes to the Sorbonne. The public anxiously waits for the historian "to produce the truth (which can be obtained only by critical analysis of sources)" he observed.[43] But it is inclined to demand that the truth "not be presented to it in a naked, fragmentary, more or less uncertain form, that is to say, as it is." It wants instead "poetic impressions, emotions, ideas."[44]

The limitations that the historical scholars in the universities had finally succeeded in imposing upon themselves would obviously not permit such a violation of the spirit of scientific scholarship. Who then would fill the gap if the professional historians proved incapable of combining a strict adherence to the canons of their craft with the ability to write history that would reach a mass audience? On this point the usually optimistic Langlois echoed his colleagues' earlier misgivings about the temptations of worldly fame.

> Everything seems to encourage the *écrivains-artistes* who undertake to speak to the general public about past men and events not to be satisfied with austere scientific sobriety: the irresistible temptation to employ their [literary] gifts, the desire to influence their contemporaries, and the very requirement that they select [facts] at random from the mass of available material (for they cannot say everything).[45]

The general public, which had been driven from the university seminar rooms, was now apparently achieving its revenge by tempting the new practitioners of academic history to betray their solemn commitment to science. By taking note of this situation and announcing its urgency, Langlois, the austere *chartiste,* was alerting his fellow scholars to an ominous development that was soon to threaten the newly-acquired prestige of the academic historical profession.

Gabriel Monod's contribution to the growing controversy concerning the historical method indicated that he had much less faith than Langlois in the possibility of achieving a genuinely objective approach to historical synthesis. His methodological observations seem to suggest a subtle shift away from his earlier faith in an objective science of history based on a critical examination of the documents and an evolution toward a position resembling that of Seignobos. Monod continued to believe that the proper objective of historical research was to "reconstitute in its historical succession *(la série des temps)* the integral life of humanity."[46] But he appreciated the partial, tentative, and imperfect character of such a reconstitution, for he realized that most of the facts of history had disappeared without leaving a trace.[47] The modern historian was therefore condemned to a vain quest for the "[general] laws that seem to be the very condition of a true science." His goal is to identify and categorize historical phenomena that repeat themselves without variation, but whatever regularities he is able to discover in the historical process can never approximate the same degree of certitude that characterizes the laws of natural science.[48] Monod had also come to suspect the presence of a subjective element in historical analysis that is determined by the "temperament [and] intellectual qualities of each historian."[49] He recognized that the past cannot be resurrected "as it really was," but only as it appears to have been to the historian living in the here and now. We can perceive historical facts only through "the knowledge that we have of the facts of the present."[50] The image that we have of the past, therefore, is formed by analogy with the present, and it is only through an attentive comparison of the indirect traces of past facts with the present facts observed directly by us that we can be able to "penetrate their character, to specify their importance, to recognize the elements of generality that link them."[51]

But this realization did not appear to dampen Monod's enthusiasm for championing the cause of the historical method, nor did it fill him with second thoughts about its claim to scientific objectivity. Like Seignobos, he had begun to express certain reservations about the "Germanic" conception of scientific history (or more accurately, the French misconception of the Germanic conception), which regarded the subject matter of history as the conscious intentions of men reflected in the surviving documents, and which therefore equated the scientific historical method with the indiscriminate piling of historical fact upon historical fact in an effort to construct a grand edifice of historical truth. He came to realize that the facts of history do not speak for themselves but require the intervention of the historian's mind to interpret them in light of his present experience in order to provide them with meaning and significance to men of his time. But he failed fully to appreciate the ominous epistemological implications of his reflections on the limitations of the historical method. The questions that he and his colleagues left unanswered posed certain theoretical problems which, if carried to their logical conclusion, threatened to undermine the very foundations of French historical science.

A question to which few of the French academic historians addressed themselves was one that had been haunting German historians and philosophers for decades: if the historian must filter his vision of the past through the prism of his personal perceptions of the present, can he be confident of possessing the same degree of objectivity that he had thought he possessed when he conceived of his role as that of resurrecting the past in its pristine form? Since he is himself a living participant in the historical process, will not his historical vision be warped by the particular environmental influences that operate on his mind to form his personal conception of present reality? That this issue was scarcely raised is indicative of the extent to which French historical thought remained relatively sequestered from the influence of the neo-Kantian critique of positivism contained in the writings of Rickert, Dilthey, Windelband, and later, Weber, which was producing an epistemological crisis in German social science during the same period.[52] When such questions did begin to surface in France after the turn of the century, they were debated largely by philosophers and sociologists and received only perfunctory attention until Raymond Aron forced open the intellectual gates to permit the influx of German theories of the philosophy of history on the eve of the Second World War.[53]

The French historians' hesitancy to confront the epistemological problem implied by the influence of subjective values on historical understanding became more conspicuous as their scholarly interests began to approach the domain in which this problem becomes most acute. In keeping with academic tradition, most of these historians had launched their careers with doctoral dissertations that dealt with topics of limited scope. Moreover, since they entered the profession at a time when history was still denied the right to apply its critical methods to the modern era, their maiden contributions to scholarship were confined to the medieval and early modern period. But toward the end of the century, when the academic historians became aware of the growing public demand for historical works of a general nature, and as the traditional prejudice against modern and even contemporary history began to dissipate,[54] an increasing number of general histories dealing with events of the recent past began to appear. And it was precisely this type of history that proved to be most susceptible to the distorting effects of the historian's own value judgments.

As critics of scientific scholarship in other nations had demonstrated, the likelihood of value-free history varies inversely with the scope of the topic under investigation. Owing to the larger number of sources (both primary and secondary) with which he must deal, the historical synthesizer is compelled to make more personal choices of inclusion, exclusion, emphasis, and interpretation than the specialist. Moreover, the historian of the recent past is much more apt to permit his personal prejudices to intrude into his historical interpretations than is the student of some distant and remote age whose controversies have long since lost their immediacy. This problem of subjectivity was compounded by the university historians' preference for political history. By treating affairs of state as the most important causal factors in historical evolution, their historical understanding was bound to be affected by their own attitudes toward the hotly-disputed political questions of the day.

It seems likely that these epistemological difficulties received such scant attention from the French academic historians because of two historical conditions, one relating to the development of their profession, and the other to the domestic political situation in France. First of all, their hesitancy to pursue such questions to their logical conclusion reflected the fact that the discipline of history had not yet passed through what Thomas Kuhn has called the stage of "normal" science; typically the first generation of practitioners are so absorbed in the practical application of the recently adopted "paradigms" of their profession that they have little time or inclination to submit the theoretical foundations of their discipline to a searching reexamination.[55] The German historians of the late nineteenth century felt free to question the methodological and epistemological assumptions that had guided historical research in their country for generations because they had inherited rather than created the system and had a minor stake in its preservation. But the French academic historians who had participated in the revolution that recently established the new models of inquiry for *la science historique* were understandably reluctant to chip away at the methodological edifice that they themselves had built.

Moreover, the relatively stable condition of the French political system in the first two decades of the Third Republic's existence contributed to the persistence of the somewhat naive faith in the possibility of objective, value-free historical study that underlay the theoretical system of the French historical school. The deep-seated political divisions for which France has long had a deserved reputation were temporarily concealed by the common commitment to redeem the national honor that had been lost in 1870, a cause that no Frenchman of the postwar period, not even a scientific historian, could think of as incompatible with the spirit of objectivity and disinterested scholarship. The problem of historical objectivity was seldom addressed until the political and religious animosities that had been submerged in the transitory consensus of the early years reappeared during the Dreyfus Affair, when the university historians were compelled to examine the political implications of their teaching and the ideological underpinnings of their scholarship. Until the advent of that political polarization, however, the conception of an objective method of historical investigation—notwithstanding the occasional doubts of a Monod or a Seignobos—reigned supreme. The unquestioned and unchallenged objective of historical study in France was to repair the spiritual damage that had been inflicted at Sedan.

5
History as Civic Instruction: The Conflict of Science and Patriotism

The didactic purpose for which the academic historical profession in France had originally been founded represented an enduring albeit unacknowledged flaw in its claim to scientific objectivity. The movement of historical reform did not emerge spontaneously from a cultural vacuum, but was an outgrowth of the military defeat and the political climate that produced the regime that came to be known as the Third Republic. It was infused from its very inception, as we have seen, with a sense of mission to accomplish a specific purpose—the rekindling of patriotic feeling in the minds of French youth—and was dependent upon an institutional instrument to achieve that purpose—the republican political regime and its educational system. The New History was ineluctibly destined to become an applied, rather than a pure, science. The French historians were thus impelled by the very nature of their mission to venture beyond the terrain of esoteric erudition into the arena of partisan politics. Just as their desire to centralize, rationalize, and professionalize the production of historical scholarship drew them into a tacit alliance of mutual benefit with the political reformers of the university system (who had been impressed by the valuable services rendered by the German historians to the fatherland), their belief in the educative function of history inevitably involved them in the heated controversies that raged throughout the 1880s over the issue of primary school reform.

The condition of French primary education in the early years of the Third Republic was hardly encouraging to the historians who were seeking to enthrone their discipline as the principal vehicle of patriotic instruction. Duruy's tentative attempts to reform the structure and curricula of the lower educational levels had failed to loosen the stranglehold of tradition. Primary education remained a voluntary, relatively neglected enterprise, still very much under the sway of clerical influence.[1] The pathetically small and ill-prepared crop of *instituteurs* graduated each year by the *écoles normales* and the generally poor quality of the history textbooks employed in the classrooms were symptoms of the spirit of indifference to historical instruction that had characterized the first decade of the new regime.

This attitude was rooted in the structure of the French political system prior to 1870. Under the Bourbon Restoration, the July Monarchy, and the Second Empire, when a restricted suffrage discouraged popular participation in political affairs, historical instruction was thought to be useful principally as a means of preparing members of the royal family for their official duties. Michelet tutored Bourbon and Orléanist princesses in his prerevolutionary days, and the education of the future Napoleon IV was entrusted to Fustel de Coulanges and later Lavisse under the Second Empire.[2] But the major burden of familiarizing the average Frenchman with his nation's heritage was borne by the institution of the family. Michelet was often read at the hearth of republican households to transmit the story of the glorious revolutionary tradition to the young generation. The Restoration and Orléanist histories that filled the private libraries of landed or moneyed families were the principal sources of historical education for the young of the *noblesse* and the *haute bourgeoisie*.[3] With the definitive establishment of universal manhood suffrage in 1876, however, the issue of educational reform became a major topic for public debate.[4] The importance of universal education to a democratic system was an article of faith for the republican elite that gradually assumed positions of political power in France after 1875. The succeeding years were dominated by efforts to broaden the scope of primary instruction until 1882, when Jules Ferry's Primary Education Law rendered education from the ages of six to thirteen free, obligatory, and "neutral" (that is, all forms of religious instruction were prohibited).

By expelling religion from the public schools, the republicans deprived French education of its traditional source of moral and patriotic indoctrination. The nineteenth century had discovered that the inculcation of patriotism was most effective when it was based upon a superior principle. Religion and the principle of royal or imperial legitimacy had formerly provided this transcendent basis of patriotism. But under the influence of the doctrines of Kantian spiritualism that were becoming popular among republican thinkers, religion was reduced to a matter of conscience, while the position of the prince was usurped by the nation that he had formerly been thought to incarnate. The conception of *la nation* as the collectivity of the citizens, one of the most cherished legacies of the Revolution, provided the political leaders of the Third Republic with the superior principle that they had been searching for. During the 1880s they succeeded in replacing the discredited theological and dynastic bases of patriotism with the nationalist credo of the revolutionary tradition.[5]

The institution of free, compulsory, and secular primary education was designed to prepare the newly enfranchised electorate for the civic responsibilities required for political participation in a democratic system. This program of citizenship training was intended to foster a national consensus based on the liberal principles embodied in the Declaration of the Rights of Man. As the public school system rapidly began to replace the church as the source of patriotic instruction, the teaching profession became, in the words of one of its most respected spokesmen, the "militia of the republican party" in every isolated hamlet of the French nation, charged with the responsibility of inculcating republican values in French youth.[6]

Ernest Lavisse was one of the first modern French historians to recognize the potential uses of history as an instrument of patriotic instruction in the public schools. He had observed during his sojourn in Germany how the teaching of history could contribute to the formation of patriotic sentiments in impressionable young minds. "The most active nations today are searching in their historical origins for proof of their *raison d'être* and a guarantee of their future," he informed his students at the opening of the Faculty of Letters of Paris in 1883. "Philologists and historians have inflamed the patriotism of the Slavs. Italy has not forgotten its glorious past . . . Germans conceive of a sort of *Germania mystique*."[7] Could France afford to remain indifferent to these movements, he asked. "Not to take the defensive would be national suicide," he concluded. "Foreign science is attacking us. It is invading our national history with false and dishonorable interpretations of it." A school of historians is "exalting Prussia and Germany and spreading hatred against the French."[8]

He saw this threat to French traditions as coming not only from without, but from within the nation as well. The disappearance of religion as the basis of patriotic instruction had left a spiritual vacuum that must be filled by new ideals based on the firmer ground of historical truth. He defended the special place that history had come to occupy in the educational life of France, pointing out that "we add to the national energy when we give a people the consciousness of its value, pride in its history."[9] Moreover, he contended that the history instructor should not be expected to observe the rules of objectivity required of other educators. One could not teach the history of France "with the equanimity that suits the rule of participles," he declared, because it deals with "the blood of our blood and the flesh of our flesh."[10] The obligation to make the fatherland "loved and understood" rests with history. Historical consciousness is necessary in order for the French student to become "a citizen and a soldier," and if he does not become "a citizen imbued with [a sense of] his duties and a soldier who loves his rifle, the [history] teacher will have wasted his time."[11]

Since the principal responsibility for providing a "civic education" belongs to the history teacher,[12] Lavisse continued, he must also help to protect French students from "the spirit of indifference and skepticism" by cultivating "the national spirit," which will replace the abandoned ideals of religious faith and monarchical loyalty.[13] His language frequently betrayed an almost Barrèsian reverence for *la patrie*, its traditions, its soil. "My children, our Fatherland is not merely a territory," he informed a group of students from his native province, "it is a human structure, begun centuries ago, which we are continuing, which you will continue . . . A natural instinct binds us to our ancestors with a sort of sacredness . . . It gives us a feeling of continuity and accompanied with the charm of long memories, it gives us that force and tranquility which rises from the deeply buried root with the ever-flowing sap."[14]

Lavisse believed that history should serve other pedagogical purposes as well. In a report submitted in 1890 to a commission on educational reform, he proposed that historical instruction also be used "to fortify the moral sentiment in French youth." He conceded that "it is not true that the just are always rewarded and the wicked always punished in history," yet insisted that the historian, the new priest of the secular republic, "not only has the right to be a moralist, he has the duty."[15] He must seek to deduce general maxims of right conduct from the great book of the past, just as the *curé* before him discovered such prescriptions in the gospels and the writings of the church fathers.

Lavisse did not display any awareness of the inherent contradiction in using the new academic discipline that he and his colleagues were defending as a science of universal validity to impart patriotic and moral values to French youth. He did concede that "the cultivation of national feeling is a delicate matter." The history teacher must strive to "fortify the natural love of the native country" but in doing so he must be careful "not to forget the man in the Frenchman" and avoid deprecating "the place of humanity."[16] Since science deals with universal man, he declared, it cannot be rendered subservient to nationalist ends. But when Lavisse attempted to relate his conception of science to the goals of education, he appeared to slip into a confused mélange of morality, patriotism, and science that increasingly characterized the movement for which he was a prominent spokesman. The educational system of France, he insisted,

> is an Institute of universal science, but it is not for that reason cosmopolitan. It belongs to a nation first of all; it honors that nation; it serves it by augmenting the value of the mind, the source of all values . . . It summarizes, expresses, and fortifies the national spirit. It is a residence of the youth, where the young people join the cult of science to the cult of the fatherland.[17]

Lavisse, like so many French educators of his generation, was able to skirt the issue of the conflict between the universality of the scientific spirit and the parochial nature of patriotic instruction because of his conviction that France, by virtue of its revolutionary heritage, occupied a special place in the world that rendered its national concerns universal. He urged French students to "take advantage of the right to love, the right to prefer France," since "to serve her is the most effective means of serving humanity."[18] To those who accused him of attempting to introduce politics into education, he replied that "it is not playing politics; it is teaching history to teach our beloved Frenchmen that they are the noblest beings, the noblest among the children of men, because they are the freest and the richest in rights."[19]

Throughout his entire life, Lavisse remained a dedicated, outspoken French patriot, and was therefore one of the few academic historians to escape the accusations of internationalism that flowed like a torrent from the ranks of the extreme right in the decade prior to World War I. But if patriotism was a constant in his intellectual development, political ideology was a variable. As one surveys the entire sweep of his career, it is difficult to avoid the conclusion that the principle that determined his political loyalties was sheer opportunism. Under the Second Empire, as we have seen, Lavisse used his personal connections with Victor Duruy's son to gain a prestigious post in the minister's office, and later in the Imperial household itself. In the years immediately following the departure of the Emperor, when a royalist or imperial restoration was far from an impossibility, he frequently expressed in private his hostility to the republican form of government. He carried on an extensive correspondence with his erstwhile pupil, the Prince Imperial, until the dashing young pretender's premature death at the hands of the Zulus in 1879. Large extracts of this correspondence, which Lavisse had deposited in the Bibliothèque Nationale before his death, were published posthumously in 1929 in the *Revue des deux mondes*, and immediately caused a scandal at his old publishing house, the Librairie Armand Colin.[20] The director unsuccessfully tried to convince Lavisse's niece to forbid further publication of his letters on the grounds that they had been written at an early age and did not reflect her uncle's mature political convictions. It is obvious why the letters caused such concern among his former associates, who wished to protect his good name. In November 1874, shortly before the passage of the constitutional laws that established the republican form of government in France, he had written to the prince suggesting that the recent elections demonstrated that "a large part of the nation is not yet decided; the day that it will decide for the Empire, which cannot be far off, the Empire will be restored."[21] Two years later, on the eve of Marshal-President MacMahon's unsuccessful challenge to the republican tradition of legislative supremacy, Lavisse informed the prospective Napoleon IV that "the Republic is full of dangers. The men are very small, ideas do not exist. Nothing is on the horizon. We are stricken with sterility. Opportunism is an excuse for impotence. Radicalism is an old mask behind which there are only base passions. The center left is sexless. What can we do with all this?" His proposed solution to these defects in the republican system reminds one of the royalist Charles Maurras's subsequent pleas to the Duc d'Orléans to stage a *coup de force:* "It is around you alone that *le ralliement* can develop."[22] Only in 1878 did he begin to have second thoughts about the likelihood of an imperial restoration. "I have little faith in the long duration of the Republic, and I am having less and less in it," he announced. "But I used to think that the Empire alone was capable of succeeding the Republic; I no longer believe that."[23] As if to hedge his bets even further, Lavisse managed to remain on friendly terms with the Orléanist pretender's uncle, the Duc d'Aumale, and was a frequent visitor to the salon of Princess Mathilde.[24]

The death of the imperial heir in 1879, together with the resignation of MacMahon in the same year, spelled the end of the hopes of the counterrevolutionary forces in France to stem the tide of republicanism. The Third Republic had demonstrated its resilience in the face of domestic adversity, and the monarchical and Bonapartist alternatives appeared to have run their course. In this fluid political situation, Lavisse again underwent a timely ideological conversion which paved the way for a meteoric rise in the academic historical profession that surpassed his rapid advancement in the closing years of the Second Empire. After two years of service at the Ecole Normale as a lecturer in modern history, he was summoned to the Sorbonne in

1880 to assist Fustel de Coulanges, and in 1888 was awarded a professorship of his own. By that time he had already established a reputation as one of the most vocal champions of the Republic.[25]

One of the features of the Republic that most appealed to Lavisse was its pedagogical policy. The educational philosophy of Jules Ferry, which reserved a preeminent place for patriotic instruction in the primary school curriculum, satisfied the single criterion that Lavisse instinctively applied to social and political institutions. His acquaintance with Gambetta and Clemenceau, whom he had met during his student days in the Latin Quarter, and his friendship with Ferry in the 1870s, convinced him that republicanism was capable of restoring pride in the fatherland and reviving the sense of national unity and purpose that had temporarily disappeared with the Second Empire.[26] In a spate of articles in professional periodicals, in his classroom lectures, and in several public speeches, Lavisse spent the decade of the 1880s attempting to "establish the new institutions and create the moral foundations of a veritable republican legitimacy" by employing the arguments of history. As Raoul Girardet has observed, he popularized the notion that the "definitive establishment of the Republic" in France was the culmination of the revolutionary process set in motion in 1789, and in an even more dramatic sense, represented "the logical outcome of twenty centuries of history."[27]

Hence Lavisse's expanded definition of history's educative function burdened it with yet a third responsibility: the encouragement of republican loyalty. In his advisory instructions to primary school history teachers, he constantly emphasized that, while an open mind must at all times be encouraged in the young *écolier,* certain "indisputable truths" of French history must be presented as axiomatic. When dealing with the era of Louis XIV, he suggested, the teacher should dwell on the excessive pride of the grand monarch, he must point out that the king was a spendthrift and a warmonger and should terminate his treatment of the period "with the story of some disaster and the portrayal of the miseries" that dominated the final years of his reign. The instructor should always strive to demonstrate the inequities of the *ancien régime,* comparing it to the spirit of liberty and equality that pervades the Third Republic. Such comparisons, he remarked, "will demonstrate to the pupils [the reality of] social progress."[28]

With regard to modern history, Lavisse was not insensitive to the particular difficulties that arise from the controversial nature of the subjects treated, but he insisted that the history teacher is justified in imparting those "indisputable truths" that have been definitively established by history. His description of the last days of the *ancien régime,* for example, typified the oversimplified treatment of the causes of the Revolution that characterized his written works. "The kingdom suffered abuses of all sorts; inequality, injustice, despotism," he declared. "Genius protested louder; it produced the French ideal of liberty, of justice, of humanity. And this was the French Revolution."[29] He suggested that the lessons covering the events of 1789-1799 reflect the unquestioned assumption that "the French Revolution made a heroic effort to substitute the rule of reason and justice" for the irrational and unjust system of the Bourbon monarchy and that by becoming a republic, France "changed its old laws in order to give itself better ones."[30]

Such a program of political reeducation necessitated a shared commitment to the Republic on the part of the *instituteurs*, and the highly centralized system of French education was admirably suited to the purpose of imposing such a uniformity of opinion on its employees. The inspectors who supervised elementary education in the *départements* were, of course, themselves products of the state-controlled system of higher education, as were the prefects and the bureaucrats at the Ministry of Public Instruction.[31] Moreover, as we have seen, the aforementioned educational reforms of the 1890s transformed the entire teaching corps—from the elementary school instructor to the chaired professor at the Sorbonne—into a single, closed corporation, designated as the *Université*. Instructors at the primary and secondary school level were trained either at the Ecole Normale Supérieure or at one of the less prestigious teacher training schools. If the history courses in the primary schools were to serve as the conveyer belts on which the principles of secular bourgeois morality, patriotism, and orthodox republicanism were to be transmitted to the younger generation, the instructors themselves would first have to be imbued with these values in their professional training. Lavisse took note of this exigency and urged the university professors to "direct the schoolmasters and lead them by the hand" in an effort to ensure their acceptance of the reigning orthodoxy.[32] Such a plea was hardly necessary since the Minister of Public Instruction, on the advice of the local prefect, appointed all members of the teaching staff and carefully prescribed the program of studies for the state normal schools.[33]

As the political preferences of those at the top of the educational hierarchy began to take hold in the lower echelons, it seemed only logical that the production of textbooks for classroom use should also originate from the same source, to ensure an even greater degree of standardization and centralized direction. Several of the most notable Sorbonne historians considered this task sufficiently important to interrupt their scholarly work to write history manuals for use in the *écoles primaires* and *lycées*. As early as 1875 Lavisse had compiled a textbook for the elementary grades that was widely used as a primer of patriotic instruction. It contained passages exhorting French schoolchildren never to forget the excruciating indemnity imposed on the fatherland by the Germans, and bristled with references to the humiliating fate of the lost provinces.[34] The famous *petit Lavisse*, which reappeared in revised editions in 1884, 1895, and 1912, became the familiar companion of millions of French pupils during the first four decades of the Third Republic.[35] It does not appear as an exaggeration to agree with two recent historians that Lavisse's sovereign authority in the university, the phenomenal success of his textbooks at all levels, and his academic and political relations made him the "pope of official history" in late nineteenth century France.[36]

Following the example set by Lavisse (and perhaps with an eye to the pecuniary rewards that could be realized from the publication of required classroom textbooks), other prominent *universitaires* got into the act. Seignobos composed a two-volume *Histoire de la civilisation* to accommodate the *lycées* for women that had been opened in 1880, and followed this up with textbook histories of the Middle Ages, the Renaissance, and the modern period.[37] Monod contributed manuals for use at the Saint-Cyr military academy, as well as a primer for use in the primary schools after the educational reform of 1909. Even Langlois suspended his aversion for history conceived on a grand scale long enough to bring out a series of texts that covered centuries of historical development.

History manuals employed in the French public school system have traditionally expressed the dominant values of the educational and political elite. Ever since the Bourbon Restoration, when the few history primers in existence were studded with denunciations of the Revolution, the partisan nature of public instruction has been so pronounced that it moved one critic to observe that "from the day that written history is given official encouragement, it is no longer history."[38] But the presumption of scientific objectivity that dominated the thinking of the Sorbonne historians in the early decades of the Republic enabled them to skirt this issue. Langlois defended the scientific and objective manner in which the official textbooks were researched and written, claiming that constant revision and correction of past errors assured a high degree of accuracy and impartiality. He insisted that they constituted objective works of scholarship which supplied "precise inventories of acquired knowledge," the distillation of decades of monographic research carried on by the leading historians of the nation, rather than propaganda tracts replete with patriotic or political themes.[39]

But independent studies of the content of the textbooks employed in the history and civic instruction courses of the French primary schools prior to the First World War suggest that quite the opposite result obtained. After examining eighty-eight of the most widely used texts, Carlton J.H. Hayes found that nearly all were written not only to acquaint French schoolchildren with the history and institutions of their country, but also to make them "love it with emotional pride and religious zeal."[40] An earlier evaluation of some seventy-five textbooks by the Carnegie Endowment concluded that most primary school manuals in France tended to exalt "military qualities" more than "civic virtues" and foster a spirit of "chauvinism" rather than a healthy patriotism.[41]

The programs of study in French primary education were similarly designed to instill patriotic sentiments in French youth, though the leading authorities on historical education took pains to deny that they had any intention of prostituting history for nationalist ends. "We hardly ever ask of history any more that it provide moral lessons or examples of good conduct," Langlois and Seignobos proclaimed. Nor do we continue to use history "to exalt patriotism or loyalism, as they do in Germany." The principal value of a science, they continued, is the degree to which it is accurate and objective, and "all we ask of history any more is [that it present] the truth." But the testimony of students who had themselves attended the history courses in the primary schools contradicted the assertions of the two eminent historians of the University of Paris. When the candidates for the *baccalauréat moderne* were asked in July 1897 "what is the purpose of history in education?" 80 percent replied, in substance, "to exalt patriotism."[42] This judgment was confirmed by Hayes's inquiry, which has shown that seven of the twelve subjects of study in French primary schools were "national" in nature, in that they possessed "a largely patriotic content" and were taught "in a conspicuously national manner." Hayes noted that historical instruction, the underpinning of the program of patriotic education, was devoted almost exclusively to French national history and treated the history of other nations only when it impinged upon the history of France, which usually meant during a war.[43]

The inherent incompatibility between the commitment to objective scholarship and the willingness to employ history for moral, patriotic, and political purposes posed few threats to the self-assurance of the academic historians throughout the remainder of the nineteenth century. Whatever abuses this type of history might have produced were effectively camouflaged within the framework of the seemingly innocuous program of civic instruction. Several decades later a member of the profession complained that "in order for history to realize the intentions of civic education, it was necessary to mutilate it, to present only certain aspects of it while neglecting the others, and this fraud alienated us from the scientific conceptions of history."[44] But no such sentiment was forthcoming from the French academic historians in the last quarter of the nineteenth century, largely because the content of historical instruction harmonized so perfectly with the universally accepted value system that the republicans had adopted to replace the authoritarian, clerical traditions of the past. As Raoul Girardet has observed, the "spirit of the new republican *civisme*" fostered the virtues of "joint responsibility, discipline, work, and foresight" as well as promoting "the cult of the fatherland, universal suffrage, and the principles of 1789."[45]

This eclectic medley of Jacobin nationalism, democratic idealism, and bourgeois moralism was the ideological diet that sustained the first generation of Frenchmen as it struggled to recover from the doldrums induced by the defeat. It was only after the reappearance of an antirepublican movement on the right and the rise of international socialism and revolutionary syndicalism on the left at the turn of the century that the ideological underpinning of the educational orthodoxy was exposed. While the rightist opposition concentrated its attacks on the republican bias that underlay the academic scholarship and teaching, the extreme left, influenced by the doctrines of revolutionary syndicalism, Marxian internationalism, Jaurèsian pacifism, and Hervéist antimilitarism, chipped away at its patriotic, jingoist, bourgeois prejudices. The republican historians, after their signal success in establishing their discipline as an objective science, were caught in this ideological crossfire.

6
The Record of Scholarly Achievement, 1876–1900

But the early decades of the Third Republic were almost totally free from such ideological controversies as later raged between the academic historians and their critics on the two extremes of the political spectrum. The politics of consensus was still the rule. The public evaluation of the academic historical profession was largely confined to a consideration of its record of scholarly production, and this judgment was universally and justifiably a favorable one. Even the most resolute defenders of the tradition of historical writing that was progressively being superseded could not gainsay the string of impressive accomplishments that the French historical profession had recorded during the last quarter of the nineteenth century. For all their troublesome doubts and uncertainties about methodology, for all their feelings of inferiority vis-à-vis their opposite numbers in Germany, the French historians succeeded admirably in the two major objectives that they had set for themselves: the creation of a discipline within the university devoted exclusively to historical scholarship and the formation of an elite community of scholars that assembled in the reformed university system the most prominent historians of the nation and the most promising candidates for discipleship.[1]

The infectious enthusiasm for rediscovering the national heritage that resulted from this mobilization of talent rubbed off on the archivists, whose preliminary labors were prerequisites for a systematic exploitation of the historical documents. Guizot, in his capacity as Louis Philippe's Minister of Public Instruction, had set the stage for the location and collocation of the surviving historical records by securing an annual credit of 120,000 francs to finance the publication of the important archival materials relating to the history of France.[2] He established the Comité des Travaux Historiques to administer this program and recruited legal historians, paleographers, numismatists, philologists, and diplomatists from the Ecole des Chartes to collect, organize, and edit the long-lost documents.[3] Circulars were dispatched to every commune requesting notification of the existence of Roman inscriptions, unpublished letters, documents, and monuments that had been discovered by private individuals.[4] This investigative activity was intensified in the last quarter of the century, as the *chartistes* and their new allies at the Sorbonne and the Ecole Pratique, supported by government subsidies, organized and opened five additional archives that had been left untouched by the earlier researchers.[5]

But while much of the groundwork for the opening of the archives had been laid earlier, it remained for modern scholars to catalogue the materials in order to make them more easily accessible to the historical researcher. The period from 1876 to 1900 saw the compilation of the great archival bibliographies that were to orient the future troops of young scholars that cascaded off the academic assembly line in search of virgin sources to exploit. This extended project was the work not of obscure technicians, but of the most renowned masters of the French historical profession and their most talented apprentices. After years of painstaking research, Gabriel Monod and his disciples at the Ecole Pratique brought out in 1888 the *Bibliographie de l'histoire de France*, which covered the period prior to the Revolution.[6] A decade later Georges Brière and Pierre Caron published the *Répertoire méthodique de l'histoire moderne et contemporaine de la France* for the nineteenth century materials. Langlois's useful *Manuel de bibliographie historique* taught hundreds of young scholars how to use these and earlier compilations to best advantage, and the *Introduction aux études historiques* that he coauthored with Seignobos was the first handbook of historical study to appear in France.[7]

It was entirely fitting that substantial progress would be made in the collection of documents relating to the French Revolution under a regime that drew its ideological inspiration from the principles of 1789. From his newly endowed chair in the History of the French Revolution, Alphonse Aulard announced his intention to supervise a major project of archival retrieval and organization that would put the documents of the revolutionary period in a state to be utilized by future scholars.[8] By the end of the century he had edited collections of documents relating to the Jacobin club and the city of Paris between 1799 and 1815, and had begun work on the surviving documents of the Committee of Public Safety, a massive undertaking that produced twenty-six volumes before he terminated it in 1923.[9] Between 1894 and 1914 the Municipal Council of Paris commissioned a published collection of the legislative acts of the Commune of Paris during the Revolution, and in 1903 the National Assembly, at the insistence of Jean Jaurès, authorized the publication of the collection of documents relating to the economic history of the Revolution.[10]

As the documents were progressively subjected to such professional scrutiny, the teams of investigators discovered a veritable gold mine of historical information. The sheer volume of material inevitably produced a trend toward narrow specialization along topical, geographical, and chronological lines. Professional societies devoted to a particular aspect of French history began to appear, and the instant success of the *Revue historique* prompted the foundation of a number of professional periodicals committed to publishing the results of scholarly research in specific areas of historical interest. In 1881 two university historians founded a periodical, *La Révolution française,* devoted exclusively to the revolutionary period. After Aulard acceded to the editorship in 1887, the review became the official forum for articles and reviews dealing with the great event, and a newly-created Société de l'Histoire de la Révolution Française assumed control of publication.[11] By the turn of the century the French historical profession had evolved into a mosaic of specialized disciplines, each with its own professional organization and organ. This trend toward specialization at times approached almost ludicrous extremes, as with, for example, the *Revue du seizième siècle,* the *Revue de la Révolution de 1848,* the *Revue Bossuet,* and the *Revue Bourdaloue.*[12]

The nature of much of the historical scholarship during this period, particularly in the form of doctoral dissertations, reflected this increasing emphasis upon restricted topics. One dedicated young *érudit* spent 1,236 pages describing the history of the Commune of Paris from May to December 1792. Philippe Sagnac, who later reached the pinnacle of success in the French historical profession, devoted over 300 pages to a historical analysis of one twenty-four-hour period, the revolutionary *journée* of 10 August 1792.[13] It was precisely such concentrated monographic scholarship that was taken as proof that the scientific organization of historical studies was beginning to bear fruit. What must surely have appeared to the nonspecialist as an unjustifiable expenditure of time and effort on topics too limited to be of any general interest was hailed by the academic historians as the epitomy of the scholarly division of labor. Each monograph, no matter how seemingly irrelevant, unimportant, and time-consuming, was seen as forming an integral part of a vast, collective, centrally-directed project of historical research. The growing number of dissertations and specialized studies constituted building blocks that would contribute to the step by step reconstruction of the imposing mosaic of the past. "Apprentices are being trained in many workshops," Lavisse noted with satisfaction, and he foresaw the day when several "valiant laborers working on various parts of the task, will explore and excavate our national history."[14] The remaining obscurities of our knowledge of the French past, he declared, can be illumined only through "a collective effort of laborers who know their job."[15]

This spirit of scientific teamwork was not limited to the restricted domain of monographic scholarship. For this was also the era of the great collaborative synthesis, a genre of history which harked back to the tradition of the *Encyclopédie*, in which a team of historians pooled their collective wisdom to produce multivolume works covering an extended period of time. Lavisse and Alfred Rambaud's pioneering *Histoire générale du IVe siècle à nos jours*, which appeared in twelve volumes between 1892 and 1901, enjoyed an immediate success and became the model of its kind. During the completion of the final volume of this ambitious project of universal world history, Lavisse turned his attention to the past of his own nation. At the opening of the new century he began to edit the massive *Histoire de France depuis les origines jusqu'à la Révolution*, which appeared in nine installments between 1900 and 1911.

This new trend toward history painted on a broad canvas by a team of trained experts was intended simultaneously to strengthen the tradition of scientific historical scholarship and to broaden its appeal. The former design was apparently based upon the misconception that a dozen historical specialists working separately to produce a series of works covering an extended period of time could collectively attain a degree of objectivity that was beyond the means of the individual scholar. In their introduction to the *Histoire générale*, Lavisse and Rambaud confidently asserted that by farming out each chapter to one of their collaborators, who "by special studies and estimable publications" had demonstrated expertise in a special area, they were insuring that the finished product would offer the double advantage of a unity of design and a diversity of talents.[16]

The notion that the personality of the individual historian could be extinguished from a work of history by increasing the number of minds that helped to produce it was not peculiar to Lavisse and his compatriots, but was a common conviction that inspired the collaborative works that were beginning to appear in all the major nations of the Western world in the same period. Lord Acton, in his famous letter to the contributors of the *Cambridge Modern History* project, expressed a similar faith in the corrective powers of collaboration.

> Our scheme requires that nothing shall reveal the country, the religion, or the party to which the writers belong.
> It is essential not only on the ground that impartiality is the character of legitimate history, but because the work is carried on by men acting together for no other object than the increase of accurate knowledge.
> The disclosure of personal views would lead to such confusion that all unity of design would disappear.[17]

Unfortunately, these new collaborative works failed to achieve the two major objectives that their editors had announced. Their goal of reaching a higher level of objectivity was thwarted from the outset, since the subjectivity of interpretation was simply multiplied by the number of collaborators. The result, in many cases, was a confusing unevenness of viewpoint. Lavisse's and Rambaud's *Histoire générale* was itself the supreme example of a work marred by inherently conflicting tendencies with respect to both ideology and methodology. For example, the editors selected Seignobos, a Dreyfusard and promoter of the conception of history as a social science, to write the general history of the Third Republic, while assigning to the anti-Dreyfusard *littérateur* and *académicien* Emile Faguet the section on the history of French letters since 1870. As might have been expected, Faguet's reflections on the state of French history betrayed a marked hostility to the very scientific historical school to which the editors and most of their other colleagues subscribed. His brief synopsis made no mention at all of the transformation of French history into a scientific, academic discipline in the latter half of the nineteenth century. Totally ignoring the academic *érudits* who had been responsible for that development, he reserved his most lavish praise for Duke Albert de Broglie, Albert Sorel, Fustel de Coulanges, Thureau-Dangin, and other historians of the old school. As if his inclusion of it in the category of letters alongside drama, poetry, and the novel were insufficient to convey his intention, he ended his piece with a description of history as a *canton de la littérature*.[18]

The quest for perfect impartiality was but a subsidiary motivation underlying the *fin de siècle* evolution toward synthetic, collaborative history. The leading French historians were as yet only vaguely troubled by doubts about the scientific and objective nature of historical scholarship. The principal reason for this shift in emphasis was the professional historians' recognition of the growing reaction against monographic history on the part of the general public. Lavisse himself was the first among the *universitaires* to signal the retreat from specialized scholarship that was to become widespread in the twentieth century. He had begun his career as a fervent advocate if not a practitioner of scientific scholarship, but his tenure at the Sorbonne was marked by a gradual evolution away from the tradition from which he had sprung. As early as 1885 he was publicly ridiculing the obsessive empiricism and the indiscriminate accumulation of facts that he claimed was characteristic of the *érudit,* who is "apt to magnify what is small, to consider as a discovery some poor novelty, to despise as mediocre that which is known, to abandon the highways for the footpaths, the footpaths for the blind alleys, and Charles Martel for Childebrand."[19] He cautioned his students to avoid an excessive preoccupation with historical detail. "If you have placed your magnifying glass on a speck of dust," he warned, "you must keep it there just long enough to make sure it is indeed a speck of dust, not one minute longer."[20]

The dean of the Sorbonne historians carried on a decade-long debate over the issue of scholarly specialization with his old friend Gaston Paris, a product of the German seminars and the Ecole des Chartes. Paris argued that French historians must make an even greater effort to adopt the monographic approach of Germanic scholarship, while Lavisse replied that they must resist the temptation to bury themselves in monographic studies, and must instead seek a happy medium between Germanic specialization and French generalization. His annual speech to the incoming students of the Sorbonne in 1895 expressed this growing concern about the problem of overspecialization.

> We are well aware that we must not make scholars out of you and nothing else. You need to have a liberal education that will enable you to choose your particular path after comparison and reflection, and that will leave you, whatever your speciality, with a view of the whole, which is so necessary for minds that do not want to be small.[21]

He went on to praise the public courses, which "deal with the big questions" and contribute to "your general education."[22] He was consistent in his defense of the tradition of *la culture générale,* even to the point of recognizing a knowledge of Latin as a prerequisite for historical study.[23]

Lavisse's own work exemplified this changing attitude toward historical scholarship. The textbooks and general histories of his later period did not "exclude the use of scholarship and scientific methods," in the words of a former pupil, yet tended to present the results of such research in "broad, solid, and attractive structures of true literary value." It was this kind of work, rather than scholarly monographs, that established Lavisse's reputation as the grand old man of the historical profession and set the stage for his election to the French Academy in 1892.[24] Seignobos and Langlois, both former protégés of Lavisse, fully recognized their mentor's deficiencies as an *érudit*. Seignobos, who was a student in Lavisse's first class at the Ecole Normale, recalled that his master had "only a very meager command of historical data" and never even attempted to impress his disciples with his erudition.[25] Langlois simply observed that though Lavisse was "a great historian in every sense of the word," he was "not a scholar."[26] He concentrated on picking out the "summits of interest," in the words of a recent critic, preferring to leave "the valleys to be explored by those students who possessed such patience and time."[27] Yet, Lavisse's uneasiness about the growing trend toward extreme specialization was shared even by those who had helped to encourage it. Seignobos and Langlois were not averse to administering a tongue-lashing to those historical scholars who were indiscriminately combing the archives for thesis topics. "If the activity of the specialists in external criticism were applied to questions the solution of which was important," they declared, "it would be more fruitful."[28]

The greatest cause for alarm in the historical profession was the growing realization that the vast bulk of historical scholarship produced by the French universities was of little interest to anyone but specialists in the field. In the case of most professions, the esoteric nature of the research conducted would hardly have constituted a cause for concern. The public had never expressed a collective desire to be kept abreast of the nature of specialized research that was carried on in the physical and natural sciences, for example, nor did the specialists in those disciplines feel obliged to advertise it. But the members of the academic historical profession, as we have seen, felt a special sense of civic responsibility that impelled them to cultivate a special relationship with the reading public. The historians' spirit of professionalism was equaled and to some extent rivaled by their sense of public responsibility. As the nineteenth century came to a close, a number of French thinkers, both inside and outside the university, began to ask whether these separate callings were in fact mutually incompatible.

These expressions of disillusionment with the nature of academic history emanated from three separate sources, but their virtually simultaneous appearance toward the end of the century signaled a major turning point in the fortunes of the historical profession in France. The earliest and most potent challenge to the position of history in the French university came from the small but rapidly proliferating band of scholars who were busy laying the foundations for the new academic discipline of sociology. A second group of hostile critics, originating in the ranks of the historical profession itself, issued a call for history to abandon its preoccupation with monographic, empirical study and forge a methodological link with the more theoretical disciplines, such as philosophy and psychology. A third group of French intellectuals, for the most part unaffiliated with the university, demanded that history be reestablished as a branch of the humanities.

The convergence of these three stands of opposition threw the school of scientific history on the defensive. No one could justifiably dispute the fine quality of the historical scholarship that was being carried on in the French university since the mid-1870s. But the academic historians had laid themselves open to criticism because of their somewhat inflated and precipitate claim to the mantle of science. In the wake of these onslaughts, they found it increasingly difficult to retain their undisputed predominance in the French university as the guardians and practitioners of the new science of man.

Part Two

Interdisciplinary Conflicts and Revised Objectives

7
The Challenge of the Science of Society

Sociology was from its inception a French science *par excellence*, but for several decades following the death of its illustrious founder, the terms "sociology" and "social science" fell into disuse in France and actually came to inspire a degree of hostility in French academic circles. Auguste Comte's reactionary political, social, and religious doctrines and the vogue of German historical scholarship in France that began in the 1860's all conspired to postpone the emergence of sociology as an academic discipline in the French university. The early decades of the Third Republic, as we have seen, were dominated by the attempts of the French historians to enthrone their discipline as the "queen of the sciences of man" in the French university system. There was little room for competition from a new discipline which had yet to develop a set of methodological principles beyond the preliminary teachings of Comte and his dispersed disciples.

The institutionalization of sociology as a major academic discipline in the last decade of the nineteenth century and the first decade of the twentieth was the result of the tireless efforts of Emile Durkheim and the handful of loyal apostles who helped spread the new gospel throughout the French academic community. Durkheim's own educational background provides few indications of the important role that he would later play in the development of French social science. His undistinguished record at the Ecole Normale—he graduated next to the bottom of his class in the *agrégation* of 1882—was presumably due to his having to take his examinations in philosophy, there being as yet no course in the social sciences at the hallowed institution that trained the educational elite of the nation. In spite of this less than impressive performance at the rue d'Ulm, Durkheim did not depart with the kinds of resentments harbored by many of the historians who had graduated earlier. He later dedicated his two doctoral theses, the first on Montesquieu and the second on the division of labor in society, to two instructors at the Ecole Normale who profoundly influenced his social thought: the historian Fustel de Coulanges and the philosopher Emile Boutroux.

After five years of service as a philosophy professor in provincial *lycées*, which he interrupted in 1885 to take a leave of absence that enabled him to spend six months studying the organization of philosophy and social science in the German universities,[1] the young *normalien* received an appointment from the Director of Higher Education, Louis Liard, to teach the first course in the social sciences at the University of Bordeaux.[2] It was indicative of the widespread resistance to this type of curricular innovation that it was first introduced at a provincial outpost far from Paris. The Sorbonne was evidently unprepared to sponsor such an unproven discipline until it had been tested at a safe distance.[3]

In a series of articles and in his inaugural lecture, Durkheim set the stage for his future campaign to win acceptance for the nascent science of society. To dispel the widespread hostility that the term "sociology" still prompted in France, Durkheim set out to disarm the opposition with a spirited campaign on two fronts. Recognizing that the greatest obstacle to the establishment of sociology as an academic discipline was the historical profession (which viewed the new science as a potential threat to its academic hegemony), he took the offensive against the academic historians.[4] He chose to address his appeal to national pride—a shrewd tactic in view of the popular belief that the French historical profession had been infected by the Germanic spirit after 1870. Fresh from a half year of observation in the centers of social science across the Rhine, he ridiculed the popular conception of German superiority in the analysis of human society, past or present. He asserted that the scientific study of society depends upon the active use of reason and rational analysis, rather than a passive surrender to the claims of the empirical data. The homeland of Descartes and Comte was better equipped than the land of Ranke and Waitz to develop a truly scientific approach to social reality.[5]

Such an appeal to French cultural chauvinism was clearly a tactical measure aimed at softening public resistance to the new discipline of sociology. But lest his critical attitude toward the German historical school be construed as an endorsement of the old literary conception of French history, which, though thoroughly discredited in the Sorbonne, still had well-placed advocates in the Ecole Normale and most of the prestigious Parisian *lycées,* Durkheim endorsed the modern French historians' repudiation of their predecessors. He dismissed the historians of the old school as products of a literary training, in which a superficial exposure to a few masterpieces prepared them to engage in the frivolous and fruitless task of applying literary methods and standards to the study of human society.[6]

But Durkheim was not interested in flailing a dead horse. He knew where the real enemy lay. The inaugural lectures rapidly developed into an indictment of the scientific school of French history that had appropriated such a large part of the academic curriculum during the past decade. He claimed that scientific history had failed to live up to the boundless expectations of its founders because its methods had proved insufficient to render it a true science. The modern trend toward monographic history, with its emphasis on the patient accumulation of an "enormous mass of facts," had prevented historians from developing the type of methodological tools appropriate to a true scientific discipline. Because they lack a priori knowledge of the nature of society and social institutions, he declared, historians have tended to produce works that are hardly more than "vile and arbitrary classifications, vain erudition, useless and dead compilations" of little interest to anyone beyond the small circle of specialists in the field. The narrow, indiscriminate, empirical approach of the modern historians, he charged, has blinded them to the necessity of employing *une idée directrice* in historical study, and has resulted in a mishmash of esoteric monographs that contribute little to a broader understanding of social problems.[7]

Sociology, he announced, is waiting in the wings to take up where history has left off. By developing a truly scientific methodology —one that does not make the mistake of equating science with the indiscriminate collection of raw data—academic sociology is uniquely capable of developing those *idées directrices* to orient the historical researcher in his specialized investigations. Enamored as he was of the division of labor in society, he extended that conception to the university. He compassionately reserved a special place for the historians as the laboratory technicians of the new science of society. Through their careful investigations of the mass of historical data, they would serve to furnish answers to the large questions posed by the sociologists, by subjecting their theories to the test of empirical verification.[8] But the threat to history's preeminent position in the academic hierarchy was unmistakable. He regarded sociology not simply as another distinctive discipline. Because it dealt with subject matter relating to the totality of human experience, it must become nothing less than the keystone of the emergent social sciences.[9]

Under the careful tutelage of Durkheim, the discipline of sociology grew by leaps and bounds in the last decade of the nineteenth century, the same period during which academic history was beginning to experience the beginnings of its first major crisis of confidence. In 1889, two years after Durkheim's groundbreaking course on the social sciences, sociology was established as an academic discipline at Bordeaux. Four years later, following Durkheim's defense of his two doctoral theses, a group of social theorists founded the first periodical of the fledgling profession, the *Revue internationale de sociologie*. In its first number the editor, René Worms,[10] described the major objectives of the new science. He carefully distinguished it from the recent attempts of some historians, such as Seignobos, to apply the methods of social science to the study of history. Worms argued that history had failed to develop a sound methodological basis for social research, especially regarding the events of the modern period, which is particularly vulnerable to the influences of the historian's personal prejudices. It had been established "with a view to serving politics," concentrating on reciting a tale of "sovereigns and wars" instead of analyzing the social determinants of human behavior, and was therefore incapable of being a "total science of societies." Sociology, on the other hand, had begun the task of developing a methodology that would avoid such pitfalls "by exclusively employing the severe procedures of science." Since the principal objective of the new discipline was to analyze "social facts" in order to discover the laws that govern them, he asserted, it alone can become the "queen of the unified [social] sciences."[11] Moreover, he declared, the scientific study of modern French society would yield prescriptive as well as descriptive results since "to study what is, is to prepare what ought to be."[12]

By the mid-nineties, this carefully orchestrated campaign on behalf of the new discipline and its approach to the study of society began to bear fruit. In 1896, Durkheim was awarded the first university chair in social science at Bordeaux and in the same year a group of young disciples who had followed him from the Ecole Normale founded what was to become the principal organ of the profession, the *Année sociologique*.[13] These events signified the emergence of a school that was beginning to pose a potential threat to the predominant position that the history profession had achieved in the French university system during the past two decades.

In the first number of the new review the young sociologists reaffirmed their differences with the historians and revealed their conception of the future role that sociology should play in the scientific analysis of society. History had forfeited its claim to leadership in the social sciences because of its excessive specialization, its emphasis on analysis at the expense of synthesis, and most important, its unwillingness to search for the laws of historical development that underlie the myriad of seemingly unrelated facts of history. What is needed in France, they declared, is a "synthetic social science" that seeks to eliminate the unique, accidental, nonrepetitive facts of the past (which so often form the subject matter of exhaustive historical treatises) while isolating the general trends and tendencies that can be derived from the study of a particular historical situation. The historical approach, which emphasizes chronology, biography, and series of unrelated events, deals only with "superficial manifestations of reality" that have little scientific usefulness. A true science searches for universal principles of causation that help the investigator to understand the general significance of his subject, and this, they proclaimed, is precisely what sociology seeks to accomplish.[14] Durkheim believed that underlying history's incapacity for formulating meaningful generalizations of scientific usefulness was its obsession with recapturing the past in its pristine form regardless of its relevance to the concerns of the present—an allegation that echoed earlier criticisms of history in Renan's *L'Avenir de la science* and Nietzsche's *Use and Abuse of History*. "Sociology proposes to itself other problems than history," Durkheim announced. It does not seek to know the defunct forms of civilization in order to reconstitute them. Like any positive science, it has primarily as its object the explanation of a reality which is close to us, and which can affect our ideas and our behavior. "That reality," he declared, is above all, "the man of today."[15]

The rapid gains recorded by the new discipline of sociology throughout the 1890s did not signify an end to the reservations that the leading members of the Sorbonne, both within and without the historical profession, harbored about the new science of society. On the contrary, by the middle of that decade influential *universitaires* and their allies were still resisting the idea that sociology constituted a legitimate academic discipline. Lucien Herr, the librarian of the Ecole Normale, wrote in the quasi-official *Revue universitaire* that the new school of social science centered in Bordeaux deserved nothing but ridicule because it based its so-called scientific analysis of society on a jumble of statistics and secondary sources and tended indiscriminately to accept all evidence "with no attempt at criticism."[16] Charles Andler, writing half a year later in the same review, complained that "sociology, such as it is constituted, can neither resolve, nor even pose," the important questions of man's behavior in society. He denounced the followers of Durkheim for "prematurely moving in a direction in which everything is obscure" and thought it absurd that they presumed to engage in a study of society without relying on the disciplines of psychology and history.[17] But by the turn of the century, as we shall see, these reservations rapidly began to evaporate, and sociology was well on its way to establishing itself as a major intellectual force in the French *Université*.

Two years before Durkheim became the first chaired professor of social science in the French university system, a scholar who straddled the chasm that separated the older discipline of history from its modern competitor in the social sciences made a valiant effort to bridge the gap. In a monumental tome entitled *De l'Histoire considérée comme science,* Paul Lacombe attempted to rescue the embattled muse Clio from the subordinate position to which the Dukheimians were attempting to banish her. His work was a serious attempt to respond to the sociologists' critique of history without lapsing into the petulant defensiveness that characterized many of the historians' rejoinders. His principal objective, as his title implies, was to postulate the conditions under which history could be regarded as a true science. He was well aware that such an attempt would ineluctably draw him into the fierce interdisciplinary rivalry that had been raging in the professional reviews since Durkheim's inaugural lectures at Bordeaux. Since his aim was to vindicate the scientific claims of history, Lacombe intentionally avoided using the term "sociology" in the title for fear of frightening off prospective readers in the historical profession. But for reasons that he later explains, he suspected that his book would probably be more helpful to sociologists than to historians.[18]

Lacombe began his defense of scientific history by defining the word "science" as it has been used in the natural and physical sciences. In its most general meaning, he declared, science represents the attempt to establish similarities among phenomena that will yield some degree of predictability based upon observed regularities in their behavior.[19] A survey of the past performance of the historical profession led him to the conclusion that history had failed to meet this test. He attributed this incapacity to the erroneous conception of the scientific method that had been nurtured by the historical scholars. By concentrating on the pursuit of historical "reality," he remarked, such scholarship had become not only a useless waste of time and energy, but an exercise in anti-intellectualism.[20] A sterile, indiscriminate empiricism must not be confused with the true scientific method, which aims at *understanding* the reality with which it comes into contact.

> As the mass of historical reality increases, the part that each scholar can assimilate becomes a smaller fragment and a narrower slice of the whole. Ever more remote from the total conception, the knowl-

edge of the scholar gradually decreases in value. It thus culminates in absolutely useless notions which in no way advance our understanding of man and the world.[21]

He traced the origin of this impasse in historical research to the historical profession's confusion of historical "reality" with historical "truth." The former concept refers to the myriad of facts that are obtainable from the documentary evidence of the past, while the latter signifies the "meaning" or "significance" of those facts. By striving to recreate historical *reality* in all its detail, the scholar is merely constructing a preliminary edifice upon which historical *truth* can be built. The enormous conglomeration of individual events that the scholar feels obligated to retrace constitutes a vast heap of historical reality, a slice of past life, which, instead of yielding a scientific understanding of the past, actually diverts the historian from his final goal. It is as if the chemist were compelled to examine every molecule of a particular compound before he could hope to understand the whole. Past reality in its entirety is no more susceptible to scientific understanding than is the whole of present reality, Lacombe insisted, and the continued pursuit of it will inevitably lead to a wild goose chase.[22]

The successful pursuit of historical *truth*, on the other hand, was a future possibility that Lacombe refused to rule out. Indeed, he believed it should become the primary preoccupation of the historian. Such a procedure depends upon the investigator's willingness to acknowledge the existence of "a hierarchy among the diverse orders of historical facts." The historian must abandon his efforts to gather relics of the past with an "excessively perfect equality of interest," Lacombe declared, and must admit that certain types of knowledge are more urgently needed by the modern world than others. Having thus liberated himself from the tyranny of research that is of "secondary importance or of no use to the present," the scholar can direct his efforts in certain predetermined directions.[23]

The postulation of a hierarchy of historical knowledge clearly implied the need for a set of principles of selection, and Lacombe suggested that history borrow such analytical criteria from the natural and physical sciences. One useful principle is what he called the "principle of similitude." The historian is interested in isolating and grouping together those occurrences in history that are demonstrably connected to other occurrences in a *given period.* Secondly, since history is a process of perpetual evolution, the historian must strive to elucidate the cause and effect relationship between occurrences in *successive periods.* Those past actions which have no discernible connection with simultaneous actions, and which appear to have been unique and nonrepeatable, Lacombe defined as "events." Those occurrences that do exhibit qualities of similarity with other actions in the same time and place and which survive and causally determine future developments, he defined as "institutions." If history is to become a true science, he argued, it must factor out the isolated, accidental, unique events of past reality, and concentrate solely on the study of institutions.[24] The ultimate aim of history is therefore not simply the reconstruction of past reality "as it really was." In Lacombe's eyes, such a procedure is utterly devoid of scientific value, and is justified solely for whatever personal satisfaction or entertainment value that might be derived from such antiquarianism. The scientific historian must restrict himself to the elaboration of general truths about social institutions and their evolutionary development throughout history. As a scientist of history, he must seek out regularities, similarities, and causal connections in man's past, just as the natural scientist searches for regularities, similarities, and causal connections in nature.[25]

Lacombe was convinced that these uniformities of human history could be discovered with the aid of the new science of psychology. Psychology has shown that mankind exhibits certain universal, instinctual needs that determine the nature of human conduct, and that all men "form their sensations, perceptions, and memories, and construct their imaginations, according to uniform modes." These "constants of human behavior," he claimed, can assist the historian in his effort to derive general patterns of human action in the past. He noted that Montesquieu, Voltaire, Turgot, Condorcet, and Comte had all practiced the method of psychological observation in order to develop a scientific definition of *l'homme général*. But he complained that this tradition was rejected by the German historicist school of the nineteenth century, which concentrated on resurrecting the unique, individual "events" of the past at the expense of more general trends, patterns, and regularities. The task of French historians, he declared, is to adopt the approach of the early social scientists in France by subjecting the individual phenomena of history to a rigorous psychological analysis that will disengage the "fundamental traits that constitute the intellectual parts of our nature."[26]

Lacombe anticipated the complaint from the historical profession that such an approach constitutes nothing less than a repudiation of the established notion that history must strive to resurrect past reality in its concrete, unique manifestations. He knew that historians did not welcome the recent attempts of the sociologists to superimpose an a priori hypothetical schema upon the raw material of the past. But he considered this intransigence self-defeating because the infinite diversity of historical phenomena produces only uncertainty and doubt in a mind that is "bereft of any [unifying] conception." The true scientist does not observe reality in a passive, uncritical manner. He employs a "formulated hypothesis, a preconceived plan of verification," to furnish him with a "principle of elimination and selection" that will limit the scope of his investigation and focus his attention on certain regularities of human behavior.[27] He urged historians to refrain from excluding such hypotheses from their definition of scientific history and to accept the definition of the scientific method as a combination of inductive and deductive reasoning. After confronting the facts of the past, the historian must proceed to the much more important task of isolating their similarities, and identifying the causal relationship among them. In order to separate the causal from the purely accidental antecedents, to avoid the logical fallacy of *post hoc ergo propter hoc,* he must deduce "the effects that each antecedent is likely to produce."[28]

Lacombe thus came to a conclusion similar to that reached by Seignobos, namely, that the mind and present experience of the historian play an active, conceptual role in recreating the truth of the past. Citing Renouvier, who had also influenced Durkheim in this regard, he emphasized the importance of "imaginative experience" in historical investigation as a necessary complement to purely empirical observation. By using the organizational principles of psychology to sift out the nonessential events from the "unlimited sea of facts" and by subsuming clusters of related facts under the category of "institutions," he declared, the historian must then strive to connect each institution to the dominant "psychic forces" of the particular time and place. Since "psychic forces" do not leave visible or tangible traces that can be analyzed empirically, the historian must rely on his imaginative powers to reconstruct them. The entities and institutions that he identifies in the past are therefore "fictitious categories *(corps fictifs)*" that link related events which are "more or less simultaneous and more or less similar."[29] Unless the historian is willing to employ such paradigms, Lacombe asserted, he is doomed to failure in his effort to become a true scientist of the past.

Lacombe injected into his work a note of pessimism regarding the possibility of transforming history into what he conceived of as a truly scientific enterprise. As hopeful as he was of developing a theory of historical causation, he remained unconvinced that it could ever be firmly established on a scientific footing. His awareness of the multiplicity of causal factors that operate on historical phenomena, together with his appreciation of the perpetual possibility that the fortuitous intervention of an individual participant could disrupt the causal connections, compelled him to conclude reluctantly that "the hope of reconstituting total causality is chimerical" and to concede that "the explanation of the effect will necessarily remain very incomplete."[30] The only way in which historians could live with these inherent limitations, he believed, was to eschew the type of sweeping generalizations indulged in by the sociologists, and to concentrate on identifying "trends" and "tendencies," rather than absolute causal connections, in historical development.

Since his definition of a science also implied the capacity for prediction, he extended his reservations about history's analysis of the past to its speculations about the future. He held that the historian's obligation to take into account the perturbative influence of "great individuals" on history precluded an infallible prediction of future trends and compelled him to remain content with describing the general tendencies he observes. Vague probability rather that precise necessity characterized the historian's predictive power. Tentative, circumspect efforts at forecasting general trends are valuable because they may suggest ways in which man can prepare for the problems that he is likely to confront in the future. But the comfort of certainty is gone.[31]

Lacombe's work represented, though perhaps unintentionally, another frontal assault on the methodological assumptions of the French historical profession, and by implication, a challenge to its newly acquired position of preeminence in the university. He was, it is true, unwilling to entrust the sociologists with the privilege of presiding over the scientific study of the past—a privilege which, he believed, they had forfeited because of their blindness to the decisive influence of individuals on historical development and their naive faith in the applicability of scientific generalizations to the events of the past. But in a deeper sense he was implicitly declaring his kinship with them in their dispute with the historians. Like Durkheim, he was proposing a scientific conception of historical study that emphasized the need to isolate the universally significant aspects of past reality for the purposes of comparison with the present and prediction of the future. Like Durkheim, he identified this conception of the scientific method with the heritage of French rationalism, contrasting it with what most French observers regarded as the "Germanic" tradition of historicism. His notion of a universal mechanistic psychology had its source in the seventeenth and eighteenth century French intellectual tradition, and his endorsement of the hypothetical, conceptualizing nature of scientific investigation was strongly influenced by Comte and his English popularizer, John Stuart Mill.

The conspicuous blind spot in Lacombe's critique was typical of much of the methodological literature of that period. Like so many of his compatriots, he ignored the neo-idealist reaction against positivism that had begun to appear in Germany. In his zeal to reassert the primacy of French *raison* and *clarté* over Germanic "pedantry," he failed to take into account the revisionist criticism from Dilthey (who had also sought to unite history and psychology to create a special branch of the human sciences), just as Durkheim tended to ignore the early work in sociological theory of Max Weber.[32]

It was supremely ironic that the first major effort to counter the attempts by the champions of sociology and psychology to appropriate the subject matter of history in France was launched by a foreigner. It almost seemed as though the native historical profession, faced with these multifarious threats to its intellectual hegemony in the universities, was temporarily incapable of defending itself. Alexandre Xénopol, a noted Rumanian historian and frequent contributor to French periodicals, produced a series of highly technical treatises on the historical method that set out to demonstrate "the perfectly scientific character" of history, and to defend it against "the accusations that are falling on it from all sides." Remarking that the detractors of the scientific conception of history base their critiques upon the alleged absence of methodological principles that has supposedly created "that state of anarchy in which history finds itself," Xénopol proposed to demonstrate not only that history does possess such fundamental principles, but also that they are no less scientific than those employed by the sciences of nature.[33]

The myth that history lacks a scientific methodology of its own, Xénopol declared, has recently gained currency because his beloved discipline has seen "its method, its goal, and its principles formulated by thinkers other than historians themselves." These attempts by nonhistorians to posit methodological principles of historical study were all born of the erroneous conviction that the principles of the physical and natural sciences can be applied to history. Hence, the burden of proof has been unfairly shifted to the historians. When they are unable to prove that their craft satisfies the methodological requirements of its sister sciences, they are unfairly asked to renounce its ultimate claim to scientific status. History, Xénopol argues, need no longer apologize for its alleged deficiencies.[34] The idiosyncratic, excessively exclusive definition that the natural scientists, physicists, and sociologists have given to the term "science" must be expanded to embrace the species of knowledge and evidence with which historians deal.[35]

Xénopol launched his project of recharting the terrain of the scientific historical method by disputing the assertion of Lacombe and the German neo-Kantians[36] that the acquisition of scientific understanding is a subjective mental activity that is separate from empirical reality. He regarded time and space not as mere "a priori categories of our understanding," but rather as "real and existent forms" with a prior, independent existence, which are "perceived and abstracted from reality by our intellect." Man's reason, therefore, is nothing less than "the reflection of the universal reason of things." Without this fundamental conception, he asserted, history would be nothing more than "an immense fantasy." It is through the mediation of these two categories of the mind, therefore, that the scientific investigator can penetrate the essence of physical reality.[37] He then proceeded to divide the sciences into two separate groups, each of which conducts investigations appropriate to its respective domain of reality. The "theoretical sciences" (under which he subsumes physics, chemistry, astronomy, psychology, sociology, economics, and so on) seek to comprehend coexistent phenomena in space, that is, phenomena which exist simultaneously in a given time period. What he calls the "historical sciences" (geology, paleontology, and so on) deal with the succession of phenomena in time. Hence, he regards history not merely as a particular branch of the sciences but rather as "a general method of conceptualizing phenomena" that submit to "the transforming influence of time."[38]

Xénopol claimed that the critics of scientific history had been led astray by their failure to distinguish between these two radically different types of scientific knowledge. He regarded Lacombe's ultimate pessimism concerning history's ability to produce airtight generalizations about historical institutions as a misplaced sentiment. History is incapable of discovering general laws applicable to phenomena in a particular time period not because of any inherent methodological defect, but because such matters are outside its sphere. The study of social institutions in a given period is the task of the theoretical sociologist. Historical analysis cannot and should not be expected to develop general laws governing a collection of "simultaneous facts;" its task is to determine "the succession of a single line of facts that are connected in the course of time."[39] The historian cannot generalize about events that succeed each other in time. A generalization assumes a similarity of elements united in a single, unchanging conception. Such similitude is impossible to obtain by linking successive groups of events, since no two facts in historical succession are ever the same.

> To demand that the historical sciences reduce their explanations to laws similar to those that govern coexistent facts is to ignore completely the character of those sciences, which have the goal not of establishing relations of similitude and coexistence, but rather the relations of difference and succession.[40]

History, in short, should not be expected to discover similarities among isolated events in a particular period; this is the task of the theoretical sciences. Science cannot be defined simply as the search for verifiable generalizations about observable reality, but must also make room for history's attempt to account for the significance of individual actions in the course of time. Xénopol accepted Lacombe's definition of science as a body of knowledge that strives to establish causal relations in reality, but rejected Lacombe's claim that the individual person or event in history cannot be considered a cause. On the contrary, he insisted that the theoretical sciences can have nothing to say about cause-and-effect relationships precisely because they are ahistorical, dealing with timeless, unchanging reality, whereas history is the science of causation *par excellence*.

> While the sciences of coexistent facts are incapable of penetrating the causes of phenomena, it is otherwise with the sciences of successive facts, of which the discovery of causes constitutes the principal attribute. Each successive fact is in essence the productive cause of the others; each one is the effect of an antecedent and the cause of a consequent.[41]

Hence, if the discovery of causation is regarded as the principal aim of the scientific method, Xénopol concludes, the scientific character of history is even "more marked than in the sciences which are called 'natural.'"[42]

At the end of this complex and rambling work, Xénopol attempted to identify the "fundamental determinants"—he carefully avoided using the term "cause"—that have influenced the progress of mankind in history. Following Taine, he acknowledged the importance of race and milieu in the formation of human character through the ages, but concluded that since each geographical area has a unique environment, and since intermarriage has practically canceled out whatever effects racial purity might have had, these two influences could not be considered natural laws of history. The three constants that he did see operating throughout human history are "the instinct of self-preservation," "evolution," and "imitation." He proclaimed that these three processes constitute the key causal elements in the development of mankind. Historical progress is the result of the inventiveness of individual geniuses and imitation by the culture. Individuals are constantly producing innovations, and the mass of humanity, driven by its monistic urge toward survival, imitates and adopts those innovations that promise to enhance the likelihood of self-preservation.[43] Since historical progress is the work of fortuitous variations based on individual innovation, he declared, Lacombe and the sociologists are wrong to subsume discrete historical events under the rubric of institutions and entities. The task of the historian is to study the origins and development of individual phenomena in succession and trace the "linkage of causes and effects" throughout history.

Xénopol cavalierly dismissed the misgivings of Lacombe and the German neo-Kantians regarding the historian's ability to escape the subjective influences of time and place in the formulation of his hypotheses. Historical science, because it is a concrete science dealing with individual, unique events, is under no obligation to concern itself with hypothetical speculations of the type employed by Lacombe, nor need it grapple with the problem of value free historical knowledge that troubled Rickert and Windelband.[44] History is able to evade these limitations because it deals with the evolution of humanity throughout the ages, a process which conforms to the logical rules that operate in the historian's own mind. He is able to chart the development of human history because his rational faculties are a direct reflection of the universal reason of phenomena.[45]

Xénopol's attempt to defend history's claim to the title of an autonomous branch of science was, in the last analysis, a failure. As Lacombe remarked in a critical review of the work, Xénopol's references to evolution, the instinct of self-preservation, and imitation as the universal laws of history themselves represented an unwitting surrender to the concepts of biology.[46] After reaffirming his conviction that the laws of psychology provide the most useful set of principles for historical study, Lacombe paused to reflect about the confused state in which history found itself. He interpreted both Xénopol's frantic effort to appropriate for history the language and concepts of Lamarckian biology and his own advocacy of classical psychology as symptoms of the historical profession's earnest quest for organizational principles and hypothetical guideposts capable of bringing order and structure to the meaningless mass of historical data being excavated from the archives. "We want to construct a definitive philosophy of history,"[47] he declared, and this offhand comment revealed the extent to which French history had come full circle by the turn of the century. The term "philosophy of history," which had been wielded as an epithet by the men who had liberated the historical profession from its subservient status as a branch of philosophy, had lost the pejorative connotation of the earlier years.

8
Henri Berr and the "Terrible Craving for Synthesis"

Paul Lacombe's reference to the French historical profession's urgent search for the principles of a philosophy of history appropriately appeared in the first number of a new review that was founded at the turn of the century for the express purpose of reversing the centrifugal trend that had brought the profession to its current impasse. Six years earlier, the founder of this review, a *normalien* named Henri Berr, had published a revealing semiautobiographical testament in the form of an exchange of letters between a Parisian student and a professor at Strasbourg to which he gave the intriguing title *Vie et science*. The letters from the student expressed Berr's own youthful disenchantment with the scientific studies to which he and his comrades had been subjected at the university. Having completed his examinations, the youth found himself despising the libraries, the books, and the university itself. Science, he had come to believe, had lost all meaning because it had been severed from the realities of life.

> This immense domain of research that concerns man appeared to me as a somber and inextricable jungle; philology with all its subdivisions, history with all its auxiliary sciences, a prodigious multiplicity of materials, so many centuries, so many peoples, so many languages, so many facts, and so many works—what were the connections, what was the purpose of all this? . . . The meaningless multitude of precise facts, the hazy hodgepodge of general ideas swirling within me; and I felt an extreme weariness.[1]

The old philosopher responded to this pessimistic outcry by reminding the student that the original purpose of the reorganization of the French universities after 1870 had been precisely to reinvigorate the intellectual life of France through the revival of science. He remarked that the university was intended to serve as "a sort of retreat where one derives the *idées directrices* and principles common to all for use in his own life." But he conceded that that original objective had been subverted in recent years due to the failure of French science to bring about the anticipated unification of knowledge.

> When I listened to people who declare that higher education, for which they make the greatest case and which they declare is imperfect in France, has as its goal the diffusion of the "scientific spirit" throughout a nation, . . . I tell myself that the true goal of this higher education is to fabricate intellectual mechanisms which are without defect but which are also without life.[2]

Since the current malaise of the younger generation is traceable to the "excess of scientific analysis" that is taught in the schools, he continued, the older generation must redefine its objectives to exclude this erroneous and perverted view of science.

The representative of the generation of 1870, writing from the occupied city of Strasbourg, refused to abandon his faith in the French universities as the center of this movement. With the university reorganization statutes still two years in the future, he dreamed of a *République universitaire* which would unify the dispersed institutions and traditions of scientific learning in Paris and promote "a hierarchy, a harmony, a common, deliberate policy" among the human sciences that would stimulate creativity and intellectual ferment. The present *Universités d'analyse,* he declared, must be converted into *Universités de synthèse.* These revamped centers of knowledge will eventually replace the outmoded religious institutions as the site where French youth can come into contact with "ultimate truth" and "communicate among themselves and with the universe." It is in this intellectual atmosphere that he hoped the new generation would be able to enter the secular church of higher learning.[3]

These sentiments were hauntingly similar to the original spirit of the historical reformers who by 1900 had succeeded in institutionalizing their discipline in the French university. In the wake of the military defeat a quarter of a century earlier, Gabriel Monod had assigned to higher education the goal of creating "the intellectual unity of the nation" by becoming "the center and the source of its intellectual life." He envisaged a university that would recruit a student elite through whose efforts alone "the scientific spirit can spread throughout the entire nation."[4] But in the last decade of the century there were those, such as Henri Berr, who began to accuse the men in control of the educational apparatus during the intervening years —and the historians in particular—of having retreated from this original goal.

It was perhaps inevitable that the university historians would fail to accomplish the sweeping objectives of the postwar period owing to the conflicting demands that had been placed upon them by their profession and their public. Fritz Stern has succinctly captured the flavor of their painful dilemma in his observation that "just as the historian was getting ready to become an academic monk, shut up in his study with his sources, the world about him sought him as a preacher."[5] Ernest Lavisse himself lamented this growing separation between the academic monk and his public clientele. The year after the publication of Berr's dialogue of despair, the patron of hundreds of Sorbonne students warned that "when an educator ignores or scorns the particular character of a generation, he in turn will be ignored and scorned by it, as though he were a man of another age in the distant past, with which youth feels no kinship."[6] We have forgotten the true purpose of education, he continued. The entire educational machine is organized to "fabricate diplomas, from the child whom we award a certificate of primary studies to a young man of twenty-five, twenty-eight, and even thirty, who solicits our *agrégations* and doctoral degrees; but neither the primary school, nor the *collège*, even less the faculties, constitute a *milieu moral*."[7]

Some of the university historians were able to wear both the academic and the clerical robes with relative ease. Lavisse rather successfully divided his time between his scholarly pursuits and the more general activities that won him such a wide audience among the members of *le grand public*, especially the young. But few *universitaires* were capable of matching the versatility of this prolific author of monographs, general histories, textbooks for primary and secondary instruction, educational critiques, articles for political, historical, and pedagogical journals and patriotic sermons for French school children of all ages. As historical research became increasingly specialized, the university historians began to feel the pressure of their manifold responsibilities. Since the apprenticeship of *lycée* instruction was normally a prerequisite for a coveted university position, the young graduate of the Ecole Normale or the Sorbonne was usually compelled to devote the early part of his career to teaching history not as a discipline in itself, but as a guide to good citizenship. But as the more ambitious of the *instituteurs* scaled the academic ladder to the pinnacle of the system, the university faculties, they quickly learned that future success in the profession depended upon their ability to demonstrate competence as scholars, rather than as inspirational teachers. It was to this end that they devoted the vast bulk of their time and energy.

This subtle reordering of priorities inevitably detracted from history's central position in the curriculum of civic education. The old vision of history as the spiritual regenerator of a defeated, divided nation had already begun to fade by the last decade of the century. As the original, more general purpose retreated from view, the academic historians began to concentrate their efforts on perpetuating the specialized body of knowledge that had been acquired by years of painstaking research and on training future professionals to carry on the tradition. By making history more scientific, they had sapped much of the strength it had previously possessed as a spiritual force. Part of the explanation could be found, as Berr insisted, in the university's overemphasis on specialization, empiricism, and analysis.[8] As one observer later remarked, education must be carried on "in the name of a principle, an idea."[9] But principles, purposes, and preconceived ideas constituted those very a priori elements that the university historians thought they had successfully banished from the realm of higher education. It was not until the beginning of the twentieth century, as we shall see, that a principle of education and scholarship began to gain widespread acceptance.

Berr's passionate reaction to the increasing specialization of knowledge reflected the influence of his intellectual mentor at the Ecole Normale, the philosopher Emile Boutroux, and, to a lesser extent, of the historian Fustel de Coulanges. Boutroux's lectures and writings represented a call to arms for all those willing to defend French thought against the corrosion of scientism. The chief target of his attacks was the dominant school of history in France, which he castigated for encouraging the indiscriminate pursuit of "unpublished texts" and "anecdotes" at the expense of historical synthesis and broader understanding. The latter process, he argued, requires an accurate appreciation of the historical material that can be achieved only through an imaginative effort to penetrate the minds of men in the past.[10] It is no mere coincidence that Durkheim and Berr, the two most vocal critics of the newly adopted methods of scientific history, had both been disciples of Boutroux.[11] Though trained in rhetoric and philosophy, Berr was converted early in his career to the belief that history, properly conceived, could become the linchpin of the new unification of knowledge in the social sciences that he hoped would bridge the gap between science and life. His dissertation, which, like Durkheim, he dedicated to Boutroux, and which was published in 1899 under the suggestive title *L'Avenir de la philosophie: esquisse d'une synthèse des connaissances fondée sur l'histoire,* furnished a program for action. He began by sounding the tocsin to announce "the contemporary crisis" of French intellectual life, and proposed a number of suggestions on how it could be rescued from its present cul-de-sac.

Like Durkheim and Lacombe, Berr insisted that the new intellectual renaissance must avoid adopting foreign models and derive its strength and its inspiration from the native traditions of France. He defined, or perhaps more accurately, redefined, science as a unified system of knowledge aiming at "an effort toward clarity," and insisted that the genius of France and the French language was particularly suited to such an enterprise. Since the principal task of science must be to account for the behavior of all things, the future savant must "weigh everything in his mind and render it intelligible." He denounced the conception of science that had dominated French intellectual life during the past three decades. "Far from replacing religion and philosophy," he declared, "science has in turn failed, and nothing has been able to replace it." In contrast to the analytical, disruptive, disintegrating tenets of that false conception of science, he declared, the guiding principal that will preside over the search for truth in his system will be to "understand everything and unify everything."[12]

Berr paid tribute to those two past masters of French history, Renan and Taine, for convincing him that their discipline could provide the principles with which to reorganize the scientific tradition in France. In his early work *L'Avenir de la science,* Renan had confidently predicted that "the future of a science of synthesis will know no bounds,"[13] and in his post-1870 reflections on *La Réforme intellectuelle et morale* of the defeated French nation, Renan remained convinced that history, conceived of as a synthetic form of knowledge, could provide the basis for that reform.[14] Taine had once defined history as "a living geometry," and this conception of a synthetic scientific history began to replace the cult of specialized studies currently in vogue. Enough of the compilers, the investigators, the analyzers, the fact-grubbers, Berr proclaimed. "It is logicians and organizers that we need today."[15]

What recommends history as the keystone of the social sciences, Berr maintained, is its unique ability to disengage the thread of causality in human affairs while remaining faithful to the living reality of human existence. As the "science of dynamic unity" history must concentrate on discovering the explanatory laws underlying the evolution of phenomena instead of wasting its energy on recovering and purifying the documents of the past. He cited the warning of Claude Bernard, the illustrious founder of the experimental method of French science, that "the simple verification of facts can never succeed in constituting a science; one could multiply the facts and observations ad infinitum and learn nothing from them." The assignment of history, if it is to comprehend the meaning of historical change, is "to return to the concept of natural laws."[16]

Berr was careful to protect himself against the damaging accusation that his proposal was nothing more than a reversion to the discredited doctrines of the philosophy of history of the past two centuries. The old theories of this tradition, from Vico to Hegel, had sought to popularize a conception of the interconnectedness of all historical phenomena and to link past, present, and future in an all-embracing, explanatory law. He credited such metaphysical theorizing with the virtue of exposing the absurdity of conducting historical analyses that do not result in a synthesis and the insignificance of facts unrelated to a general schema. But what disqualified it from serious consideration by scientific historians in the present era was its overly-ambitious aim to establish this schema a priori, and to construct the synthesis prematurely, before the completion of the analytical stage. Hence the various theories of the philosophy of history can be viewed as nothing more than "metaphysical" doctrines of little use for the present.[17]

But the historical school that succeeded them was equally uncongenial to the necessities of the modern world. He complained that the reaction against the tradition of the philosophy of history after the middle of the nineteenth century had resulted in the victory of "erudition" and the tradition of monographic research. One need only scan the list of the books that appear each year and the number of periodicals that roll off the presses to become alarmed at the direction historical study is taking, he declared. It is both impossible and unnecessary to know everything about the past, yet the historians continue to excavate with indiscriminate enthusiasm.

> Perpetual repetition is ridiculous; human energy must not be wasted at random or without any apparent result; historical research must ultimately come to an end. In order for that to happen, it must, without ceasing to be scientific, respond to the preoccupations that had caused the philosophy of history to be born.[18]

History, in short, if it is to be a useful discipline, must abandon its minute, parochial preoccupations, and seek to discover the empirical laws that underlie human progress. He attributed the rapid progress of sociology as an academic discipline to the impasse in historical studies caused by the professional historians' inability to proceed beyond the analytical stage of historical scholarship.

Berr then turned his attention to the science of sociology, which had begun to pose such a threat to the position of history in the academic system. He found the infant discipline excessively presumptuous and pretentious, a "rough-hewn science" which abounds in grand generalities that are unsupported by empirical evidence. Yet, like Lacombe, he had come to history from the outside, so had no professional interest in defending the independence of the discipline against the inroads of the Durkheimians.[19] Historians and sociologists, he suggested, should forge a working alliance instead of coexisting at swords' point, for they can both serve each other while serving the scientific interests of the nation. Indeed, he contended that history could discover its *raison d'être* "only through sociology" while history alone could help sociology to "confirm its findings" and therefore "become efficacious." Neither is a true science in itself, he claimed, but the two are complementary aspects of a unified science of society that is simultaneously speculative and practical, which he hoped would revive and transform the old discredited philosophy of history. He never specified which party was to possess controlling interest in the partnership, though he did imply, in an earlier article, that history was best equipped to preside over the unification of the social sciences.[20]

In his autobiographical dialogue Berr's Strasbourgeois professor had urged that the unification of scientific knowledge in France be effected under the auspices of the university system.[21] Two years after the appearance of this work French higher education passed through the final stage of the reorganization plan that Duruy had first mapped out during his tenure at the Education Ministry.[22] As we have seen, the disparate faculties in Paris were finally unified and reconstituted under the heading of *Université* and the immediate effect was to centralize the teaching of social science in the Latin Quarter. It almost appeared as if Berr's call for an *Université de synthèse* in Paris had found a receptive audience in the higher reaches of the republican government. Hence, by 1899 Berr could speculate with more optimism and confidence about the prospects for an academically sponsored center for historical synthesis. La Nouvelle Sorbonne was an ideal site for such an enterprise. Funded, directed, and staffed by the state, it could, much like the church in the Middle Ages, fulfill the dual role of collecting and organizing the existing knowledge of man and nature and educating future generations in the methods by which that knowledge might be preserved and transmitted.

> The State should intervene above all to hasten the Synthesis, to promote Science—not that vain, fragmentary science, but a united, conquering science. . . . The State must be the total educator, the educator of mature adults as much as possible, but especially the

educator of the new generations . . . To all those who are in search of beliefs, to all those who deliver themselves or are delivered to it, it should give those beliefs, if it has them to give.[23]

But Berr's plans for the new university were the premature pipe dreams of an outsider. As a professor of rhetoric at the *lycée* Henri IV, he was far removed from the inner sanctum of the academy and taught an obsolete subject that was rapidly losing all semblances of academic respectability. Appropriately, the publication of his dissertation in 1899 was greeted with scorn or indifference by the guardians of the official orthodoxy. Gabriel Monod dismissed Berr's proposal to establish history as the foundation of synthetic knowledge as "just another eclecticism in which all knowledge becomes a monism."[24] One could hardly have expected the academic historians to receive with enthusiasm suggestions for university reform from a secondary school instructor who had been trained in the suspect discipline of rhetoric by that notorious critic of the university and its methods, Emile Boutroux.

Faced with this lack of receptivity to his program among the historians of the university, Berr decided to emulate Victor Duruy, who had earlier circumvented the academic opponents of his reforms by creating an institution outside the university structure to carry them out. As the new century began, Berr and a select group of associates founded the International Center for Synthesis and launched a new organ of historical opinion, the *Revue de synthèse historique.* In the programmatic statement that appeared in the first number of the new review, its founder reaffirmed his conviction that history must transcend the narrow confines of monographic scholarship and concentrate on developing a sound methodological and conceptual framework for the systematic study of man. Only in this way, he declared, could it redeem the pledges of the early historical reformers to make history the foundation of a unified system of scientific knowledge. Acutely conscious of the academic historians' distaste for the process of theoretical generalization, he followed the example of Lacombe and took pains to assure them that he was not merely a mouthpiece for the sociologists. "The word theory should not give alarm," he declared. "It does not presuppose, it absolutely does not presuppose, vague, excessively general speculations put forth by thinkers who have never been working historians."[25]

But if one hand was extended in friendship to the historical establishment, the other pointed the finger of accusation. He asserted that a new definition of science must replace what he regarded as the defective conception favored by the historical profession. We are doing a disservice to the word science, he declared, when we abandon scientific historical investigation to "routinism and empiricism." While agreeing with them that theoretical speculations must be verified by empirical investigation, he warned the historians that theories and hypotheses cannot be dispensed with.[26]

He paid the requisite tribute to the great contributions of the historical reformers in the postwar years, endorsing the *Revue historique*'s declaration of war on the propensity for unverified speculation and a priori generalization that was responsible for the deficiencies of historical scholarship in the past. But he reminded the French historians of the rapid advances of sociology in recent years and attributed them to its ability to "respond to the permanent demand for general ideas." He claimed that sociology's success was in part due to the fact that it "reintroduced philosophy into history" and praised its practitioners as the heirs of the German and French philosophical tradition of the late eighteenth and early nineteenth century. It was the great merit of the Durkheimians at the *Année sociologique*, he asserted, "to have applied a precise, experimental, comparative method to historical facts." He agreed with Lacombe that sociological analysis is defective because it neglects the role of individuals in shaping the events of the past. Only the historian can give proper attention to the individual peculiarities that produce variations in history and that explain even the most general social transformations. But he warned that historians must no longer turn their backs on the conceptual apparatus developed by the social sciences, which can assist them in understanding the basic human needs to which social institutions are a response.[27]

Berr correctly anticipated the historical profession's resistance to his attempt to introduce the theoretical, synthetic approach of the social sciences into historical research. There are talented men, he noted, "who cannot think of science except in terms of detailed research, and who, since detail is infinite, push forward this research of theirs only to see the goal recede before them." These same scholars "pity the rash souls who wish to move outside the limits of what they themselves have studied and aspire to a comprehensive view." They regret that the human mind is "periodically seized with a terrible craving for synthesis, to the detriment of patient analytical work." They are baffled and troubled by the fact that every thirty or forty years humanity succumbs to this temporary insanity that it mistakes as a normal activity.[28] But it was an insanity, as two recent scholars have observed, that had already crept into the academy itself. It was the sociologists of the *Année sociologique* who were responsible for proposing to French scholars in the late nineteenth century "the model of a science with vast ambitions, which they could not help but contrast with the cramped program" of the academic historians, and which provided them with the hope of identifying the structures and laws of social development and of addressing historical problems on a grand scale.[29]

The "terrible craving for synthesis" that periodically afflicts the public mind recurs so regularly, Berr pointed out, precisely because it is deep-seated in the human psyche. Moreover, it serves a higher function as the justification for scientific activity itself. "If science were only the satisfying of a curiosity, for retrospective reporting," Berr asserted, "it would be singularly futile. The collector of facts is no more admirable than the collector of stamps or shells. Synthesis is useful, even morally, in giving us a conception of the dignity of science."[30] Berr's plea for a new scientific synthesis included a demand that the wedge that had been driven between science and life be removed. Theory and practice, thought and action, scholarship and worldly activity must be reconciled, and both will derive benefits from the reconciliation. Life will be enriched and instructed by the lessons derived from the scientific study of the past, and the writing of history will regain its reputation as a worthwhile activity in the eyes of the French public.[31] He specifically reiterated his defense of his new proposal against the inevitable allegation that it was a camouflaged reversion to the metaphysical, a priori tradition of the philosophy of history.

> Let no one fear a return to the philosophy of history, by which is meant—for the word itself is not intrinsically bad—a priori metaphysics, clouds in theory and, consequently, utopias in practice. It would be unfortunate to confuse generalizations born of fantasy or ratiocination with those based on acquired knowledge. It is a science that we wish to practice here, true science, science in its entirety. None may enter here who does not bring with him a sound method.[32]

Emile Boutroux, his old master at the Ecole Normale, appended to Berr's programmatic statement a brief essay on "History and Synthesis," which attempted to provide the philosophical underpinning for his protégé's new undertaking. After citing his former colleague Fustel de Coulanges' celebrated maxim, "il faut toute une vie d'analyse pour une heure de synthèse," the philosopher posed the question: is it legitimate to establish a journal devoted to historical synthesis before all the monographic facts of history are recorded? Due to the legacy of Baconian empiricism, he pointed out, modern man has been led to assume that all scientific generalizations must originate in the facts themselves and cannot derive from the hypothetical speculations of the investigator. But even the British empiricist school has come to realize that induction is not the sole means of establishing a universal law. He quoted John Stuart Mill to the effect that "to pass from a fact to a law, we are under no obligation to exhaust our analytical knowledge of cases in which the fact has occurred . . . [In] certain cases, the consideration of a single example is sufficient to establish a universal proposition."[33]

Boutroux entreated French historians to abandon their blind faith in empiricism and to adopt the new imaginative approach to history. "The conditions that the empiricists postulate do not exist," he maintained.

> Human thought is not presented with isolated materials that it must assemble by adding an external cement. Human thought, from the moment that it is first employed, perceives things as parts forming wholes and wholes divided into parts . . . The progress of thought involves the more and more distinct consciousness of the rapport that exists within things between the one and the many, between the identical and the diverse.[34]

The purpose of historical scholarship, therefore, is to make some sense out of the junk heap of the past by isolating from the mass of documents "certain classes of facts considered particularly worthy of living in the memory of men." It is the duty of the historian, therefore, to inform his readers of the significance of the results that he has obtained. This function of condensation and simplification must be carried out by those who know how to "transmute facts into ideas without losing anything of their substance." The procedure of establishing general propositions is illegitimate and dangerous only if it is conducted according to abstract principles with no reference to "concrete and living science."[35]

The academic historians greeted the new review with the same lack of enthusiasm that had infused their reception of Berr's dissertation a year earlier, except that the weapon of the boycott replaced the critical rejoinder. During the years before it began to achieve world-wide renown for the catholicity of its interests and the profundity of its analyses, the principal contributors to the *Revue de synthèse historique* came almost exclusively from intellectual circles outside the academic historical profession. The ranks of philosophy and sociology were particularly well represented, with Boutroux, Durkheim, and Lacombe earnestly pursuing the epistemological questions that they had raised in earlier writings. The Durkheimian François Simiand used the pages of Berr's review to propose "the annexation of history, disencumbered of the accidental, the biographical, and the narrative, by a sociology of the constants of human evolution."[36] Those historians who did participate in the intense methodological debates that enlivened the review were mostly foreigners, such as Karl Lamprecht and Benedetto Croce, who had themselves been spearheading an intellectual counterrevolution against the positivist methods and assumptions of historical scholarship in their own countries. The sociologists in particular flocked to the new periodical like iron balls to a magnet. The Durkheimians soon began to publish summaries of the *Revue*'s leading articles in their own organ, the *Année sociologique*.[37] What better way to advance the claims of their own profession than to invoke the authority of a periodical dedicated to the renovation of the competing discipline of history?

In his monumental *La Méthode historique appliquée aux sciences sociales*, Charles Seignobos had insisted that the inherent subjectivity of the historical method caused by the inevitable intervention of the mind of the historian did not detract from the scientific character of the method.[38] A year later his confederate Charles Victor Langlois contributed his own defense of scientific theory based on similar arguments. He acknowledged that when the historian attempts to embrace vast quantities of raw data, he must "choose, emphasize certain facts to the exclusion of others," in order to render them intelligible to the reader. He therefore regarded it as inevitable that the author of a general work of history will "impress the mark of his personality on his work." But the recent advances in the development of source criticism have so mitigated the effects of this subjectivity, he claimed, that the historian is "now protected from his own imagination by the accumulation of incorruptible, solid realities that the scholars have laboriously erected around him."[39]

Langlois denied that history had any reason to apologize for the defects ascribed to it by its professional competitors. He chided his colleagues for passively acquiescing in the sociologists' campaign to gain custody of "the rational study of historical phenomena." He accused the Durkheimians of being for the most part poorly prepared for such a task, and denounced them for reintroducing into historical study "the habits of an intemperate philosophism." Modern scholars must never be permitted to forget the disappointing failures of the discredited philosophy of history, which presumed to formulate laws of historical development, he declared. The modern historian need not feel that he must compete with the sociologists on the terrain of theory, for he has no interest in dealing with such metaphysical abstractions as historical laws. His role is that of a "reporter" of past events and nothing more.[40]

But despite the historians' ostracism and the sociologists' encroachments, Berr did not abandon his dream of establishing a synthesis of knowledge founded on historical study. He renewed his overtures to the historical profession, attempting to stimulate interest in the growing theoretical controversies that were simmering in the pages of the review. In 1904, one such major effort to involve the academic historians in these debates regarding the future of their own discipline fell on deaf ears. The *Revue de synthèse historique* dispatched an opinion poll to all the leading professors of history in France, soliciting their views on a variety of methodological questions relating to scholarship and teaching. The disappointing response to this questionnaire was itself an indication that the profession still looked askance at the new group. None were received from the Ecole des Chartes and the Ecole Pratique des Hautes Etudes, and the great names from the Sorbonne were conspicuously missing from the list of respondents.[41]

The replies that were received by the review virtually ignored the problems of historical methodology that were raised in the questionnaire. One such question asked whether courses on methodology, such as the one offered by Seignobos and Langlois at the Sorbonne, should be instituted at the provincial universities. The respondents were almost uniformly hostile to this proposal. Charles Petit-Dutaillis, the great historian of the medieval monarchy, contended that a few lessons should suffice to acquaint the historian with the methodological problems of historical research, and declared that excessive emphasis upon methods might introduce him to "a number of theories and systems that he might poorly assimilate and apply incorrectly."[42] Georges Desdevises du Dézert displayed a similar distrust of methodological training, agreeing that a limited number of lectures on the subject are all that should be required.[43]

Berr interpreted this apparent decline in professional history's interest in theoretical and methodological problems as a reflection of the growing resistance to the invasion of theory (that is, philosophy) in the sacred realm of empirical history. For all his characteristic charity, his sense of indignation at this trend soon became apparent. His ironic, almost sarcastic reaction to the historians' indifference to methodological questions expressed his increasing pessimism about the possibility of converting them to his cause.

> All that is true; a few rapid lessons are sufficient; the historical method can be taught in a few days; that is why so many historians do not succeed in killing the metaphysician that is within them, and why so many scholars commit methodological errors. Do they expect us to create *agrégés* and *licenciés* according to the most expeditious procedures? Methodology is obviously useless, nay, harmful; let us permit the students to read their textbooks and a few "great works" in peace. Do they want to teach the youth *history* or the métier of the historian? These are not exactly synonymous.[44]

Later in the same year Berr made one last attempt to gain a hearing within the academy for his plea for a coordinated program of methodological instruction and scientific synthesis. The opportunity presented itself in 1904 when a wealthy society lady endowed a chair in historical methodology at the Collège de France.[45] Louis Liard, the vice rector of the University of Paris, who was an avid reader of Berr's review, encouraged the apostate historian to throw his hat in the ring. Such a prestigious platform on the periphery of the *Université* would have enabled Berr to initiate in history what Bergson had begun in philosophy from the same lectern: a systematic counterattack against the reigning tradition of positivism. While it was unlikely that he would reverse the dominant intellectual tendencies of the Sorbonne professoriate, he would at least have gained access to a wider audience among the young generation that was flocking to Bergson's weekly indictments of philosophical positivism.

As was customary in French academic circles, Berr was expected to drum up support for his candidacy through personal visits and written solicitations to the faculty. One such letter to a noted scholar revealed that Berr's vision of a university-sponsored center for scientific historical synthesis was not yet dead. He appealed for greater cooperation between social scientists and historians, claiming that the time had come to "react against the excess of analysis" which had resulted in leaving historical scholarship "bare, without coordinating principles or clear aims." A new history must be inaugurated that avoids the defects of the positivist approach of the past, without falling into the a priori trap of the philosophy of history or the seductions of sociology, which overemphasizes the social aspect of human life.[46]

The creation of the new chair in historical methodology reflected the increasing interest in that subject, which Berr had played such a large part in stimulating. But his candidacy was passed over by the Ministry of Public Instruction and its academic advisers. The recipient of the honor, despite his advanced age, was Gabriel Monod. The *universitaires* had succeeded in installing one of their own, the very man who had led the reaction against the philosophical tradition of history over a quarter of a century ago.[47] Significantly, the incumbent of the new chair spent the bulk of his time lecturing on Michelet and the divergent legacy of his historical work, and never got around to discussing the historical method, the topic for which the chair had been created.[48]

Undaunted by this setback to his career plans, Berr resumed his proselytizing efforts. The academic historians could use their contacts at the education ministry to immunize the lecture hall against the infection of synthetic history, but it was not so easy to quarantine the written word. Increasing numbers of young history students read the new journal and were strongly influenced by the assaults on historical positivism that they encountered in its pages. Lucien Febvre, who at the time was about to embark upon a long and fruitful career in history (and later to found a review of his own dedicated to liberating French history from the positivist tradition), has recorded the enormous impact of Berr's periodical on the new generation of historians. His words bear an eerie resemblance to those of the disillusioned Parisian student in Berr's earlier dialogue. He recalled that he and his *promotion* of prospective historians "were beginning to find our studies banal, and were just about to quit when, in 1900, our interest was refired by the appearance of the *Revue de synthèse historique*."[49] Henri Irenée Marrou, who also subsequently helped the French historical profession to shatter the positivist chains of the past, paid tribute to Berr's review for enabling the neo-Kantian criticism of Dilthey, Rickert, and Weber to reach a French audience, however small, though he claimed that the "positivist prejudices" that even Berr was unable totally to escape sterilized the effort.[50]

These retrospective testaments indicated that the members of the young generation of history students in the French universities who began to question the positivist assumptions of their masters were compelled to look outside the walls of the academy for alternative approaches to the study of the past. This situation did not change significantly until the last decade of the Third Republic's existence, when the *Revue de synthèse historique*, the *Annales* of Marc Bloch and Lucien Febvre, and the rediscovery of German philosophical thought all helped to loosen the grip of nineteenth century positivism. Marrou himself recalled that when he arrived at the Sorbonne in 1925 he was greeted by

> the weak but still convincing voice of old Seignobos (Lucien Febvre and Marc Bloch were still exiles in Strasbourg); positivism was still the official philosophy of the historians . . . We had to wait until 1938 and the two resounding theses of Raymond Aron before the critical philosophy of history was finally integrated into French culture.[51]

In 1902, two years before Berr's candidacy for the chair in historical methodology at the Collège de France was rejected, Emile Durkheim, another discovery of the ubiquitous Louis Liard, had finally received the long-awaited call to the Sorbonne. Though he was originally hired as a substitute for Ferdinand Buisson in the chair of Science of Education, he was permitted to devote half of his lectures to sociology. His subsequent academic advancement was rapid and dramatic. When Buisson's chair fell vacant in 1906, Durkheim was chosen as the successor, and his lectures on pedagogy were declared the basic course required of candidates for a teaching degree.[52] This forum gave the Durkheimians a commanding influence on the thinking of the next generation of university and secondary school instructors.

As sociology began to achieve notoriety and intellectual respectability in French academic circles, the pleas of Berr, Lacombe, and others for a joint, cooperative venture between the historians and social scientists gradually discovered a sympathetic audience in both disciplines. Though many historians continued to resist the temptation to integrate their craft into the broader framework of the social sciences, the unfolding of political events slowly coaxed them out of their isolation and plunged them into the public arena. As we shall see, this new trend toward public involvement helped to restore to the historical profession the sense of relevance, purpose, and coherence that it had temporarily lost.

9
The Dissolution of the Republican Consensus

The publication of Emile Zola's celebrated letter "J'Accuse" in January 1898, which charged the French army and its supporters in the Ministry of War with the crime of intentionally suppressing evidence favorable to a hapless Jewish officer who had been convicted of treason three years earlier, set in motion a chain of events that eventually led to a complete reversal of the verdict. But the more immediate consequence of the reopening of the Dreyfus case was the creation of the Dreyfus Affair. In the last two years of the nineteenth century there appeared in French politics something that had not been in evidence for some time: a renewal of vigorous political activity on the extreme right. Catholics, monarchists, neo-Bonapartists, authoritarian nationalists, and a motley assortment of professed anti-Semites all used the pretext of national honor (which they claimed was being tarnished by the supporters of Dreyfus) to challenge the political dominance of the republican party. Soon the fate of Dreyfus, as Alfred Cobban observed, came to be bound up with the survival of the Third Republic itself.[1] The parties of the left, on the other hand, began to see in the issue of Dreyfus's unjust treatment an opportunity to strike a decisive blow against the vestigial sources of anti-republican sentiment in the church and the military.

The prior public pronouncements and political activities of the university professoriate in general and the historical profession in particular gave no indication of the position they were likely to adopt vis-à-vis the ensuing confrontation between the defenders of the Republic and its opponents on the right.[2] The single common trait that the leading members of the academic historical profession had exhibited in their past writings and political activities was a deeply felt patriotism. But it was a patriotism of the 1870 vintage, forged in the spirit of *revanche*. Despite its original identification with the republicanism of Gambetta, Jules Simon, Paul Bert, and others, the cult of the fatherland quickly developed into a virtually universal sentiment, unconnected to any specific political creed.[3] As the purveyors of this eclectic brand of patriotism in a period of ideological consensus, most influential academic historians were able to avoid committing themselves to a fixed political position. They preferred to devote their energies to the relatively noncontroversial task of promoting the single ideal that was shared by all Frenchmen from the royalist right to the radical left. Their cooperation with the republican state in the quarter century after Sedan was based on a devotion to the revival of French patriotism and a sober recognition of mutual advantage rather than on ideological affinity.

Gabriel Monod had launched his academic career as a well-connected citizen of the Bonapartist Empire, and had never distinguished himself as an outspoken champion of the Third Republic in its early years. Lavisse, as we have seen, maintained his contacts with the Imperial pretender until shortly before the latter's death in 1879. His appearances at royalist salons, together with his occasional references to the weakness of republican institutions, might easily be interpreted as a preference for a more authoritarian type of system than that which had evolved in France after 1875. He made no effort to come to the defense of the Republic during the Boulanger crisis, and his close ties with the French army at the outset of the Dreyfus Affair—he was moonlighting as an instructor in history at the Saint-Cyr Military Academy at the time—made it unlikely that he would join hands with the promoters of antimilitarism among the Dreyfusards. Similarly, Seignobos and Langlois, the two most prominent members of the second generation of historians committed to the reform of their profession, had begun their rise to prominence during what has been called the Orléanist phase of the Third Republic and had never distinguished themselves as outspoken supporters of the republican system. Indeed, the former, whose father was a centrist deputy in the monarchist-dominated National Assembly elected in 1871, had been hostile to the republican regime during his youth, and identified with the Orléanist faction of the monarchist movement that was campaigning for a royal restoration before 1875.[4]

Patriotic fervor, which had served as the litmus test of republicanism in 1871, was hardly a criterion of political sympathies in the changed situation of the *fin de siècle*. Indeed, the old republican spirit of *revanche* had been usurped by the standard bearers of the new right: Déroulède, Barrès, and later, Maurras. Since the French Revolution, nationalism had been a distinctly republican creed. But in the writings of Barrès during the 1890s that term began to take on connotations that sharply distinguished it from the old-fashioned patriotism of Gambetta, Mazzini, and Kossuth. He spiced it with a potent dose of anti-Semitism and antiparliamentarianism, and added an appeal to a Caesarist *chef* to assume control of the French state in order to defend the integrity of the Fatherland.[5]

No one could have predicted with certainty the part that the university historians would play in the unfolding drama of the late 1890s that pitted the self-proclaimed nationalists of the revived right against the established regime. Though their service to the educational system implied an acceptance of the Republic, could one rule out the possibility that the French historians who had risen to prominence in the aftermath of Sedan might discover in patriotism and Germanophobia a basis for agreement with the nationalists who were posing as the defenders of the French army against its detractors in the government? Was the patriotic prose of Lavisse's *Tu seras soldat*, for example, significantly different from the most extreme, blood-and-soil rhetoric of Barrès, Bourget, and Déroulède?

The publication of Zola's letter forced the members of the university to choose between the principle of national honor and the ideal of republican defense, and the earliest responses left no doubt as to which cause exerted the stronger appeal. The first flurry of protest at Dreyfus's unjust treatment emanated from the offices of the most prominent members of the historical and sociological professions —Aulard, Lanson, Croiset, Victor Basch, Louis Havet, Henri Hauser, Durkheim, Bouglé, Mauss, Andler, Buisson—and the membership list of the Dreyfusard Ligue pour la Défense des Droits de L'Homme read like a directory of the Parisian academic establishment.[6] Aulard served as vice-president of the Ligue in France and was a member of the executive council of the International Federation of the Leagues of the Rights of Man.[7] Gabriel Monod and his former colleague at the Ecole Pratique, the historian-politician Gabriel Hanotaux, were tortured by doubt about the army's allegations of treason from the very beginning, and this doubt developed into certitude of innocence when Monod put to good use the expertise in paleography and diplomatics that he had acquired in Germany to determine to his own satisfaction, by comparing the *bordereau* to samples of the captain's handwriting, that Dreyfus could not have authored it.[8] As late as November 5, 1897, he had written to a friend explaining his hesitancy to publicize his belief in Dreyfus's innocence because he felt that his own position as a Protestant would blunt the effect of his pronouncement. But as soon as his conscience compelled him to realize that such an attitude would reflect cowardice on his part, he joined the ranks of the Dreyfusards by the end of the year,[9] and rapidly became a leading advocate of revision.[10] Seignobos, one of the original signers of the "Appeal of the League for the Defense of the Rights of Man and Citizen" that appeared in the Bastille day issue of *Le Siècle*, was so outspoken in his Dreyfusard sympathies that he occasionally had to be rescued from anti-Semitic mobs that invaded his classroom. So did Croiset, who became dean of the Sorbonne, or "Dreyfus Dean," as the enemies of the Republic put in, in 1898.[11]

Contrary to popular opinion, however, the academic historical profession did not rally en masse to the Dreyfusard banner. One conspicuous absentee from the front ranks of the defenders of the Republic was Ernest Lavisse. His only significant journalistic involvement at the height of the imbroglio, an article in his *Revue de Paris*, was an innocuous appeal for "national reconciliation" based upon the hybrid ideal of bourgeois patriotism that he had been promoting for decades. He severely criticized those who leapt into the *Affaire* "without knowing anything about the trial," and who sought to take from it "whatever flattered and confirmed a previously held conviction." He complained that the controversy was poisoning the political atmosphere of the moderate Republic, driving the Dreyfusards into the camp of "socialists, revolutionaries, and anarchists" while forcing "conservatives of all nuances" into an alliance with the enemies of the Republic.[12] He called upon the two parties to the dispute, which he claimed were at odds because of "a dreadful misunderstanding," to patch up their quarrel in the interests of the nation, complaining that "so many men are capable of torturing themselves for noble sentiments." Offer to the Fatherland "the sacrifice of your hatreds," he implored them, in a characteristic attempt to patch up unresolvable differences with a comforting platitude, "and then soothe yourself with the idea that, together, all of you are France."[13]

Less innocuous was the behavior of the historian-politician Alfred Rambaud (who had presided over the reorganization of the French university system as Minister of Public Instruction in 1896 and was currently coediting the *Histoire générale* series with Lavisse) and of Gustave Fagniez (the cofounder, with Monod, of the *Revue historique*). To the consternation of their associates in the historical profession, Rambaud became a charter member of the anti-Dreyfusard League of the French Fatherland,[14] and Fagniez became an active sympathizer of the anti-republican Action Française movement.[15] But aside from these notable exceptions, the leading historians of the university stood four square behind Dreyfus. The Sorbonne, the Ecole Normale, the Collège de France, and the Ecole Pratique provided most of the shock troops, while the Faculty of Law, which might have been expected to lead the campaign for justice and right, remained largely on the sidelines.[16] Throughout the two remaining years of the nineteenth century, the *universitaires* plunged into the unfamiliar world of mass meetings, political rallies, and journalistic polemics. A decade later Pierre Leguay observed that a new spirit of political involvement had begun to emanate from the faculties of the New University, which by then "had no greater fear than to be isolated, to lose contact with real life."[17] The old gap between science and life that Berr had lamented a few years earlier was being narrowed. The spirit of public involvement had once again infiltrated the academy, not in the form of a commitment to promote patriotism through an innocuous program of civic instruction, but in the form of a call to arms to defend the embattled Republic against the hostile forces in its midst.

The Dreyfusard movement responded with effusive expressions of gratitude to the university's newly-discovered passion for political activism. The Radical Republican press, which had formerly expressed a certain suspicion of the elite character of the reformed university system, applauded the new spirit of *engagement* that had apparently impregnated the academic intelligentsia. In late January 1898, Clemenceau's *L'Aurore* publicly welcomed the politicization of the *Université*, declaring that it is a joy to see it "affirming with such vigor its fidelity to the ancient traditions of liberalism, reason, and justice, which are its pride and honor." The example it has just given, the article continued, should reassure all those who, "deceived by certain affectations of skepticism and snobbery [in the university], feared that its generous vitality was numbed."[18] As far as the French left was concerned, the university's behavior during the Dreyfus Affair had vindicated it before the bar of popular opinion, and thus achieved, as Pierre Leguay observed, the objective that the *universitaires* had been hoping for: "the reconciliation of *le haut enseignement des lettres* and democracy."[19]

The Dreyfus case catalyzed another dramatic transformation in public attitudes that left an indelible imprint on the French historical profession. The French army's sordid role in the conspiracy to deny the accused captain a fair trial set off a wave of antimilitarism on the left that reached a crescendo after the turn of the century. Moreover, since the officer corps and its civilian accomplices chose to wrap themselves in the tricolor, these antimilitarist and pacifist sentiments frequently metamorphosed into criticism of the doctrine of patriotism itself. This growing opposition to the well-established tradition of bourgeois patriotism was accelerated by the conspicuous presence of the leading French members of the Second International in the front ranks of the Dreyfusards, who were waging a running battle with the self-proclaimed integral nationalists on the right. The new spirit of internationalism had been transported to the inner chambers of the National Assembly by the fifty-odd socialist deputies who were elected in 1893, and by the end of the 1890s its effect began to be felt among the generation of prospective schoolmasters who were graduating from the universities. Several young history instructors, in particular, were attracted to the new cause and came to regard their classrooms as ideal platforms from which to promote it. If their masters could invoke the heritage of 1789 in support of their patriotic teachings, were not the members of the new generation of *instituteurs* equally entitled to trace the origins of the doctrine of internationalism to the cosmopolitan ideals of the French Revolution?

The *promotions* of history instructors graduated from the teacher training schools around the turn of the century were subjected to influences far different from those that had operated on their predecessors in the profession. The spirit of wounded patriotism that pervaded the French teaching corps in general and the history section in particular during the early years of the Third Republic had already begun to give way to a more cosmopolitan mood. The history teacher of the 1870s and 1880s had tended to regard his task as that of emulating the performance of his Germanic counterpart, whose service in the cause of patriotic education had played such an important role in the movement of unification that achieved its objective at France's expense in 1871. To the *instituteur* who began his career in 1900, the Franco-Prussian War was but a vague memory that was obscured by contemporary distractions. For the young man in search of a fighting faith to fire his imagination, the rise of international socialism and its more extreme offshoot, revolutionary syndicalism, offered the promise of universal peace and international brotherhood as an attractive alternative to the traditional exaltation of the fatherland and the ritualistic references to the lost provinces and the necessity of their liberation. Such disparate developments as the ratification of the Russian alliance (which was thought to have enhanced the prospects for world peace by compelling the German war planners to confront the likelihood of a two front war as a deterrent to aggression), the acquisition of a vast colonial empire in Africa and Southeast Asia, and the first minimal efforts at international arbitration represented by the Hague Conference of 1899, all helped divert French attention from the ancient obsession with the *outre-Rhin*.[20]

It was inevitable that this evolution toward internationalism would have an unsettling effect upon the French historical profession. It was the history teachers, after all, who had been designated by the educational reformers of the Third Republic as the principal executors of the program of patriotic instruction that was designed to reawaken the spirit of national pride, a program that had already degenerated into the basest form of indoctrination by the early 1880s. During Jules Ferry's tenure as Minister of Public Instruction, for example, 20,000 copies of Paul Déroulède's militaristic *Chants du soldat* were distributed to primary school teachers for use in the lower grades, as were copies of Lavisse's *Tu seras soldat*.[21] If the younger generation of *instituteurs* was to participate in the new movement of internationalism, it would have to come to terms with the patriotic aspects of its professional heritage.

The *instituteurs'* function as the official promoters of patriotism was preserved for the remainder of the century. In 1886 the Association des Anciens Elèves de l'Ecole Normale de la Seine voted to affiliate with Déroulède's League of Patriots after rejecting a competing offer to join a mildly internationalist organization called the French Society of Peace Through Education.[22] Even as late as 1899, in the wake of the Dreyfus controversy, there were indications that the teaching profession was still loyal to the old republican tradition of *revanche*. In September, a monument was erected in the courtyard of the Ecole Normale of Laon honoring three schoolteachers from Aisne who had been executed by the German occupiers in 1870 for organizing the local *francs-tireurs*. This monument to pedagogical patriotism had been financed by a subscription to which over 50,000 *instituteurs* had contributed. The *Revue de l'enseignement primaire* reprinted an engraving of the three martyrs and applauded the "vibrant flame of patriotism" that had burned at the inauguration ceremony. Later in the year the same journal published poetry invoking the glorious exploits of Jeanne d'Arc and nationalistic songs employing heroes of French history as their themes.[23]

But as the generation of 1900 began to replace the generation of 1870 in the lower and middle echelons of the teaching profession, it bore the stamp of the new mood of antimilitarism that had been forged in the burning fires of the Dreyfus Affair and fueled by the spirit of internationalism that emanated from the small but increasingly militant and vocal trade union movement. More and more of the younger *instituteurs* began to attach greater significance to their participation in the campaign to unionize French schoolteachers than to their traditional function in the state educational bureaucracy. And since the unionization campaign brought them into contact with the revolutionary, antipatriotic sentiments that pervaded the international socialist movement and the syndicalist labor organization, the

Confédération Générale du Travail, these two callings would present an insoluble conflict of loyalities.

The growth of trade unionism among French schoolteachers occurred in three phases. Sporadic efforts to organize the *instituteurs* into a nationwide professional society between 1887 and 1898 were frustrated by the unrelenting hostility to the principle of teacher unionization displayed by a succession of Opportunist governments. The 1884 law authorizing the formation of professional associations had inspired the formation in 1887 of a Syndicat des Instituteurs et Institutrices, and the first congress of the new organization in the same year established a committee to prepare the groundwork for the creation of a single national union embracing all public school teachers in France. But Minister of Public Instruction Spuller scuttled the idea on September 20, 1887, in a ministerial circular that denounced the proposal for a national teachers' association as ill-conceived and unnecessary. In a period when the *instituteur* was still a loyal servant of the republican state in its struggle to destroy the influence of the Catholic church in primary education, the mere expression of governmental opposition to unionization was sufficient to squelch the proposal for the remainder of the century.[24]

The foundering of these early attempts to establish a national organization of public school teachers did not impede the proliferation of local and regional societies devoted to the defense of professional interests and to the provision of such innocuous services as mutual assistance funds and credit unions. In the course of the 1890s the number of these mutual benefit societies, or *Amicales,* increased from twenty-five to sixty, a trend which reflected a growing sentiment among several *instituteurs* in favor of some type of professional organization. This extensive activity on the local level resulted in a renewed appeal for a nationwide teachers' association during the turbulent national election campaign of 1898. The sentiment for unionization grew in intensity during the effort among primary school teachers to raise funds to commemorate the famous three martyrs of 1870. Many teachers began to realize for the first time that they constituted a professional corps with a community of interests. In response to these growing demands, 120 delegates representing 52 regional teacher associations assembled in the city hall of Laon on August 19, 1899, to discuss the idea of organizing a national conference to which all regional Amicales would be invited. The Laon conference scheduled such a meeting for the following year in Paris and set up a permanent organization to establish plans and priorities.[25]

The Paris conference of 1900 represented a major turning point in the history of teacher unionism in France for two reasons. The first dramatic innovation was the abrupt reversal of the republican government's former disapproval of the principle of a national teachers' organization. Education Minister Georges Leygues bestowed the Waldeck-Rousseau government's official blessing on the *Amicales'* convention by agreeing to preside at the closing session and by endorsing the general aims of the fledgling organization. The second deviation from previous practice occurred when participants at the conference openly discussed pedagogical questions, such as the place occupied by history in the curriculum of primary education, which had formerly been under the exclusive jurisdiction of the Ministry of Public Instruction.[26]

Both these developments were indicative of a new trend in French education that became more pronounced in the following year. On July 1, 1901, the Chamber of Deputies amended the 1884 law so as to grant total freedom of association to all professional groups in French society, a move that was widely interpreted as authorizing the unionization of government employees. Several new teacher associations sprouted almost overnight in response to this liberalized law of association. The 1901 conference of *instituteurs* at Bordeaux formed a national Fédération des Amicales d'Instituteurs and established a permanent commission to keep each new regional grouping abreast of the parent organization's activities. Moreover, the delegates to this conference not only resumed the discussion of pedagogical issues that had been initiated in the previous year, but proceeded to pass resolutions informing the Ministry of Public Instruction of the conference's views on a variety of pedagogical subjects. The most controversial of these resolutions was one that criticized the inordinate attention devoted to military events in primary school history courses and urged an end to the practice of preaching "a bellicose chauvinism" in the classroom.[27] Within the short span of three years, the teaching profession in France had succeeded in surmounting government hostility to unionization, forming a permanent national organization of public school teachers that was independent of government control and establishing the right of *instituteurs* to pass judgment on the pedagogical policies of the state educational authorities.

This burgeoning spirit of independence within the teaching corps reappeared at the 1903 national congress of the Amicales at Marseilles, as did expressions of the government's willingness to tolerate it. Premier Emile Combes, whose current campaign against the Catholic church and its teaching orders depended upon the active support of the *instituteurs*, attended the congress in person to express his ministry's gratitude to the public school teachers for serving as the foremost "advocates of the Republic" and the staunchest guarantors of the established regime.[28] Such a characterization was no mere exercise in exaggerated flattery. The teachers' association had loyally supported the government in its recent campaign on behalf of the democratic laic republic, and the state, in turn, had been impelled to endorse the principle of teacher unionism in order to insure the continuation of that support.[29] But the Dreyfus Affair, which had served temporarily to dispel the aura of mutual hostility and suspicion that had existed between the government and the new teacher organization by uniting the two parties in the common effort to preserve republican institutions, generated a by-product that ultimately contributed to the disruption of that tenuous truce. A small but growing minority within the teachers' association had responded enthusiastically to the antimilitarist sentiments expressed by some of Captain Dreyfus's more staunch supporters, and this increasing antipathy for the army gradually evolved into a more general hostility to the very principle of patriotism that had sustained the Republic for the past two decades.[30]

While this spirit of antimilitarism and antipatriotism continued to grow on the left, the right had succeeded in appropriating the banner of nationalism that had been borne by the defenders of the Republic in its early years. Consequently, the more pacifistically inclined members of the teaching profession were beginning to fear that their continued participation in the civic education programs in the primary schools was serving the cause of those rightist apostles of jingoism and *revanche,* such as Barrès, Bourget, and Deroulède, who were campaigning for a military rematch with the German Empire.[31] Thus, as the teaching profession closed ranks to defend the Republic against its real or imagined enemies in the sacristies, the barracks, and the elegant flats of the Faubourg Saint Germain, several of its recent recruits were also intent on ridding their own house of the scourge of superpatriotism that they had inherited from their predecessors.[32] These new sentiments finally surfaced at the Marseilles Congress of the Amicales, at which several younger delegates shocked their more moderate colleagues by singing the *Internationale* and staging noisy demonstrations in support of a militant program of trade unionism along the lines suggested by the syndicalist labor organization, the Confédération Générale du Travail, which had been founded in 1895. By the end of the congress a combative minority had formed a separate organization within the ranks of the Amicales, called L'Emancipation de l'Instituteur, and proceeded to organize regional associations and found a newspaper of that name.[33]

The new Emancipation faction began to speak out against the system of "administrative slavery" which entrusted government directors, inspectors, and prefects with almost unlimited authority to rule on the nomination, promotion, and transfer of teaching personnel and empowered the education ministry to determine the content of classroom curricula.[34] The general objective of the new group was to gain for all members of the teaching profession complete autonomy within the governmental hierarchy and to restore their "full material and moral independence" from meddling bureaucrats. Convinced that the cautious leadership of the Amicales was incapable of pursuing such ambitious goals, the Emancipation militants asserted the right of the teaching corps to form a labor union in the modern sense of the term, a right that had not yet been formally acknowledged by the republican government.[35]

Though the Ministry of Public Instruction continued to oppose the principle of unionization, it shied away from a direct confrontation over the issue. Any effort to press it at that time would have run the risk of alienating large segments of the teaching profession as well as elements within the Socialist movement (which upheld the *instituteurs'* right to unionize) at a time when the support of both groups was needed in the final skirmishes of the anticlerical campaign. But the government's reluctance to act enabled the militant teachers to present it with what amounted to a *fait accompli.* Throughout 1904 and 1905 several teachers' associations reconstituted themselves into *syndicats* and deposited their bylaws at the local Bourses du Travail (labor exchanges founded in 1892 which represented a nationwide symbol of working class solidarity).[36] In the December 1904 elections for the departmental councils of primary education, Emancipation candidates swamped their Amicalist opponents in several constituencies, winning all seven seats in the Paris region, after conducting campaigns in which the right to unionize was the principal issue.[37]

Coupled with this growing sentiment in favor of unionization was a corresponding demand that the teaching corps sever its traditional ties to the French state and establish contact with the nascent international labor movement. By July 1905, the organ *L'Emancipation* was describing the *instituteur* as an "exploited proletarian" whose interests coincided with those of the working class.[38] In November of the same year the leadership of the rebel teachers' group issued a "Manifesto of Unionized Schoolteachers" which denounced the schoolmaster's former role as an agent of *l'état* and a promoter of *la patrie.* "It is not in the name of the government, even the republican government, nor in the name of the state, nor even in the name of the French people that the *instituteur* dispenses his teaching," it declared. "It is in the name of truth." This bold assertion was accompanied by a renewed demand for total independence from governmental control and an announcement of the group's intention to enter the Bourses du Travail and to seek formal affiliation with the Confédération

Générale du Travail (C.G.T.). These militants waged a propaganda campaign in the pages of the pedagogical press throughout 1905, urging local Amicales to reorganize themselves as *syndicats* and hailing the Emancipation organization as the embryo of a national Fédération Nationale des Syndicats.[39]

The new mood of defiance and militancy within the ranks of the teaching profession did not go unnoticed or unchallenged. The renegade *instituteurs'* frequent assaults on the tradition of patriotic instruction in the primary schools, not to speak of the rhetoric of revolutionary syndicalism that adorned their public pronouncements, provoked a predictable torrent of invective from the center and the right. As early as 1903 *Le Temps* and *Le Journal des débats* had denounced the delegates to the Marseilles Congress who had sung the *Internationale,* "a song of insurrection," and each new reference to the schoolmaster's obligation to the international workers' movement elicited similar responses.[40] In April 1904, *L'Eclair, La Liberté, La Croix, L'Univers,* and other organs of conservative opinion devoted inordinate attention to an "appeal to patriotic *instituteurs*" issued by a small group of disgruntled teachers who accused their militant brethren of betraying "the spirit of the French Revolution, the laic and patriotic spirit" with their affronts to the fatherland.[41]

Emile Bocquillon, one of the drafters of the patriotic manifesto, subsequently founded a new organization, L'Union des Instituteurs Patriotes, and a new pedagogical journal, *L'Ecole patriote,* both of which were dedicated to defending the tradition of civic education that the syndicalist teachers were seeking to destroy.[42] Bocquillon berated the major pedagogical periodicals for serving as the "conscious or unconscious accomplices of the antipatriotic movement" that was sweeping the teaching profession.[43] His subsequent writings, which sought to expose the "crisis of patriotism in the schools," drew enthusiastic endorsements from several former inspectors and directors of primary education, and the august guardians of French tradition in the Académie française expressed their collective concern about the alleged crisis by awarding his first book on the subject the coveted Prix Montyon in 1906.[44]

The syndicalist appeal for affiliation with the C.G.T. prompted further rejoinders from the rightist press. *L'Eclair* accused the teaching corps of harboring "collectivist, revolutionary, and international" sentiments.[45] *Le Temps* chimed in with the same charge, and urged the government to suppress all attempts by the *instituteurs* to form *syndicats.*[46] The socialist newspaper *L'Humanité* was one of the few political journals to endorse the militants' demands.[47] Their November 1905 manifesto was met with a conspicuous silence from the three official mouthpieces of the left wing coalition in power, *La Petite République,* the organ of the *socialistes de gouvernement, Le Radical,* and Clemenceau's *L'Aurore*.[48] The refusal of the leftist parties in the governing coalition to endorse the policy of *instituteur* syndicalism signified an important shift in attitude that was to have unpleasant consequences for the militant union leaders in the following years.

The elections of 1906 recorded a major political victory for the Radical party and for its allies in the newly-unified socialist camp. With some 406 deputies of the left as against 180 of the right sitting in the new Chamber, the long campaign against the church successfully completed, the army purged of its antirepublican elements, and the Dreyfus verdict officially reversed, the Radical Republic appeared to be firmly established and the forces of reaction definitively vanquished. This success in liquidating the threat of counterrevolution from the nationalist right released the subsequent Radical ministries from the necessity of tendering tacit approval of teacher unionism in return for political support, and enabled them to concentrate on quelling the forces of revolution represented by the syndicalist elements within the teaching profession. The appearance in 1906 of Georges Sorel's inflammatory *Reflections on Violence* and the C.G.T.'s adoption of the Amiens Charter, which reaffirmed the doctrine of the general strike, in the same year rendered a governmental counterattack virtually inevitable. After the Tangier incident in 1905, the growing fear of Germany gradually began to supplant the receding fear of a clerico-military plot against the Republic, and it was the extreme left, not the nationalist right, that appeared to pose the greatest threat to French internal security in the face of mounting pressures from abroad. The teaching corps, which had played a major role in the Republic's victory over the army, the church, and the forces of integral nationalism and anti-Semitism between 1898 and 1905, was itself destined to bear the brunt of the repressive policy adopted by the regime when the issue of teacher unionization surfaced in the second half of the decade.

When the central committee of the newly formed Fédération des Syndicats de l'Enseignement officially asserted its right to enter the Bourses du Travail on February 21, 1907, the Clemenceau government seized this opportunity to justify punitive action. On March 11 it sponsored an amendment to the association acts of 1884 and 1901 which specifically denied organizations of public school teachers the right to strike and to join the Bourses. The syndicalists retorted with an open letter to the premier accusing him of seeking to transform the *instituteurs* into slaves of the state, which they described as a "tyrannical and sanguinary monster." At its second national congress at Nantes in the same month the Fédération voted unanimously to affiliate with the C.G.T., a decision which, combined with the public insult to Clemenceau, provoked a wave of governmental repression that culminated in the dismissal of several union leaders.[49]

This new crackdown on the militant teachers was not entirely without precedent. An *instituteur* who dared to lecture revolutionaries at the Parisian Bourse du Travail on the evils of war during the German Emperor's provocative visit to Morocco in 1905 received a stiff censure from the authorities. In April of the same year François Thalamas, a history instructor who was later to become a *bête noire* of the nationalist right, was transferred from the *Lycée* Condorcet after invoking the lessons of history to deny the existence of God, assert the impossibility of miracles, and suggest that Jeanne d'Arc had suffered from "auditory hallucinations that she declared to be voices of terrestrial origin."[50] But it was another *lycée* professor of history, Gustave Hervé, whose heretical beliefs regarding hitherto sacred French traditions provoked the most acrimonious controversy. Hervé was one of the most vocal participants in the vociferous debates on pacifism and the doctrine of the international general strike against war that enlivened the annual congresses of the Second International after 1900. He achieved early notoriety with the suggestion that French soldiers transfer the tricolor from the barracks to the nearest dunghill. His vendettas against the military and the ideal of patriotism in the trade union press and in his own newspaper, *La Guerre sociale*, reflected French socialism's increasingly internationalist orientation, though few followers of Jaurès ever went so far as to endorse Hervé's dictum, "Notre patrie, c'est notre classe."

At the turn of the century, after declaring that the history textbooks employed in the French schools were tainted with chauvinist biases,[51] Hervé published his own manual, *L'Histoire de France et de l'Europe*. The appearance of this controversial volume, which contained unconcealed attacks on practically every historical tradition cherished in France, became an instantaneous cause célèbre in French political life. After several syndicalist *instituteurs* distributed the book to their students, the government decided that it could no longer tolerate such an egregious perversion of the original purpose of historical instruction. Following repeated attacks upon the work from conservative newspapers, the heated debate over pedagogical patriotism reached the floor of the Chamber of Deputies on June 3, 1904, when a rightist deputy interpellated the Combes government on the issue of "internationalism in the schools." The resulting furor forced the Minister of Public Instruction to concede that Hervé's manual "is not a history book, it is a book of polemics,"[52] and after the Chamber voted 468 to 47 to prohibit its use in the public schools, he ordered it off the departmental lists.[53] In June 1905 the Municipal Council of Paris voted 47 to 6 to forbid the purchase of the work for use in the city's schools.[54]

Despite these official efforts to silence the new voices of antimilitarist internationalism in the classroom, the movement continued to gain force. Not only did Hervé's book find its way into the hands of French schoolchildren through the extralegal agency of sympathetic instructors,[55] but other antimilitarists began publishing works of a similar stripe. Moreover, this new element began to infiltrate the editorial staffs of the pedagogical press. By 1902 Hervé and his followers had gained control of the *Revue de l'enseignement primaire*, which boasted a clientele of over 30,000 elementary school teachers. The periodical rapidly abandoned the patriotic stance that it had taken as late as 1899. By 1903 it was publishing the words of the *Internationale* on the demand of a large number of its readers, with an accompanying article announcing that many members of the teaching profession frequently sing it.[56] A year later it reversed its former position vis-à-vis the three martyred *instituteurs* of 1870, accusing them of excessive chauvinism for leading the resistance to the German occupation.

It was this type of activity that prompted the Clemenceau ministry to institute repressive policies that were more extensive, better coordinated, and more vigorously pursued than those of its predecessors. Their end result was to drive a wedge between the republican government and the syndicalist wing of the teaching profession that remained until the outbreak of the First World War. The spirit of all-out warfare suffused the polemical exchanges between state and school for the remainder of the decade. The syndicalist periodicals continued to fulminate against the Radical ministry for reducing the *instituteur* to a position of servitude and imposing on the French pupil "prefabricated formulas that totally destroy his initiative and independence." They confidently announced that the mounting forces of "a liberating syndicalism" will dispossess the state apparatus of its powers and create a "moral and civic education adapted to the needs of the working class."[57] The government responded with a vigorous defense of the hierarchical system of the state *Université* and the necessity of imbuing the teaching profession with "the official principles" of the Republic. *Le Radical* ominously announced that "we are waging war—and we are waging it pitilessly—against ideas that are destructive of the fatherland." Even the moderate socialist organ *La Petite République* came to the defense of the government against the syndicalist militants.[58]

An even more radical critique of the educational system was forthcoming from the tiny but conspicuous band of anarchists in France, who dismissed the syndicalist proposal for total autonomy within the existing political system as an ineffective panacea that would merely perpetuate the enslavement of the working class by the bourgeois state. The anarchists attacked the *école laïque* as a fraudulent symbol of democracy that served the interests of the ruling class by forming "perfect republicans, submissive citizens, and enthusiastic patriots" as well as "obedient workers and disciplined soldiers." They denounced the prevalence in the primary schools of history manuals and citizenship primers that promote "the consecration of great warriors and illustrious cretins, the glorification of the fatherland, the grandeur of France, the glory of the Republic" and teach "respect for teachers, bosses, leaders; respect for property, the flag, authority."[59] This perception moved one anarchist critic to describe the public school teachers in France as "the intellectual cops of the capitalist classes"[60] and another to remark that the Republic's victory over the church in the educational controversies of the past several years had merely substituted one tyranny for another. "The laic dogma has replaced the religious dogma," he observed. "Has anything changed?"[61] The anarchist alternative to the "specious" autonomy within the system of the *école laïque* proposed by the syndicalist *instituteurs* was the formation of "free schools" outside the state educational system. Sponsored by both syndicalists and anarchists, several such schools appeared in the first decade of the twentieth century, and one lasted from 1904 to 1917.[62]

Such developments would have been of negligible importance had they been isolated instances of extremist sentiments confined to the leftist fringes of the syndicalist movement in France. But the evidence suggests that they were indicative of a growing trend of uneasiness throughout the entire teaching profession about its official function as the transmission belt of patriotism. An informal opinion poll conducted in 1899 revealed a widespread sentiment of antimilitarism among French intellectuals in general and those attached to the university in particular.[63] In 1902 *La Petite République* sponsored an essay contest on the subject of whether the textbooks employed in the public schools were in keeping with "the requirements and aspirations of the modern spirit." The jury, which was headed by Ferdinand Buisson, the former director of higher education, awarded first prize to the response of a Parisian schoolteacher entitled "Unmasking the Poisoners." The winning essay mercilessly indicted Lavisse's manuals of civic education, especially the widely used *Tu seras soldat,* for promoting a spirit of superpatriotism and contributing to an *éducation d'Apaches.*[64]

Spurred by the antimilitarist sentiments of the teachers' syndicalist movement, an ever-increasing number of young schoolmasters enlisted in the campaign to rid the public schools of the scourge of patriotic indoctrination. At its Amiens Congress in September 1904, the Ligue de l'Enseignement voted overwhelmingly to drop its motto,

"Pour la Patrie, par le Livre, par l'Epée," and a spokesman justified this action on the grounds that the slogan had been adopted during the period when France was occupied by the German army and was being bled by reparations demands. "We did not want to declare ourselves conquered," he explained, "but that belongs to history."[65] In the same year a large contingent of primary school instructors attending a Congress of Peace Through Law at Nîmes went even further, praising the "acts of courage" of those who had refused to bear arms for *la patrie*.[66] In 1905 the Sorbonne historian Gustave Lanson publicly acknowledged that "the evil exists. A certain number of *instituteurs* . . . in reaction against nationalism, have plunged into internationalism, which they summarily and brutally interpret as the negation of the fatherland."[67] By the end of the decade one noted professor could publicly assert that "40 percent of the French teachers are speaking out against the fatherland and 50 percent never speak of it [at all]."[68]

The internationalist *instituteurs* were the first members of the history profession to raise the issue that had remained dormant for so many years: the incompatibility between history's professed commitment to scientific objectivity and the services that it was expected to render to the program of patriotic instruction in the public school system. In 1905 the fourth congress of the *Amicales* at Lille adopted as the order of the day a resolution stipulating that the organization was dedicated to "preserving the scientific character of historical instruction, that is to say, avoiding making it systematically serve the construction of a social ideal and the cultivation of certain sentiments." The purpose of this declaration, according to a subsequent observer, was to remind the history teacher of his duty to "teach history for its own sake, without subordinating it to the purposes of moral, civic, or patriotic edification."[69] This reaction against the tradition of patriotic education within the teaching profession was not confined exclusively to syndicalist circles. When the widow of Paul Bert, the architect of Ferry's civic instruction programs and a symbol of the effort to emulate the successful program of patriotic indoctrination employed in the German schools, attempted to commission a biography of her husband as part of a collection of historical biographies, the editor of a major publishing house turned her down on the grounds that his chauvinistic brand of patriotism was too controversial.[70]

By the beginning of the second decade of the twentieth century, the French teaching profession, the social institution that had been given custody of the patriotic ideal and the republican creed since the days of Ferry, was riddled with what the state could not help regarding as antipatriotic and, in some cases, anti-republican sentiments. The

Fédération des Syndicats de l'Enseignement, which in 1906 boasted only twelve affiliate *syndicats* and 1,000 active members, was coordinating the activities of fifty *syndicats* and 3,000 members by 1912. Though the more moderate Fédération des Amicales still commanded the loyalty of more than three times that number,[71] it was compelled to adopt a more militant stance in order to prevent its younger members from defecting to its syndicalist competitor.[72] At the Lille Congress of the Fédération des Amicales in 1905, for example, the teachers present adopted a resolution declaring that a citizen is under no obligation to fight for his country unless "it be the object of a brutal aggression."[73]

The movement to establish a nationwide teachers association, which had begun in the last decade of the nineteenth century as a modest effort in defense of narrow professional interests, blossomed into what one observer has summarized as a feeling of "solidarity with the working class, a violent critique of the state, and a desire to reorganize society" that affected the entire French teaching corps.[74] The fact that schoolteachers were beginning to evidence interest in affiliating with the C.G.T., an organization committed to sabotaging France's military policy, overthrowing its political regime, and destroying its economic system, caused at least one noted pedagogue to wonder whether the *instituteurs* were capable of continuing to exercise their function as "the guardians of order, the enemies of all disturbing novelties, the preachers of respect and resignation, the ingenious artisans of social conservation" or whether they were destined to become "agents of protest and agitation."[75]

The apparent increase of antipatriotic attitudes among primary and secondary school instructors prompted an outburst of recrimination in nationalist circles. Maurice Barrès railed against the success of antipatriotism in "academic milieux," complaining that while German schoolmasters continue to preach the cult of the fatherland, the vast majority of French *instituteurs* are "impregnated with pacifism." Alcide Ebray, a republican diplomat who resigned his post in protest against the dismissal of Delcassé in the wake of the first Moroccan crisis, extended this indictment to the *universitaires,* whose "antipatriotic and antimilitarist" sentiments, while not as outrageous as those emanating from the classrooms of the *écoles primaires,* were actually more dangerous because they were expressed with more "elegance and distinction." Georges Grosjean, a nationalist deputy, lambasted the "mandarins" at the Sorbonne for setting a subversive example that had begun to inspire treason throughout the entire *Université*. He accused the historians in particular of succumbing to the allurements of internationalism while their German, English, and Italian counterparts continued to glorify their respective national traditions.[76]

Such efforts by spokesmen of the French right to lump distinguished university professors together with syndicalist militants in the primary schools betrayed a gross lack of discrimination and a propensity for blurring important distinctions. It is true, nevertheless, that the respectable, established historians in the universities were not entirely unaffected by the new directions in which their younger colleagues in the lower levels had begun to move. When Hervé appeared before the Cour d'assises of Auxerre in November 1901 to answer charges of publicly insulting the armed forces, he was accompanied by a bevy of *universitaires* who signed a declaration proclaiming that they shared "all the ideas" of the accused. Charles Seignobos himself sent a warm letter of support.[77] Alphonse Aulard also rushed to the defense of the embattled internationalists in the teaching corps. He supported those *instituteurs* who sang the *Internationale* at their professional meetings, claiming that the *Marseillaise* and the *Internationale* were both expressions of the "republican soul of France."[78]

Few of the university historians sympathized either with the doctrines of international revolution that were preached by the more militant members of the socialist movement or with the extreme antipatriotism promoted by the *Hervéists*. They were for the most part humanitarian liberals, whose internationalism and pacifism was of the gentle, idealistic variety that predominated at the Hague Peace Conference of 1899. When his own *Manuel de morale et d'instruction civique* came under attack in the Chamber by a leading nationalist deputy and founding member of the anti-Dreyfusard League of the French Fatherland, Gabriel Syveton, for its allegedly antipatriotic passages, Aulard, who was later to preside over the Association Française pour la Societé des Nations,[79] responded by redefining the term patriotism to make room for the internationalist spirit that he believed to have been ushered in with the new century.

> In the name of the ideal of human solidarity, in the name of the doctrine of the United States of Europe, of the United States of the world, we internationalist patriots, we partisans of disarmament, we enemies of war, demand that French policy apply itself to the peaceful return [of the lost provinces] if such is their will.[80]

He was thus careful to justify the French claims to Alsace-Lorraine not on the familiar anti-German grounds, but by invoking the principle of self-determination, which he described as "the true tradition of the French Revolution." For Aulard, the solution to the problem of the lost provinces was not to be found in the shrill calls for military intervention that had been emanating from Barrès, Déroulède, and others. The only hope for a just peace resided in the establishment of the United States of Europe on the basis of popular consent. The Germans' principal sin was that they annexed Alsace-Lorraine without consulting the local population, thereby violating the principle of national self-determination established during the French Revolution.[81] By redefining the doctrine of patriotism in this way, Aulard was able to embrace the cause of the eastern provinces without having to depart from the revolutionary republican heritage and play into the hands of the authoritarian nationalists.

Aulard envisaged the role of the schoolmaster as that of instilling in the minds of the youth not the lessons of superpatriotism, but of the original "principles of 1789." The benign influence of the school, he observed, has already "rendered the republic more republican" and it was largely thanks to the instructors that "the bourgeois, conservative republic of Thiers" has been transformed into "a democratic, laic republic."[82] The teaching corps will continue to teach patriotism, he announced, but it will be the patriotism of the French Revolution, which is a patriotism "without braggadocio," a patriotism of "enlightened men who have a fear of war."[83] He defended the notion of "pacifist education," which he claimed had been formulated by "the philosophes of the eighteenth century" and the heroes of 1793, who were "humanitarians and internationalists, partisans of the Universal Republic, enemies of narrow patriotism."[84]

Charles Victor Langlois, long the most insulated and least *engagé* member of the Sorbonne inner circle, hailed the incipient spirit of internationalism that appeared in French higher education at the turn of the century. He criticized the historians of the old school (without mentioning names) who had been animated by the desire to justify parochial patriotism.[85] He was pleased to herald the demise of the old dream of transforming the French universities into centers of historical research, modeled after the German universities and devoted to the glorification of the fatherland and its cultural traditions. "All the universities in the world," Langlois observed with approval, "are now working fraternally" in an "immense and collective labor of which each claims only a small part."[86] He later pushed this tolerant, cosmopolitan approach to the very limits of French *amour-propre*.

> What people would dare to claim a sort of intellectual, artistic, or scientific hegemony over the world such as it is? It used to be sufficient to know everything that was written in French; today, men of letters in every country are familiar with the masterpieces of all peoples, including even the Russians and Scandinavians, and no one is content any longer with his national literature.[87]

This new faith in the international unification of knowledge and culture was symptomatic of the receptivity to foreign influences that the Parisian universities had begun to develop since the late 1890s. By the end of the first decade of the twentieth century, as we have seen, the Sorbonne began to acquire a world-wide reputation as a center of higher learning that restored much of the prestige that it had lost since the end of the Middle Ages. The rapid influx of foreign scholars transformed the Latin Quarter into what a visiting English student later described as a "curious cosmopolis."[88] The presence of these foreigners, with their strange new ideas and unfamiliar customs and life styles, helped bring an end to the cultural isolation that the university reformers had earlier decried.

In an article on "The International Organization of Historical Studies," an American historian later observed that this spirit of international understanding emerged slowly and with great difficulty in the French historical profession. He attributed this resistance to the importance that had been attached to national history throughout the nineteenth century, as well as to the tendency toward an extreme specialization which gripped the French profession during the same period.[89] Nevertheless, in the late 1800s, certain hints at a broader internationalist spirit began to appear. Lavisse and Rambaud's *Histoire générale* included chapters by foreign scholars, and Monod's *Revue historique* began to print special bulletins written by non-French historians, including Germans. Meanwhile, historians from different countries were beginning to evidence a lively interest in each other's work, and calls began to arise for the planning and organization of international conventions at which views on scholarship and teaching could be exchanged. The Congrès Internationale d'Histoire Diplomatique, held in The Hague in 1898, was the first such international conclave for historians. The second international congress in 1900 heard pleas from several participants for the creation of a permanent international society for historians in all fields. A few months later, by popular demand, the Congrès Internationale d'Histoire Comparée was born. In 1903 the Congress met in Rome and adopted the name Congrès Internationale des Sciences Historiques. At this Rome Congress, the keynote speaker warned against "the danger of writing [history] with an excess of nationalism" and insisted on "the essential unity of [world] history.[90]

Thus, as the French Third Republic entered its fourth decade, the disruptive events of the *fin de siècle* had guaranteed that it would face a domestic situation which was far different from that which had obtained since its birth. In its early years, the new regime had surprised most European observers by achieving a speedy national recovery and by securing widespread acceptance of democratic political institutions amidst a continent of monarchies and empires. The old counterrevolutionary ideologies that had previously competed with the republican idea for public favor—Bonapartism, clericalism, and the two branches of royalism—appeared to have lost their former appeal by the end of the 1870s. Similarly, the revolutionary mystique that had helped to overturn regimes in 1830 and 1848, and which had plunged Paris into civil war in 1871, seemed to have been domesticated by the Third Republic, under which the term "radicalism" had become a synonym for moderation in social and economic policy. But the Dreyfus case reopened the Pandora's box of extremist ideologies that had enlivened the French political landscape in the earlier part of the century. A revived royalist movement under the leadership of Charles Maurras appeared on the right end of the political spectrum alongside the new nationalism of Maurice Barrès and the authoritarian Caesarism of Paul Déroulède. The hierarchy of the Catholic church ended its brief truce with the laic republic by reasserting its opposition to the major institutions of French democracy. Meanwhile, the seeds of an antirepublican brand of international socialism, pacifism, anarchism, and revolutionary syndicalism were being sown on the left.

The historians of the university, as we have seen, had not remained immune from the unsettling effects of this dramatic turn of events. The disintegration of the old republican ideal—that eclectic mélange of bourgeois patriotism, anticlericalism, and moderate social reformism that they themselves had been so active in promoting—forced many members of the profession, particularly in the lower echelons, to reassess the function of history in public education. The reaction against its use as a source of patriotic instruction was largely a belated acknowledgement of the undeniable fact that the cause of "national honor" had been appropriated by the New Right.[91] International cooperation and understanding" became the watchword of increasing numbers of republican intellectuals eager to disassociate themselves from the cause of patriotism that had been so intimately identified with the Third Republic in its infancy.

When the historians and sociologists in the university rallied to the cause of Captain Dreyfus, they had implicitly opted to become *engagés* in the defense of the Republic in what they feared was its hour of danger, and the triumph of the Dreyfusard cause seemed to be a vindication of that decision. But once that hour of immediate danger had passed, the resulting ideological fissures remained, and leading members of the university came to believe that these divisions within French society could no longer be papered over with the comforting but increasingly empty platitudes of the past. Many within their ranks, who had entered the arena of partisan politics to defend the established regime during the Dreyfus Affair, began to see their future task as one of formulating new principles and proposing new doctrines that could serve as the ideological underpinnings of a new republican legitimacy.

10
Social Science and the Restoration of the Republican Synthesis

The collapse of the republican consensus and the sharpening of ideological conflicts during the Dreyfus Affair, together with the appearance of extremist movements and ideologies which challenged the legitimacy of republican institutions in the early years of the twentieth century, caught the historians in the French universities by surprise. As the architects of the civic education program in the schools, they were particularly disheartened by the recent revelations of its defects as a mechanism of socialization. Several highly-placed *universitaires* began to wonder if the "principles of '89," which had served as the basis for those citizenship programs, were less than ideal foundations of social cohesion. The logical inconsistency of basing a social and political system upon an ideology that both sanctified the rights of the individual citizen vis-à-vis his society and authorized him to question the legitimacy of the regnant political regime in the name of some higher ideal had not been apparent in the early years of the Republic, when the system suffered few organized challenges to that legitimacy. Marshal MacMahon's and then General Boulanger's unsuccessful campaigns against the youthful regime in the first two decades of its existence merely served to confirm the viability of republican institutions during that period. But the deep social, political, and religious divisions that appeared during the Dreyfus Affair and continued on into the new century convinced many intellectual supporters of the Republic that a supplementary source of consensus would have to be discovered if the republican system was to weather the ideological storms that had begun to brew.

Philosophers and social scientists in France had been pondering the need for a new moral code to replace the well-worn principles of the French Revolution as the underpinning of social cohesion long before the outbreak of the Dreyfus Affair. One school of philosophers in particular had developed an elaborate theory of social solidarity during the 1880s and the first half of the 1890s. Henri Marion, a disciple of the neo-Kantian philosopher Charles Renouvier, published his *De la Solidarité morale* in 1880, and was selected to be the first occupant of the chair of the Science of Education at the Sorbonne in 1883 after service on the Conseil Supérieur de l'Instruction Publique. Also in 1880, the Renouvierist philosopher Alfred Fouillée brought out his *La Science sociale contemporaine,* which called for the liberation of sociology from the a priori, deductive methods of the philosophy of history and the adoption of the experimental, a posteriori, inductive methods of the natural sciences. Both argued that the firmest basis of social solidarity in modern industrial society is extreme specialization and the division of labor, tendencies which they believed would increase the mutual interdependence of each unit in the social organism in the same manner that the division of functions of the various organs in the physiological organism enhance its viability.[1] But Marion's untimely death in 1896 and Fouillée's premature retirement from his post as *maître de conférences* at the Ecole Normale in 1879 due to bad eyesight and poor health removed them from the center of French intellectual life. Their preliminary speculations about the scientific bases of social equilibrium remained on the periphery of French social thought until the end of the century.[2]

But the problem of ensuring social stability continued to lurk beneath the deceptively tranquil surface of the Third Republic throughout the 1890s. The Boulangist plot, despite its failure, had revived the specter of a man on horseback rescuing France from its popularly elected regime, and the activities of such Boulangist propagandists as Maurice Barrès and such authoritarian patriots as Paul Déroulède kept alive the idea of a military coup long after the demise of the general himself in 1891. The appearance of Edouard Drumont's Anti-Semitic League in the year of Boulanger's fall resurrected an old cause to which a renascent antirepublican right could rally, as it did a few years later during the Panama scandal. At the other end of the political spectrum, the foundation of the Second International in Paris on the centenary of the French Revolution (at which gathering a majority of the delegates were Frenchmen), the unanticipated election of fifty socialist deputies to the Chamber in 1893, the upsurge of anarchist agitation that resulted in the assassination of the president of the Republic the following year, and the formation of the militantly syndicalist General Confederation of Labor in 1895, all helped to reawaken the old fears of a Red Republic that still haunted middle class voters who remembered the winter and spring of 1871. Coupled with these fears was the general realization among many Radical politicians that the appearance of socialist and trade union movements reflected a growing sentiment in favor of state intervention to redress social grievances, a sentiment that they could no longer afford to ignore, lest they risk a mass defection of disillusioned and embittered wage earners to the fledgling parties of the extreme left.[3]

In the year 1897 Léon Bourgeois, a republican politician who had observed these ominous developments at first hand—in the past decade he had headed, among others, the Ministries of Education, Interior, and Justice and served as prime minister—published a slim volume entitled *La Solidarité*. In this work he remarked that modern industrial society had produced two systems of thought that were inimical to social cohesion: the laissez-faire, social Darwinist doctrine of the struggle for existence among individuals, and the socialist doctrine of the life-and-death conflict between the two major classes. Bourgeois proposed that these obsolete, socially disruptive ideologies be supplanted by a new social theory stressing the scientific basis of the values of solidarity, mutual cooperation, and altruistic interdependence.[4]

His book was advertised as an objective analysis of the recent trends toward instability in French society and purported to offer a scientific program for the reestablishment of social equilibrium. But its descriptions and prescriptions were clearly intended also to provide a scientific justification for the Radical Party's newly adopted program of moderate reformism, which rejected the socialist ideology of class conflict while promoting interventionist measures designed to correct the most glaring social abuses that gave rise to leftist agitation and to rally Radicals and moderate Socialists to the support of piecemeal reform.[5] The biological doctrine of the interdependence of the various parts of a living organism, applied to the social organism, provided the Radical program with a scientific veneer that distinguished it from the ideological doctrines of the past. In order to establish its kinship with French republican traditions, Bourgeois represented his new doctrine as an offshoot of the philosophy of the Enlightenment and "the culmination of the social and political theory to which the [French] Revolution had given the world its first formulation."[6] But the concept of solidarity had "an inspiring scientific appearance without a trace of ideology," asserted Charles Gide, an intellectual ally of Bourgeois. "Unlike liberty, equality and fraternity, solidarity is not a high-sounding word, nor is it a mere ideal. It is just a fact, one of the best established facts of history and experience."[7] To its proponents, the ideal of social solidarity seemed to provide "an impregnable foundation for an extended version of the ideals of the French Revolution by going beyond sentimental fraternity to the facts of interdependence."[8]

Durkheim's social theory coincided perfectly with these doctrines of solidarity, and the conclusions of his *Division of Labor in Society*, which was published in 1893, closely resembled those reached independently by solidarist thinkers such as Marion, Fouillée, and Bourgeois. The solidarist philosophers and the Durkheimian sociologists had both been profoundly influenced by the writings of Renouvier, both had close contacts with the emergent Radical Party, and both recognized the value of the educational system as a means of communicating the new doctrine to the masses. According to Durkheim's disciple Maurice Halbwachs, the founder of French academic sociology introduced his discipline into the Sorbonne "through the narrow door of pedagogy," and believed education to be "the most efficacious means that a society has at its disposal to form its members in its [own] image."[9]

The almost simultaneous publication of Bourgeois's book and the outbreak of the Dreyfus Affair transformed the theoretical abstractions of the solidarist and sociological schools into a practical political doctrine. The French politicians who called themselves "Radicals" began to achieve a predominant position in French political life after 1898, and soon thereafter, with the crucial assistance of supporters in the intelligentsia, began to promote the solidarist ideology as the basis of a new republican consensus. At the International Congress of Social Education, held at Paris under government auspices in September of 1900 as part of the *Exposition Universelle,* Radical politicians, university professors, civil servants, and primary school teachers met to devise ways of introducing the new doctrine of solidarity in the state education system.[10] Appropriately, Bourgeois served as president of the congress and directed the discussion.[11]

The most important consequence of the congress was the formation of the Ecole des Hautes Etudes Sociales in December of the same year.[12] The declared objective of the new school, which had no formal ties to the degree-granting faculties, was to promote the teaching of social science in higher education, but the subsequent *conférences* and pamphlets that it sponsored were replete with proposals for the utilization of solidarist theory as the basis of a new moral system for the Third Republic. Durkheim and Célestin Bouglé traveled from Bordeaux and Montpellier respectively to lecture at the new school, and the team at the *Année sociologique* forged a working alliance with the solidarist thinkers and Radical politicians who dominated the administrative council of the institution. Among them were Alphonse Darlu, Inspector General of Public Instruction; Ferdinand Buisson, who had succeeded Marion as professor of the Science of Education at the Sorbonne in 1896 after having spent seventeen years institutionalizing the Third Republic's educational innovations from his post as the Director of Primary Education; Minister of Commerce Alexandre Millerand; and Félix Alcan, the publisher of the *Année sociologique* and many of the scholarly works of the leading historians and sociologists.[13] The solidarist doctrine was quickly adopted with the greatest enthusiasm by numerous teachers at every level of the French educational system. It soon found its way into textbooks and classroom lectures, and the enrollment of the Ecole increased dramatically in its first decade.[14]

Shortly after the first congress of the Ecole des Hautes Etudes Sociales, the Radical and Radical-Socialist party was constituted as a permanent political organization, and the spokesmen for the new political grouping eagerly endorsed the solidarist ideology.[15] Following the elections of May 1902, which gave the *Bloc Républicain* its first clear-cut majority, the men who had helped to formulate and promote the new solidarist and sociological doctrines were suddenly swept into positions of political and academic power. Bourgeois was elected president of the Chamber of Deputies, Buisson surrendered his professorship of the Science of Education to become Chairman of the Education Committee of the Chamber, Bouglé was summoned from Montpellier to the Sorbonne, and Durkheim was hired as Buisson's temporary replacement and named to the powerful University Council.[16] In 1906 Durkheim officially inherited Buisson's chair and had his course declared mandatory for all candidates for a teaching degree. Though he had the title of his chair changed to the Science of Education *and* Sociology in 1913, he continued to reserve at least a third of his teaching for pedagogical subjects.[17] It is hardly an exaggeration to remark that the founder of modern French sociology, who taught simultaneously at the Sorbonne, the Ecole Normale, and the Ecole des Hautes Etudes Sociales, exercised a veritable domination over the French educational system during the decade prior to the First World War.[18]

The academic historians, already ensconced in positions of power and influence throughout the university system, were confronted with a vexing dilemma as they reviewed the circumstances surrounding the rapid rise to prominence of their erstwhile competitors, the sociologists. Throughout the last quarter of the nineteenth century, as we have seen, they had helped to devise and put into practice a program of historical education designed to promote the sentiment of patriotism as an antidote to the despair caused by the defeat of 1870. But once the Dreyfus Affair and the ideological conflicts that followed it had exposed the sores of the body politic that had been festering throughout the 1890s, the defense of *La République* became an even more pressing concern than the regeneration of *La Patrie*. The new priority, which assumed a greater urgency when antirepublican movements of both left and right appeared at the turn of the century, was to develop a new moral basis for a republican consensus and communicate it to the young generation. As early as 1895, Lavisse had called attention to the emergent conflict between the principles of liberty guaranteed by the Declaration of the Rights of Man and the requirements of social order. He declared that France needed to "organize" her democracy by encouraging respect for established laws and by "creating new customs through education." This could no longer be achieved, he announced, by reviving the "vague philosophies" of the past, which encouraged the free exercise of the mind and produced an "ideal" on which one could base one's program for "modifying the real." The modern social theorist must abandon such "theological" and "metaphysical" approaches and submit his mind to the "discipline of science," which alone is capable of producing a "renewal of the moral life" of the Third Republic.[19]

Yet participation in such a campaign would require the historians to patch up their interdisciplinary quarrel with the sociologists, who had already begun to promote a system of moral education based neither on the principles of bourgeois patriotism nor on the Declaration of the Rights of Man, but on the solid lessons of modern science. Occasional friendly pourparlers were forthcoming from the sociologists, a courtesy which rendered the idea of an alliance between history and sociology somewhat less distasteful to the historians. By the turn of the century Durkheim had moderated his earlier criticism of history as a discipline, and in time began to hail the historical approach as a useful conceptual tool in social research. There is present in each living human being today, he declared, "the man of yesteryear" who forms the "unconscious part" of his nature. He cautioned the present-oriented social scientist against neglecting the centuries of historical development "in the course of which we were formed and from which we result." Durkheim conceded that historical study is an essential preliminary step in the process of understanding human behavior in modern society, because it sheds light on the formative influences that have determined the nature of present social reality. History, thus conceived, is not therefore a frivolous and pointless exercise in nostalgia. The social scientist takes leave of the present to examine the nature of social institutions of the past not for their own sake, but in order to learn about the origins and development of contemporary institutions.[20]

Durkheim also became a staunch defender of history's privileged position in the curriculum of the educational system, particularly at the lower levels. In the opening lectures from his chair in the Science of Education at the Sorbonne during the 1902–1903 academic year, he declared that since sociology was still too "undeveloped" to be of use in the primary and secondary school program, history as a subject that is "closely akin to sociology" represented the best available method of acquainting the student with the reality of social life. The sole condition that he imposed upon history was that it abandon its traditional emphasis on the role of individual actors and concentrate on demonstrating to the student how historical change is the result of "collective and anonymous forces."[21] In accordance with this new tolerant attitude toward history, the sociologists and solidarist philosophers who directed the Ecole des Hautes Etudes Sociales willingly opened its doors to their colleagues in the historical profession. Alfred Croiset, the historian of classical antiquity who had become dean of the Sorbonne in 1898, was one of the founding members and served as the first president of the Council.[22] As a leading member of the Conseil Supérieur de l'Instruction Publique, he organized a series of investigations between 1900 and 1903 dealing with questions of educational reform which had been discussed at the Ecole. Lavisse, Seignobos, and Gustave Lanson were frequent participants in its periodic *conférences,* the transcripts of which were published by Félix Alcan, a member of the governing board of the school.[23]

What united the historians and the sociologists of the French university system in a common purpose was their commitment to preserve the social order of the Third Republic. During the polemical battles of the Dreyfus Affair, most of the major historians at the Sorbonne rubbed shoulders with the sociologists in the Dreyfusard organizations, and both groups came to realize that their interdisciplinary squabbles paled beside the overriding need to defend the Republic and provide it with a new moral system.[24] Some years later Célestin Bouglé, Durkheim's right-hand man, recalled how the ideological conflicts of the *fin de siècle* helped to forge a common bond between the sociologists and their former detractors in other disciplines.

> Politics was never foreign to these sudden changes of fortune [for the sociological movement]. The shock of the Affair occurred. Sociologists and antisociologists found themselves on the same side. Now at last, not only did they have better things to do than to fight among themselves, but, faced with the common adversary,

they came to understand that they were serving the same ideal. The team at the *Année sociologique* . . . did their duty as "intellectual" citizens. All were bent on demonstrating, on the morrow of the Affair, that they had perceived the breadth of the problem posed and had an inkling of the necessary reconstructions.[25]

Gabriel Monod later remarked that the intellectuals who joined the Dreyfusard cause were fighting not merely to bring justice to a wronged individual, but also to fortify the fatherland with a vigorous new tradition of "civic training and republican education." Former antagonists "forgot their past quarrels" and joined forces to promote "the ideas of patriotic defense and social reform."[26]

Several thinkers in France, as we have seen, had been suggesting for over a decade that the disciplines of history and sociology resolve their differences and cooperate on the basis of a common commitment to promote the cause of social science. But just as the early attempts by Duruy and his colleagues to create a historical profession met with only limited success until the military disaster of 1870 provided the impetus for a full-scale campaign of educational and professional reform, it required the threat of a radical disruption of the social fabric of the Third Republic to convince the historians and the sociologists of the necessity to pool their efforts in pursuit of a common objective.

The controversy sparked by the Dreyfus Affair soon evolved into a Manichean confrontation between what had come to be viewed by both sides as the "two Frances"—the revolutionary and the counter-revolutionary traditions that together represented the dual legacy of 1789. The social institutions inherited from the *ancien régime,* the army, the church, and what was left of the old aristocracy, lined up against the latter-day custodians of the revolutionary idea, the Radicals, Socialists, anticlericals, and Freemasons. Once the issues had been posed in terms of competing historical traditions, historical arguments inevitably came to play an important role in the continuing controversy. As a consequence, the historians in the university were presented with the opportunity to acquire a renewed sense of purpose for their craft. In alliance with the sociologists, they could help to furnish the defenders of French democracy with the requisite intellectual ammunition. As was the case in their earlier efforts on behalf of French patriotism, the vehicle for transmitting the new message to the populace was to be the public school system. "We live in a representative and laic democracy," Seignobos observed in the wake of the Affair. "Our students are all destined to become voters. Since history is the true civic instruction, it is on the professors of history that the old mission of providing the political instruction of future citizens devolves."[27]

The guiding spirit of this monolithic educational system was to be the doctrines of modern science. In a lecture delivered at the Ecole des Hautes Etudes Sociales in the winter of 1902–1903, Seignobos traced the historical origins and development of the scientific moral system that had been established in the French university. He paid tribute to Victor Duruy for having initiated the assult on the "verbal" and "aristocratic" character of higher education in the closing years of the Second Empire. He praised the early efforts to introduce "the study of contemporary reality" in the curriculum of the secondary schools, and hailed the democratic and laic system of primary education and its teaching corps, which, he noted with approval, had been transformed into "state personnel."[28] The subsequent reforms of higher education, he declared, had been accomplished both in the "spirit of the Revolution" and in the "scientific spirit of the nineteenth century," for the purpose of responding to "the needs of a democratic and rationalist society."[29] He defended the highly centralized apparatus in which the republican government determined the number and types of faculty positions to be created and the titular professors of the faculty involved recommended prospective candidates to the ministry. "Science," Seignobos observed, is represented by the professorial body, while "Society" is represented by the ministry. "It is difficult," he concluded, "to imagine a more rational mechanism."[30]

The completion of the trend toward educational centralization in the early years of the twentieth century had several important effects on the nature and scope of historical teaching and scholarship. One immediate consequence of this process was a dramatic increase in interest in modern and contemporary history, a development that was a natural consequence of the historians' recent involvement in the current controversies in French politics. But this new orientation of historical studies had several obstacles to surmount. In a work entitled *The Present State of Modern Historical Studies in France*, published in 1901, Pierre Caron and Philippe Sagnac, two of the most promising alumni of the new school of academic history, complained that while the scientific approach to historical scholarship had long flourished in ancient and medieval studies because of the antiquarian nature of the subject matter, most historians had shied away from topics of modern history because of the dissension that such studies would inevitably provoke. They pointed out that the Ecole des Chartes and the Ecole Pratique des Hautes Etudes had skirted the controversies of modernity by restricting their scholarly investigations to historical periods whose partisan disputes had long since subsided.[31]

At the Ecole des Chartes, between 1890 and 1900, Caron and Sagnac observed, only 34 of the 142 theses presented in fulfillment of the requirements for the *diplôme d'archiviste* dealt with modern subjects. Though this was a slight improvement over the earlier period —between 1865 and 1875 none of the 98 theses presented ventured beyond the Middle Ages—it nevertheless reflected a hesitation on the part of both professors and students to confront the special problems inherent in modern history. Similarly, at the Ecole Pratique, of the more than forty *conférences* conducted in its history and philology section, only two were devoted to the post-1500 era. Sagnac and Caron urged that seminars devoted to that neglected period be established on the model of the laboratories in ancient and medieval studies, and that sections on modern history (covering the period from the Reformation to the French Revolution) and contemporary history (devoted to the post-1789 era) be established in the faculties of letters of the universities. To encourage scholarly production in modern history, they founded the *Revue d'histoire moderne et contemporaine* in 1899 and the Société d'Histoire Moderne two years later.[32]

Caron's and Sagnac's complaint about the continued lack of student interest in modern history at the beginning of the first decade of the twentieth century, if justified at that time, would have been unwarranted by the end of the decade. The activities of the Société d'Histoire Moderne and the *Revue d'histoire moderne et contemporaine*, together with Rambaud's lectures and seminars in modern and contemporary history at the Sorbonne, had stimulated a lively interest in this hitherto forbidden subject by that time. In a statistical study of the number of theses submitted at the Sorbonne for the certificate of advanced study *(mémoires du diplôme d'études supérieures)*, Ferdinand Lot determined that interest in modern history was increasing markedly at the expense of medieval history:

Mémoires du diplôme d'études supérieures submitted at the Sorbonne

	1907	1908	1909
Modern history	11	17	20
Medieval and Religious history	4	5	5

Source: Ferdinand Lot, *Diplômes d'études, étude de statistique comparée*, p. 24.

At the pre-doctoral level, at least, the old prejudice against modern history appeared to be on the wane.

Sagnac and Caron were confident that an impartial, objective study of modern history could be initiated in the doctoral program at the Sorbonne. The source of this optimism was their belief that a precedent had already been established by Alphonse Aulard in his course on the History of the French Revolution. They contended that Aulard and his protégés had set out to study the events of the Revolutionary epoch "rationally and scientifically" with the intention of exposing the falsehoods of the "counterrevolutionary and revolutionary legends" that had been popularized by ideologically motivated writers in the past. The results of this research were incorporated in dozens of doctoral dissertations produced by the disciples of Aulard, as well as in articles appearing in the official periodical of the Aulardian school, *La Révolution française*. If the objective methods of scientific history could be applied to such a controversial period as the Revolutionary era, they asked, was it unreasonable to expect scholars to cast off their remaining inhibitions and proceed to subject the entire sweep of modern history to a systematic scientific analysis?[33]

One important obstacle to such an enterprise that troubled them was the independent tradition of nonscientific history writing which the nineteenth century reformers had succeeded in banishing from the university only to see it reaffirm its viability and vitality in other centers of French culture, including the independent newspapers and literary reviews, the *Académie Française* and the other branches of the *Institut de France*. Since the writing of history had long been considered within the competence of the amateur and the dilettante, the academic historians were much harder pressed than their brethren in other disciplines to achieve public recognition of their title to the exclusive patent on historical production. These nonacademic centers of historical writing formed a sort of counterintelligentsia outside the university. It differed from its academic counterpart not only in its methodological approach to historical study (by clinging to the old conception of history as a branch of art, literature, and philosophy rather than as a social science), but also in ideology (which tended toward conservatism and, in some extreme cases, outright antirepublicanism).[34]

The existence of an independent branch of the intelligentsia, which refused to endorse the prevailing methods and doctrines developed in the university, and which was engaged in the popularization of methods and ideologies overtly antagonistic to them, represented a stumbling block to the bold project of the academic historians and sociologists to establish *la science historique* and *la science sociale* as the twin keystones of the new republican orthodoxy. A successful campaign to restore an ideological consensus would be compelled either to silence the recalcitrant branch of the intelligentsia that proposed an alternative methodology or ideology, or to render it ineffective by stigmatizing it in the public mind as unworthy of serious consideration.

The academic historians' commitment to the liberal values of tolerance and intellectual freedom led them to choose the latter alternative. Caron and Sagnac spearheaded the attempt to challenge the scholarly credentials of those modern historians who dared to deviate from the methods and doctrines of the academic historical school. They attacked the commercially successful works of the historian Franz Funck-Brentano for adding nothing of value to the cumulative knowledge of historical scholarship. These and other such historical vulgarizations, they declared, were written "hastily, without criticism, with the purpose of lauding the *ancien régime,* in the most complete ignorance of the essential documents." They accused the directors of the Société d'Histoire Contemporaine, an organization of nonacademic historians founded in 1890 which competed with their own Société d'Histoire Moderne et Contemporaine, of selecting for publication in their society's journal documents which "inspire aversion for the men and the accomplishments of the Revolution" and give expression to the "counterrevolutionary passions" of the society's editorial board.[35] They had similar unkind words for literary periodicals that catered to the simple tastes of the general public and ignored the principles of scientific scholarship. These journals, they charged, publish book reviews that were products of "pure journalism" and thus "without scientific value."[36]

As disciples of Aulard, Caron and Sagnac felt obliged to deliver the *coup de grâce* to the most notorious scholarly threat to their master's historical interpretations of the French Revolution. They denounced as superficial the work of Albert Sorel and his pupil Albert Vandal, which disputed the conclusions of the Aulard school regarding the consequences of Revolutionary and Napoleonic policies,[37] and dismissed Louis Madelin's studies of the First Empire as undocumented exercises of the literary imagination.[38] They concluded that the study of modern history in France was divided into two competing schools, the one "confessional and often reactionary, conservative, always dominated by the name of Taine," the other "rationalist, attempting to apply to all subjects a rigorously objective method." Under the auspices of Aulard, they remarked, the latter group of historians had "completely renovated the political history of the French Revolution" during the past twenty years, and "totally reformed historical teaching" in the French universities by establishing the scientific historical method "founded on the reasoned and critical use of sources."

Sagnac and Caron declared that their purpose in founding the *Revue d'histoire moderne et contemporaine* had been to assemble "on a strictly scientific terrain and to the exclusion of simple amateurs," all the historians of the modern era who are committed to the "scientific method." They left no doubt as to where such scholars were to be found. While the "literary" historians at the *Institut* and its various academies have produced numerous works that are "too often strikingly mediocre," they declared, the historians in the university have already begun to study modern history in a "truly objective and scientific manner." Caron proudly observed that 86 of the 159 members of the Société d'Histoire Moderne were academics, a consequence, he assumed, of the "reputation of exclusiveness" enjoyed by the society on account of its bylaws, which exclude "popular historians and ordinary contributors to newspapers and periodicals with large circulations." The two editors lamented the continued presence and popularity of these

> subjective historians—we cannot say that they constitute a school, since with them everything is left to individual caprice, passions, and above all, the interests of the writers—those who consider history an art rather than a science, an exercise within the competence of any dilettante, and who, instead of confining themselves to the critical and exact determination of the facts, lose themselves in vain political or religious declamations.[39]

In an implicit reference to the commercial success enjoyed by Sorel, Vandal, Taine, Madelin, Funck-Brentano, and others, they complained that the works of amateur historians appeal to the general public because of their literary and artistic aspects which lead one to assume the existence of "serious substantive qualities." The survival of this unscientific spirit has thus produced a plethora of useless works of history that serve merely to encumber historical scholarship and complicate the task of the bibliographer. Caron and Sagnac attacked all historians who use a "philosophical system" to orient their scholarship in a "predetermined direction" and who permit themselves to "see the facts and read the documents only through certain forms of thought." They called upon all "objective historians" to resist the temptation to seek "laws of the general evolution of humanity" and to be content with the "determination of historical facts."[40]

They proudly remarked that the new generation of scholars who had received a "solid university education" were prepared to serve as an antidote to this discredited type of history writing, having been trained to be objective and to apply a precise method to their historical investigations. A few years later Aulard explained in greater detail how the academic historical profession would enforce the rules and regulations governing the scholarly treatment of the controversial events of the Revolutionary epoch. He noted with satisfaction that the works of Taine and other impressionistic historical studies by amateurs, dilettantes, and *littérateurs* had been thoroughly discredited by the young historical school that had gained control of the major periodicals and organizations of the profession, and declared that they would not be permitted to infect the minds of future scholars, as they had infected minds in the past. He even went so far as to decree that any candidate for the doctorate at the Sorbonne who dared to cite Taine as an authority on a question of historical fact would be disqualified. It infuriated him that the methods and doctrines Taine popularized still possessed great authority, particularly among the general public, which remained ignorant of the many defects of his scholarship.[41]

If modern history in general was subject to such exploitation by skillful dilettantes with a flair for the catchy phrase or the engrossing style, the history of literature had long been the most vulnerable prey of all. The function of literary criticism in France had traditionally been monopolized by the journalists and critics on the staffs of the independent reviews and dailies, and there was nothing to suggest that these gentlemen were prepared to surrender their ancient prerogative. But in the early years of the twentieth century the university began a concerted effort to absorb the tradition of literary scholarship. Gustave Lanson, a former protégé of the literary critic Ferdinand Brunetière who had graduated to the Sorbonne in 1900 after years of obscurity as a professor of rhetoric in various *lycées*, established a tradition of historical scholarship which sought to apply scientific standards to the history of literature and expose the unscientific nature of journalistic literary criticism. He complained that the history of literature had for too long suffered from an "excess of liberty" which enslaved it to the vagaries of "individual caprice." French literary criticism, he charged, has refused to recognize that "discipline, healthy discipline, [and] exact methods," are the sole means of comprehending and explicating works of literature. Frenchmen have for too long been wedded to the discredited tradition of deductive, impressionistic criticism, believing that "ideas," "logic," and a little "talent" are sufficient for writing such history. They have produced fantasies of historical interpretation which are models of Cartesian logic expressed in the most engaging of styles, but which contain little factual or truthful information about the authors being studied.[42]

Lanson was happy to announce that the history of literature was being transformed from a journalistic indulgence into an academic discipline, and that except for a few remaining "games of dilettantes" and "prejudices of fanatics,"[43] it was fast becoming a branch of social science. Like historical study in general, literary history had begun to draw inspiration from the principle of intellectual unity which affirms the existence of an objective, scientific conception of past reality that abolishes differences of interpretation and ideological preconceptions. There is no longer, he insisted,

> a science of party, a monarchist or republican, Catholic or Socialist science. All men from a given country who participate in the scientific spirit affirm thereby the intellectual unity of their father-

land. For the acceptance of a given discipline establishes a communion among men of all parties and all beliefs. The acceptance of the results produced by the loyal obedience to this discipline . . . and the acceptance of the sovereign arbitration of the methodological rules removes the bitterness from disputes and furnishes the means for putting an end to them.[44]

By acquiring a monopoly on the production of scientific works of historical, literary, and social criticism, and by defining the nature and scope of that criticism so as to exclude from consideration works that stray from the methodological and doctrinal orthodoxy that they had established, Lanson and his colleagues hoped to rely on the prestige of science to neutralize the threat to the new intellectual unity posed by the literary intelligentsia outside the university, which tended to line up on the political right.[45]

There was little need to go to such extremes to insure against the appearance of such criticism from within the academy, for the simple reason that decisions regarding appointment, promotion, and financial assistance for research purposes were made by ministerial committees dominated by the very men who were committed to maintaining the doctrinal and methodological orthodoxy of the reformed university.[46] This institutional encouragement of academic consensus was reinforced by another tendency at work in the French university. The contention of the Durkheimians and the solidarist philosophers that a division of labor in society was the firmest guarantee of the maintenance of social cohesion began to achieve widespread acceptance in university circles in the opening years of the twentieth century. But this doctrine of extreme specialization, as we have seen, had been applied to the intellectual labor at the Sorbonne for decades, particularly in the history department. It had long been an article of faith in the creed of the academic historians that monographic specialization was the ideal means of extinguishing the subjective prejudices of the individual scholar (thereby precluding his adopting impressionistic interpretations of the historical evidence that might conflict with the objective, scientific truth).

Such a policy appeared especially appropriate to the subjects of literature and modern history, which were particularly susceptible to the distortions of the *partis pris* of the individual scholar. "All our methods have been instituted to neutralize the deceptive powers that are within us," declared Lanson, referring explicitly to the history of literature. They help us to "separate the subjective elements from the objective *connaissances*," to "restrain" our imagination and "filter" out everything that prevents us from producing an "exact representation" of historical reality.[47] The function of such self-effacement, he asserted, was to reduce to an absolute minimum the part played by "personal sentiment" in a work of literary history. The scientific historian, therefore, must eschew broad, generalizing studies of past masterpieces in favor of "studies of manuscripts, collation of editions, discussion of authenticity and attribution, chronology, bibliography, biography, and the search for sources."[48]

Charles Victor Langlois, the most consistent defender of the event-oriented approach to historical analysis, pushed this notion of scholarly impersonality to its ultimate extreme. "I am more and more persuaded that the best method of communicating to the public the truly assimilable results of our research is not to write history books," he declared;

> it is to present the documents themselves, purified of the material faults that have crept into them . . . The man of today who writes about the past necessarily adds something to the document that he employs; but what? his personal reflections that he imposes on the reader. Now these reflections are both useless and dangerous . . . The true role of the historian is to put the people of today in contact with the original documents that are the traces left by the people of yesterday, without mixing anything of himself in them.

In any case the historian who insists on departing from the documents is "protected against his own imagination by the heap of incorruptible, immovable realities with which the *érudits* have furnished him."[49] It was passages such as these that moved subsequent critics of the scientific school of French history to accuse Langlois of "debasing history into mere erudition." A modern philosopher of history has complained that the eminent Sorbonne historiographer "no longer dared to write history at the end of his career, but was content to offer his readers merely a selection of facts . . . as if the choice of selected evidence were not already a very considerable intrusion of the author's personality, with his particular orientations, prejudices, and limitations."[50]

But Langlois and Lanson were not alone in promoting the ideal of scientific scholarship as an iron-clad guarantee against error, exaggeration, and speculative imagination. Even Ernest Lavisse, who could never have been accused of displaying caution or restraint in his own discursive expositions, did not hesitate to require such scrupulosity of his disciples. In his inaugural lecture at the official opening of the reformed Sorbonne in November 1896, he informed the assembled students that the price they would be expected to pay for the privilege of attending the revered center of higher learning was submission to the "scientific spirit," which he described as "the everpresent censor of our actions and our thoughts."[51]

Similar sentiments were voiced on behalf of *modern* and *contemporary* history by Caron and Sagnac, who insisted that in history as in other sciences the "division and specialization of labor" represented the most satisfactory means of forestalling the emergence of the idiosyncratic, speculative spirit that disqualifies much of the historical work carried on outside the university. They proposed that more reviews of "limited, highly specialized interest" be created in order to encourage this trend toward monographic specialization among modern historians, and urged scholars to divert more of their energy to such unexciting but necessary tasks as the compilation of bibliographical guides and manuals. In order to prepare prospective historians for the painstaking labor and self-abnegation that is required by the profession, they argued, the universities must devote less time to verbal lessons and more to textual criticism conducted in smaller classes wherein the student's scholarly work could be "directed, regulated, and oriented" by "authorized masters." Only in this way will a sufficient number of highly trained young *érudits* be available to produce historical work that is "methodological and collective, that is to say, fully scientific."[52] The old notion that a talented historian could single-handedly embrace and reconstruct a historical event or period was rapidly falling into disrepute.[53]

The conflict between such a restrictive conception of the historian's *métier* and his acceptance of a broader social obligation did not go entirely unnoticed within the historical profession, particularly in view of the recent criticisms directed at the positivist preoccupations of historical scholarship. In the concluding chapter of his massive *Manuel de bibliographie historique,* Charles Victor Langlois noted that several theorists of the social sciences had begun to accuse the academic historical scholars of failing to adapt their craft to the needs of the present by postponing indefinitely the establishment of general conclusions. They chided historians for posing "insignificant questions" and for avoiding those which admit of "general, scientific solutions that can be incorporated into Social Science." He conceded that historical scholars had tended in recent years to overlook the possible uses to which their labors might be put for the "advancement of the knowledge of man and the world."[54]

But Langlois did not hesitate to defend the historian's predilection for the monograph and his penchant for the irrelevant and inconsequential. Most historians pursue their scholarly endeavors for "the pleasure of working," he observed, insisting that "historical studies have a *raison d'être* within themselves."[55] The historical record comprises much material that lacks any apparent significance for modern man, yet the historian is "instinctively impelled to collect, with the same seriousness, all the traces that subsist."[56] He specifically dismissed Paul Lacombe's proposal that historians replace the indiscriminate approach of monographic scholarship with the search for institutional regularities that might yield generalizations of use to social science. Langlois accused the champions of "*l'histoire-science,* considered as an auxiliary to Social Science" of having substituted vain exhortations for serious efforts to put their theories into practice. "They have a persuasive and very engaging manner of saying, 'Let's get going,'" he declared, "but they are making no progress and are hardly attempting to make any." The most important accomplishments in the field of history, he concluded, were represented by the preparatory work undertaken by the dozens of anonymous scholars who have been laboring in the archives to "put the documents in a state to be utilized." This was the type of work that provided history with its justification for existence. The true task of the historian is to

> establish the authenticity of the documents, classify them, catalogue them, and then make a bibliography to orient scholars. France needs to make a collection of documents like the *Monumenta Germaniae Historica,* and fortunately we have vast permanent workshops in which certain texts are subjected to systematic scrutiny.[57]

Langlois had nothing but contempt for popular vulgarizations addressed to the general public, which displayed little interest in monographic scholarship. He labeled these works "'history books,' in the narrow and vulgar sense of the expression," which were produced for popular consumption and were usually replete with "impressions, judgments, and affirmations, [but] not proofs." Academic scholars ought to confine themselves to establishing the authenticity of archival documents and preparing them for future exploitation, and should resist the temptation to adduce sweeping generalizations and heuristic prescriptions from the evidence.[58] Hence, while the sociologists and a growing number of historians were beginning to conceive of the scientific approach to the study of history as a process of framing hypotheses and producing general conclusions, Langlois stubbornly clung to the old positivist definition of science that he had learned from the philologists, paleographers, and archivists at the Ecole des Chartes.

Langlois's plea that academic history confine itself to monographic analysis instead of venturing into the realm of social theory left him isolated among his colleagues. The French historians' success in establishing their craft as a major academic discipline by the end of the nineteenth century was hardly the type of experience that would inspire sentiments of humility and prudence. Moreover, their recent alliance with the sociologists had propelled them into the arena of social theorizing, and the Durkheimians had welcomed them into the fold and proclaimed the utility of the historical method in all fields of social research. Contrary to Langlois's advice, the first decade of the twentieth century marked the emergence of a concerted effort on the part of the university historians to convince their sister disciplines in the faculties of letters to accept the historical method as the methodological foundation of the social sciences and to adopt it in their own scholarly research. This campaign eventually resulted in what a contemporary observer described as an "invasion of history" at the Sorbonne.[59] In the very year that the last volume of Langlois' *Manuel de bibliographie historique* appeared, his associate Seignobos brought out his *La Méthode historique appliquée aux sciences sociales*, which rapidly became the bible of the new faith.

Seignobos hailed the recent unification of the formerly autonomous subdivisions of the humanities and social sciences in the Faculty of Letters. He considered the centralized university system an appropriate site for the establishment of a common set of methodological regulations to govern historical scholarship, particularly the more challenging operation of historical synthesis. He believed that such an assemblage of rules would complement the procedures established for the auxiliary sciences (philology, paleography, diplomatics, and so on) that had already refined the methods of historical analysis. But what seemed most promising of all to Seignobos was the potentially universal application that he envisaged for the historical method. Once it has been perfected, he asked, why should it be confined to the discipline of history? No social science can ever hope fully to comprehend social facts, he remarked, for a fact immediately becomes a past fact, leaving only a trace of its existence. All empirical knowledge about man's behavior in society is therefore historical. The historical method is, in effect, a general method of human reasoning that can be employed in the various disciplines of social science outside the realm of history.[60] He was convinced that he had discovered within his own discipline a universal method for comprehending human behavior that could liberate the human sciences from the confusion, uncertainty, and self-doubt in which they were currently floundering and place them on an equal footing with the sciences of nature. By avoiding the twin extremes of the positivists' indiscriminate collection of unrelated facts and the metaphysical speculations of the philosophers of history, he believed, the process of historical synthesis could establish a middle ground in which controlled hypotheses of historical development would produce universally valid generalizations about human behavior.

Earlier in his career, Seignobos had established a link between the historical method as he defined it and a particular branch of the empirical sciences. He divided the latter into two distinct groups, which he labeled, respectively, the "descriptive" and the "physical" sciences. To the latter category he assigned mathematics and physics, both of which, he claimed, belong to the realm of human thought that deals with an eternal reality that is absolute and unchangeable, and can be designated symbolically by formal mathematical symbolism (such as that employed by analytic geometry or calculus). Geology, botany, and zoology, on the other hand, since they deal with an evolving reality, with phenomena that are transformed by the development of time, employ the same "indirect" or "descriptive" methods of history. Whereas the physical sciences deal with the "eternal present," the descriptive sciences confront the constantly evolving present, which instantly becomes the past.[61]

Seignobos therefore regarded the historical method as the organizing principle of this second type of scientific reasoning. The process of evolution that underlies the descriptive sciences is continuous (whether in the historical, geological, botanical, or zoological domain). It can therefore be assumed that present experience (that is, in the case of history, the historian's present as represented by his understanding of his own culture and society) is directly connected to the historical experience that he is attempting to recapture. The basis for this continuity is the absolute, unchanging nature of human thinking. Though the epiphenomena of social, economic, religious, and political institutions emerge, evolve, and decline in the historical process, the phenomenon of human thought is a constant throughout history. The historical observer is therefore justified in using the analogical method to understand the past.[62]

For Seignobos, the laws established by psychology to describe the mechanism of human thought constituted the surest guides to assist the historian in his task of historical understanding. He must seek to uncover the psychological processes that motivate the behavior of historical actors.[63] The documents studied by the historian are mere "symbols" which are "useful only through the mental operations that they produce, through the images that they evoke."[64] The historian of medieval labor history, for example, "does not see a single worker or a single tool of the Middle Ages; he operates only on the images that these things represent in his mind, and he represents them only by analogy with the workers and the implements of the present world that he knows to be analogous."[65]

Seignobos came to believe that by borrowing selected concepts from social psychology, the historical method can become the universal method of social science. Indeed, he had long been convinced that it was "the sole method [that is] applicable to all the descriptive studies of social and psychological phenomena." It is appropriate "not only to the so-called historical sciences, which deal with past phenomena," he declared, but also to "whoever is studying human societies, [whether past or present]."[66] Even Langlois, who stubbornly denied that historical study was capable of discovering regularities of human behavior that could be reduced to explicit scientific formulations, was sympathetic to the historians' desire to embrace the totality of human experience. Part of the reason for the popularity of history, he conceded, was the universal desire to "know scientifically the origins and genealogy of what is" and to discover "the modes if not the laws of becoming."[67] Though he sternly disapproved of efforts to employ history for such purposes, he understood the motivations of the leading academic historians in France who, during the first few years of the twentieth century, had begun to build bridges to the major theoretical social sciences, sociology and psychology, with the intention of establishing a unified science of human behavior in France.[68]

If the improved relationship between history and the newly-established social sciences resembled a marriage of mutual convenience, history's position vis-à-vis the older, humanistic disciplines of the Faculty of Letters could more accurately be described as one of systematic usurpation. The study of theology had succumbed to the hegemony of the historical method even before the advent of the academic historical profession, during the period when the biblical criticism of Ernest Renan subjected the masterpieces of Judeo-Christian thought to the iconoclastic scrutiny of historical analysis. This trend was accelerated by the anticlerical attitudes and policies of the Third Republic. The University of Paris, which had begun as a theological college and achieved early notoriety largely owing to its theological scholarship, had abolished its Faculty of Catholic Theology altogether in 1885.[69] So discredited was theology as an intellectual discipline that it became virtually moribund until the revival of Thomist thought in the twentieth century under the auspices of Jacques Maritain.[70]

Philosophy, the ancient queen of higher learning, which had been under attack from the scientific school of historical scholarship throughout the last half of the nineteenth century, also suffered a dramatic decline in prestige. It must have seemed to many French academic philosophers that the new schools of history, sociology, and psychology were hovering around its decaying carcass eager to carve out what each regarded as its deserved share. But while the historians had already established a firm antiphilosophical position which they were only beginning to moderate, the latter two social sciences had frequently emphasized their kinship with the philosophical tradition. Many of the pioneers in both sociology and psychology had been trained in the arts of Minerva, as we have seen, and their conversion to these newly-established fields of study did not require a repudiation of their intellectual origins.[71] Indeed, the two dominant philosophical traditions in France, the Cartesian rationalism inherited from the golden age of French thought and the Kantian idealism introduced by Renouvier after 1870, were both much more compatible with the theoretical, generalizing spirit of the new sciences of man than they were with the more empirical, a posteriori approach of academic history. Durkheim and the other founders of French sociology who had been nurtured on philosophy unabashedly acknowledged the influence of Descartes, Kant, Renouvier, and the solidarist philosophers. Both Durkheim and his associate Célestin Bouglé frequently invoked the authority of philosophy to buttress their sociological doctrines. The latter declared that academic sociology was serving to renovate French philosophy and described the new social science as a "philosophical effort" to produce an explanatory theory of human development.[72]

That the philosopher Emile Boutroux, perhaps the most respected living symbol of the resistance to the positivist methods of history in the French university,[73] received the dedication of Durkheim's *Division of Labor in Society* and was named the first president of the Ecole des Hautes Etudes Sociales suggests the esteem in which philosophy was held by the promoters of the new social sciences. It was the theoreticians of scientific history, not the champions of academic sociology and psychology, who had insisted not only on transforming philosophy into the history of philosophy, but also on stigmatizing its methodology as a metaphysical, unscientific remnant of a bygone era that could contribute little to a deeper understanding of man and his place in society.[74]

For the most part, the academic philosophers, who had long been fighting to protect the independence and integrity of their discipline against the progressive encroachments of the academic historians, eagerly grasped the hand of friendship that was tendered by the social scientists. While the antagonism between history and philosophy persisted, the sociologists and philosophers forged a working alliance that strengthened the position of both disciplines. Though some historians, as we have seen, were beginning to conquer their traditional distrust of theory, most philosophers continued to view the historical method that had been developed in the French universities as a challenge to the philosophical approach to human questions and therefore a threat to the vitality of French learning. And as the number of university chairs in history began to increase in direct proportion to the decline in the number of chairs in philosophy at the turn of the century,[75] an intense professional rivalry heightened the bitterness of the epistemological dispute between philosophy and history.

The most convincing exposition of the philosophers' case against history as the basis of modern education and scholarship appeared in a highly polemical work entitled *La Réforme de l'enseignement par la philosophie,* by Alfred Fouillée, the prematurely retired philosopher who had influenced Durkheim and the solidarists. Fouillée, whose theory of social causation emphasized the determinative role of ideas in human development,[76] believed that a carefully organized system of education was absolutely essential to the dissemination of those ideas that the state considered important from the national point of view. "Education should not be a simple acquisition of knowledge," he had earlier declared, "but a cultivation of living forces with a view to assuring the supremacy of the highest idea-forces *(idées-forces).*[77] In regard to the achievement of this objective, Fouillée was convinced, like Nietzsche,[78] that the historical approach to education was a fraud, and that history had totally forfeited its right to replace philosophy as the foundation of higher culture and learning. "The historical method, improperly erected into a universal method" of education and scholarship, he boldly asserted, has constituted the greatest intellectual error of the nineteenth century.[79] He recalled the years after 1870 when France had been in dire need of an educational policy aimed at "positive reconstruction" that would bind the spiritual wounds and restore national self-confidence. Philosophy might well have been expected to furnish the intellectual basis for a positive, integral doctrine that would unite Frenchmen and give them faith in the future of their nation, he observed. But instead, the educators and scholars of the French University fell under the influence of the "critical, negative, and destructive" spirit of scientific history, which contributed to a trend toward "universal disintegration" that had a disastrous effect on the formation of young French minds.[80]

Part of the explanation for this pervasive "intellectual anarchy" and "skepticism," Fouillée believed, resided in the inherently contradictory proposition that an integral doctrine of education and scholarship could be based on the lessons of history. The assumption that precise analogies can be drawn between past and present events, as well as the claim that prediction of the future can be based on observation of the past, were both central to the argument that the historical method represents the appropriate pedagogical tool for restoring intellectual unity to French culture. Yet the French historians' acceptance of the Germanic, "evolutionary" conception of historical reality as "eternally moving" and "forever changing," Fouillée argued, belies their affirmation of the integrative function of historical study. No science, in the proper sense of the term, can be founded on "the particular and the ephemeral," he pointed out, yet historians persist in rooting their educational philosophy in just such shifting sands.[81]

He claimed that the scientific historians themselves had become plagued with second thoughts about their claim to the title of educators of the French nation after coming to realize "the vanity and the inutility of their 'science.'" He charged that the familiar positivist justification of historical study as the search for "the facts" of the past has become a half-hearted defense, since the historian now recognizes that his perception of the past is distorted by "the ideas and sentiments of his epoch," and that it is only through his "political, religious, economic, or moral" preconceptions that he comes into contact with "what he calls the facts."[82] He reminded his Gallic readers that the homeland of the so-called science of history across the Rhine had produced a "school of lies in which the patriotic end justifies the means," and noted that in French schools an objective approach to the study of the past had become impossible because the putative lessons of history that the historian adduces are merely expressions of his personal, subjective opinions. "If he is a monarchist, he [the historian] will demonstrate to you through history the danger of republics; if he is a republican, the dangers of monarchies." From the moment that the historian ventures to elicit an instructive conclusion or develop a heuristic generalization from the infinite mass of facts that constitute the historical evidence, he has departed from history properly so-called and is expressing ideas, declared the philosopher of the *idée-force*. There is no more ideological science than history, and there is no science which "deals less with facts."[83]

Fouillée argued that historians have sought to evade the disquieting implications of this situation by rushing off in two opposite directions. One group, which believes in the possibility of reconstructing past reality through the use of imagination and thought, yet which is intent on minimizing the distorting influence of subjective personal preferences, has been forced into an increasing reliance upon the theoretical schema, ideal types, and paradigms employed by sociology. The only value of history thus conceived, he declared, is in "furnishing sociological solutions." Another group, concerned about preserving the historian's self-image as the impartial collector of the facts of history, has retreated even further into a preoccupation with the "more or less unimportant details of monographic scholarship," thereby transforming history into a sort of "navigation without a compass on an ocean of facts without a law." How, he asked in an earlier work, can one expect to derive meaningful guides to thought and action from a discipline that is swamped by "the details of dry and *ipso facto* uninteresting facts"? Those who have opted for the former escape route, he contended, have tacitly conceded the subservience of history to the theoretical social sciences. Those who have chosen the latter have merely accentuated the trend toward the isolation of history and the disintegration of French social thought. But the salient point was that both trends struck Fouillée as indicative of history's incapacity to provide intellectual sustenance to minds that were becoming increasingly "devoid of directing principles."[84]

Having made short shrift of history's claim to pedagogical utility, Fouillée proceeded to reassert the competing claim of philosophy. Instead of encouraging the parrot-like memorization of facts, names, and dates, and instead of "crushing individuality under the weight of a mnemonic erudition and a bookish science," a philosophically-based education would require reflection, inventiveness, and above all, speculative imagination. Whereas today's historical specialists have "cut the tree of science from its roots in order to gather the immediately edible fruits," philosophy has retained its interest in the universal and profound aspects of human existence. It alone is capable of providing rational precepts to mankind in the postreligious era which avoid the twin pitfalls of excessive specialization and ideological polemic. Fouillée hoped that philosophy and its recent offsprings, sociology and psychology, would succeed in wresting control of French education from the historians. The twentieth century would thenceforth abandon its preoccupation with the past and concentrate on the present and future and would soon become "the century of social science." Moreover, this alliance of philosophy and social science would be uniquely capable of successfully combatting the antidemocratic tendencies that had begun to threaten the moral unity of the French Republic. Philosophy and social science can provide "the veritable civic and democratic education," because they introduce "unity, simplicity, and generality" in the educational process. Unlike history, which bores students with its dreary litany of unconnected events, a philosophically-based social science will be capable of "provoking interest and even enthusiasm" in the students. Nothing, he concluded, in a ritualistic genuflection to French *amour-propre,* could be more appropriate to the fatherland of Descartes.[85]

Such bold reassertions of philosophy's role in French education and scholarship grew out of the eagerness on the part of many French philosophers to identify their ancient discipline with the emerging school of modern social science, and of the social scientists' reciprocal willingness to embrace the philosophical tradition that had been repudiated by the academic historians. As a result of this mutual cooperation, French philosophy succeeded in retaining its position as a respectable field of study in the modern university, while the social scientists of the Durkheim school, in the words of Henri Peyre, "oriented French sociology, for better or for worse, toward philosophy."[86]

But during the very period that the philosophical tradition was recovering from the half-century long effort of the scientific school of academic history to supersede it, the historians had already launched a new campaign to annex another discipline in the Faculty of Letters. It was a year before the publication of Fouillée's denunciation of the historical method and its pretensions to universal applicability that Gustave Lanson was summoned to the Sorbonne to extend the scientific historical method to the field of literary studies. As we shall presently see, this attempt by the university historians to absorb the literary tradition in France was confronted with two institutional stumbling blocks. The first was the persistence of the tradition of classical learning in the Ecole Normale Supérieure and in the system of secondary education, both of which institutions had retained a certain measure of independence from the centralized educational apparatus that had been constructed during the past quarter century. The second was the bevy of *littérateurs* who had succeeded in preserving the classical literary tradition outside the university structure.

The academic historians had traditionally dealt with this latter group of writers either by ignoring them or by ridiculing their work as unscientific, impressionistic, and subjective. Their independence and prosperity were guaranteed by their close connections with the world of Parisian journalism, the literary reviews, and the custodians of classical culture in the *Institut*. But the other barrier to the absorption of literary criticism by the historical method—the classical tradition that had been preserved in the Ecole Normale and the *lycées*—was susceptible to a direct and decisive assault. Ever since 1863 students in secondary education had been able to enroll in a special section concentrating on science and modern languages, but were still held responsible for the classical subjects included in the examination for the *baccalauréat*, the qualifying degree for entry into higher education. Critics had been hammering away at the inferior position of the modern curriculum in the *lycées* and the privileged status of the Ecole Normale throughout the last quarter of the nineteenth century.[87] The culmination of this campaign came in 1902, when the modern curriculum attained legal parity with classical studies in secondary education. Obsolete literary subjects such as rhetoric were downgraded, and a year later the Ecole Normale was deprived of its autonomy and absorbed by the University of Paris.[88] Durkheim's course in scientific pedagogy, now open to *normaliens*, began to attract prospective *instituteurs* who might have taken more traditional courses in earlier days. Ernest Lavisse, who had received what he regarded as an insufficiently scientific education at the rue d'Ulm forty years earlier, was named director of the revamped school. The battle lines had been drawn between scientific scholarship and classical culture, and it quickly became evident that the opening skirmish in the struggle between these two competing intellectual traditions would be fought over the issue of secondary education, which until 1902 had succeeded in preserving the classical curriculum of the *ancien régime*.

The educational reformers of the Third Republic did not shy away from this inevitable confrontation with the classical curriculum of the *lycées*. Indeed, they welcomed it, for they realized that if they were to succeed in establishing a new scientific morality in modern France, they would have to deprive the secondary schools of their traditional autonomy and renovate the pedagogical methods and curricula that predominated there. They had already succeeded in transforming the universities and the elementary schools into their image of a modern educational system,[89] and had long complained that the nature and objectives of education in the *lycées* was totally at variance with the reigning educational philosophy. The curriculum was dominated by the traditional subjects of a classical education—Latin, Greek, rhetoric, and philosophy—and virtually no attention was paid to modern subjects such as geography, living languages, and science. This classical curriculum had originally been designed to accommodate the needs of the predemocratic age, in which a tiny elite of leisured gentlemen constituted the educated class. Acquaintance with the literary masterpieces of Greco-Latin antiquity (preferably in the original language) and familiarity with general philosophical concepts, aesthetic taste, logical thinking, and precision in expression were deemed sufficient preparation for adult life.[90] The wisdom of the ancients was thought to represent a better guide for conduct in the modern world than anything developed in the intervening centuries. The defenders of this venerable system of secondary education had come to regard it as the last remnant of classical culture to resist the onslaught of academic barbarism that had already triumphed in university circles. In the words of an alumnus of the exclusive *lycée* Henri IV who was later to become the literary editor of the *Revue des deux mondes*, nothing was "less *scolaire*, in the narrow sense of the term," than the classical education offered at the Parisian *lycées*, and nowhere was there a more conspicuous absence of the type of "absurd, narrow, boring, pedantic men" who had recently gained control of higher education.[91]

The architects of university reform waged an uninterrupted war against what they considered the obsolete, unscientific program of French secondary education throughout the first decade of the twentieth century. Even the passage of the Education Reform Act of 1902, which deprived Greek and Latin of their privileged status in the *lycée* curriculum and greatly weakened rhetoric, did not blunt their criticism.[92] As late as 1910 Lavisse was warning incoming Sorbonne students that they were "leaving the hands of distinguished humanists [in secondary education], whose lessons you must now forget in order to become scientists."[93] Seignobos continued to inveigh against the remnants of the verbal and aristocratic approach to learning that persisted in secondary education. By stressing rote memorization of texts and placing a premium on rhetorical and stylistic perfection at the expense of a "direct view of realities," he complained, the *lycées* continued to produce an elite of refined dilettantes, while neglecting the important task of preparing the average student for the practical skills required by modern industrial society. He praised the recent reforms for introducing the "modern idea of practical scientific education," which he saw as merely the first victory in the important campaign to transform French learning from a system serving "a clerical and aristocratic society that wished to form priests and gentlemen" into one appropriate to the democratic system of the twentieth century which must strive to produce "citizens and workers."[94]

Durkheim was also active in the campaign to replace the old aristocratic system of secondary education with a program that was better suited to an industrial system and a democratic political order. In a course entitled The History of Teaching in France, which he conducted during the 1904–1905 academic year, he took note of the intellectual disarray of secondary education, remarking that no new faith had emerged to replace the recently displaced classical tradition. He accused the secondary education system of overemphasizing verbal and rhetorical skills and denounced it for perpetuating the archaic notion that the ability to explicate literary masterpieces represented the most important indication of intelligence. "To acquire science," he pointed out, "is not the same thing as acquiring the art of communicating it." He protested that the formal exercises that constituted such an important part of the *lycée* education in no way contributed to the understanding of human nature, since they encourage abstract thought which has no relation to "a determinate object." "One does not reflect in a void," he announced. Correct ideas can arise only from "putting the intellect in contact with reality." The two objects to which "it is possible to attach thought" are man and nature, yet neither are dealt with by the traditional classical disciplines. The latter is within the sphere of competence of the physical and natural sciences, while the former belongs to the science of man.[95]

Durkheim, therefore, agreed with Seignobos that humanistic education could justify its existence in the modern world only by demonstrating its usefulness in preparing students for the social reality that they would confront as citizens. This would require the abandonment of the traditional type of classical education, which strove to impart general culture instead of preparing students for specialized careers in modern society. Instead of seeking to provide citizens with useful knowledge in a particular *métier*, it sought to form Renaissance men. "Man is socially useful," Durkheim declared, "only if he assumes his share of the common work, that is to say, if he practices a profession." By emphasizing practical, technical subjects rather than a diffuse, ambiguously defined general culture, education must train the future citizen and worker to perform precise tasks that will be required of him in the complex industrial system he is about to enter.[96]

Such specialized training would serve not only to improve the opportunities of each citizen to achieve a secure position in the socioeconomic system, but also would strengthen the cohesiveness and moral unity of that system, which, according to Durkheimian theory, was a function of the division of labor.[97] The worker who knows his precise position in the complex hierarchy of the social organism understands what is expected of him in the performance of his social function, for which he has been specially trained. He will thereby be more apt to regard his individual destiny as indissolubly linked to the social collectivity. As a consequence, he will be less likely to suffer from the anomic *malaise* that afflicts individuals who have not been adequately prepared to occupy a particular position in the labor force of society and who are therefore unable to become integrated into the social organism.

Alfred Croiset proposed a similar model of utilitarian education. He recognized the need to replace the antiquated ethical doctrines of Christianity and classical culture with a modern system of scientific education. The underpinning of the new system, of course, was to be the ideas derived from the French Revolution. But he warned that those individualistic principles must be tempered by an emphasis on the importance of mutual cooperation and social harmony. Individual initiative and self-reliance must be encouraged, since they are the motor of political and economic progress, but they must not be permitted to prevent the coordination of activities in the interest of the common good. "The isolated man is nothing," the dean of the Sorbonne observed. "He is worth something only through his union with the society of which he is a part." The necessary solidarity among the citizenry is the primary source of consensus and social cohesion.[98] A system of secondary education which prepares the student for his specialized social and economic role is therefore an essential institution in modern industrial society.

The classical system of learning that had dominated the *lycées* for centuries was wholly inappropriate to this new conception of the goal of secondary education. The principal objective of classical learning—the dissemination of general culture, the formation of what the French writers of the seventeenth century called *l'honnête homme* (the well-rounded gentleman)—was a reflection of the classical view of human nature as a fixed, invariable essence unaltered by influences of time and place. The generalizations about man that were first proposed by the Greek and Roman humanists of antiquity were thought to be universally and eternally applicable. This humanistic world view was especially appealing to Frenchmen, since they had long been taught to regard their native culture as the heir to classical civilization. Its timeless verities had been enunciated by the ancient Greeks, diffused throughout the Western world by the Romans, rediscovered by the Italian humanists of the Renaissance, and ushered into the modern world by the French writers of the seventeenth and eighteenth centuries.

It was precisely this special claim to universality and eternity that the historians and sociologists of the Sorbonne were seeking to discredit. Durkheim contended that classicism rested on two erroneous assumptions concerning the nature of man. The first was that human nature is always and everywhere identical and does not admit of essential variations according to different historical periods and geographical milieux. It was this belief in "one single form of mentality and morality for the entire human race," he pointed out, that constituted the immovable rock upon which the philosophes of the seventeenth and eighteenth centuries based their abstract, a priori speculations. The second assumption was that the philosophy and literature of Greco-Roman antiquity express timeless, universally valid truths about the human experience that cannot be superseded and therefore constitute the best possible guides for present behavior.[99]

Durkheim explained that both axioms of the classical creed are defective because they reduce man to his logical aspect alone and fail to consider him as a historically determined phenomenon. He called for the adoption of a revised conception of man together with up-to-date methods of teaching it, declaring that the classical view of human nature was incompatible with the "recent results attained by the historical and social sciences." He boldly asserted that the ancient belief in the immutability of human nature had been demolished by the lessons of history, which reveal that mankind has undergone such profound transformations that it is both superficial and misleading to speak of "man" in a general, universal sense. Since history demonstrates that there have been as many ethical systems as there have been types of societies, modern man must abandon the notion of that "abstract and general man" that represented the ideal type of the seventeenth century and strive to penetrate the extreme complexity and variability of human nature as it has been manifested in different periods and places.[100]

Durkheim also urged modern scholars and educators to discard the obsolete conviction that universal principles of human behavior were definitively expressed for eternity in the writings of classical antiquity. To hold to such a belief would require that one efface the imprint of time and detach those writings from the particular milieu that produced them. Historical scholarship has revealed that the social ideals of ancient Greece and Rome were parochial, temporary values that reflected the particular social conditions that prevailed in a given time and place. Classical culture, he declared, must be regarded as a product of history that was gradually constructed over an extended period of time rather than as a spontaneously generated standard of human conduct of eternal and universal applicability.[101]

Durkheim's major complaint about the classical view of man was that it was totally devoid of pedagogical utility. Its dependence on Greek and Roman models of thought and behavior prevented the student from confronting the vast "spectacle of the diversity and infinite variability of human nature." But he was even more alarmed about what he considered its implicit ideological assumptions that rendered it incompatible with the spirit of democratic society. A doctrine which conceives of human nature as part of a static reality of arrested forms that can be "expressed once and for all in a formula" implies that man has already attained the limit of his creativity and is condemned to repeat himself to perpetuity. This view of human nature, communicated to the future members of France's intellectual elite through the secondary education system, has encouraged them to regard existing social institutions as indestructable and to distrust any attempt to modify them as an "unrealizable and dangerous utopia."[102]

Durkheim voiced the hope that this discredited humanistic conception of man as a finite, limited entity would be replaced by the view of man established by recent historical research, which has shown that humanity is susceptible to infinite variation and transformation. With the aid of historical study, he proclaimed, we must convey the conception of man as an "infinitely flexible and Protean force, capable of assuming the most diverse forms, under the pressure of constantly changing circumstances." By demonstrating that existing social institutions were products of a particular period and particular conditions and will give way to others in due course, history confronts the student with the reality of gradual, evolutionary improvement. Such a doctrine will encourage a sanguine faith in orderly progress without inspiring "revolutionary intemperance," since it teaches that every historical transformation has taken place with great difficulty and has been accomplished "under the empire of necessity."[103]

This evolutionary, Whiggish conception of human history was an appropriate social theory for the Radical Republic. It sanctified the tradition of moderate progress under the benevolent tutelage of the democratic state and rejected the twin extremes of revolutionary socialism and the reactionary ideologies of the latter day defenders of the *ancien régime*. Accordingly, Durkheim regarded the evolutionary, historical conception of human nature as a useful tool in democratic education. By dramatizing both the possibilities and the limits of human progress, a historical education inculcated the twin virtues of flexibility and patience. The historical sciences and the social sciences, he declared, are intimately linked in this enterprise, and share a common purpose: the discrediting of the classical view of man, and the suppression of the educational apparatus that perpetuated it.[104]

The new emphasis on practical, specialized, and utilitarian education during the first decade of the twentieth century in France seemed to herald a retreat not only from classical humanism, but from the hallowed tradition of Cartesian rationalism as well. In a speech entitled "The Needs of Democracy in Matters of Education," Alfred Croiset explained why Frenchmen must liberate themselves from their past reliance on the *esprit de finesse* of Cartesianism in order to become "rigorously realist." He scolded Frenchmen for their aptitude of generalizing which frequently impelled them to ignore the hard, crude facts. "We love general ideas. Scattered facts do not interest us," he lamented. "We are eager to derive from the facts a system which we strive to make clear, logical, harmonious, in conformity with an ideal of geometric or classical elegance that we carry within us." Frenchmen, he remarked, are infatuated with words and ideas without realizing that words are only symbols and ideas are of value only by their "conformity with things."[105] Both words and ideas tend to conceal reality from us, he warned. One cannot attain "realistic knowledge *(savoir réellement)*" merely by creating impressive logical or verbal constructions, but rather one must attempt to "penetrate deeply into reality, to model one's ideas on this reality." In order to accomplish this feat of historical understanding, we must begin in a "state of preliminary submission" to the facts instead of seeking to "accommodate the facts to our fantasies and passions." We must resist the temptation to construct philosophical systems that coordinate facts and give them meaning. Our taste for classical regularity too often tempts us to construct too hastily an "elegant and fragile edifice of ideas."[106]

Similar expressions of this narrowly empiricist conception of scientific historical study continually cropped up in the writings of the academic historians in France. In a speech entitled "The Scientific Spirit and the Method of Literary History," Gustave Lanson remarked that it is not certain procedures that historians must borrow from the natural sciences, but rather their spirit, which he described as "disinterested curiosity, severe probity, laborious patience, and submission to the fact." Despite the many differences that distinguish scientific history from the sciences properly so-called, he declared, the single common denominator is that "our object is the facts, . . . present and past reality."[107]

Such an attitude represented a reaction against the two major traditions of historical writing that had preceded the scientific historical tradition in France: the generalizing, a priori, rationalist school of the eighteenth century, personified by Voltaire, and the subjective, impressionistic, Romantic school of the nineteenth century, represented by Michelet. Both were guilty, in the eyes of the modern historians, of seeking to impose their own principles and values upon the raw data of history. Yet, as we have seen, the university historians themselves were hardly ideological eunuchs. They not only subscribed to particular political beliefs with varying degrees of enthusiasm, but were committed to communicating those beliefs to their students.[108] How could these men comfortably combine an austere devotion to the facts with a commitment to defend and promote the principles of republicanism and democracy in their classrooms?

In a lecture entitled "The Unity of Principles in Public Education,"[109] Dean Croiset provided a suggestion of how these seemingly conflicting callings might be reconciled. He again took note of the deplorable absence of guiding principles in the Third Republic, and suggested that more energy be expended to ensure that the appropriate values be communicated to French youth through the schools. "Every regime has attempted to make the ideas upon which it was founded prevail in public education," he observed. But because they were usually too blatant in their attempt to compel adherence to their ideas, past regimes have tended to bring about the opposite result from the one intended. The clerical education of the eighteenth century produced the deistic and agnostic philosophes, the Napoleonic *Université* nurtured the Restoration liberals, the Voltarianism of the July Monarchy provoked the clerical reaction of the 1850s, and the Second Empire spawned a generation of republicans. As an astute student of history, Croiset rejected the idea of establishing an official ideology for the Third Republic, an "orthodox history, an orthodox philosophy . . . a scientific doctrine controlled by the state" as an unnecessary affront to the principle of intellectual freedom that was, in any case, likely to breed opposition.[110]

Yet Croiset was by no means prepared to promote a neutral approach to education whose guiding principles would be "submerged in insignificant facts." While avoiding the more blatant types of propaganda, he declared, public education must nevertheless propose to the student an ideal and a faith lest it abandon him to a life of nihilism. And the only ideal that could escape the distorting influences of personal prejudices is that of science. "The love of scientifically established truth" is itself an admirable principle of education, he asserted. It is wrong to regard the methods and objectives of science as something dry and cold.[111] Science is an ideal capable of inspiring the "purest and most powerful enthusiams" in the young citizen of French democracy. "The almost religious love of scientific truth," he announced,

> raises minds that are otherwise rather ordinary above themselves and communicates to them a grandeur which they would seem incapable of at first glance. That scientific faith, furthermore, is essentially republican and democratic . . . since the republic and democracy must be regarded as a social state in which the progress of all is assured by the free exercise of thought.[112]

Croiset was satisfied that the history teacher who relies on the principles of science as a pedagogical tool has no need to present his students with dogmatic judgments about the past in order to convince them of the superiority of democratic institutions. A simple narrative of the significant historical facts, bereft of any preestablished hypothesis, would accomplish the same objective. Suppose the teacher is explaining Luther and Calvin, the eighteenth century, and the Revolution, he proposed.

> If he is a democrat and a republican, as I hope he is, he has no need to produce grand theories which would prove nothing. Democracy is a fact; let him analyze the deep-seated causes that have produced it, . . . let him make [the student] grasp the historical reasons that have rendered the Republic possible and necessary. Let him make the student see the facts clearly. The conclusions will automatically follow. No sermon, however eloquent, is more valuable for the formation of minds and practical efficacity than the simple exposition of well-established facts.[113]

No society has ever been able to maintain itself without relying on a moral system, he declared. But the "law of fraternal and republican solidarity," the doctrine of civic morality that we must communicate to our young generation, must be taught in a positive and scientific spirit, based on the facts of history. "The more the ideal derives from the facts," he concluded, "the more education will be positive." Thus, the teacher is provided with the means to escape the Scylla of a state doctrine and the Charybdis of total neutrality by relying solely on the facts established by scientific history. It is in this way that we can most effectively contribute to "the progress of democracy and the Republic."[114]

Gustave Lanson repeated this familiar litany in a speech calling for a "national education with a scientific basis." He noted that the goal of humanistic education should be to service the needs of democracy by producing citizens who possess "love for the laws and the fatherland." Since the teacher is forming not only minds, but also citizens, he must provide a "moral and social commentary" on the assigned readings. But no sermons are necessary; indeed, he must scrupulously avoid the temptation to surrender to the spirit of dogmatism and to engage in fanatical proselytism. His principal concern should be to disengage and develop certain *hautes leçons* from the readings through a process of historical explanation. Lanson even went so far as to suggest that grammatical study could be put to "the service of democracy."[115]

But it was Durkheim, of course, who displayed the most unshakable faith in science as the principal source of moral instruction. Morality is first and foremost concerned with reality, he announced in his Sorbonne lectures on the science of education. "The actions it demands of us concern beings and things that actually exist around us. Consequently, . . . the clearer our notion of reality, the more apt we are to behave as we should. It is science that teaches us what is. Therefore, from science, and from it alone, must we demand the ideas that guide action, moral action as well as any other."[116]

It was not a simple matter for the Sorbonne reformers to cover themselves with the mantle of science in order to demonstrate their relevance to modern democratic society. They had themselves received conventional classical educations, and had been trained in the humanistic disciplines. None, with the notable exception of Langlois, had enjoyed the benefits of specialized instruction in the Ecole des Chartes or the Ecole Pratique. Aulard and Lanson were former professors of rhetoric, Lavisse and Monod were *normaliens* trained in traditional prescientific disciplines, and Croiset was a classical scholar. For such men of letters to gain public acceptance as scientists necessitated a wholesale repudiation of their intellectual origins.

Ernest Lavisse, a product of a classical *lycée* training and an equally literary and classical education at the unreformed Ecole Normale, led the scramble for rehabilitation. In a self-deprecating oration appropriately entitled "Souvenirs d'une éducation manquée," he dutifully recited a tale of regrets about his own intellectual training. He confessed that years of immersion in the classics had left him without "a precise knowledge of anything," since no one had ever bothered to explain to him the pedagogical value of the compulsory exercises in Greek and Latin translations. He had learned to despise philosophy for its lifeless abstractions, and rhetoric for compelling him to deliver polished, convincing, and persuasive recitations on people and events he scarcely understood. He was discouraged from cultivating an interest in science since it was distrusted and relegated to an inferior level in the curriculum.[117]

Lavisse dismissed his preparation for the *baccalauréat* at the Ecole Normale as a "wasted year." The most promising students in his *promotion* were compelled to concentrate on literary or philosophical subjects, since little else was available to them. After declaring history as his major field, he was given assignments on complex historical subjects without ever receiving any instructions about how to explicate a historical text or determine its authenticity. The possibility of applying scientific methods to historical research was never broached, since history was universally considered a branch of literature. While other students enjoyed observing old Louis Pasteur at work in his laboratory, Lavisse lamented, he and his fellow *littéraires* had been conditioned to dismiss such empirical procedures as inappropriate to historical research.[118]

It was the recognition of these glaring defects in their own education, Lavisse declared, that had motivated the members of his generation to mount the recent campaigns to reform secondary and higher education in France. Using the revamped university as the focal point for these reforms, he and his colleagues were injecting the classical methods and curriculum with a lethal dose of the scientific spirit in order to "protect the new generations from the errors of which they [the members of his own generation] were the victims." Describing the conflict with classical education as "the quarrel of the ancients and the moderns," he insisted that such a goal could be accomplished by causing the scientific spirit of the university to penetrate every aspect of education.[119]

Similar confessions of wasted schooldays and defective preparation were to emanate from other converted *littérateurs* within the course of the decade. In an article also entitled "Une Education manquée"—the similarity of language almost suggests a prior coordination of efforts—Alfred Croiset asserted that his revulsion against the mandatory exercises in Latin discourse was so intense that it turned the future Hellenist and Sorbonne dean into an unenthusiastic, undistinguished student.[120] Gabriel Monod seldom missed an opportunity to express his disdain for the unscientific approach to historical scholarship and teaching of two *littérateurs* and former luminaries at the rue d'Ulm whom he had once called *maître*, Michelet and Fustel de Coulanges.[121] Lanson, who as late as 1894 was still ridiculing the notion of applying scientific methods to the history of literature,[122] did public penance at a banquet of the Société de l'Histoire de la Révolution in the spring of 1906. As a "professor of rhetoric and a *littérateur*," he declared at the beginning of this speech, "I am ashamed to speak to you of historical work, of the historical method. Finding myself beside my dear colleague, Aulard, whom I love and venerate for the fine model of scientific life that he offers to all studious men, I sense how insufficient is my right to be here." His only consolation was to recall that Aulard himself, the man who for the past twenty years had done so much to establish the scientific approach to the study of the Revolution, was also a former rhetorician. "What a rehabilitation for professors of rhetoric," he exclaimed. "And what a lesson!"[123] For his part, Aulard was only too willing to disown the written work of his prescientific period. In the 1905 edition of his earlier treatise on the orators of the French Revolution, the book that had been responsible for his selection as the first occupant of the new Sorbonne chair in Revolutionary history, he confessed that he had approached his subject from a literary point of view and remarked that, were he to rewrite the book, he would employ a more rigorous method, provide more extensive documentation, and strive to attain "a more objective impartiality."[124]

There was a distinctly political flavor to the *universitaires'* indictment of the literary tradition that had been rooted out of higher education during the nineteenth century and was in the process of losing its position in the secondary schools. The epithets "clerical" and "aristocratic," which Seignobos frequently hurled at the old system, were juxtaposed against references to "democratic society," "citizens," and "workers," which he applied to the new. His objectives were to remind the French public that the literary tradition of French education was a surviving remnant of the *ancien régime* and to establish a link between scientific education and democratic society. For he recognized that while the discoveries in the physical sciences had established their social utility and had therefore gained the support of "public opinion and the public powers," the social sciences "do not have practical applications in the ordinary sense" and hence are in a less favorable position. He therefore regarded it as vitally important for the future of his profession to discover practical uses to which "the study and the teaching of the sciences of man can be put."[125]

Seignobos presented a defense of social science that he felt would appeal to the public powers in a democracy. He maintained that the citizens of a democratic society require an educated elite to tutor them in the requisite civic responsibilities. Man is by nature "neither liberal nor democratic nor rational," he noted, but rather is "authoritarian, aristocratic, mystical . . . naturally conservative, inclined to respect the powers, beliefs, and privileged [positions] established by tradition."[126] In order to preserve public faith in the democratic ideals of freedom and equality, he declared, a continuous effort would be required to combat the natural conservatism of man. The educators whose function it is to form citizens of a democratic polity will have to develop a clear understanding of the "instincts, passions, prejudices, and habits of humanity" in order to liberate modern man from his own instinctual limitations. It is this necessity to defend the values of democracy and science against the forces of tradition which, in Seignobos's eyes, justified the study of social science in a democratic nation.[127] The scientific study of human institutions, therefore, implied not the unprejudiced search for truth, but rather the creation of a blueprint for inculcating students with a preordained set of verities revealed by the enlightened educational elite of the nation, whose mission it is to rescue the citizenry from the darkness to which it has been consigned by its human frailties.

But Seignobos worried that the French public might be left with the impression that the *universitaires* themselves belonged to an exclusive mandarinate, a misconception that could jeopardize their reputation as promoters of the democratic idea. Whereas the philosophers and historians of the Enlightenment had prepared the way for the democratic revolutions of the eighteenth century, he noted, the literary elite of the nineteenth century had come to despise democracy, fearing the untutored barbarians who, once enfranchised, would proceed to destroy the social institutions devoted to the preservation of "the higher life of the intellect." In response, the common people understandably came to regard humanistic culture as "a luxury of privileged men who need the support of an aristocratic society." It is no wonder, he concluded, that the people have occasionally viewed higher education with suspicion and hostility. He was surprised that democracy has not displayed even more rancor toward it.[128]

The democratic masses had already learned to accept the existence of a scientific tradition because of the material benefits that they received from scientific research. Seignobos was convinced that the humanities and social sciences could win similar public approval by renouncing their ties to the literary tradition (which was identified in the public mind with the frivolous, aristocratic education of dilettantes) and by identifying with the scientific tradition, which was regarded as an ally of modern democratic society.

> Perhaps the "Sciences" [which have] always [been] popular, have covered "Letters" with their prestige. But since the direct sympathy of the public powers alone can assure the future of our establishments, it would be imprudent to allow them to be taken for luxury institutions, remnants of an aristocratic regime. On the contrary, we must emphasize the services that they can render in preparing intelligent servants of democracy.[129]

We began this chapter by remarking that the domestic tensions that gripped France during the Dreyfus Affair presented the French academic historians with a dilemma. Should they strive to preserve their intellectual purity by maintaining a position of strict neutrality in the contemporary ideological warfare that threatened the unity and viability of the Third Republic? Or should they attempt to demonstrate the relevance of their scholarship to the problems of modern French society by placing their services at the disposal of the republican state, even at the price of betraying their obligation to the higher truths of science? Their solution to this problem was very similar to the manner in which they resolved the conflict of science and patriotism that we examined in Chapter 5. The historians in the immediate postwar period had resolved the inherent contradiction in their professed objectives by insisting that patriotic instruction and the promotion of the scientific spirit went hand in hand because the national interest of France and the objectives of modern science were identical. Similarly, the historians of the early twentieth century established a connection between the epistemology of science and the political system of democracy. Instead of directly confronting the dilemma posed by their conflicting allegiances to science on the one hand and politics on the other, as contemporary social scientists such as Max Weber were doing in Germany, the French historians reiterated their earlier denial that such a conflict existed.

By the end of the first decade of the twentieth century, the influential historians in the French universities had succeeded in broadening the scope of the historical method to include virtually all the branches of the sciences of man, a strategy which received the tacit support of their former competitors, the sociologists. But their efforts to introduce the historical method to the discipline of literature provoked an unexpectedly vigorous opposition from the traditional defenders of French letters. As the citizens of what they proudly regarded as the motherland of literary culture in the Western world, Frenchmen took great pride in their literary tradition, which continued to flourish in the twentieth century as a result not of governmental subsidy or academic encouragement, but of public patronage. The independent band of *littérateurs* who operated out of the *Institut* and its various academies, the Parisian newspapers, and the literary reviews, the members of that branch of the French intelligentsia that observers were fond of calling "the Republic of Letters," stubbornly resisted the incursion of the historical method into their traditional domain. In the eyes of many of them, the university historians' attempt to establish the universality of the methods of scientific history, as well as the effort to use the tools of their craft for political purposes, represented a serious threat to the viability of French culture in the modern world.

The most memorable criticism of the reformed university and its resident historians on behalf of the literary intelligentsia flowed from the pen of an independent-minded writer who had prematurely ended his student career at the Ecole Normale after two years of intellectual and spiritual deprivation. Despite his disillusionment with French higher education, Charles Péguy did not regard his departure from the university in the autumn of 1897 as a final repudiation of his education heritage. He intended to return at some future date to complete his formal academic training and fulfill his dream of occupying a university chair after a much-needed respite to think and write on his own.[130] He subsequently submitted a proposal for a thesis topic at the Sorbonne which was ambitiously entitled "De la Situation faite à l'histoire dans la philosophie générale du XIXe siècle."[131] As a perceptive member of the postwar generation, he was acutely aware of the important place that history had occupied in the transformation of French intellectual life since 1870. Though he never returned to resume work toward his doctoral degree, his interest in this proposed thesis topic never waned. Many of the lengthy, rambling articles that appeared in the *Cahiers de la quinzaine,* the fortnightly review that he founded at the turn of the century, were fragmentary attempts to redeem his earlier pledge to explain the influence of historical writing on the *Weltanschauung* of nineteenth century France. That he chose to evaluate the legacy of professional history in France from the vantage point of an academic drop-out operating out of a tiny bookshop in the shadow of the Sorbonne rather than as a dutiful disciple of an eminent *universitaire* was itself a reflection of his contempt for the practitioners of what he called *la science historique moderne.*

The bill of particulars of Péguy's indictment of the academic historical profession constituted, in large measure, a repetition of the criticisms that had previously emanated either from dissident members of the profession or from philosophers and social scientists who resented history's preeminence in the university system. His denunciation of the "presumptuousness" of the historians for seeking to comprehend the infinite complexity of past reality through the examination of the surviving documents,[132] his complaints about their preoccupation with the insignificant details of historical research at the expense of a deeper understanding,[133] and his indignant refutation of their claim that the methods of the natural sciences could be transported to the historical sciences,[134] revived objections that had already been raised elsewhere by the turn of the century.

What distinguished Péguy's counteroffensive against the tradition of historical learning in France were two novel allegations. Whereas earlier critics had derided the academic historical profession for spawning a generation of narrow-minded pedants isolated in the ivory tower with their noses riveted to the scholarly grindstone, Péguy was among the first to accuse the university historians of the opposite sin. Following their admirable intervention on the side of the Republic during the Dreyfus Affair, he charged, the intoxicating effects of political influence and power had caused them to abandon their former commitment to scholarly disinterestedness and objectivity. Their science had degenerated into a rigid ideological doctrine that served the interests of the regnant regime, and they shamelessly used their power to grant scholarships, degrees, and promotions, together with their contacts with their political allies, to reward younger scholars who subscribed to the tenets of their school and to punish those who did not.[135] But the second and most ominous aspect of Péguy's assault on the university historians was his description of the new republican ideology that they were busy promoting as a subversive, German-inspired threat to French culture and tradition, a charge that surely must have startled those academic historians who had labored to establish their discipline as the keystone of the postwar patriotic revival.[136]

Péguy's record as a personal friend and ideological ally of the politically advanced members of the university, together with his continual reaffirmation of his loyalty to the Republic, placed him in a curiously ambivalent position. His tirades against the "intellectual party" were the anguished protests of a disillusioned devotee of the republican mystique who felt betrayed by his former comrades-in-arms, whom he accused of abandoning the cause of truth and justice in favor of a cynical scramble for position and power. His isolated position between the Radicals, who controlled the governmental machinery after 1902, and their enemies on the right, who were seeking to dislodge them, left him politically unaffiliated, without a large constituency among the French public. As one biographer put it, Péguy was "an alumnus of the Ecole Normale without a degree, a professor without a chair, a master without disciples, a leader without followers, a poet without readers, a publisher without clients, a socialist without a party, an orator without an audience and a mystic without religion."[137]

The practical consequence of this public pose was the lasting impression of a cranky, idiosyncratic, ineffectual voice of despair which proposed no coherent ideology that could move men to action, save a sort of purified republicanism that struck many observers as the unrealistic pipe dream of an incurable mystic. Péguy's inability to situate himself precisely on the political spectrum and his unwillingness to recruit an organized political following diminished the effectiveness of his critique of the French university and its historical tradition. When he fell at the battle of the Marne at the beginning of the First World War, he died a prophet ignored, a critic unheeded.

It was not until the appearance of the antirepublican, unabashedly royalist movement L'Action Française that a systematic, ideological campaign was mounted against the academic intelligentsia. The new movement was fortunate to have secured the services of a veteran member of the *Université*, Pierre Lasserre, who undertook the assignment of spearheading the royalist onslaught against the republican university during the decade before the First World War. Speaking with the authority of one who, unlike Péguy, had received numerous academic honors, studied with the university's most illustrious members, taught in secondary schools for a decade, and completed a doctoral thesis at the Sorbonne, Lasserre subjected his former mentors and colleagues to a barrage of criticism from his influential post as a regular contributor to the movement's daily newspaper and an occupant of an "endowed chair" in the Institut d'Action Française, a sort of royalist Sorbonne financed with private funds.

From the spring of 1908, when he joined the editorial staff of the royalist journal, to his departure in the summer of 1914, Lasserre played the role of the royalist Pied Piper of the Latin Quarter, attempting to entice Parisian students to spurn their professors at the republican university and march to the tune of L'Action Française. As the resident *universitaire* of the movement, Lasserre pursued his youth crusade with a vengeance. During the winter of 1908–1909, he delivered over thirty lectures from this chair at the Institute in which he exposed what he called "The Official Doctrine of the University."[138] He waged an extended campaign in the daily newspaper against some of the most notable (and in his view, notorious) historians at the Faculty of Letters, accusing them of abandoning the sacred tradition of French letters for the subversive doctrines of German science.[139] In 1909 he took revenge on Dean Alfred Croiset of the Sorbonne, who, with Aulard, had irreparably damaged his academic career by denying him the requisite *mention très honorable* at his thesis defense. To the delight of antirepublican students throughout the Latin Quarter, he published a putative exposé of the scholarly deficiencies and political fanaticism of the revered Hellenist.[140] He argued the royalist case against the university at numerous public debates before youthful audiences frequently numbering in the thousands. The content of his addresses seldom departed from a single theme: the necessity to root out the nefarious methods and doctrines that had infiltrated French higher education through the mediation of the Durkheimian social scientists and the scientific historians.[141]

The hinge on which Lasserre hung his indictment of the "official doctrine" of the reformed university was the alleged threat that it posed to the classical culture of France. The frequency with which the dichotomy of the modern (or scientific) and classical (or literary) traditions appeared in his writings signified that the royalist movement's opposition to the republican university had crystallized around the issue that had divided the French intelligentsia since the furor concerning the Educational Reform Act of 1902: should France replace her tradition of classical learning with a modern approach that incorporates the doctrines and methods of social science and scientific history? By posing as the defenders of classical culture, Lasserre and the other members of the Action Française were able to acquire a measure of respectability in the eyes not only of impressionable young denizens of the Latin Quarter seeking a cause to defend, but also of many nonroyalist members of the French literary intelligentsia who were intent on preserving the cultural tradition on which they had been nurtured. That such eminent representatives of the literary world as Proust, Gide, Apollinaire, Valéry, Malraux, and Thibaudet could speak highly of the literary doctrines of the Action Française is dramatic testimony to the efficacy of its appeal.[142]

Pierre Lasserre may have been the most persistent, prolific, and outspoken critic of the historians and social scientists of the French university to emerge from the ranks of the rightist literary intelligentsia in the decade prior to World War I, but his was by no means an isolated voice of discord emanating from that political and cultural milieu. On the contrary, it would hardly be an exaggeration to say that the university was subjected to an uninterrupted cacophony of criticism from the intellectual spokesmen for political and literary conservatism ever since it declared its republican sympathies during the Dreyfus Affair and openly acknowledged its positivist and modernist prejudices during the campaign for educational reform. Owing to the efficiency of its organization, the enthusiasm of its adherents, and the air of intellectual certainty that informed its ideology, the Action Française paced the other rightist groups in this offensive against the modern spirit and institutional innovations of the New University. Charles Maurras, Lasserre's superior in the royalist movement, seldom missed an opportunity to give the "Sorbonnards" what he considered to be their just due, though his scattered writings on the subject were characteristically weighted more heavily on the side of invective and *ad hominem* denunciation than on the side of doctrinal or methodological criticism.[143] The latter obligation was frequently discharged by Lasserre's former classmate Louis Dimier, an art historian and former *lycée* professor who conducted a vitriolic propaganda campaign against the academic historical profession in the royalist Institute, of which he was the director. Dimier set out to rectify what he described as the university's attempt to distort French history,[144] and sought to identify the reactionary ideology of the Action Française with the teachings of French historians whom he identified as counterrevolutionary precursors of the movement, including such luminaries as Taine, Renan, and Fustel de Coulanges.[145]

A second group of writers in the authoritarian-nationalist camp, though not orthodox royalists in the strict sense of the term, echoed many of the criticisms that Lasserre and the Maurrasians had been directing at the political doctrines and positivist methods of the French University. Ever since the publication of his influential novel *Les Déracinés* (which recorded the fictional tribulations of seven youths who were torn from the nourishing traditions of provincial life and deposited in the desiccating milieu of the Latin Quarter), Maurice Barrès had been on the warpath against academic scientism, which he saw dissolving the affective bonds that tie men to each other, to their native province, and to the memories of their ancestors.[146] His fellow novelist Paul Bourget was a frequent defender of the traditions of classical learning and Catholic morality and a persistent detractor of the positivist spirit of academic social science, not only in his novels,[147] but also in the occasional guest lectures that he delivered at the Institut d'Action Française.[148] Henri Massis, a converted Catholic writer and future disciple of Maurras, caused a momentary furor in prewar French intellectual circles with a spate of articles and books (written in pseudonymity with Alfred de Tarde in the name of "the youth of today") which denounced the scientific spirit of French higher education and called for a return to the teachings of the classics and the church.[149] Even before his brief flirtation with French royalism prior to the First World War, Georges Sorel, who invariably sat next to Péguy at Bergson's Friday afternoon lectures at the Collège de France,[150] expressed antipathy for the "intellectualist," "positivist," and "scientific" tradition that had overtaken academic history in France during the past half-century,[151] and denounced the "oligarchy of *érudits*," who "flatter the popular masses in order to dominate the state."[152] Jules Lemaître and Ferdinand Brunetière, who were, with Emile Faguet, the reigning masters of French literary criticism at the turn of the century, both displayed a marked hostility to the academic intelligentsia and the political ideology and scholarly methodology that it promoted.[153]

It was no mere coincidence that, with the exception of Péguy, the most outspoken critics of the university in the literary world became sympathizers of L'Action Française. Once the most prominent historians and social scientists of the university chose to identify their scientific educational innovations with the cause of the Radical Republic, it was understandable that the luminaries of the ancient literary fraternity should react to what they regarded as the usurpation of their traditional role by gravitating to the only major political movement that espoused the cause of literature against science and the cause of the French fatherland against the "destructive" forces of Radical republicanism.[154] Nor was it coincidental that the bulk of the literary intelligentsia sided with the enemies of the Republic during the Dreyfus Affair and its aftermath. For once the *littérateurs* perceived the new republican consensus that was being sought by the academic intelligentsia and its political allies as a threat not only to the religious and military traditions of France, but also to her tradition of classical culture, it was inevitable that they would cast their lot with the priests and soldiers who were struggling to preserve the remnants of the *ancien régime* in the hostile environment of the modern world. The "Republic of Letters" and what Albert Thibaudet was to call the "Republic of Professors" continued to coexist in an atmosphere of mutual recrimination until the summer of 1914, when both groups joined the sacred union of all Frenchmen that a foreign threat alone could create and sustain.

Epilogue

We began this study by detailing the process whereby the ancient art of history writing, which had long flourished in French culture as an avocation of amateurs and an adjunct of literature and philosophy, was gradually severed from its traditional connections, transformed into an academic profession, and hailed as the keystone of the human sciences in the reformed French university. We explored the dynamic tension between these somewhat grandiose hopes of establishing history on a scientific footing and the parallel ambitions of the university historians to serve first as the catalysts of a renewed national self-confidence after the humiliation of 1870, and later (in partnership with the sociologists) as the promoters of a refurbished political ideology for twentieth century France. We concluded our treatise with a cursory reference to the growing criticism of the methods, the doctrines, even the spirit of the New University, and its historical profession in particular, that had begun to emerge from within the ranks of the literary intelligentsia after the turn of the century.[1]

It is important to bear in mind that much of the opposition to the new tradition of historical scholarship in the French university was prompted by motives that were primarily ideological in nature. Charles Péguy, for all his claims to the title of a free-floating spirit devoted solely to transcendent and eternal truths, was fired by more parochial loyalties to church and fatherland. Nor could the numerous efforts by fellow *littérateurs,* after Pierre Lasserre's break with L'Action Française, to portray the former royalist militant as an impartial devotee of higher values succeed in effacing the antirepublican, anti-Semitic tone of his prewar attacks on the university.

But to recognize the ideological motivations of the most vociferous critics of that institution does not automatically absolve it of all responsibility for the heated controversy that engulfed it in those years. On the contrary, it is difficulty to avoid drawing the conclusion that the university historians unwittingly contributed to their own vulnerability to the immoderate and often unjust criticism from their detractors on the right by their own exaggerated and premature assertions that they had developed an objective method of scientific analysis that would banish subjectivity from historical scholarship. It required only a modest expenditure of effort on the part of their political enemies to strike a damning balance sheet contrasting the bold professions of scientific impartiality that adorned their programmatic manifestoes and public pronouncements with the egregious absence of it in much of their written work.

The burden of redeeming the pledges made in the name of their profession was not a light one, yet they appear to have borne it with relative ease. In spite of their conflicting prescriptions for the proper uses and objectives of historical study and the assaults mounted against them from outside the profession, all of which might easily have given rise to troublesome uncertainties and self-doubts about the nature of their mission, one cannot help but receive the impression of a serene self-confidence among the leading academic historians of France at the point at which this study concludes. Yet, in retrospect, the years of the First World War must be viewed as a concluding chapter in the story of the era that has served as the subject of this book. By the time hostilities had ceased, it had become evident that the tradition of historical learning established by the professional historians during the past five decades had been transformed in several important respects. The first illusion to be dispelled in the heat of world conflict was the unqualified assumption that the modern historian had achieved a level of impartiality that shielded him from the distorting influences of patriotic feeling. Like their counterparts in Germany, the French historians rapidly abandoned their prewar commitment to higher truths in the summer of 1914 and surrendered to the basest form of jingoist hysteria during the next five years. The xenophobic tone of their wartime writings, particularly those of Aulard and Lavisse, belied their earlier projects for international brotherhood and understanding, as well as their devotion to historical objectivity.[2]

In the course of the 1920s, another prewar illusion that had been entertained by the French academic historians began to crumble. The old program for the establishment of a republican consensus on the basis of the lessons of history began to receive, for the first time, a challenge from intellectual critics on the left. After the Russian Revolution and the appearance of a Communist movement in France, a new generation of leftist historians, inspired by Aulard's erstwhile protégé Albert Mathiez, began to criticize the underlying assumptions of republican history, particularly those that had postulated a historical connection between the doctrines of the French Revolution and the ideology of the Radical party.[3] These renegades on the left, whose base of operations remained within the university, were soon joined by a group of journalists and free lance writers outside the university who attacked the university historical profession from the vantage point of the right. Jacques Bainville, Pierre Gaxotte, Louis Bertrand, Franz Funck-Brentano, and other adherents or sympathizers of the French royalist movement exploited their own personal connections with well-heeled Parisian publishing houses such as that of Arthème Fayard and pandered to the French public's taste for popular history to bring out a series of commercially successful works whose unmistakably royalist coloration did not prevent their authors from achieving both commercial success and a respectable position in the French literary world.[4]

Of even greater significance was the more broadly-based reaction against the positivist methods of historical scholarship that set in during the interwar period and quickly spread to every corner of the French academic world. Though the revolt against positivism appeared much later in France than it did in Germany and Italy, it swept across the French intellectual landscape like a forest fire once the first spark had been ignited. When the French historians who had survived the war began to reconstruct the shattered edifice of historical scholarship in their country, as H. Stuart Hughes has recently observed, they sought to emulate not the founding fathers of the academic historical profession treated in this study, but rather two writers who had never acquired a large following in prewar university circles: Jules Michelet and Henri Berr.[5] The latter's *L'Evolution de l'humanité*, a collaborative, multivolume series of general histories which was launched in 1913 and began appearing in 1920, achieved for this early and largely unheeded critic of positivist methods and the monographic approach to historical study the universal respect that had been repeatedly denied him before the war. The impulsion to go beyond the documents, together with the urge to conquer the distrust of historical generalization, both of which had led Berr to found his *Revue de synthèse historique* at the turn of the century, were much in evidence in the works that appeared in his series. This was synthetic history at its best, animated by a passion for recapturing the complexity of past epochs through the broad sweep of historical narrative.

But it was left to two early contributors to the *Revue de synthèse historique* and the *Evolution de l'humanité* collection, Marc Bloch and Lucien Febvre, to spearhead what Hughes has called a "full-scale assault on the citadels of French historiography."[6] In their early writings they had already begun to address topics that their forebears in the historical profession had eschewed—psychological states of mind, collective memories, religious experiences, and other historical phenomena whose traces cannot be discovered in documents alone but must be recreated in the mind of the historical investigator through a process of imagination and intuition.[7] A decade after Berr had launched his collaborative enterprise, Bloch and Febvre founded the *Annales d'histoire économique et sociale,* and proudly acknowledged the editor of the *Revue de synthèse* as their intellectual godfather. Febvre later observed that "the renovation of historical studies in France was paradoxically the achievement of a literary man enamored of philosophy who, owing to these tendencies, was able to escape the narrowness and limitations of the spirit of specialization." As for the theoretical and methodological contributions of his predecessors in the academic historical profession, the editor of the *Annales* could scarcely conceal what seem to be his rather unduly harsh disapproval.

> Always the same idea; the facts, the little pieces of the mosaic, totally distinct, totally homogeneous. An earthquake has dislocated the mosaic; the pieces are buried in the ground; let's dig them up and above all be careful not to miss a single one. Collect them all, no need to chose among them . . . Our masters said these things as though . . . all history writing were not a process of choice . . . A historian who calls for the pure and simple submission to the facts, as if the facts were not of his own creation, as if they had not been selected by him . . . does not deserve to be considered a historian.[8]

The new review was soon to restore France to the front ranks of historical scholarship in the Western world by liberating French history from the positivist strictures and monographic proclivities of its recent past. It assembled historians, economists, sociologists, and other social scientists for an exchange of views on a broad range of substantive and methodological questions relating to historical problems.[9] But the leadership of the *Annales* took pains to ensure that the new group would not become merely the latest gathering of academic specialists sequestered from external influences in the privacy of their studies. Lucien Febvre in particular was anxious to emphasize the utility of history to the society in which it is written, and to repudiate the professional historian's tendency to isolate himself from the general public under the pretext of striving for scientific accuracy and scholarly integrity. He proudly described his celebrated biography of Luther as a work of "popularization," and pointedly reminded the professional historian of his obligation to address himself to the general public in order to prevent journalists and amateurs from stepping in to meet the need.[10]

Somewhat later, a third aspect of the French academic historical tradition gradually began to come under attack. The *universitaires'* tendency to ignore the issues raised by the philosophy of history —most conspicuously, the problem of historical knowledge and its limitations—received its first major challenge in the late 1930s, when Raymond Aron's writings on the subject inspired a growing interest in the epistemological problems that historians across the Rhine and the Alps had been wrestling with for decades. With the appearance of Henri Irenée Marrou's *De la Connaissance historique* in 1954 (the year of Henri Berr's death), the philosophy of history had fully regained the respectable position in French intellectual discourse that it had occupied in the first half of the nineteenth century. Questions of historical periodization, the relation of hypothesis to fact, and the possibility of scholarly objectivity once again became the subject of investigation.

Finally, the new generation of French historians gradually began to reveal an additional shortcoming in the earlier approach to historical analysis, namely, the preoccupation with political events at the expense of an adequate understanding of the underlying social and economic processes. The political orientation of the founders of professional history in France was an ineluctable consequence of their conception of the nature and purpose of historical study. It flowed directly from their preoccupation with elucidating historical events through an examination of the documents that record them, for most memorable events are political in nature (wars, peace conferences, changes of regime, and so on) and the most reliable documents that preserve them for posterity generally exist in governmental archives. Similarly, their willingness to use the lessons of history to instill patriotism and, later, republican loyalty, in French school children led them to attach greater significance to political developments. Seignobos himself conceded this bias in 1924 in the preface to his *Histoire politique de l'Europe contemporaine,* observing that the war and its aftermath had obliged historians to recognize the extent to which "the superficial phenomena of political life" were merely the tip of a vast iceberg composed of "the profound phenomena of economic, intellectual, and social life."[11] The preliminary groundwork for a systematic investigation of the socioeconomic substructure of French history had been laid during the quarter century before the war. Jaurès convinced the Chamber of Deputies to finance the retrieval and accumulation of documents relating to social and economic developments during the French Revolution. The historical writings of Jaurès, Henri Hauser, Emile Levasseur, and a handful of other pioneers anticipated the great socioeconomic studies of modern French historiography, while *La Revue d'histoire des doctrines économiques et sociales* (founded in 1908 and renamed *La Revue d'histoire économique* in 1914) began to consider historical questions that later dominated the pages of the *Annales*. But aside from these few exceptions, the French historical profession turned a collective deaf ear to the controversies of a socioeconomic nature that were currently raging in the German universities. The appearance of a French Sombart, Weber, or Troeltsch had to await the advent of the interwar period, when Bloch, Febvre, and Ernest Labrousse established social and economic history on a firm footing and demonstrated the limitations of conventional political history.

The historians in this study who lived on into the interwar period, such as Seignobos, Lanson, Lavisse, and Aulard, saw the historical doctrines that they had formulated come under attack for ideological reasons from both left and right, saw their positivist conception of historical methodology subjected to severe criticism from historians such as Berr, Febvre, and Bloch as well as from philosophers and social scientists outside the profession, and saw their interest in political history superseded by a new preoccupation with understanding the broader, socioeconomic processes of the past. It is possible that they experienced the feeling of regret that often haunts intellectual innovators at the end of their careers, when they begin to witness the supersession of their pioneering work by their successors.[12]

But if such was their sentiment, it was not entirely justified. For the new course that the academic historical profession embarked upon after the First World War came close to fulfilling at least one of their earliest and fondest dreams: that of establishing history as a highly respected discipline in the French university. The renaissance of French historical studies in the interwar period was a result not only of the tireless labors of the scholars of social history at the *Annales*, the economic historians working with Labrousse and others, and the historical synthesizers surrounding Berr, but also of the disarray in which academic sociology found itself in the twenties and thirties. The Durkheimian school had suffered a noticeable decline in vitality and coherence after the loss of more than half its members on the battlefield and the death of its guiding spirit in 1917. *L'Année sociologique*, the official mouthpiece of the sociological profession in France, appeared only twice throughout the 1920s—the first postwar issue in 1925 and a sparse volume in 1927—and then discontinued publication altogether. In the next decade the *Année* group split into five sections, each dealing with a separate branch of social research. These centrifugal tendencies impeded the sociologists' attempts to maintain a coherent point of view and, more important, to recruit followers to carry on the tradition, with the result that the better students in the social sciences tended to flock to other disciplines.[13] Just as the sociologists had capitalized on the weaknesses of academic history in the prewar era to advance their own professional ambitions, the historians became the principle beneficiaries of sociology's crisis in the interwar decades.[14]

But while the historians moved in to fill the vacuum that the sociologists had left, they did so not by reasserting history's former claim to autonomy as an academic discipline and to the uniqueness of its methodology. Instead, they resolved to build bridges to the social sciences and to integrate their methods and approaches into historical study. Whereas American historians and social scientists continue, for the most part, to coexist at swords' point, their French counterparts have tended to emphasize their areas of mutual agreement and to minimize their differences. The result has been decades of reciprocal cross-fertilization to the benefit of both disciplines, without the customary apprehension that such cooperation would compromise the professional goals for which each had fought with such determination.

It is too early for a definitive judgment regarding whether the historical school treated in this study can be credited with having inhibited or contributed to the revival of historical studies in modern France. Did the members of that school unwittingly perform a disservice to the scientific historical tradition by burdening it with a conception of the scientific method which, being defective, delayed its acceptance in French culture? Though this remains a distinct possibility, I am inclined to adopt the tentative view which emphasizes the continuity between the founders of the academic historical profession in France and the heirs to that tradition in the interwar period. Moreover, it seems possible to detect evidence of the duration of their influence long after the Second World War as well. For an important part of their legacy continues to thrive in the study rooms of the sixth section of the Ecole Pratique des Hautes Etudes, which was established under Febvre's leadership in 1947 as a center for scholarly research where historians and social scientists could assemble under the same roof in pursuit of a common goal. The enormously prolific and influential group of scholars who have gathered there represent the finest tendencies of historical scholarship and social research. By avoiding the twin extremes of a propensity for unsubstantiated speculation and excessive generalization (which their professional forebears combatted so tenaciously and effectively throughout their careers) and the commitment to a narrow, indiscriminate empiricism (to which the historians discussed in this study frequently succumbed), and by refusing to view their work as the scholarly adjunct of some political, patriotic, or moral ideal, the *érudits* of the *sixième section* may have begun to approach the elusive goal that escaped their predecessors: that of transforming history into something approximating a science. That the bold but premature hopes of the scholars who founded the historical profession in the French university a century ago have come closest to realization under the auspices of the institution that represented the earliest fruit of their reformist impulse is perhaps the most dramatic and appropriate monument to their great vision.

Appendices
Notes
Works Cited
Index

Appendix A

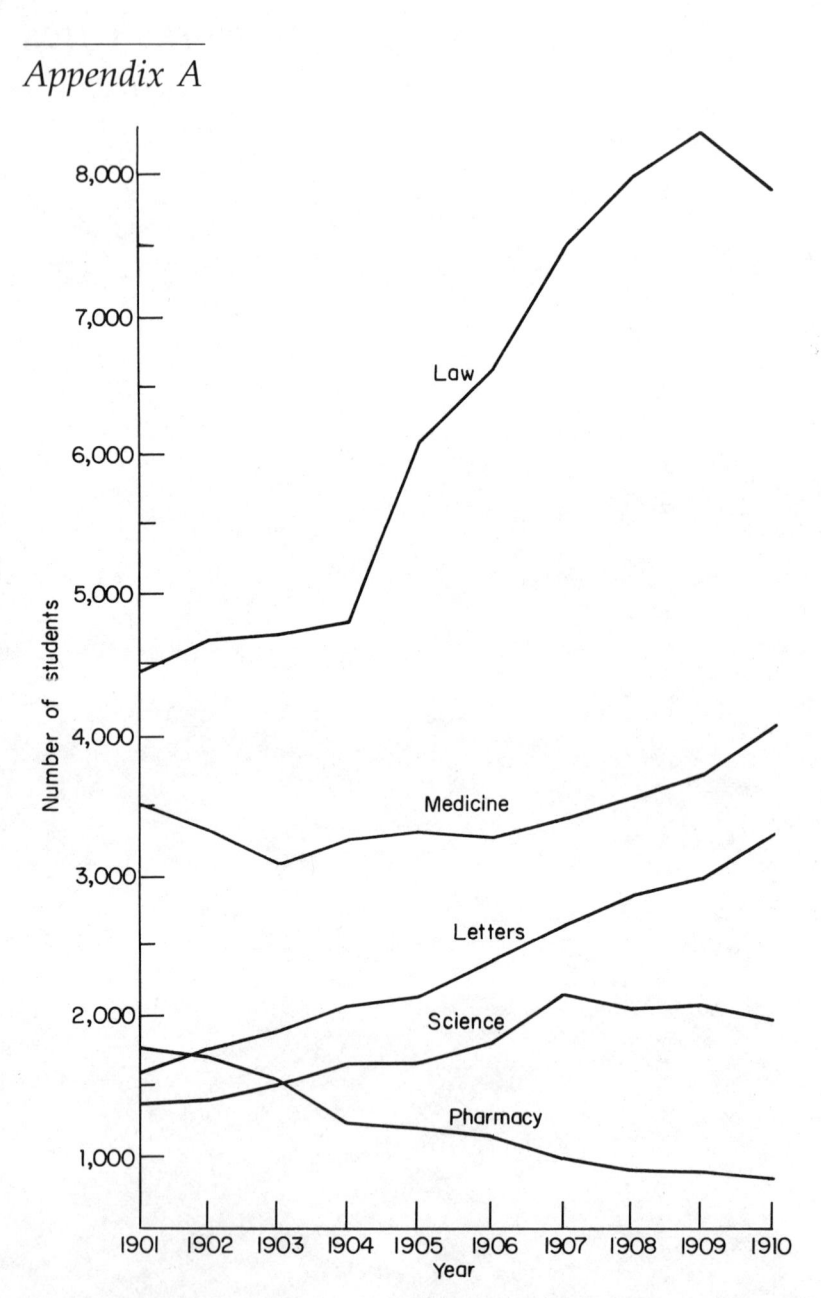

Number of students enrolled in each faculty, University of Paris, 1901–1910.

Source: *Ministère de l'instruction publique. Enquêtes et documents relatifs à l'enseignement supérieur. Rapports des conseils de l'Université pour l'année scolaire 1911–1912*, p. 14.

Appendix B

Teaching positions in history, French and German universities, 1904–1905

Category	French provincial universities	Paris	Total for French universities	German universities
Ancient history	8	9	17	33 (7)[a]
Medieval history	12	13	25	35 (14)
Modern history	13	7	20	44 (15)
Medieval-Modern	—	—	—	29 (7)
Local history, etc.	12	—	12	11 (4)
Total	45	29	74	152 (47)

Source: Ferdinand Lot, "L'Enseignement de l'histoire et de l'histoire de l'art dans les universités d'Allemagne et de France," *Bulletin de la Société d'histoire moderne,* 21 (February 1904), 115–116.

[a] Parentheses indicate number of *Privatdozenten* included in figures for German universities.

Increase in number of teaching positions in history, French and German universities, 1895–1896 to 1904–1905

	1895–1896	1904–1905
French provincial universities	36	45
Parisian institutions (Sorbonne, Ecole Normale, Ecole des Chartes, Ecole Pratique, Collège de France)	21	29
Total French universities	57	74
German universities	134	152

Source: Lot, *La Faculté de philosophie, recherches statistiques,* p. 10, and Lot, "L'Enseignement de l'histoire," pp. 115–116.

Appendix C

Teaching positions (professeur, professeur adjoint, maître de conférences, chargé de cours) in nonscientific disciplines, French universities, 1895–1896

Institution	Philosophy and Pedagogy	Classical Philology	Classical Archeology	Ancient History	History and Auxiliary Sciences	History of Modern Art	Geography
Sorbonne	6	7	1	2	7	1	3
Ecole Normale	2	5	—	1	2	1	1
Collège de France	3	2	2	—	—	1	1
Ecole des Chartes	—	—	—	—	6	1	—
Ecole Pratique	3	6	2	1	2	—	—
Ecole du Louvre	—	—	1	—	—	2'	—
Ecole des Beaux Arts	—	—	—	—	—	3	—
Total for Paris	14	20	6	4	17	9	5
Total for provinces	22	49	8	5	31	—	11
General total	36	69	14	9	48	9	16

Source: Lot, *La Faculté de philosophie, recherches statistiques*, p. 8.

Sanscrit and Comparative Grammar	German Philology	English	French Literature and Romance Philology	Antiquities and Oriental Philology	Slavic Philology	Egyptology	Total
1	2	2	9	—	—	1	42
—	1	—	2	—	—	—	15
2	1	—	2	6	1	1	22
—	—	—	1	—	—	—	8
4	—	—	2	6	—	2	28
—	—	—	—	1	—	2	6
—	—	—	—	—	—	—	3
7	4	2	16	13	1	6	124
3	16	12	31	3	1	2	194
10	20	14	47	16	2	8	318

Appendix D

Teaching positions in nonscientific disciplines, German universities, 1895–1896

University	Philosophy and Pedagogy	Classical Philology	Classical Archeology	Ancient History	History and Auxiliary Sciences	History of Modern Art	Geography
Berlin	13	8	7	7	12	7	4
Bonn	6	5	1	1	4	3	2
Breslau	3	6	1	1	5	2	1
Erlangen	3	3	1	—	2	—	1
Freiburg	5	3	1	1	6	2	1
Giessen	3	2	1	—	2	—	1
Göttingen	4	5	—	1	5	2	1
Greifswald	2	3	2	1	5	—	1
Halle	6	6	2	2	5	1	3
Heidelberg	2	3	2	1	8	1	1
Jena	5	3	1	1	3	—	1
Kiel	3	2	1	1	4	1	1
Königsberg	2	5	—	2	3	2	1
Leipzig	9	3	3	3	12	5	4
Marburg	4	3	1	2	5	—	1
Munich	4	7	1	2	10	3	1
Münster	3	4	1	—	3	2	1
Rostock	1	2	1	—	1	—	—
Strasbourg	3	4	2	3	4	4	2
Tübingen	4	3	1	—	3	1	—
Würzburg	3	2	1	1	2	1	1
Total	88	82	31	30	104	37	29

Source: Lot, *La Faculté de philosophie, recherches statistiques*, p. 10.

Sanscrit and Comparative Grammar	German Philology	English Philology	Romance Philology	Antiquities and Oriental Philology	Slavic Philology	Egyptology	Total
7	8	2	4	7	1	2	89
3	4	2	2	2	—	1	36
2	4	2	2	3	2	—	34
1	1	—	1	1	—	—	14
3	3	2	3	1	—	—	31
1	1	2	3	—	—	—	16
2	3	2	2	3	—	1	31
1	3	1	1	3	—	—	23
3	7	2	5	3	—	—	45
3	6	2	2	2	—	1	34
3	3	1	1	3	—	—	25
2	5	2	2	1	—	—	25
2	3	1	2	2	—	—	25
3	6	1	3	6	4	2	64
1	3	1	3	1	—	—	25
3	5	1	2	2	—	—	41
1	3	1	1	—	—	—	20
—	1	—	2	1	—	—	9
2	4	3	3	5	—	1	40
2	1	1	2	1	—	—	19
1	2	—	2	—	—	—	16
46	76	29	48	47	7	8	662

Appendix E

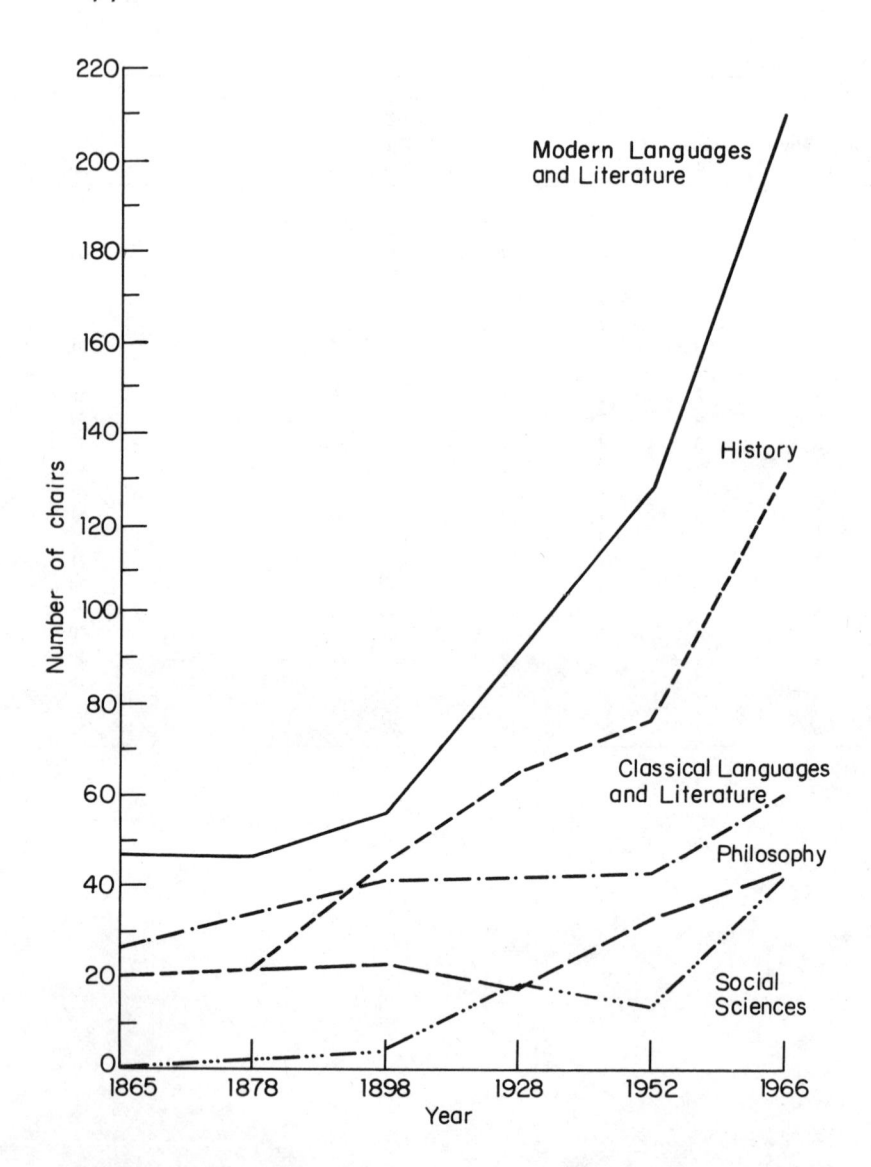

Number of chairs in Paris and provincial faculties, Ecole Normale Supérieure, Collège de France, 1865–1966.

Source: Terry N. Clark, *Prophets and Patrons: The French University and the Emergence of the Social Sciences* (Cambridge, Mass.: Harvard University Press, 1973), p. 31.

Appendix F

Theses submitted for the diploma of advanced studies (diplôme d'études supérieures), faculties of letters of French universities, 1907–1909

University	Philosophy 1907	Philosophy 1908	Philosophy 1909	History and Geography 1907	History and Geography 1908	History and Geography 1909
Aix	—	2	3	—	—	—
Besançon	2	1	2	—	1	—
Bordeaux	2	2	3	2	1	3
Caen	1	2	—	3	3	3
Clermont	—	1	—	3	2	4
Dijon	—	—	2	2	4	5
Grenoble	1	—	—	—	—	—
Lille	1	3	3	—	5	3
Lyon	1	6	2	5	9	8
Montpellier	3	1	1	—	—	—
Nancy	—	—	1	2	2	3
Poitiers	—	1	1	—	1	1
Rennes	3	—	—	1	4	2
Toulouse	3	1	2	1	—	2
Total	17	20	20	19	32	34
Paris	12	22	18	31	30	22
General Total	29	42	38	50	62	56

Source: Ferdinand Lot, *Diplômes d'études et dissertations inaugurales. Etude de statistique comparée* (Paris: Champion, 1910), p. 11.

Inaugural dissertations submitted for the doctor of philosophy degree, faculties of philosophy of German universities, 1906–1908

	Philosophy			History			Geography and Ethnology		
University	1906	1907	1908	1906	1907	1908	1906	1907	1908
Berlin	1	5	7	20	29	32	3	5	4
Bonn	2	5	6	9	12	9	5	3	5
Breslau	1	—	2	5	8	6	—	—	1
Erlangen	16	16	19	—	6	3	4	3	—
Freiburg	1	1	2	6	6	19	—	—	2
Giessen	1	—	5	3	—	2	4	2	1
Göttingen	—	1	2	5	12	15	—	1	2
Greifswald	1	1	—	7	17	9	1	—	—
Halle	2	6	1	10	8	7	8	3	2
Heidelberg	7	7	5	10	9	6	—	3	—
Jena	6	5	7	8	6	10	4	6	3
Kiel	1	—	1	—	1	2	2	2	3
Königsberg	2	2	—	1	2	3	—	1	2
Leipzig	11	8	7	20	18	11	6	4	5
Marburg	—	2	—	5	4	7	3	1	2
Munich	6	7	8	5	10	7	—	—	2
Münster	3	1	2	22	17	16	1	—	2
Rostock	3	—	1	—	—	—	3	—	3
Strasbourg	2	2	3	4	6	4	—	1	—
Tübingen	2	4	1	7	5	5	2	—	—
Würzburg	2	1	3	3	2	2	—	2	—
Total	70	74	82	150	178	175	46	37	39

Source: Lot, *Diplômes d'études et dissertations inaugurales. Etudes de statistique comparée*, p. 12.

Appendix G

Foreign students enrolled in the Faculty of Letters of Paris,

Academic year	Men	Women	Total
1902–1903	136	194	330
1903–1904	187	223	410
1904–1905	243	282	525
1905–1906	263	428	691
1906–1907	337	569	906
1907–1908	351	711	1062
1908–1909	419	731	1150
1909–1910	540	789	1329

Source: *Ministère de l'instruction publique. Enquêtes et documents relatifs à l'enseignement supérieur. Rapports des conseils de l'Université pour l'année scolaire 1910–1911* (Paris: Impr. Nationale, 1912), p. 64.

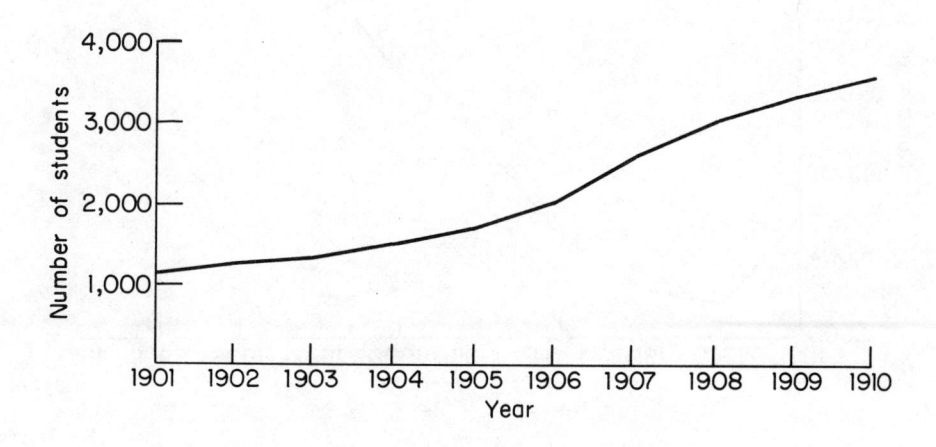

Foreign students enrolled in all faculties, University of Paris, 1901–1910.
Source: *Ministère de l'instruction publique, 1911–1912,* p. 13.

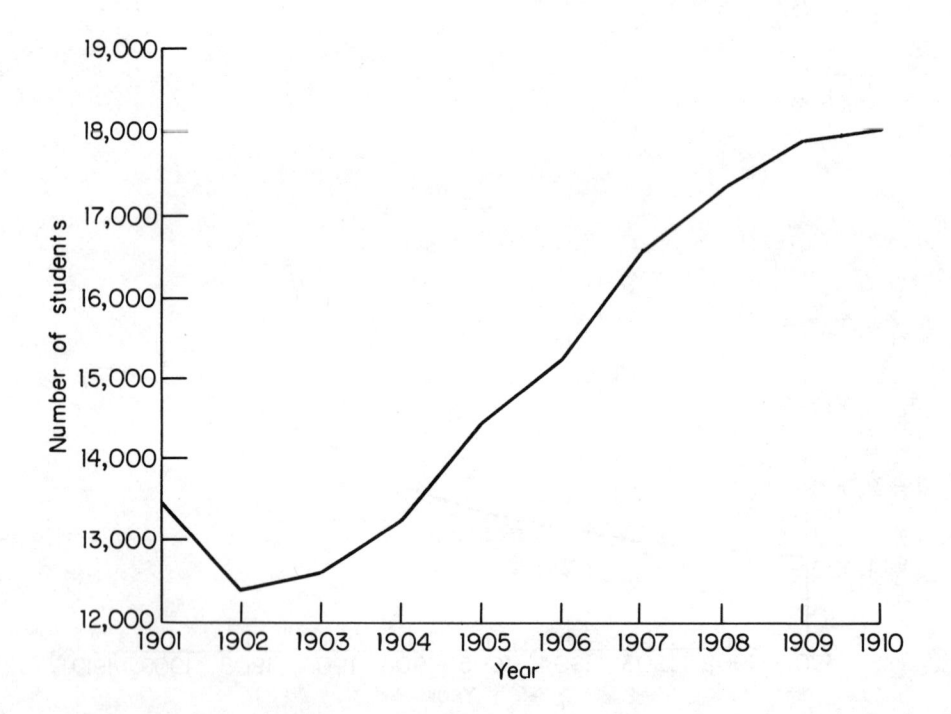

Students (French and foreign) enrolled in all faculties, University of Paris, 1901–1910.
Source: *Ministère de l'instruction publique, 1911–1912*, p. 13.

Appendix H

Course offerings in history departments of selected Parisian institutions of higher learning, 1914

Faculty of Letters of Paris (Sorbonne)
  Ancient history
  Ancient history of the Far East
  Archeology
  Auxiliary sciences of history
  Byzantine history
  Colonial history
  Greek history
  Historical method
  History of Christianity in ancient and medieval times
  History of Christianity in modern times
  History of Christian thought and literature from the sixteenth to nineteenth century
  History of music
  History of the civilization of the Far East
  History of the French Revolution
  History of the Hebrew religion
  Medieval history
  Modern and contemporary history
  Modern political and diplomatic history
  Roman history

Ecole Nationale des Chartes
  Archival management
  Bibliography
  Diplomatics
  History of civil and canon law of the Middle Ages
  History of the political, administrative, and judicial institutions of France
  Medieval archeology
  Paleography
  Romance philology
  Sources of the history of France

Ecole Pratique des Hautes Etudes, 4th section
  Ancient history of the Far East
  Assyrian philology and antiquities
  Byzantine and modern Greek philology
  Comparative grammar
  Dialectology of Roman Gaul
  Egyptian philology and antiquities

Epigraphy and Greek antiquities
General and comparative phonetics
Greek philology
Historical geography
History
History of contemporary doctrines of physiological psychology
History of economic doctrines
Latin epigraphy and Roman antiquities
Latin philology
Literary history of the Renaissance
Oriental archeology
Paleography
Romance languages and literature
Sanscrit, Hebrew, Arabic

Source: *Les Universités et les écoles françaises. Renseignements généraux* (Paris: Office Nationale des Universités et Ecoles Françaises, 1914), pp. 75–76, 83, 85.

Notes

Prologue

1. See H. Stuart Hughes, *The Obstructed Path: French Social Thought in the Years of Desperation, 1930-1960* (New York: Harper & Row, 1966), p. 19, and J. H. Plumb, in *New York Times Book Review,* December 31, 1972, p. 8.

2. See the complaint of David H. Fischer in the preface to his *Historians' Fallacies* (New York: Harper & Row, 1970).

3. See Terry N. Clark, "Emile Durkheim and the Institutionalization of Sociology in the French University System," *Archives européennes de sociologie* (1968), pp. 58-59 for a discussion of the greater difficulty involved in creating new disciplines in French universities than in those of England and the United States.

4. Fritz Stern, ed., *The Varieties of History* (Cleveland: World Publishing Co., 1965), p. 21.

5. Leopold von Ranke, *The Theory and Practice of History,* ed. Georg G. Iggers and Konrad von Moltke (New York: Bobbs-Merrill, 1973), pp. xii, xix-xx.

6. W. M. Simon, *European Positivism in the Nineteenth Century* (Ithaca, N. Y.: Cornell University Press, 1963), p. 3.

7. For the purposes of this study we may ignore the use of the term "positivism" in the narrow Comtean sense.

8. Georg G. Iggers, "The Crisis of the Conventional Conception of Scientific History," unpub. manuscript.

9. Norman F. Cantor and Richard I. Schneider, *How to Study History* (New York: Crowell, 1967), pp. 247-248.

10. Lucien Febvre, "Sur une forme d'histoire qui n'est pas la nôtre," *Annales*, 3 (1948), 21-24.

11. See Fritz K. Ringer, *The Decline of the German Mandarins: The German Academic Community, 1890-1933* (Cambridge, Mass.: Harvard University Press, 1969), pp. 102-103.

12. See Allan Mitchell, "German History in France after 1870," *Journal of Contemporary History*, 2 (July 1967), 85. It appears that Fustel de Coulanges, perhaps the most gifted French historian of his generation, was prevented from exercising a greater influence over the new school of French historians at the Sorbonne because of failing health (which caused frequent absences from the classroom) and an authentic *érudit*'s distaste for academic politics (see AN,F17 20780, Fustel de Coulanges Dossier), though he was one of the first to recognize the need to improve the quality of historical instruction in the faculties of letters (see Fustel to Duruy, 22 January 1868, *ibid*.). Professor Martin Siegel is currently exploring the connections between Fustel and his "cluster" of disciples at the Ecole Normale Supérieure.

13. See, for example, Clark's "Emile Durkheim and the Institutionalization of Sociology," as well as his recent work, *Prophets and Patrons: The French University and the Emergence of the Social Sciences* (Cambridge, Mass.: Harvard University Press, 1973); Ben-David's and Awraham Zloczower's "Universities and Academic Systems in Modern Societies," *European Journal of Sociology*, 3 (1962), 45-84, and Ben-David's *The Scientist's Role in Society* (Englewood Cliffs, N.J.: Prentice-Hall, 1971).

14. Fischer, *Historians' Fallacies*, p. 161.

15. Particularly in the writings of Ben-David, whose analysis of scientific innovation, while differing with Kuhn's in several important respects, touches on many of the problems raised in *The Structure of Scientific Revolutions* (Chicago: University of Chicago Press, 1962).

16. *American Historical Review*, 78 (April 1973), 370-393.

17. I do not propose to become involved in the raging controversy over whether Kuhn's speculations on the growth of scientific knowledge are applicable to the social sciences, or indeed, whether they are philosophically valid at all. For a lively discussion of this debate see Imre Lakatos and Alan Musgrave, eds., *Criticism and the Growth of Knowledge* (Cambridge, Mass.: Harvard University Press, 1970).

18. I have found particularly useful for heuristic purposes Ben-David's concept (which is also employed by Edward Shils) of the "center" of scientific research as well as Clark's model of the "cluster" of innovative researchers who band together to form a "school."

1. Prelude to Reform: 1866-1870

1. Charles Victor Langlois and Charles Seignobos, *Introduction aux études historiques* (Paris: Hachette, 1898), p. x.

2. Victor Duruy, *Notes et souvenirs: 1811-1894*, I (Paris: Hachette, 1902), p. 69. See also Roger L. Williams, *The World of Napoleon III, 1851-1870* (New York: Collier Books, 1962), p. 178.

3. Duruy, *Notes*, p. 70.

4. See Henry E. Bourne, *The Teaching of History and Civics in the Elementary and Secondary School* (New York: Longmans, Green and Co., 1902), p. 41; Langlois and Seignobos, *Introduction,* appendix I; Jean Ehrard and Guy Palmade, eds., *L'Histoire* (Paris: Colin, 1964), p. 68.

5. Williams, *The World,* p. 190. Ernest Lavisse, a close associate of Duruy, recalled that the minister was fond of comparing the role of the "professor in his chair" to that of the "priest at his altar." Ernest Lavisse, *Un Ministre: Victor Duruy* (Paris: Colin, 1895), p. 100.

6. Duruy, *Notes,* pp. 202ff, 301. See *Les Statistiques de l'enseignement primaire, moyen, et supérieur* (Paris: Delalain, 1870) pp. 644–739 for the results of the inquiry on French higher education.

7. Paul Frédéricq, *L'Enseignement supérieur de l'histoire: notes et impressions de voyage* (Paris: Alcan, 1899), p. 73. For a similar assessment see Emile Durkheim's introduction to *La Vie universitaire à Paris* (Paris: Colin, 1918), p. 16.

8. *Circulaires et instructions officielles relatives à l'instruction publique, ministère de S. Exc. M. Duruy* (Paris: Delalain, 1870), pp. 652–654. See also Charles Victor Langlois, *Questions d'histoire et d'enseignement* (Paris: Hachette, 1902), p. 161.

9. Louis Liard, *L'Enseignement supérieur en France, 1789–1893,* II (Paris: Colin, 1894), p. 282. See also Lavisse, *Un Ministre,* pp. 63–64.

10. *Administration de l'instruction publique (de 1863 à 1869), Ministère de Son Exc. M. Duruy* (Paris: Delalain, n.d.), pp. 717–719.

11. *Ministère de l'instruction publique. Statistique de l'enseignement supérieur, 1865–1868* (Paris: Impr. Impériale, 1869) p. xxiii. See also Liard, *L'Enseignement,* pp. 292–293.

12. Duruy to Napoleon III, 6 August 1863, reproduced in Duruy, *Notes,* pp. 197–198.

13. *La Vie universitaire,* p. 143. See also *Institut de France. Académie des sciences morales et politiques. Séances et travaux,* 60 (1900), pp. 265–266.

14. Mortimer D'Ocagne, *Les Grandes Ecoles de France* (Paris: Hetzel, 1887), pp. 350–354.

15. *Ministère de l'instruction publique. Statistique de l'enseignement supérieur, 1865–1868,* pp. 498—511. Langlois and Seignobos, *Introduction,* Appendix II. Liard, *L'Enseignement,* p. 402.

16. See Abel Lefranc, *La Fondation et les commencements du Collège de France, 1530–1542* (Paris: Presses Universitaires de France, 1932).

17. See Duruy, *Circulaires,* pp. 653–654.

18. See Maurice Prou, *L'Ecole des Chartes* (Paris: Picard, 1921), D'Ocagne, *Les Grandes Ecoles,* pp. 213–219.

19. See Clark, "Emile Durkheim," pp. 58–59, for a discussion of obstacles to academic innovation peculiar to the French educational system.

20. *Administration de l'instruction publique,* p. 646.

21. *La Vie universitaire,* p. 183.

22. Georges Desdevises du Dézert and Louis Bréhier, *Le Travail historique* (Paris: Librairie Bloud, 1907), p. 13.

23. Liard, *L'Enseignement,* p. 294.

24. Lavisse, *Un Ministre,* p. 81.

25. See Charles Bémont, "Gabriel Monod," in *Ecole Pratique des Hautes Etudes, section des sciences historiques et philologiques, annuaire, 1912-1913*, p. 10. Albert Delatour, *Institut de France. Académie des sciences et politiques. Notice sur la vie et les travaux de M. Gabriel Monod,* meeting of 9 January 1915, p. 20.

26. *Ministère de l'instruction publique. Statistique de l'enseignement supérieur, 1865-1868,* pp. xxiv-xxv. See also Charles Andler, *Vie de Lucien Herr* (Paris: Rieder, 1932), p. 32.

27. For discussions of this relatively obscure but extremely influential scholar, see Gabriel Monod, *Gaston Paris* (Nogent-le-Rotron: Impr. de Daupeley-Gouverneur, 1903) and J. Bédier and M. Rocques, *Bibliographie des travaux de Gaston Paris* (Paris, 1903).

28. Pierre Leguay, *La Sorbonne* (Paris: Grasset, 1910), p. 10.

29. See Jean-Paul Sartre, *What Is Literature?* trans. Bernard Frechtman (New York: Harper & Row, 1965), pp. 80ff for a provocative analysis of the changing function of the writer in the modern world.

30. Leguay, *La Sorbonne,* pp. 13-16. See also Charles Victor Langlois, *Manuel de bibliographie historique* (Paris: Hachette, 1896), pp. 317ff, and Henri d'Arbois de Jubainville, *Deux manières d'écrire l'histoire* (Paris: E. Bouillon, 1896), wherein the author distinguishes between the "literary" or "a priori" method and the "experimental" or "a posteriori" method of historical writing.

31. Cited in Ehrard and Palmade, eds., *L'Histoire,* pp. 54-55.

32. Harry Elmer Barnes, in his *A History of Historical Writing* (New York, Dover Publications, 1962), p. 250, remarked that French historians during this period were denied the opportunity to exercise a Rankean-type influence on subsequent generations of scholars because they "lacked the power wielded through a long continued seminar."

33. Prou, *L'Ecole des Chartes,* p. 5.

34. Leguay, *La Sorbonne,* p. 47.

35. Louis Halphen, in *Histoire et historiens depuis cinquante ans: méthodes, organisation et résultats du travail historique de 1876 à 1926,* I (Paris: Alcan, 1927), p. 149. For a list of the original faculty of the historical section of the Ecole Pratique see *Ministère de l'instruction publique. Statistique de l'enseignement supérieur, 1865-1868,* p. 4.

36. The original board of editors included Paul Meyer, Charles Morel, Gaston Paris, and Hermann Zotenberg. *Revue critique d'histoire et de littérature,* 1 (6 January 1866). Zotenberg retired two years later.

37. *Revue critique* (14 April 1866), p. 234.

38. *Ibid.,* pp. 236-238.

39. Langlois and Seignobos, *Introduction,* p. 113.

40. Lavisse, *Un Ministre,* pp. 82-83.

41. Langlois and Seignobos, *Introduction,* pp. 113-114.

42. *Revue critique* (1866), pp. 366-367.

43. *Revue critique* (1868), pp. 243-247.

44. *Revue critique* (1869), pp. 1-3.

45. *Revue des questions historiques,* 1 (1866), p. 5.

46. See *Revue critique* (1866), pp. 234-238, and d'Arbois de Jubainville, *Deux Manières,* pp. 185ff.

47. *Revue des questions historiques,* 1 (1866), p. 7.
48. *Ibid.,* p. 6. Though no specific names were mentioned, the reference to "renowned authors" was clearly aimed at antagonists of the Catholic monarchies such as Thierry and Michelet.
49. Christian Pfister, "Le Cinquantenaire de *la Revue historique,*" in *Histoire et historiens depuis cinquante ans* (Paris: Alcan, 1927), p. vii.
50. *Revue des questions historiques,* 1 (1866), pp. 6–9.
51. The reviewers of the *Revue critique* frequently took note of the deteriorating situation of higher education in France and issued appeals for far-reaching reforms. See, for example, *Revue critique* (1866), p. 120.
52. Cited in André Bellesort, *Les Intellectuels et l'avènement de la Troisième République* (Paris: Grasset, 1931), pp. 60–61.
53. Delatour, *Notice,* p. 19.
54. *Revue critique* (1867), p. 19.

2. History's Role in the Regeneration of the Fatherland

1. G. P. Gooch, *History and Historians in the Nineteenth Century* (London: Longmans, 1952), p. 108.
2. Delatour, *Notice,* p. 17.
3. For a brilliant treatment of this school of historiography see Georg G. Iggers, *The German Conception of History* (Middletown, Conn.: Wesleyan University Press, 1968), chap. 5.
4. Gabriel Monod, *A la Mémoire de M. le Professeur Georges Waitz* (Nogent-le-Rotron: Impr. de Daupeley-Gouverneur, 1886), pp. 3–4.
5. Delatour, *Notice,* pp. 17–18.
6. Charles Bémont, "Gabriel Monod," *Revue historique,* 110 (May–August 1912), pp. v–vi, quoting Monod.
7. Pfister, in *Histoire et historiens,* II, viii–ix.
8. Gabriel Monod, *Allemands et Français* (Paris: Sandoz et Fischbacher, 1872), p. 138. See also Gabriel Monod, *Portraits et souvenirs* (Paris: C. Lévy, 1897), pp. 75, 203–204, for further evidence of his tenderness toward Germany during this period of his career. At the beginning of the twentieth century, after being subjected to a barrage of criticism from the nationalist right for his allegedly pro-German sentiments, Monod endeavored to defend himself by publishing in *Le Temps* a letter that he had written to Michelet in 1866 which expressed serious reservations about the German conception of history. See *Le Temps,* 5 September 1900.
9. Ernest Lavisse, Dedication, *Etudes d'histoire du moyen âge* (Paris: Cerf & Alcan, 1896), p. xii. Delatour, *Notes,* p. 19. Monod to Duruy, 8 Sept. 1868, in Archives Nationales, F17 file (hereafter abbreviated as AN,F17), 21982, Gabriel Monod Dossier.
10. Bémont, in *Ecole Pratique annuaire,* pp. 10–11.
11. Monod, *Portraits et souvenirs,* p. 316. Paul Farmer has analyzed the growing popularity of the German model of higher education in French circles during the nineteenth century. See his "Nineteenth Century Ideas of the University," in Margaret Clapp, ed., *The Modern University* (Ithaca: Cornell University Press, 1950), pp. 16–17.

12. Frédéricq, *Notes*, p. 80.
13. Delatour, *Notice*, pp. 22–23.
14. Bémont, in *Revue historique*, 110 (May–August 1912), p. vi. AN, F17 25893, Alfred Rambaud Dossier.
15. See Joseph Bédier, *Hommage à Gaston Paris. Leçon d'ouverture du cours de langue et de littérature françaises du moyen âge, prononcée au Collège de France, le 3 févr. 1904* (Paris, 1904). AN, F17 25874, Gaston Paris Dossier.
16. See Paul Vidal de la Blache, "Notice sur la vie et les oeuvres de M. Alfred Rambaud," *Mémoires de l'académie des sciences morales et politiques de l'Institut de France*, XXVII (Paris: Firmin-Didot, 1910).
17. Lavisse letter, October 1865, in Charles Seignobos and others, *L'Education de la démocratie: leçons professées à l'Ecole des Hautes Etudes Sociales* (Paris: Alcan, 1907), pp. 28–29n.
18. Lavisse, Dedication, *Etudes d'histoire*, p. xii.
19. Donald F. Lach, "Ernest Lavisse," in Bernadotte Schmitt, ed., *Some Historians of Modern Europe* (Port Washington, N.Y.: Kennikat Press, 1966), p. 242. See also Lavisse, *Un Ministre*, p. 73.
20. Duruy, *Notes et souvenirs*, p. 233.
21. Lavisse, *Un Ministre*, pp. 71, 164.
22. Except for Monod's brief stint at the lycée de Laval in the mid-1860s, all three managed to avoid service in secondary education. See Christian Pfister, in *Revue historique*, 110 (May–August 1912), p. xxiv.
23. See E. N. Anderson, *Nationalism and the Cultural Crisis in Prussia, 1806–1815* (New York: Octagon Books, 1966), pp. 16–17.
24. Quoted in Claude Digeon, *La Crise allemande de la pensée française, 1870–1914* (Paris: Presses Universitaires de France, 1959), p. 372.
25. Gabriel Monod, *De la Possibilité d'une réforme de l'enseignement supérieur* (Paris: Ernest Leroux, 1876), p. 10.
26. Ernest Lavisse, *La Fondation de l'Université de Berlin à propos de la réforme de l'enseignement supérieur en France* (Paris: Hachette, 1876), p. 39.
27. Monod, *De la Possibilité*, p. 43.
28. Delatour, *Notice*, pp. 25–26.
29. Gaston Deschamps, *La Malaise de la démocratie* (Paris: Colin, 1899), p. 166.
30. Ernest Lavisse, *Questions d'enseignement national* (Paris: Colin, 1885), pp. xxiv–xxv.
31. Lavisse, *La Fondation de l'Université de Berlin*, p. 31.
32. (Paris: Hachette, 1875).
33. See Lach, "Ernest Lavisse," in Schmitt, ed., *Some Historians*, p. 243.
34. Digeon, *La Crise allemande*, p. 365.
35. Monod, *Allemands et Français*, p. 67.
36. Iggers, *The German Conception of History*, p. 91.
37. The ambivalent attitude of the French intellectuals toward their German counterparts after 1870 is treated at length in Digeon, *La Crise allemande*, passim.
38. See Bellesort, *Les Intellectuels*, pp. 59–60.
39. Monod, *De la Possibilité*, p. 22.
40. *Revue historique*, 1 (1876), p. 27.

41. *Ibid.*, pp. 28-29.
42. *Ibid.*, p. 29.
43. Leguay, *La Sorbonne*, p. 44.
44. Monod, *De la Possibilité*, pp. 12-13.
45. See Ben-David, *The Scientist's Role in Society*, p. 103, and Ehrard and Palmade, *L'Histoire*, p. 68.
46. Monod and Lavisse in particular proved to be quite adept at adjusting their political loyalties to the requirements of their career. See below, chaps. 5 and 9.
47. See Ehrard and Palmade, *L'Histoire*, pp. 49-65 for a discussion of the ideological uses of history in France since the Revolution.
48. See Herbert Butterfield, *The Whig Interpretation of History* (New York: Norton, 1965) for a critical analysis of this type of historical writing.
49. Robert A. Kann treats the general theme of counterrevolutionary ideology in his *The Problem of Restoration* (Berkeley: University of California Press, 1968), as does Arno Mayer in his *Dynamics of Counterrevolution in Europe: 1870-1956* (New York: Harper Torchbooks, 1971). The writings of Taine are the most notable examples of the counterrevolutionary uses of history in France after 1870. I am currently at work on a study of the rebirth of counterrevolutionary history in twentieth century France.
50. See Fritz Stern, *The Politics of Cultural Despair: A Study in the Rise of the Germanic Ideology* (Berkeley: University of California Press, 1961), pp. 183-266, for an excellent treatment of Arthur Moeller van den Bruck, a popularizer of this type of historical conception in Germany.
51. See Herbert Marcuse, *Reason and Revolution* (Boston: Beacon Press, 1964), pp. 10ff.
52. Ehrard and Palmade, *L'Histoire*, pp. 57, 68. See also Peter Stadler, *Geschichtschreibung und historisches Denken in Frankreich, 1789-1871* (Zurich: Berichthaus, 1958), pp. 102-117, and Stanley Mellon, *The Political Uses of History: A Study of Historians in the French Restoration* (Stanford: Stanford University Press, 1958), pp. 12-17.
53. Louis Halphen, *L'Histoire en France depuis cent ans* (Paris: Colin, 1914), pp. 21-22.
54. *Ibid.*, p. 23. See also Stadler, *Geschictschreibung und historisches Denken*, pp. 141-151, and Friedrich Engel-Janosi, *Four Studies in French Romantic Historical Writing* (Baltimore: Johns Hopkins University Press, 1955), pp. 88-120.
55. Edmund Wilson, *To the Finland Station: A Study in the Writing and Acting of History* (Garden City, N.Y.: Doubleday, 1953), pp. 12-26.
56. See Mellon, *The Political Uses of History*.
57. See Paul Farmer, *France Reviews Its Revolutionary Origins: Social Politics and Historical Opinion in the Third Republic* (New York: Octagon Books, 1963).
58. See *Revue critique* (September 1871).
59. *Revue historique*, 1 (January-June 1876), 25.
60. *Ibid.*, p. 26.
61. *Ibid.*
62. *Ibid.*, p. 28.
63. *Ibid.*, p. 29.
64. *Ibid.*, p. 32.

65. *Ibid.*
66. *Ibid.*, p. 33.
67. *Ibid.*, p. 35.
68. *Ibid.*, p. 36.
69. Among the most notable contributors were Duruy, Fustel de Coulanges, Lavisse, Paris, Ernest Renan, Albert Sorel, and Hippolyte Taine. See *ibid.*, pp. 2-3. Such a diverse group of historians could scarcely be characterized as a "school."
70. Quoted in Stern, ed., *The Varieties of History*, p. 173.
71. *Ibid.*, p. 174.
72. See Halphen, in *Histoire et historiens depuis cinquante ans*, I, 148, for a list of the journals and professional societies that appeared in France after 1876.
73. *Revue historique*, 1 (January-June 1876), 29-30.

3. The Institutionalization of Historical Study in the New Sorbonne

1. See Mitchell, "German History in France after 1870," pp. 81-99.
2. Monod, *De la Possibilité*, pp. 31-32. See also Monod, in *Institut de France. Académie des Sciences Morales et Politiques. Séances et travaux*, 60 (1900), 266.
3. Monod, *De la Possibilité*, p. 38. For a description of the dispersion of courses in the historical and social sciences in the Parisian university system see Henri Hauser, *L'Enseignement des sciences sociales* (Paris: Chevalier-Maresq, 1903), pp. 89-220.
4. See Henry E. Guerlac's perceptive essay, "Science and French National Strength," in Edward M. Earle, ed., *Modern France* (Princeton: Princeton University Press, 1951), pp. 81-105. For a discussion of the emergence of the German universities as centers of scientific research at the middle of the nineteenth century see Ben-David, *The Scientist's Role in Society*, pp. 108-121.
5. Durkheim, *La Vie universitaire à Paris*, p. 17.
6. Ben-David, *The Scientist's Role in Society*, pp. 15, 99. See his appendix, where he attempts to quantify the shifts in centers of scientific publications and discoveries.
7. See Robert Flint, *History of the Philosophy of History* (New York: Scribner, 1894), p. 617, and John A. Scott, *Republican Ideas and the Liberal Tradition in France, 1870-1914* (New York: Columbia University Press, 1914), pp. 91-94.
8. Leguay, *La Sorbonne*, pp. 28-29.
9. Ferdinand Lot, *La Faculté de philosophie en Allemagne et les facultés des lettres et des sciences en France. Recherches statistiques* (Paris: Colin, 1896), p. 20.
10. Ernest Lavisse, *Essais sur L'Allemagne impériale* (Paris: Hachette, 1888), p. 276.
11. Charles Seignobos, *Le Régime de l'enseignement des lettres* (Paris: Impr. Nationale, 1904), pp. 6-7.
12. Leguay, *La Sorbonne*, pp. 41, 79.
13. See the publication of the annual budget of the Ministry of Public Instruction in the *Revue internationale de l'enseignement*.
14. See Ernest Lavisse, "La Société d'Enseignement Supérieur. Actes de la Société," *Revue international de l'enseignement* (January 5, 1881), p. 105.

15. *Ministère de l'instruction publique. Direction de l'enseignement supérieur. Règlements des universités* (Paris: Impr. Nationale, 1897), pp. 31–56.

16. *Ibid.*, pp. 1–31.

17. Croiset became dean of the Sorbonne in 1898, less than two years after the reform of higher education. Lavisse became director of the Ecole Normale in 1903 after that institution was annexed by the University of Paris. All in all, between 1870 and 1919, the history profession produced two deans of the Sorbonne (Wallon and Croiset) and three directors of the Ecole Normale (Fustel de Coulanges, Lavisse, and Lanson).

18. *Ministère de l'instruction publique. Statistique de l'enseignement supérieur, 1865–1868,* p. 4. See also Paul Frédéricq, "The Study of History in Germany and France," *Johns Hopkins University Studies in History and Political Science,* VIII (May-June 1890), 95.

19. The *licence* was a professional certificate roughly equivalent to an undergraduate degree from a first-rate American university and usually required at least two years of study.

20. Alfred Croiset, in *La Vie universitaire à Paris,* pp. 37, 59.

21. Clark, *Prophets and Patrons,* p. 23.

22. See Vidal de la Blache, "Notice sur la vie et les oeuvres de M. Alfred Rambaud," pp. 122–137.

23. The *agrégation* was not a degree, but a competitive examination for a teaching post in secondary education or, in a more advanced form, for a professorship in the faculties of law, medicine, or pharmacy.

24. Lavisse, "Le Concours pour l'agrégation d'histoire," pp. 150–151, Jean Bonnerot, *La Sorbonne* (Paris: Presses Universitaires de France, n.d.), pp. 9–57.

25. Frédéricq, *Notes,* p. 97.

26. See Lavisse, in *Revue internationale de l'enseignement,* 13 February 1881; hereafter cited as *RIE.*

27. Leguay, *La Sorbonne,* p. 12. For the organizational statutes of the new university, see *Ministère de l'instruction publique. Direction de l'enseignement supérieur. Règlements des universités. Décret du 21 juillet 1897* (Paris: Impr. Nationale, 1897). The use of the term *Université* after 1896 referred to the union of the formerly separate faculties. The original term, Université de France, which was coined by Napoleon and abolished in 1850 (though it continued to be used informally thereafter), referred to the entire educational system in France, including the primary and secondary schools and the various scholarly academies.

28. Clark, *Prophets and Patrons,* p. 79.

29. Bédier, "Sur l'oeuvre de Gaston Paris," p. 21. AN, F17 25874, Paris Dossier.

30. See *Etudes romanes, dédiées à Gaston Paris par ses élèves français et ses élèves étrangers des pays de langue française* (Paris: Bouillon, 1891) and *La Société amicale Gaston Paris. Bulletin,* 1903–1904 and 1905 for a list of his former students.

31. Lavisse, "Le Concours pour l'agrégation d'histoire," p. 146.

32. See Vidal de la Blache, "Notice sur la vie et les oeuvres de M. Alfred Rambaud," pp. 135–141; AN, F17 25893, Rambaud Dossier.

33. Lavisse, "Ouverture des conférences de lettres et philologie et d'histoire," *RIE* (November 15, 1883), pp. 1139–1140.

34. He served as Minister of Public Instruction from 1875 to 1876 and dean of the Sorbonne from 1876 to 1888.

35. Mitchell, "German History in France after 1870," pp. 85–86.

36. Pierre Leguay, *Universitaires d'aujourd'hui* (Paris: Grasset, 1912), pp. 36–37.

37. The list of Monod's protégés includes most of the leading members of the French historical profession before the First World War. The dedication of a volume of essays commemorating his election to the presidency of the fourth section of the Ecole Pratique in 1895 was signed by 150 former students including Charles Bémont, Emile Bourgeois, Georges Desdevises du Dézert, Gustave Fagniez, Gabriel Hanotaux, Henri Hauser, Camille Jullian, Ferdinand Lot, Charles Petit-Dutaillis, Christian Pfister, Henri Pirenne, Maurice Prou, and Philippe Sagnac.

38. Cited in Delatour, *Notice*, p. 41.

39. See Mitchell, "German History in France after 1870," p. 83.

40. See below, chap. 5.

41. Alphonse Aulard, "Leçon d'ouverture du cours d'histoire de la Révolution française à la faculté des lettres de Paris," *Etudes et leçons sur la Révolution française*, 1 (Paris, 1901), pp. 18–28.

42. As a top-level bureaucrat in the Ministry of Foreign Affairs from 1866 to 1876 and thereafter secretary to the president of the Senate, Sorel had been privy to much archival material that had previously been unavailable for scholarly scrutiny. See Farmer, *France Reviews Its Revolutionary Origins*, p. 45.

43. Alphonse Aulard, *Taine: historien de la Révolution française* (Paris: Colin, 1907), pp. 327, 330. The major reference here is to Taine's *Origines de la France contemporaine*.

44. See Pierre Caron and Philippe Sagnac, *L'Etat actuel des études d'histoire moderne en France* (Paris: Revue d'histoire moderne et contemporaine, 1902), p. 39.

45. He wrote his *petite thèse* in Latin on Asinius Pallion.

46. His only major work was a study of the orators of the revolutionary assemblies entitled *L'Eloquence parlementaire pendant la Révolution française*.

47. Léon Cohen, "Alphonse Aulard," *Revue universitaire*, 1 (1929), p. 304.

48. Georges Lefebvre, "L'Oeuvre historique d'Albert Mathiez," *Annales historiques de la Révolution française*, 9 (1932), pp. 98–102.

49. Aulard, "Leçon d'ouverture," p. 16.

50. His definitive *Histoire politique de la Révolution française* appeared in 1901. He was also to become the principal adviser to the Ministry of Public Instruction on matters relating to modern historical teaching and scholarship, and a member of the committee on diplomatic archives of the Ministry of Foreign Affairs.

51. The best accounts of Aulard's life and career can be found in Georges Belloni, *Aulard: historien de la Révolution française* (Paris: Presses Universitaires de France, 1949); Pierre Flottes, "Aulard professeur," *La Revue française*, 81 (1928); H. Chobaut, "L'Oeuvre d'Aulard et l'histoire de la Révolution française," *Annales historiques de la Révolution française*, 6 (1929), 1–4; Louis Gottschalk, "Professor Aulard," *Journal of Modern History*, 1 (1929), 85–86; and Cohen, "Alphonse Aulard." See also AN, F17 22600, Aulard Dossier.

52. *Enquête de 1865. Archives du Ministère de l'Instruction Publique,* cited in Liard, *L'Enseignement supérieur en France,* II, 284.
53. Lavisse, *Questions d'enseignement national,* pp. 94–95.
54. Ernest Lavisse, "Ouverture des conférences de lettres et philologie et d'histoire," *RIE* (November 15, 1883), pp. 1143, 1153.
55. *Ibid.,* pp. 58–59.
56. *Ibid.,* p. 93.
57. Ernest Lavisse, "Le Concours pour l'agrégation d'histoire," *RIE* (February 15, 1881), pp. 150–151; Frédéricq, *Notes,* p. 95; and Othon Guerlac, "Ernest Lavisse, French Historian and Educator," *South Atlantic Quarterly,* 22 (January 1923), 23.
58. Lavisse frequently referred to the "battles" that the "army" of scholars in the French university were fighting against the defenders of the antiquated system of higher learning that had been inherited from the past. It appeared almost as though the French professors were preparing to reenact the war of 1870, using the modern weapons of scholarship that they had appropriated from their Germanic conquerors in order to reverse the outcome.
59. See Langlois, *Questions d'histoire et d'enseignement,* p. 159, and Lavisse, *Questions d'enseignement national,* p. xxii.
60. Lavisse, "Ouverture des conférences," pp. 1132–1134.
61. Guerlac, "Ernest Lavisse, French Historian and Educator," p. 38.
62. For a discussion of these objections see Ernest Lavisse, "La Faculté des Lettres de Paris," *RIE,* April 15, 1884; Antoine Benoist, "La Réforme de l'enseignement supérieur," *ibid.,* March 15, 1884, pp. 282–292; and M. Stapfer, *ibid.,* February 15, 1884, pp. 157–174.
63. M. Crouslé, in *La Revue générale,* March 15, 1884.
64. See Frédéricq, *Notes,* pp. 53–60, 119–120.
65. For statistical analyses of the increase in the number of students and professors in the faculties of philosophy (the equivalent of the French faculties of letters) in the various German universities during the last half of the nineteenth century see Wilhelm Lexis, *Die deutschen Universitäten* (Berlin: A. Asher, 1893), pp. 118–121, 146–148. See also Wilhelm Lexis, *A General View of the History and Organization of Public Education in the German Empire,* trans. G. J. Tamson (Berlin: A. Asher, 1904), pp. 14–50.
66. Henry Wickham Steed, *Through Thirty Years, 1892–1922* (Garden City, N.Y.: Doubleday, Page & Co., 1924), pp. 38, 48–49.
67. William H. Schofield, *Les Universités de France et d'Amérique* (Paris: Colin, 1896), pp. 5–6.

4. *In Search of* La Méthode Historique

1. Charles Seignobos, "Ernest Lavisse," *La Revue universitaire,* 9 (1922), 60. Supported by one of the *bourses d'études* that the government had begun to award (and which his mentor Lavisse secured for him), Seignobos spent two years at various German universities, including those of Göttingen, Berlin (where Ranke and Sybel were still teaching), Leipzig, Munich, and Heidelberg. Seignobos to Ferry, 3 April 1879, in AN, F17 23801, Seignobos Dossier.
2. See Leguay, *Universitaires d'aujourd'hui,* pp. 145–148.

3. See G. H. McNeil, "Charles Seignobos," in Schmitt, ed., *Some Historians,* pp. 477–492; Leguay, "M. Seignobos et l'histoire," *Mercure de France,* 88 (1910), 38; and AN, F17 23801, Seignobos Dossier.

4. Seignobos, "L'Enseignement de l'histoire dans les universités allemandes," *RIE,* 1 (15 June 1881), 563–600. Monod, Lavisse, and the other editors added a *caveat* in a footnote to this article expressing serious reservations about its conclusions, which proved to be rather critical of the German conception of historical study. Their reluctance to endorse his criticisms was undoubtedly a reflection of their own respect for the German tradition.

5. *Ibid.,* pp. 595–600.

6. Charles Seignobos, "L'Enseignement de l'histoire dans les facultés," *RIE,* 8 (15 July 1884), 36.

7. *Ibid.,* p. 111.

8. McNeil, "Charles Seignobos," in Schmitt, ed., *Some Historians,* pp. 477, 480.

9. Langlois and Seignobos, *Introduction aux études historiques,* p. xvi.

10. Charles Seignobos, *La Méthode historique appliquée aux sciences sociales* (Paris: Alcan, 1901), p. 116.

11. *Ibid.,* p. 1.

12. *Ibid.,* p. 3.

13. This emphasis on "purifying" historical documents by means of source criticism, as well as the residual urge to apply the metaphors of the laboratory sciences to historical study, was reflected in his admonition to his students: "Gentlemen, one must sterilize one's instruments before using them." Cited in Henri Massis, *Evocations* (Paris: Plon, 1931), p. 59.

14. Seignobos, *La Méthode historique,* p. 5.

15. Seignobos and Langlois, *Introduction aux études historiques,* p. 193.

16. *Ibid.,* pp. 196–197.

17. *Ibid.,* p. 218.

18. *Ibid.,* pp. 225–226.

19. *Ibid.,* pp. 228, 245–246.

20. That his dissatisfaction with the dominant methodological assumptions did not cause him to endorse alternative approaches appears to represent an exception to Kuhn's dictum that "the decision to reject one paradigm is always simultaneously the decision to accept another."

21. *Ibid.,* pp. 247–249.

22. *Ibid.,* pp. 272–273.

23. *Ibid.,* p. 272.

24. *Ibid.,* pp. 115, 262.

25. *Ibid.,* p. 89.

26. *Ibid.,* pp. 93–95, 115.

27. *Ibid.,* pp. 95ff.

28. *Ibid.*

29. *Ibid.,* p. 112.

30. *Ibid.,* p. 10.

31. *Ibid.,* pp. 92–95.

32. Leguay, *Universitaires d'aujourd'hui,* pp. 216–220. The most important of these auxiliary studies in Langlois's opinion were paleography, chronology, and diplomatics. See Langlois, *Manuel de bibliographie historique,* p. vii.

33. Leguay, *La Sorbonne*, pp. 63–66.
34. Langlois, *Questions d'histoire et d'enseignement*, pp. 150, 152, 159.
35. Charles Victor Langlois, *Les Etudes historiques* (Paris: Larousse, 1915), p. 16.
36. *Ibid.*, p.18
37. See Charles Victor Langlois and C. Stein, *Archives de l'histoire de France* (Paris: Picard, 1891).
38. Langlois, *Questions d'histoire et d'enseignement*, pp. 163–164.
39. *Ibid.*, p. 164.
40. *Ibid.*, p.165. Lavisse also regarded the increased quantity of doctoral dissertations produced in French universities as a measure of the success of the new programs. See Lavisse, *Questions d'enseignement national*, pp. xxi–xxii.
41. *Ibid.*, p. 232.
42. *Ibid.*, p. 223.
43. *Ibid.*, pp. 226–227.
44. *Ibid.*
45. *Ibid.*, p. 226.
46. Gabriel Monod, *La Méthode en histoire* (Evreux: Charles Herissey et Fils, n.d.), p. 1.
47. *Ibid.*, p. 1–2.
48. *Ibid.*, pp. 3–4.
49. *Ibid.*, p. 5.
50. *Ibid.*, p. 18.
51. *Ibid.*, p. 18–19.
52. See Ehrard and Palmade, *L'Histoire*, p. 86.
53. Henri Irenée Marrou, *De la Connaissance historique* (Paris: Editions du Seuil, 1959), pp. 21–22.
54. See Mitchell, "German History in France after 1870," pp. 83–84.
55. See Kuhn, *The Structure of Scientific Revolutions*, pp. 10–22.

5. *History as Civic Instruction: The Conflict of Science and Patriotism*

1. See D. W. Brogan, *The Development of Modern France*, I (New York: Harper Torchbooks, 1966), pp. 158ff.
2. Monod, *Michelet à l'Ecole normale* (Paris: Hachette, 1895), p. 15; Siegel, "Science and the Historical Imagination: Patterns of French Historical Thought, 1866-1914," Ph.D diss., Columbia University, 1965, p. 16. In keeping with this tradition, the French literary historian Gustave Lanson was hired in 1886 to serve as the private tutor of Nicholas II of Russia.
3. Lavisse tells of how he learned about the Napoleonic wars at the knee of his grandmother. Ernest Lavisse, *Souvenirs* (Paris: C. Lévy, 1912), pp. 103–106.
4. Universal suffrage was, of course, inherited from the Second Empire, but in that plebiscitary regime it served chiefly as a means of ratifying the policies previously decided upon by the Emperor and his advisers.
5. See Louis Legrand, *L'Idée de patrie* (Paris: Hachette, 1897), pp. 269–270.
6. Ferdinand Buisson, in *La Grande Revue*, 10 November 1909, p. 26. Buisson, who served as director of primary education, professor of the Science of Education at the Sorbonne, and chairman of the Chamber of Deputies Educa-

tion Committee, exercised perhaps the greatest influence on the organization of primary education of any French educator-politician. A representative selection of his educational thought, particularly his view of the schoolmaster as the "pioneer of democracy," can be found in Ferdinand Buisson and F. E. Farrington, eds., *French Educational Ideals of Today* (Yonkers-on-Hudson, N.Y.: World Publishing Co., 1919), pp. 128–137.

7. Reprinted in *RIE*, 11 (15 November 1883), 1151.
8. *Ibid.*, p. 1152.
9. Ernest Lavisse, quoted in Georges Grosjean, *L'Ecole et la patrie* (Paris: Perrin, 1906), p. 3.
10. *Ibid.* This sentiment was echoed by Louis Legrand, a member of the *Conseil d'Etat*, who urged that history be employed for patriotic purposes in the schools. Historical instruction "should not remain purely scientific," he declared. "It should preach and propagate the cult of the fatherland." Legrand, *L'Idée de patrie*, p. 274.
11. Ernest Lavisse, *L'Enseignement de l'histoire à l'école primaire* (Paris: Colin, 1912), pp. 29–30, 32.
12. Ernest Lavisse, *A Propos de nos écoles* (Paris: Colin, 1895), p. 79.
13. *Ibid.*, p. 80.
14. Lavisse address to students in Nouvion-en-Thiérache, August 1905, reprinted in Buisson and Farrington, eds., *French Educational Ideals of Today*, pp. 94, 98–99.
15. *Ibid.*, pp. 78–79.
16. *Ibid.*, p. 157.
17. *Ibid.*
18. *Ibid.*, p. 101.
19. Lavisse, in *Manuel général de l'instruction primaire*, February 19, 1898, reprinted *ibid.*, p. 108.
20. See C. L. d'Espinay de Briort, "Une Correspondence inédite: le prince impérial et Ernest Lavisse, 1871–1879," *Revue des deux mondes* (April 1929), pp. 555–591.
21. Lavisse to Prince Imperial, 14 November 1874, *ibid.*, p. 560.
22. Lavisse to Prince Imperial, 18 February 1877, *ibid.*, p. 576.
23. Lavisse to Prince Imperial, 30 April 1878, *ibid.*, p. 586.
24. See Guerlac, "Ernest Lavisse, French Historian and Educator," pp. 27ff, and Pierre Nora, "Ernest Lavisse: son rôle dans la formation du sentiment national," *Revue historique*, 228 (July 1962), 80ff.
25. Guerlac, "Ernest Lavisse: French Historian and Educator," p. 28; Lach, "Ernest Lavisse," in Schmitt, ed., *Some Historians*, p. 247.
26. Lach, "Ernest Lavisse," in Schmitt, ed., *Some Historians*, p. 242; Guerlac, "Ernest Lavisse, French Historian and Educator," p. 26.
27. Raoul Girardet, ed., *Le Nationalisme français, 1871–1914* (Paris: Colin, 1966), pp. 80–81.
28. Lavisse, *L'Enseignement de l'histoire à l'école primaire*, p. 16.
29. Buisson and Farrington, eds., *French Educational Ideals of Today*, p. 93.
30. Lavisse, *L'Enseignement de l'histoire à l'école primaire*, pp. 8, 16.
31. Brogan, *The Development of Modern France*, I, 154–155.
32. Lavisse, *Questions d'enseignement national*, pp. xxiv–xxv.

33. Carlton J. H. Hayes, *France: A Nation of Patriots* (New York: Columbia University Press, 1930), p. 57.
34. Ernest Lavisse, *Histoire de France: cours élémentaire* (Paris: Colin, 1875), p. 175.
35. Girardet, ed., *Le Nationalisme français*, p. 80.
36. Ehrard and Palmade, *L'Histoire*, p. 74.
37. McNeil, "Charles Seignobos," in Schmitt, ed., *Some Historians*, p. 480.
38. Albert Cahuet, "La Réaction des historiens contre les manuels d'histoire," *L'Illustration*, 20 May 1933, p. 110.
39. Langlois, *Les Etudes historiques*, pp. 16–17.
40. Hayes, *France: A Nation of Patriots*, p. 52. See the valuable digest of the most widely used elementary school textbooks that appears in Appendix A, pp. 343–399.
41. *Enquête sur les livres scolaires d'après guerre.* Conciliation nationale, Bulletin No. 3 (La Flèche: Depôt des Publications de la Conciliation, 1924), p. 30.
42. Langlois and Seignobos, *Introduction aux études historiques*, pp. 288–289.
43. Hayes, *France: A Nation of Patriots*, pp. 43–44.
44. M. Guignebert, in *L'Enseignement public* (January 1927), p. 10.
45. Girardet, ed., *Le Nationalisme français*, pp. 80–81.

6. *The Record of Scholarly Achievement: 1876–1900*

1. For a chronological summary of the major innovations in the discipline of history between 1876 and 1900, with particular emphasis on the French historical profession, see *L'Histoire et ses méthodes* (Paris: Gallimard, 1961), pp. 1624–1635.
2. Halphen, *L'Histoire en France depuis cent ans*, p. 195.
3. See Barnes, *A History of Historical Writing*, pp. 213–214.
4. *Ibid.*, p. 62; Maurice Prou, in *La Vie universitaire à Paris*, p. 209.
5. Halphen, in *Histoire et historiens*, I, 154–155. By the year 1891 the French government was spending 71,000 francs to support research at the Ecole des Chartes and 75,000 francs to finance historical scholarship at the Ecole Pratique. Beginning in the last decade of the nineteenth century, an annual appropriation of 145,000 francs underwrote the cost of continuing the publication of the Documents inédits de l'histoire de France, a project begun under Guizot. See J. Franklin Jameson, "The Expenditures of Foreign Governments in Behalf of History," in *American Historical Association, Annual Report (1891)* (Washington, D.C.: Government Printing Office, 1892), p. 36.
6. Bémont, in *Ecole Pratique annuaire*, 1912–1913, pp. 18–19. In 1889 a group of scholars began publishing a monthly collection of the most significant documents that had been retrieved. See *Archives historiques, artistiques, et littéraires. Recueil de documents curieux et inédits* (Paris: Bourlaton, 1889–1914).
7. Halphen, in *Histoire et historiens*, I, 156–157.
8. Aulard, "Leçon d'ouverture du cours d'histoire de la Révolution française à la faculté des lettres de Paris," pp. 18–28.
9. H. Chobaut, "L'Oeuvre d'Aulard et l'histoire de la Révolution française," pp. 1–4.

10. Farmer, *France Reviews Its Revolutionary Origins*, pp. 59–60.
11. James Godfrey, "Alphonse Aulard," in Schmitt, ed., *Some Historians*, p. 59; Farmer, *France Reviews Its Revolutionary Origins*, p. 60.
12. Halphen, *L'Histoire en France depuis cent ans*, pp. 171–172; Bémont, in *Ecole Pratique annuaire*, 1912–1913, p. 76; Langlois, *Les Etudes historiques*, p. 18. Monod, *De la Possibilité*, pp. 45–46; *Histoire et historiens*, pp. 154ff, 171ff.
13. Halphen, *L'Histoire en France depuis cent ans*, pp. 167–168.
14. Lavisse, *Questions d'enseignement national*, p. xxii.
15. *Ibid.*
16. Ernest Lavisse and Alfred Rambaud, eds., *Histoire générale du IVe siècle à nos jours* (Paris: Colin, 1892–1901), I, 1.
17. Quoted in Stern, ed., *The Varieties of History*, p. 248.
18. Lavisse and Rambaud, eds., *Histoire générale*, XII, 1–51, 626–628.
19. Lavisse, *Questions d'enseignement national*, p. 14.
20. Lavisse, quoted in Guerlac, "Ernest Lavisse, French Historian and Educator," p. 32.
21. Lavisse, *A Propos de nos écoles*, p. 117.
22. *Ibid.*
23. See Lavisse, *Questions d'enseignement national*, p. 90.
24. Guerlac, "Ernest Lavisse, French Historian and Educator," p. 32.
25. Seignobos, "Ernest Lavisse," p. 260.
26. Charles Victor Langlois, "Ernest Lavisse," in *La Revue de France*, 5 (1922), 472.
27. Lach, "Ernest Lavisse," in Schmitt, ed., *Some Historians*, p. 253.
28. Langlois and Seignobos, *Introduction aux études historiques*, p. 110.

7. The Challenge of the Science of Society

1. Like the major academic historians in France, the future founders of academic sociology received scholarship grants from the Ministry of Education to study across the Rhine. Célestin Bouglé, Maurice Halbwachs, and Georges Davy made the hegira in addition to Durkheim. Clark, "Emile Durkheim and the Institutionalization of Sociology," p. 43.
2. Liard had discovered Durkheim in the pages of Ribot's *Revue philosophique*, to which Durkheim contributed articles on German philosophy in 1887. For a description of the new course at Bordeaux, see Harry Alpert, "France's First University Course in Sociology," *American Sociological Review*, 2 (1937), 311–317.
3. For an informative interpretive treatment of Durkheim's early career see H. Stuart Hughes, *Consciousness and Society* (New York: Knopf, 1958), pp. 278ff. For more extensive accounts see Harry Alpert, *Emile Durkheim and His Sociology* (New York: Russell and Russell, 1939); Robert Bierstedt, *Emile Durkheim* (New York: Dell, 1966); Robert A. Nisbet, ed., *Emile Durkheim* (Englewood Cliffs, N.J.: Prentice-Hall, 1965); Steven Lukes, *Emile Durkheim: His Life and Work* (New York: Harper and Row, 1973); and Dominick LaCapra, *Emile Durkheim: Sociologist and Philosopher* (Ithaca: Cornell University Press, 1972).

4. He also carried on a running battle with the psychologists, insisting that the ultimate principles of human behavior were social rather than individual. Clark, "Emile Durkheim and the Institutionalization of Sociology," p. 61. See also Daniel Essertier, *Psychologie et sociologie* (Paris: Alcan, 1927).

5. Quoted in Siegel, "Science and the Historical Imagination," p. 130. Durkheim had come under the influence of the neo-Kantian philosopher Charles Renouvier early in his intellectual career. He was therefore one of the few French academic social scientists who succeeded in incorporating into his social theory the neo-Kantian critique of positivism that Renouvier and Antoine Cournot had launched in the early years of the Third Republic. See Antoine Cournot, *Considérations sur la marche des idées et des événements dans les temps modernes*, 2 vols. (Paris: Hachette, 1872) and Flint, *History of the Philosophy of History*, pp. 642-655.

6. *RIE*, 15 (1888), 46.

7. "Cours de science sociale, leçon d'ouverture," *RIE*, 15 (1888), 45-47.

8. *RIE*, 15 (1888), 47.

9. Clark, "Emile Durkheim and the Institutionalization of Sociology," p. 51. For the ongoing territorial disputes with history see Robert N. Bellah, "Durkheim and History," in Nisbet, ed., *Emile Durkheim*, pp. 153-176, and Célestin Bouglé, "L'Année sociologique," *Les Pages libres*, 353 (October 1907), 340-345.

10. Worms headed what Terry Clark calls a separate "cluster" of researchers in the field of sociology, and regarded Durkheim and his followers as professional rivals. Clark, "Emile Durkheim and the Institutionalization of Sociology," pp. 37-38, and Clark, *Prophets and Patrons*, pp. 67, 147-154.

11. *Revue internationale de sociologie*, 1 (January-February 1893), 4-5.

12. *Ibid.*, pp. 1-2, 16.

13. For a detailed description of the organization and principal activities of this important center of sociological research see Terry N. Clark, "The Structure and Functions of a Research Institute: The *Année sociologique*," *Archives européennes de sociologie*, 9 (1968), pp. 72-91.

14. *Année sociologique*, 1 (Paris, 1896-1897), p. v, quoted in Siegel, "Science and the Historical Imagination," p. 137.

15. Quoted in Henri Peyre, "Durkheim: The Man, His Time, and His Intellectual Background," in Kurt H. Wolff, ed., *Essays on Sociology and Philosophy* (New York: Harper & Row, 1964), p. 16. For an analysis of the methodological disagreements between historians and social scientists during this period see François Simiand, "Méthode historique et science sociale," *Revue de synthèse historique*, 2 (1903), 1-57.

16. *Revue universitaire* (December 1894).

17. *Revue universitaire* (May 1895).

18. Paul Lacombe, *De l'Histoire considérée comme science* (Paris: Librairie Hachette, 1894), p. viii.

19. *Ibid.*, p. 1.

20. *Ibid.*, p. x.

21. *Ibid.*, p. xi.

22. *Ibid.*, pp. x-xii.

23. *Ibid.*, p. xiii.
24. *Ibid.*, pp. 9–10.
25. *Ibid.*, pp. 4ff.
26. *Ibid.*, p. 4. He hoped that in the future these behavioral regularities could be traced to the elemental biological needs, which could be discovered by studying the anatomical structure of the organs and the nervous system of man. He frequently cited the great Scottish psychologist Alexander Bain for scientific support for this approach. *Ibid.*, pp. 4, 34.
27. *Ibid.*, p. 54.
28. *Ibid.*, pp. 62–63.
29. *Ibid.*, pp. 64, 66, 248.
30. *Ibid.*, pp. 250–252.
31. *Ibid.*, pp. 369–370.
32. Edward Tiryakian, "A Problem for the Sociology of Knowledge: The Mutual Unawareness of Emile Durkheim and Max Weber," *Archives européennes de sociologie,* 7 (1966), 330–336. See Hughes, *Consciousness and Society,* p. 281 for a discussion of Durkheim's intellectual insularity.
33. A.-D. Xénopol, *Les Principes fondamentaux de l'histoire* (Paris: Ernest Leroux, 1899), pp. i–iii.
34. *Ibid.*, p. 24. The author chides Seignobos as a typical representative of the modern historians who are filled with doubts about the methods of their profession and hasten to apologize for its shortcomings.
35. *Ibid.*, pp. 26–27. He cited Dilthey's *Einleitung in die Geisteswissenschaften* (Berlin, 1883), p. 6, which had earlier denounced the positivists for formulating scientific hypotheses according to conceptions borrowed from the natural sciences. See Hughes, *Consciousness and Society,* pp. 192–200.
36. Xénopol was one of the few participants in the methodological debates within the French historical profession who addressed himself to the epistemological issues raised by the neo-Kantian school in Germany.
37. Xénopol, *Les Principes fondamentaux de l'histoire,* p. 1.
38. *Ibid.*, p. 19ff. Xénopol was not the first historian to establish an epistemological connection between history and geology on the basis of their common concern with evolution. Ernest Renan had earlier praised the German historians for regarding their discipline as "parallel to geology" in that it records the evolution of man in the same way that geology records the evolution of the planet. See Ernest Renan, "L'Instruction supérieure en France," *Revue des deux mondes* (1 May 1864).
39. *Ibid.*, p. 26.
40. *Ibid.*
41. *Ibid.*, p. 44.
42. *Ibid.*, p. 48.
43. *Ibid.*, pp. 72–75, 85, 131, 143, 302, 149. Xénopol's rather tortuous defense of the scientific nature of historical study borrowed from a wide variety of sources. His belief in the importance of race and environment is derived from the works of Le Bon and Taine, whom he acknowledges, and his three "natural laws of history" are reminiscent of Walter Bagehot, Gabriel Tarde, and Alfred Fouillée, whom he does not.

44. A.-D. Xénopol, *La Notion de "valeur" en histoire* (Versailles: Impr. Cerf, 1906), pp. 23, 47.
45. Xénopol, *Les Principes fondamentaux de l'histoire,* pp. 64, 332.
46. The American historian Harry Elmer Barnes also recognized this fact and identified the Rumanian scholar as an advocate of history conceived as a "genetic social science." Barnes, *A History of Historical Writing,* p. 321.
47. Lacombe, "La Science de l'histoire d'après M. Xénopol," *Revue de synthèse historique,* 1 (July–December 1900), 37, 51; hereafter cited as *RSH.*

8. Henri Berr and the "Terrible Craving for Synthesis"

1. Henri Berr, *Vie et science: lettres d'un vieux philosophe strasbourgeois et d'un étudiant parisien* (Paris: Colin, 1894), p. 97.
2. *Ibid.,* pp. 132, 171–172.
3. *Ibid.,* pp. 178–180.
4. Monod, *De la Possibilité,* p. 30.
5. Stern, ed., *Varieties of History,* p. 12.
6. Lavisse, *A propos de nos écoles,* p. 245.
7. *Ibid.,* pp. 246–247.
8. See Martin Siegel, "Henri Berr's *Revue de synthèse historique,*" *History and Theory,* 9 (1970), 324.
9. M. Guignebert, *L'Enseignement public* (January 1927), p. 10.
10. Emile Boutroux, *Etudes d'histoire de la philosophie* (Paris: Alcan, 1897), pp. 8–9.
11. Another attentive listener of Boutroux's at the rue d'Ulm was Bergson, and after the former graduated to the Sorbonne in 1885 young Charles Péguy was introduced to Pascal at Boutroux's lectures there. The extent to which Berr, a member of the Ecole Normale's *promotion* of 1881, was influenced by Fustel de Coulanges, the guiding spirit of the school in the 1880s, remains largely unexplored. Professor Martin Siegel has been combing the archives of the Ecole Normale in search of evidence of this Fustel-Berr connection. The results of this research are scheduled to be presented in a paper at the 1974 convention of the American Historical Association.
12. Henri Berr, *L'Avenir de la philosophie: esquisse d'une synthèse des connaissances fondée sur l'histoire* (Paris: Hachette, 1899), pp. 8, 11–12, 19–21.
13. Berr, *Vie et science,* p. 204.
14. See Ernest Renan, *La Réforme intellectuelle et morale* (Paris: Calmann-Lévy, 1872), pp. 95–110.
15. Berr, *Vie et science,* pp. 213, 220.
16. Berr, *L'Avenir de la philosophie,* p. 362.
17. *Ibid.,* p. 418.
18. *Ibid.,* pp. 418–419.
19. See Siegel, "Henri Berr's *Revue de synthèse historique,*" p. 326.
20. Berr, *L'Avenir de la philosophie,* pp. 424, 431; Berr, in *La Nouvelle Revue* (1890), pp. 517–523. The numerous suggestions for a union of history and sociology that surfaced in the 1890s went unheeded largely because both disciplines viewed each other as professional competitors. But this mutual

hostility began to dissipate after the turn of the century, when the two professions began to discern reasons for cooperation. See below, chap. 10.

21. Berr, *Vie et science,* pp. 6ff.

22. Duruy had later proposed to the Senate, of which he had become a member, that France establish "une grande université parisienne." Unfortunately, the proposal was made on July 14, 1870, a day before the French government took the decision to declare the war that was to bring down the Second Empire.

23. Berr, *L'Avenir de la philosophie,* p. 492.

24. Gabriel Monod, in *Revue historique,* 70 (1899), 99.

25. *RSH,* 1 (July–December 1900), 1, reprinted in Stern, ed., *Varieties of History,* p. 250.

26. *RSH,* 1 (July–December 1900), 2.

27. *Ibid.,* p. 4.

28. *Ibid.,* pp. 6–7.

29. Ehrard and Palmade, eds., *L'Histoire,* p. 84.

30. *RSH,* 1 (July–December 1900), 7.

31. Siegel, "Henri Berr's *Revue de synthèse historique,"* pp. 323–324; Barnes, *A History of Historical Writing,* p. 319.

32. *RSH,* 1 (July–December 1900), 7–8.

33. Emile Boutroux, "Histoire et synthèse," *ibid.,* pp. 9–11.

34. *Ibid.,* p. 11.

35. *Ibid.,* p. 12.

36. Ehrard and Palmade, eds., *L'Histoire,* p. 85.

37. See vols. 2, pp. 146–147; 5, pp. 138–140; 6, pp. 129–130; 8, pp. 162–164; 9, pp. 135–137; 10, pp. 176–179. Siegel, "Henri Berr's *Revue de synthèse historique,"* p. 328.

38 Seignobos, *La Méthode historique,* pp. 3–5.

39. Langlois, *Questions d'histoire et d'enseignement,* p. 226.

40. *Ibid.,* pp. 233, 239–240, 211.

41. *RSH,* 9 (1904), 10 (1905). The absence of Gabriel Monod's response was particularly conspicuous, since it was he who had originally suggested that such an inquiry be conducted.

42. *RSH,* 10 (1905), p. 191.

43. *Ibid.*

44. *Ibid.,* pp. 191–192.

45. *Revue historique,* 110 (May–August 1912), pp. xxii–xxiii.

46. B. N., MS, N.A.F., 24432, cited in Siegel, "Science and the Historical Imagination," pp. 210–212.

47. See Gabriel Monod, *La Chaire de l'histoire au Collège de France* (Paris: Editions de la Revue politique et littéraire et de la Revue scientifique, 1906), for the opening lecture. Monod paid a left-handed compliment to Berr by hailing the appearance of "the first special review devoted to historical synthesis" without mentioning the editor's name.

48. Delatour, *Notice,* p. 45. See Monod, *La Vie et la pensée de Jules Michelet: cours professé au Collège de France* (Paris: Champion, 1923).

49. *RSH,* 26, p. 228. For biographical details see AN, F17 23815, Berr Dossier.

50. Marrou, *De La Connaissance historique*, pp. 21–22.
51. *Ibid.*, p. 22. He was referring, of course, to Aron's ground-breaking *Introduction to the Philosophy of History*, which was appropriately subtitled *An Essay on The Limits of Historical Objectivity*, trans. George J. Erwin (Boston, Beacon Press, 1961).
52. Leguay, *La Sorbonne*, pp. 107–110. See also Henri Massis and Alfred de Tarde [Agathon], *L'Esprit de la Nouvelle Sorbonne* (Paris: Mercure de France, 1911), p. 99.

9. The Dissolution of the Republican Consensus

1. Alfred Cobban, *A History of Modern France*, III (New York: Braziller, 1965), p. 54.
2. Several writers have called attention to the French intelligentsia's ambivalent attitude toward the Republican regime during the last quarter of the nineteenth century. See Bellesort, *Les Intellectuels*, pp. 130–131, 158–159, 220, 234, and Scott, *Republican Ideas and the Liberal Tradition in France*, pp. 95–96.
3. Ehrard and Palmade, eds., *L'Histoire*, pp. 74–75.
4. See Leguay, "M. Seignobos et l'histoire," p. 37.
5. Barrès first used the term "nationalism" in this modern, reactionary sense in an article entitled "La Querelle des nationalistes et des cosmopolites," *Le Figaro*, 4 July 1892. For a provocative treatment of Barrès' "protofascist" tendencies, see Robert Soucy, *Fascism in France: The Case of Maurice Barrès* (Berkeley: University of California Press, 1972). Zeev Sternhell's *Maurice Barrès et le nationalisme français* (Paris: Colin, 1972) emphasizes the racist, anti-Semitic aspects of Barrès nationalism.
6. See *Le Siècle*, 14 July 1898 and E. de Haime, *Les Faits acquis de l'histoire* (Paris: Stock, 1898), pp. 338–340. Largely as a result of a misreading of Charles Péguy, the notion that French intellectuals were united in support of Dreyfus has persisted. Quite to the contrary, a majority of the French Academy signed the anti-Dreyfusard manifesto that appeared in the December 31, 1898, issue of *Le Soleil*. An appeal to "the people" from the anti-Dreyfusard *Ligue de la Patrie Française*, dated January 5, 1899, appeared above the signatures of some of the leading members of the literary intelligentsia, including Ferdinand Brunetière, François Coppée, Henri Houssaye, Albert Sorel, and Albert Vandal. The central committee that was set up in a general assembly on January 20 included the composer Vincent d'Indy, the historian Alfred Rambaud, as well as the future Action Française militants Maurice Pujo and Henri Vaugeois. Archives Nationales F7 12721, 1898–1900, Ligue de la Patrie Française. A brochure published by the critic Jules Lemaître in the name of the League on January 19, 1899, listed as members the painter Degas, the critics Francisque Sarcey and André Bellesort, and the publisher Honoré Champion, as well as the future leaders of the royalist Action Française: Pujo, Léon Daudet, Frédéric Amouretti, and Charles Maurras. Jules Lemaître, *Première Conférence* (Paris: Bureau de la Patrie Française, 19 January 1899), deposited in Archives Nationales F7 12721, 1899–1900, Ligue de la Patrie Française. These membership lists reflect the first public split between the independent literary and artistic intellectuals and the members of the Université. See below, chap. 10.

7. Godfrey, "Alphonse Aulard," in Schmitt, ed., *Some Historians,* p. 61.
8. Monod, Preface to Frank Puaux, *Vers la Justice* (Paris: Fischbacher, 1906), pp. iv–v.
9. See Monod's letters to Haime, 5 Nov. 1897 and 21 July 1898, in Haime, *Les Faits acquis de l'histoire,* pp. xv, 214–216, as well as the anonymous work by a former student of Monod's entitled *La Verité historique* (Paris, 1900).
10. See Gabriel Monod [Pierre Molé], *Exposé impartial de l'Affaire Dreyfus* (Paris, 1898), and AN, F17 21982, Monod Dossier.
11. Charles Péguy, "L'Argent suite," in *Oeuvres complètes,* XIV (Paris: Editions de la Nouvelle Revue Française, 1932), pp. 95-97 and *L'Action Française* (5 January 1909).
12. *Revue de Paris* (October 1899), pp. 648–649, 654–655.
13. *Ibid.,* pp. 667–668. Lavisse to Poincaré, 1 Aug. 1898, BN, MS, N.A.F., 16006.
14. Archives Nationales F7 12721, 1898–1900, Ligue de la Patrie Française.
15. Eugen Weber, *Action Française* (Stanford, Calif.: Stanford University Press, 1962), p. 36.
16. For a discussion by an unsympathetic observer of the Ecole Normale's participation in the *Affaire* see Hubert Bourgin, *De Jaurès à Léon Blum: L'Ecole normale et la politique* (Paris: Fayard, 1938). For a more balanced account see Robert Smith, "L'Atmosphere politique à l'Ecole normale supérieure à la fin du XIXe siècle," *Revue d'histoire moderne et contemporaine,* 20 (April–June 1973), 248–268.
17. Leguay, *La Sorbonne,* p. 175.
18. *L'Aurore* (28 January 1898).
19. Leguay, *La Sorbonne,* p. 180.
20. M. Mitard, "Le Rôle de l'enseignement historique," *L'Enseignement public,* No. 10 (November 1927), p. 377.
21. Grosjean, *L'Ecole et la patrie,* p. 3; Paul Pilant, *Le Patriotisme en France et à l'étranger* (Paris: Perrin, 1912), pp. 158–159.
22. Grosjean, *L'Ecole et la patrie,* pp. 4–5.
23. Emile Bocquillon, *Pour la Patrie* (Paris: Vuibert et Nony, 1907), p. 8; *Revue de l'enseignement public* (4 June 1899, 3 September 1899, 10 September 1899). Emile Bocquillon, *La Crise du patriotisme à l'école* (Paris: Vuibert et Nony, 1905), p. 4.
24. Max Ferré, *Histoire du mouvement syndicaliste révolutionnaire chez les instituteurs: des origines à 1922* (Paris: Société universitaire d'éditions et de librairie, 1955), pp. 24–26; Anonymous, "Histoire de la fédération d'enseignement," unpublished manuscript, pp. 3–4.
25. Ferré, *Histoire du mouvement,* pp. 26–27; Ferdinand Buisson, *Nouveau Dictionnaire de pédagogie* (Paris: Hachette, 1911), p. 53. For a description of the structure and function of the *Amicales* by members themselves see F. Bernard and others, *Le Syndicalisme dans l'enseignement* (Avignon: Ecolé Emancipée, 1924).
26. Ferré, *Histoire du mouvement,* pp. 27–28.
27. *Ibid.,* pp. 29–30, 56; *Revue de l'enseignement* (20 April 1902).
28. Ferré, *Histoire du mouvement,* pp. 32–33.
29. *Histoire de la fédération d'enseignement,* p. 7; Ferré, *Histoire du mouvement,* pp. 43, 45, 81.

30. Ferré, *Histoire du mouvement,* pp. 62–63.
31. See Ferdinand Buisson, in *La Grande Revue* (10 November 1909), pp. 39–40.
32. *Enquête sur les livres scolaires,* pp. 31–32.
33. Ferré, *Histoire du mouvement,* pp. 33, 56, 61; M.-T. Laurin, in *Le Mouvement socialiste,* no. 150 (1 March 1905).
34. *L'Emancipation de l'instituteur* (November 1904).
35. *L'Emancipation de l'instituteur* (December 1903).
36. Ferré, *Histoire du mouvement,* pp. 75–77.
37. Georges Duveau, *Les Instituteurs* (Paris: Editions du Seuil, 1957), pp. 142–146.
38. *L'Emancipation de l'instituteur* (July 1905).
39. *L'Humanité* (24 November 1905). James M. Clark, *Teachers and Politics in France* (Syracuse: Syracuse University Press, 1967), pp. 11–12.
40. *Le Temps* (20 August 1903); *Journal des débats* (10 August 1903).
41. See *L'Avant-garde pédagogique* (1 April 1904); Bocquillon, *La Crise du patriotisme à l'école,* pp. 117–121.
42. *L'Ecole patriote* (20 July 1904).
43. Bocquillon, *La Crise du patriotisme à l'école,* p. 24.
44. *Ibid.,* p. viii; Bocquillon, *Pour la patrie,* pp. xxiv, 21–24, 52.
45. *L'Eclair* (25 October 1905).
46. *Le Temps* (21 October, 25 November 1905).
47. See the favorable comments in *L'Humanité* (26 and 30 October, 24 November, and 18 December 1905).
48. Ferré, *Histoire du mouvement,* pp. 95–97.
49. *L'Emancipation de l'Instituteur* (March 1907); Clark, *Teachers and Politics,* p. 12; Anonymous, *Les Instituteurs syndiqués et la classe ouvrière* (Paris, 1907), p. 52; Ferré, *Histoire du mouvement,* pp. 104–108; Duveau, *Les Instituteurs,* p. 150.
50. Ferré, *Histoire du mouvement,* pp. 64–65; *Revue de l'enseignement primaire* (9 April 1905).
51. See the reprint of Hervé's speech at the trial of Parisian antimilitarists in December 1905, in which he denounced the history manuals that "manipulated the facts of national history for the greater glory of the fatherland" and inspired "race hatred, national vanity, and idolatry of the sword." Gustave Hervé, *Patriotism and the Worker* (New Castle, Pa.: I.W.W. Publishing Bureau, 1912), pp. 6–7.
52. Bocquillon, *La Crise du patriotisme à l'école,* pp. 117–121.
53. Grosjean, *L'Ecole et la patrie,* pp. 11, 18.
54. *Le Temps* (29 June 1905).
55. Bocquillon, *La Crise du patriotisme à l'école,* p. 253; Grosjean, *L'Ecole et la patrie,* p. 11.
56. *Revue de l'enseignement primaire* (2 and 11 October 1903); *Enquête sur les livres scolaire,* pp. 31–32.
57. Charles Martel, in *Revue de l'enseignement* (15 March 1908); E. Glay, in *Revue de l'enseignement* (21 February 1909); Ferré, *Histoire du mouvement,* p. 149.
58. *Le Radical* (16 April 1907); *La Petite République* (11 April, 14 May 1907).
59. *L'Anarchie* (2 December 1909).
60. *L'Anarchie* (9 December 1909).
61. Stephen MacSay, *Vers l'Education humaine: la laïque contre l'enfant*

(Mons: Impr. Générale, 1911), p. 82. See also G. Abraham, in *L'Anarchie* (6 January 1910), and J. Maitron, *Histoire du mouvement anarchiste en France* (Paris: Sudel, 1951), p. 327.

62. Ferré, *Histoire du mouvement*, pp. 56–57.

63. *Enquête de l'Humanité nouvelle sur le militarisme* (Paris: Schleicher, 1899). See also Henri Massis, *La Guerre de trente ans* (Paris: Plon, 1940), pp. 5–6, 39, for further references to antimilitarist sentiment in the prewar Sorbonne.

64. Bocquillon, *Pour la patrie*, pp. xxiv–xxv. See the article by T. Laurin in the November 19, 1910, number of *L'Ecole Emancipée*, the official organ of the National Federation of Public School Teachers of France, for an example of syndicalist hostility to the republican and bourgeois biases of history textbooks.

65. Bocquillon, *Pour la patrie*, p. 5.

66. Grosjean, *L'Ecole et la patrie*, pp. 30–31; Pilant, *Le Patriotisme en France*, pp. 152–153.

67. Gustave Lanson, "Le Patriotisme et l'école," *Revue bleue* (16 September 1905). See also Maurice Kahn, "Enquête sur le syndicalisme dans l'enseignement primaire," *Les Pages libres*, 337 (15 June 1907), 338 (22 June 1907), 339 (29 June 1907), 340 (6 July 1907), and 341 (15 July 1907).

68. Gabriel Séailles, "Patrie et patriotisme," *La Grande Revue* (25 July 1910), pp. 260–261. See also Herbert Tint, *The Decline of French Patriotism: 1870–1914* (London: Weidenfeld & Nicholson, 1964).

69. *L'Enseignement public* (July–December 1927), p. 377.

70. Bocquillon, *La Crise du patriotisme à l'école*, p. 5.

71. An estimated 9,500 teachers belonged to the Amicales, out of roughly 120,000 schoolteachers in France; hence, approximately 10 percent belonged to one or the other of the two teacher organizations. Ferré, *Histoire du mouvement*, p. 126. These membership figures are distorted by the fact that several schoolteachers belonged to both groups simultaneously. Clark, *Teachers and Politics*, pp. 11–12.

72. Ferré, *Histoire du mouvement*, pp. 124–126, 305.

73. Bocquillon, *Pour la patrie*, p. xxix. This resolution was later attacked in the *Journal des débats* as a prime example of "minimum patriotism."

74. Ferré, *Histoire du mouvement*, p. 213.

75. Ferdinand Buisson, in *La Grande Revue* (10 November 1909), pp. 42–43, 46.

76. Barrès's introduction to Pilant, *Le Patriotisme en France*, pp. v, vii–xii; Alcide Ebray, *La France qui meurt* (Paris: Société Française d'Imprimerie et de Librairie, 1910), p. 240; Grosjean, *L'Ecole et la patrie*, pp. 23, 33, 39, 61. For similar criticisms of this developing trend in the teaching profession see Georges Goyau, *L'Idée de patrie et l'humanitarisme* (Paris: Perrin, 1902), pp. xx–xxi, xxviii, 333–334. Whether the doctrines of antipatriotism were as widespread in education circles as these rightist critics claimed is debatable. Eugen Weber suggests that antipatriotism had become the rule among primary schools in particular by 1903. Weber, *The Nationalist Revival in France, 1905–1914* (Berkeley: University of California Press, 1968), p. 23.

77. Grosjean, *L'Ecole et la patrie*, p. 27; *La Petite République* (November 12, 15, 16, 1901); Pilant, *Le Patriotisme en France*, p. 180.

78. Alphonse Aulard, *Polémique et histoire* (Paris: Edouard Cornély et Cie, 1904), p. 58.
79. Godfrey, "Alphonse Aulard," in Schmitt, ed., *Some Historians*, p. 61.
80. Aulard in *La Depêche de Toulouse* (1 October 1902).
81. Aulard in *Action* (20 December 1903).
82. Aulard had served as both president and vice-president of the Mission Laïque Française.
83. Aulard, *Polémique et histoire*, pp. 379, 139–140.
84. Aulard, in *l'Aurore* (6 March 1904).
85. Langlois, *Questions d'histoire et d'enseignement*, pp. 215–216.
86. *Ibid.*, p. 151.
87. Charles Victor Langlois, "La Tradition de la France," Speech delivered at the University of Chicago, October 1904, reprinted in Langlois, *Questions d'histoire et d'enseignement*, 2d ed. (Paris: Hachette, 1906), pp. 24–25.
88. Steed, *Through Thirty Years*, p. 36.
89. Waldo J. Leland, "L'Organisation internationale des études historiques," in *Histoire et historiens*, II, 741.
90. *Ibid.*, pp. 751–755. See *Annales internationales d'histoire*, Congrès de la Haye, no. 1 (Paris, 1899). These sentiments were echoed at the Berlin (1908) and London (1913) congresses.
91. See Tint, *The Decline of French Patriotism*, pp. 70–114, for a discussion of the evolution of French patriotism from left to right during the last two decades of the nineteenth century.

10. Social Science and the Restoration of the Republican Synthesis

1. See Alfred Fouillée, *La Science sociale contemporaine*, 2d ed. (Paris: Hachette, 1885), pp. 78–80, 379–380, 382–383.
2. For an informative discussion of the development of the solidarist movement in France see Scott, *Republican Ideas and the Liberal Tradition in France*, pp. 157–186. Also useful in this regard is J. E. S. Hayward, "Solidarity: The Social History of an Idea in Ninteenth Century France," *International Review of Social History*, 4 (1959), 260–284.
3. Hayward, "Solidarity," pp. 279–280.
4. See Scott, *Republican Ideas and the Liberal Tradition in France*, pp. 171–172. For a description of Bourgeois's life and thought see Hayward, "Solidarity," and Scott, *Republican Ideas and the Liberal Tradition in France*, pp. 169–170.
5. Scott, *Republican Ideas and the Liberal Tradition in France*, pp. 158, 177. "The aim of *Solidarité* was not social equality, the abolition of capitalism and the inauguration of socialism," Scott observes, but rather that of "making only those social concessions that would avert the danger of revolution."
6. Léon Bourgeois, *La Solidarité*, 7th ed. (Paris: Alcan, 1912), p. 4.
7. See Charles Gide, "The Solidarists," in Charles Gide and Charles Rist, *A History of Economic Doctrines* (London: Heath and Co., 1909), p. 593, cited in Brian Turner, "Emile Durkheim: The Social Functions of Social Science," unpublished paper, Columbia University, Department of Anthropology. I am indebted to Mr. Turner's paper for calling to my attention several of the works cited in this chapter.

8. Hayward, "Solidarity," p. 281.

9. Introduction to Emile Durkheim, *L'Evolution pédagogique en France* (Paris: Presses Universitaires de France, 1969), pp. 1–2. In his opening lecture from his chair in the Science of Education at the Sorbonne, Durkheim reminded his audience that the purpose of education was social rather than individual in nature, that is, it should seek to imbue the pupil with the accepted principles of his society rather than to release within him the latent energies that pre-existed in his mind. "The man whom education should realize in us is not the man such as nature has made him," he declared. It is rather the man such as "society wishes him to be." Emile Durkheim, *Education and Sociology*, trans. S. D. Fox (New York: The Free Press, 1956), pp. 115–116, 122.

10. Scott, *Republican Ideas and the Liberal Tradition in France*, p. 179.

11. See *L'Ecole des Hautes Etudes, 1900–1910* (Paris: Alcan, 1911), and Scott, *Republican Ideas and the Liberal Tradition in France*, pp. 179–180. For the reports of the proceedings of the congress see Ministère du Commerce et l'Industrie, *Congrès international de l'éducation sociale* (1900), procès-verbal sommaire (Paris, 1902). Other speakers at the Congress included Seignobos, Buisson, the economist Charles Gide, and Durkheim.

12. The Ecole des Hautes Etudes Sociales was actually an offshoot of the Collège Libre des Sciences Sociales, which was founded by a wealthy heiress named Jeanne Weill, who wrote under the pseudonym "Dick May."

13. See Scott, *Republican Ideas and the Liberal Tradition in France*, pp. 181–183, and *L'Ecole des Hautes Etudes Sociales*.

14. Gide and Rist, *A History of Economic Doctrines*, p. 593. See also Dom Besse, *Les Religions laïques* (Paris: Nouvelle Librairie Nationale, 1913).

15. See Gaston Maurice, *Le Parti radical* (Paris, 1929), p. 27; Scott, *Republican Ideas and the Liberal Tradition in France*, pp. 157, 179–180.

16. Clark, "Emile Durkheim and the Institutionalization of Sociology," p. 42.

17. Paul Fauconnet, Introduction, Durkheim, *Education and Sociology*, p. 27; Clark, "Emile Durkheim and the Institutionalization of Sociology," pp. 54–55.

18. See Clark, *Prophets and Patrons*, pp. 162–195.

19. Lavisse, *Un Ministre*, pp. 136–138.

20. Durkheim, *L'Evolution pédagogique en France*, pp. 18–21. Comte had earlier defined history as "dynamic sociology" and suggested that history alone was capable of establishing "a true rational connection in the sequence of social events in such a manner as to permit . . . a certain systematic prevision of their subsequent unfolding." Quoted in Ehrard and Palmade, *L'Histoire*, p. 70.

21. Emile Durkheim, *Moral Education*, trans. E. K. Wilson and H. Schnurer (Glencoe, Ill.: The Free Press, 1961), pp. 275–277.

22. It was rumored that Mme. Weill (Dick May), the patroness of the Ecole des Hautes Sociales, was Croiset's mistress. See Clark, *Prophets and Patrons*, p. 195.

23. See, for example, *L'Education de la démocratie: leçons professées à l'Ecole des Hautes Etudes Sociales par MM. Lavisse, Croiset, Seignobos, Malapert, Lanson, Hadamard* (Paris: Alcan, 1907); Croiset and others, *Enseignement et démocratie*

(Paris: Alcan, n.d.); and *Les Applications sociales de la solidarité* (Paris: Alcan, 1904). The speeches by the solidarists were collected and published as *La Solidarité* (Paris: Alcan, 1902).

24. We have seen in the previous chapter that Durkheim, Bouglé, and Mauss, the triumvirate of academic sociology, joined the leading university historians in the League for the Defense of the Rights of Man and the Citizen, the principal Dreyfusard organization.

25. Célestin Bouglé, "L'Année sociologique," *Les Pages libres,* 353 (5 October 1907), 347.

26. Monod, Preface to Puaux, *Vers la justice,* pp. xiii–xiv.

27. Seignobos, "L'Enseignement de l'histoire comme instrument d'éducation politique," cited in Pierre Lasserre, *La Doctrine officielle de l'Université* (Paris: Mercure de France, 1912), pp. 360–362.

28. Seignobos, "L'Organisation des divers types d'enseignement," in *L'Education de la démocratie,* pp. 107–114.

29. *Ibid.,* pp. 17–20.

30. *Ibid.*

31. Pierre Caron and Philippe Sagnac, *L'Etat actuel des études d'histoire moderne en France* (Paris: Revue d'histoire moderne et contemporaine, 1902), p. 16.

32. *Ibid.,* pp. 17–20. Other leading members of the Society included Monod, Lavisse, Aulard, Lanson, Mathiez, Hauser, and Andler. See *RIE,* 42 (1901), 242, and *La Société d'histoire moderne. Statuts, liste de membres, communications, publications* (Paris: Société d'histoire moderne, 1904).

33. *Ibid.,* p. 39. Caron's and Sagnac's defense of their master Aulard's scholarly objectivity appeared in the same year (1901) that saw the publication of Aulard's *Histoire politique de la Révolution française,* a work that was at the time universally praised as a model of scientific scholarship. Several years were to pass before the book came under criticism from conservative critics for its ideological nature.

34. Pieter Geyl employs this distinction between the historians of the Académie and the historians of the Université in his *Napoleon: For and Against* (New Haven: Yale University Press, 1949), pp. 356–420. Very few historians—Lavisse was a notable exception—were able to plant a foot in each camp.

35. Caron and Sagnac, *L'Etat actuel,* p. 34.

36. *Ibid.,* pp. 23–24.

37. *Ibid.,* pp. 39–40, 77. Both Sorel and Vandal hailed from royalist milieux and became charter members of the anti-Dreyfusard League of the French Fatherland. Archives Nationales F7 12721, 1898–1900, Ligue de la Patrie Française. Bellesort, *Les Intellectuels,* pp. 67–68. In addition, Sorel and Vandal had been lecturing at the Ecole Libre des Sciences Politiques, which had been founded by Taine and others after the Franco-Prussian War and quickly began to attract scholars with conservative tendencies. Funck-Brentano had already proved to be a man of the right and later aligned himself with the Action Française. See Archives Nationales F7 13206, no. 2; February 1930.

38. Caron, in *Revue d'histoire moderne et contemporaine,* 17 (1912), 315.

39. Caron and Sagnac, *L'Etat actuel,* pp. 22–23, 89. Pierre Caron, "La Société d'histoire moderne," *Revue de synthèse historique,* 8 (April 1904), 245.

40. *Ibid.*, pp. 89-90.

41. Aulard, *Taine: historien de la Révolution française*, p. viii.

42. Gustave Lanson, "L'Esprit scientifique et la méthode de l'histoire littéraire," reprinted in *Etudes Françaises*, 1 (1 January 1925), pp. 33-34. See also Leguay, *Universitaires d'aujourd'hui*, pp. 65-104 and AN, F17 23927.

43. *Ibid.*, pp. 35-36. This is doubtless a reference to his former mentor at the Ecole Normale, Ferdinand Brunetière, who converted to Catholicism at the turn of the century after having joined the two other leading literary critics of France, Emile Faguet and Jules Lemaître, in opposing revision of the Dreyfus verdict. When the Ecole Normale was absorbed by the University of Paris in 1903, Brunetière was the only professor at the rue d'Ulm whose appointment was not renewed, a circumstance that was obviously related to his religious and political activities.

44. *Ibid.*, pp. 36-37. For Lanson's definition of the scientific methods of literary history see his *Essais de méthode, de critique, et d'histoire littéraire* (Paris: Hachette, 1965).

45. See Pierre Moreau, *La Critique littéraire en France* (Paris: Colin, 1960), chap. 10, for a brief treatment of the leading members of this literary fraternity.

46. See Clark, *Prophets and Patrons*, pp. 10, 25-27.

47. Lanson, "L'Esprit scientifique et la méthode de l'histoire littéraire," pp. 34-35.

48. *Ibid.*, p. 34.

49. Charles Victor Langlois, *La Vie en France du moyen age* (Paris: Hachette, 1908) pp. i-iii; Langlois, *Les Etudes historiques* (Paris: Larousse, 1915), p. 233.

50. Marrou, *De la Connaissance historique*, p. 54.

51. Quoted in Lach, "Ernest Lavisse," in Schmitt, ed., *Some Historians*, p. 39.

52. Caron and Sagnac, *L'Etat actuel*, pp. 16-17.

53. Caron, in *Revue d'histoire moderne et contemporaine*, 17 (1912), 315-318.

54. Langlois, *Manuel de bibliographie historique*, pp. 580-581.

55. David H. Fischer has effectively deflated this familiar defense of historical study in his *Historians' Fallacies*, pp. 309-310.

56. Langlois, *Manuel de bibliographie historique*, p. 581.

57. *Ibid.*, p. 582, 571-574. The historians at the university did not neglect the need for more general summaries of the evidence accumulated by the monographic scholars. But such "vast syntheses," Caron and Sagnac contended, cannot be written by individual scholars, who must "resign themselves to writing more or less important monographs," which are mere "points of departure for future syntheses." The broad, general works that depart from the empirical evidence to offer interpretations and conclusions can be written only "in collaboration." Indeed, the entire nature of historical work ought to become more "collective," they contended, for it is essential that "the workers, instead of producing in isolation, get to know each other better" so that the historical labor will be "more collective, more methodical, and consequently more similar to scientific work properly so called." They were confident that such collaborative efforts would drastically reduce the number of errors and that historical production, "instead of being left to chance, will develop in a less confused manner," with the result that the

"progress of historical knowledge will become more rapid and more certain." Caron and Sagnac, *L'Etat actuel,* pp. 5–6, 90.

58. Langlois, *Manuel de bibliographie historique,* pp. 577–578. See also his "L'Histoire au XIXe siècle," *La Revue bleue* (25 August 1900).

59. Leguay, *La Sorbonne,* p. 52.

60. Seignobos, *La Méthode historique,* pp. 95ff.

61. Seignobos, "Les Conditions psychologiques de la connaissance en histoire," *Revue philosophique de la France et de l'étranger,* 24 (July–December 1887), 3–6.

62. *Ibid.,* pp. 4, 13–21.

63. Seignobos, *La Méthode historique,* p. 109. See also Seignobos, "Les Conditions psychologiques," pp. 22, 171.

64. Seignobos, *La Méthode historique,* p. 116. It is apparent that Seignobos, Lacombe, Berr, and others who urged history to employ the laws of human behavior established by psychology actually meant social psychology. They did not appear interested in applying the methods of individual psychology to explain the actions of historical personages (as Erik Erikson and others have since attempted to do). They appear to have been primarily concerned with elucidating the thought and behavior of groups of individuals in the past. In this sense they were precursors of the modern investigators of the *mentalités populaires* associated with the school of Lucien Febvre and Marc Bloch.

65. *Ibid.* This doctrine of "historical analogy" had already been formulated in his *Introduction aux études historiques.* See above, chap. 2.

66. Seignobos, "Les Conditions psychologiques," pp. 3–4.

67. Langlois, *Manuel de bibliographie historique,* p. 34.

68. It should be noted that history had already established an intimate connection with the new science of geography. Lavisse and Rambaud invited the distinguished geographer Vidal de la Blache to contribute the opening chapter to their *Histoire générale,* and when the history instructors in the secondary school founded their first professional society, they opened its membership roles to geography teachers.

69. In order to permit imitators of Renan to continue scientific and historical studies of religious texts, a fifth section devoted to Les Sciences Religieuses was added to the Ecole Pratique in 1886. Within two decades this section was swarming with Durkheimians led by Marcel Mauss, who treated all religions, whether primitive or Western, as social facts to be analyzed from a scientific point of view. See Clark, *Prophets and Patrons,* pp. 45–47.

70. See Hughes, *The Obstructed Path,* chap. 3.

71. See Peyre, "Durkheim," p. 31.

72. Célestin Bouglé, Introduction to Emile Durkheim, *Sociologie et philosophie* (Paris: Alcan, 1924), pp. v, viii. This is a collection of Durkheim's writings on the subject dating from 1898. For an earlier expression of Bouglé's hostility to history and his defense of sociology's kinship with philosophy see his "L'Année sociologique," pp. 340–345.

73. Excluding Bergson, who addressed largely nonacademic audiences at the Collège de France.

74. It is worth noting that many psychologists in nineteenth century France had also begun their careers in the philosophical profession, and

that they never revised the title of French academic psychology's leading theoretical journal, La Revue philosophique.

75. For the comparative figures on the number of new chairs created in the French university system during this period see Clark, Prophets and Patrons, pp. 30–33.

76. See his La Morale des idées-forces (Paris: Alcan, 1908).

77. Alfred Fouillée, Education from a National Standpoint, trans, W. J. Greenstreet (New York: Appleton & Co., 1897), p. 27.

78. See Nietzsche, "The Use and Abuse of History," pp. 92–94.

79. Alfred Fouillée, La Réforme de l'enseignement par la philosophie (Paris: Armand Colin, 1901), p. 24.

80. Ibid., pp. 10, 3–4. He blamed Renan for beginning the process by which philology and criticism replaced philosophy as the science matrice of French learning. Ibid., p. 304.

81. Ibid., pp. 23–24, 17–18. He specifically rejected Seignobos's analogical method, arguing that very little in the remote past is analogous to the events of the present. He did, however, accept that method for the recent past, since the "sociological and psychological conditions have hardly changed during the past several years." Ibid., p.19.

82. Ibid., pp. 16–17, 10–11.

83. Ibid., pp. 20–21, 11–12, 25–26; Fouillée, Education from a National Viewpoint, pp. 223–225.

84. Ibid., pp. 17–18, 28, 4, 24. Fouillée, Education from a National Viewpoint, pp. 218–220.

85. Ibid., pp. 71–76, 78–79, 82–85, 210, 206–209. See also Fouillée, Education from a National Viewpoint, pp. 218–225.

86. Peyre, "Durkheim," p. 31.

87. For a representative sampling of opinion regarding the issue of lycée curriculum reform in the early years of the Third Republic see Mgr Cullivier-Fleury, La Réforme universitaire (Paris: Claye, 1873), Raoul Frary, La Question du latin (Paris: Librairie Cerf, 1885), and Gustave Lanson, L'Université et la société moderne (Paris: Colin, 1902).

88. Clément Falcucci, L'Humanisme dans l'enseignement secondaire en France au XIXe siècle (Toulouse: Privat, 1939), p. 518.

89. The last great victory of the modernists over the classicists at the university level came in 1904 with the repeal of the requirement that the petite thèse (minor doctoral thesis) be written in Latin. Aulard had waged a battle against the Latin requirement for several years and had even gone so far as to insert criticism of it in his comments on students' doctoral defenses. See Philippe Sagnac, "Le Doctorat de M. Sagnac," La Revue française, 36 (1899), 7, and Paul Gautier, "Le Doctorat de M. Gautier," La Revue française, 44 (1903), 174–175.

90. See Falcucci, L'Humanisme dans l'enseignement secondaire, for a comprehensive description of the classical curriculum of French secondary education prior to 1902 and Alexandre Ribot, La Réforme de l'enseignement secondaire (Paris: Colin, 1900), pp. 41–68, for the statement of the Radical Republicans' case against the old system by the principal proponent of the 1902 act in the National Assembly.

91. André Chaumeix, *Le Lycée Henri Quatre* (Paris: Gallimard, 1936), p. 137.
92. See Phyllis H. Stock, "New Quarrel of Ancients and Moderns: The French University and Its Opponents, 1899–1914," Ph.D. dissertation, Yale University, 1965, pp. 2–15, for a brief summary of the debates concerning the Education Reform Act. For the official transcript of the parliamentary commission's inquiry into the subject of secondary school reform, see *La Commission de l'enseignement. Chambre des députés, session de 1899, Enquête sur l'enseignement secondaire,* 7 vols. (Paris, 1899).
93. Quoted in *Le Temps* (26 October 1910).
94. Seignobos, "L'Organisation des divers types d'enseignement," in Lavisse and others, *L'Education de la démocratie,* pp. 104–107, 114–115. Seignobos's portrayal of the elitist nature of French secondary education was entirely accurate. In 1882 education was made compulsory for ages six through thirteen, a requirement that most students fulfilled at the eight-year école primaire. Full-time education beyond the primary school was limited to a tiny elite that could afford to enroll in expensive special preparatory schools which provided instruction in the classical subjects that were inadequately taught in the primary schools.
95. Durkheim, *L'Evolution pédagogique en France,* pp. 10–11, 15, 362–367.
96. *Ibid.,* pp. 359–361.
97. Raymond Aron has succinctly described Durkheim's concept of "organic solidarity" as the conviction that "consensus, or the coherent unity of the collectivity, results from or is expressed by differentiation. The individuals are no longer similar but different and . . . it is precisely because the individuals are different that consensus is achieved." Raymond Aron, *Main Currents in Sociological Thought,* II, trans. R. Howard and H. Weaver (Garden City, N.Y.: Anchor, 1970), pp. 11–12.
98. Croiset, "Les Besoins de la démocratie en matière d'éducation," in Lavisse and others, *L'Education de la démocratie,* pp. 63–66. He specifically mentioned Bourgeois's doctrine of "solidarity" as an appropriate philosophical basis for this social cohesion.
99. Durkheim, *L'Evolution pédagogique en France,* pp. 368–370.
100. *Ibid.,* pp. 368–373.
101. *Ibid.,* pp. 375–377.
102. *Ibid.,* pp. 376–377.
103. *Ibid.*
104. *Ibid.,* pp. 370–372.
105. Croiset, "Les Besoins de la démocratie," in Lavisse and others, *L'Education de la démocratie,* pp. 48, 51.
106. *Ibid.,* pp. 48–49, 51–52.
107. It is interesting to note that Henri Poincaré, the scientist and mathematician who, along with Pierre Duhem, had been challenging the assumptions of scientism in the natural sciences, was in the audience. Lanson, "L'Esprit scientifique et la méthode de l'histoire littéraire," pp. 21–38. For a discussion of the antipositivist and antimechanistic currents in the natural sciences during this period see Isaac Benrubi, *Sources et courants de la philosophie contemporaine en France,* II (Paris: Alcan, 1933), pp. 32ff.
108. See above, chap. 9.

109. Croiset, "L'Unité des principes dans l'enseignement public," in *L'Education de la démocratie*, pp. 69–98.

110. *Ibid.*, pp. 72–75.

111. This is precisely the claim advanced by Nietzsche against scientific history in his "The Use and Abuse of History," pp. 30–31.

112. Croiset, "L'Unité des principes dans l'enseignement public," pp. 77–83.

113. *Ibid.*, pp. 90–91.

114. *Ibid.*, pp. 95–96.

115. Lanson, "Les Etudes modernes dans l'enseignement secondaire," in *L'Education de la démocratie*, pp. 169–170, 181–182.

116. Durkheim, *Moral Education*, pp. 273–274.

117. Lavisse, "Souvenirs d'une éducation manquée," *L'Education de la démocratie*, pp. 4–11.

118. *Ibid.*, pp. 16–21.

119. *Ibid.*, pp. 22, 29–31.

120. Alfred Croiset, "Une Education manquée," *La Suisse universitaire* (May 1903).

121. Though Monod had earlier bemoaned the fact that history would become "a science in the true sense of the word" only with "great difficulty" and will always have to confine itself to "partial philosophical generalizations," he insisted that it should be "penetrated with the scientific spirit." What troubled him about Michelet's philosophical approach to history was that it "gave such an important place to human autonomy that it excluded in advance any scientific conception of history." Gabriel Monod, *Les Maîtres de l'histoire: Renan, Taine, Michelet* (Paris; Lévy, 1894), pp. ix–xi. He also criticized Michelet for abandoning careful scholarship for polemical oratory after transferring from the Ecole Normale to the Collège de France in 1838. Monod, *Michelet à l'Ecole Normale*, p. 22. Monod had begun to take note of Fustel's scholarly inaccuracies as early as 1875. See Monod, "M. Fustel de Coulanges et son ouvrage sur les institutions de l'ancienne France," *La Revue politique et littéraire* (1 May 1875), pp. 1037–1043 and (15 May 1875), pp. 1077–1083. See also Alphonse V. Roche, *Les Idées traditionalistes en France de Rivarol à Charles Maurras* (Urbana, Ill.: University of Illinois Press, 1937), p. 85, and Jane Herrick, *The Historical Thought of Fustel de Coulanges* (Washington D.C.: Catholic University Press, 1954), pp. 97–98.

122. See, for example, the preface to his *Histoire de la littérature française* (Paris: Hachette, 1895), p. vi, in which he condemns the notion of "imposing the scientific form on literature" as a "baleful superstition." He insisted that literature cannot be comprehended scientifically, but must be "cultivated" and "loved," and denounced those scholars who "do not read, but analyze, and think it sufficient to convert into note cards all the printed material that they get their hands on." Pierre Leguay notes that Lanson's change of heart regarding the applicability of scientific methods to the history of literature reflected the influence of the philologist Gaston Paris, who replaced Brunetière as Lanson's spiritual mentor in the 1890s. See Leguay, *Universitaires d'aujourd'hui*, p. 97.

123. Reprinted in *La Révolution française* (1906), p. 479. The republican

politicians who sponsored the educational reform bill of 1902, which ended the predominance of classical subjects in the *lycée* curriculum, frequently invoked the authority of the numerous Sorbonne professors who had received a classical education but supported the curriculum revision. See Ribot, *La Réforme*, pp. 63–64, on Lavisse, and p. 74, on Croiset.

124. Alphonse Aulard, *Les Orateurs de la révolution: l'assemblée constituante* (Paris: E. Cornély, 1905).
125. Seignobos, *Le Régime de l'enseignement des lettres*, pp. 7ff.
126. *Ibid.*, pp. 8–9.
127. *Ibid.*
128. *Ibid.*, pp. 10ff.
129. *Ibid.*
130. Daniel Halévy, *Charles Péguy and Les Cahiers de la Quinzaine*, trans. Ruth Bethell (London: Dobson, 1946), p. 84.
131. See "Sur les thèses en Sorbonne de Péguy," *Amitié Charles Péguy*, no. 76 (1960), p. 29.
132. See Péguy, "De la Situation faite au parti intellectuel dans le monde moderne," Cahier of December 2, 1906, in *Oeuvres complètes*, III (Paris: Editions de la Nouvelle Revue Française, 1927), pp. 118–133; "De la Situation faite à l'histoire et à la sociologie dans les temps modernes," *Cahiers de la quinzaine*, 8th ser. 3 (1906), 11–14; and "Zangwill," in *Oeuvres complètes*, II (Paris: Editions de la Nouvelle Revue Française, 1922), p. 200.
133. See Péguy, "Clio I," in *Temporal and Eternal*, trans. Alexander Dru (New York: Harper & Brothers, 1958), pp. 114, 335, and "Langlois tel qu'on le parle," in *Oeuvres complètes*, XIII (Paris: Editions de la Nouvelle Revue Française, 1931), pp. 305–307.
134. Péguy, "Zangwill," pp. 217–218, and "A Nos Amis, à nos abonnés," p. 373.
135. Péguy, "Un Nouveau Théologien, M. Fernand Laudet," in *Oeuvres complètes*, XIII, 136, 146–147, and "De la Situation faite au parti intellectuel devant les accidents de gloire temporelle," in *Oeuvres complètes*, III, 178–179, 200.
136. Péguy, "L'Argente suite," pp. 137–141, and "A Nos Amis, à nos abonnés," pp. 95, 110.
137. Robert Avice, *Péguy, pélerin d'éspérance* (Bruges, 1947), p. 53.
138. See Lasserre, *La Doctrine officielle de l'université*.
139. See, for example, his attacks on Lanson and Croiset in *L'Action française* (5 January 1909) and on Aulard, Seignobos, and Durkheim in *L'Action française* (23 November 1909).
140. See Lasserre, *Alfred Croiset* (Paris: Nouvelle Librairie Nationale, 1909).
141. See the F7 12862 and 12863 files of the Sûreté, Archives Nationales, and the A 31950 files of the Préfecture de Police, Département de la Seine, for attendance estimates and summaries of proceedings compiled by police spies.
142. See Weber, *Action Française*, pp. 111, 118–189, 518–519.
143. See, for example, his vicious attack on Gabriel Monod's Germanic character in his *Quand les Français ne s'aimaient pas*, 2d ed. (Paris: Nouvelle Librairie Nationale, 1926), p. 62. A more balanced critique of the university's

surrender to the doctrine of scholarly specialization can be found in his *Avenir de l'intelligence* (Paris: Nouvelle Librairie Nationale, 1909).

144. See Louis Dimier, *Les Préjugés ennemis de l'histoire de France* (Paris: Nouvelle Librairie Nationale, 1917). The F7 12862 series of the Sûreté files in the Archives Nationales and the A31950, 77E, A31805, 24E, and A1.343 files of the Préfecture de Police, Département de la Seine, contain descriptions of Dimier's speeches at royalist meetings during this period.

145. Louis Dimier, *Les Maîtres de la contre-révolution au dix-neuvième siècle* (Paris: Nouvelle Librairie Nationale, 1907).

146. See Maurice Barrès, *Les Déracinés* (Paris: Plon, 1947), and his *Cahiers*, VIII (Paris: Plon, 1930), p. 4.

147. See, for example, his attack on positivism in the dedication to *Le Disciple* (Paris: Nelson, 1935).

148. Barrès also occasionally served as a guest lecturer at the royalist Institute.

149. See Henri Massis and Alfred de Tarde [Agathon], *L'Esprit de la Nouvelle Sorbonne; Les Jeunes Gens d'aujourd'hui* (Paris: Plon-Nourrit, 1913); and the articles by the same authors, under the same pseudonym, in *L'Opinion* (July–August 1910). Agathon's attacks on the French university were preceded by a series in the same paper by François Albert entitled "La Sorbonne germanisée." See *L'Opinion* (July 18 and August 8, 1908).

150. Hans A. Schmitt, *Charles Péguy: The Decline of an Idealist* (Baton Rouge, La.: Louisiana State University Press, 1967), p. 113.

151. See Georges Sorel, *Le Système historique de Renan* (Paris: G. Jacques, 1905), pp. 5–9, as well as his *Reflections on Violence*, trans. T. E. Hulme and J. Roth (Glencoe, Ill.: The Free Press, 1950), pp. 50, 162.

152. Cited in Barrès, *Mes Cahiers*, III, 53–54.

153. See the various references to Lemaître as a hostile critic of the university in general and the historical profession in particular in the A31805, 24E and A31950, 77E series of the Préfecture files. See also Ferdinand Brunetière, *Les Ennemis de l'âme française* (Paris: Hetzel, 1899) and his *Après le Procès: réponse à quelques "intellectuels"* (Paris, 1898).

154. See Weber, *The Nationalist Revival in France, 1905–1914* and Stock, "New Quarrel of Ancients and Moderns."

Epilogue

1. I am preparing an extended study of this "rebellion of the *littérateurs*" which is intended as a companion volume to this book.

2. See Lavisse's articles in *La Revue de Paris* (November 1914), pp. 1–9; (January 1915), pp. 5–15; (February 1915), pp. 673–693; (May 1915), pp. 225–235; (January 1916), pp. 5–14; (April 1916), pp. 673–680; (July 1916), pp. 5–10; (October 1916), pp. 669–676; (December 1917), pp. 779–790; (January 1918), pp. 65–75; and (November 1918), pp. 449–452. For a description of Lavisse's hostile behavior toward the German negotiators at the Paris Peace Conference, where he served as chairman of a committee to investigate territorial claims, see J. T. Shotwell, *At the Paris Peace Conference* (New York, Macmillan, 1927), p. 14. For critical accounts of Lavisse's and Aulard's wartime attempts to bend history to the purposes of propaganda see Georges

Demartial, *La Guerre de 1917: comment on mobilisa les consciences* (Paris, Editions des cahiers internationaux, 1922); Barnes, *A History of Historical Writing,* p. 278; and Mitchell, "German History in France after 1870," pp. 95–100.

3. Farmer, *France Reviews Its Revolutionary Origins,* pp. 89–97.

4. All three contributed best selling works of popular history to Fayard's series *Les Grandes Etudes historiques,* and all were elected to the French Academy. Franz Funck-Brentano, another fellow traveler of the Action Française and contributor to the Fayard series, was a member of the Institute.

5. See Hughes, *The Obstructed Path,* pp. 21–29.

6. *Ibid.,* p. 29. Febvre began writing for the *Revue* in 1907, Bloch in 1912.

7. See Lucien Febvre and Henri Berr, "History," *Encyclopedia of the Social Sciences,* VII (New York, Macmillan, 1935), p. 361. For a description of the efforts by Febvre, Bloch, Georges Lefebvre and others to embrace the problems of collective psychology in their works see Georges Duby, "Histoire des mentalités," in *L'Histoire et ses méthodes* (Paris: Gallimard, 1961), pp. 937–966.

8. Lucien Febvre, "De La Revue de Synthèse aux Annales," *Annales,* 7 (July–September 1952), 291; Febvre, "Sur une forme d'histoire qui n'est pas la nôtre," *Annales* 3 (1948), 23–24.

9. Marc Bloch and Lucien Febvre, "A nos lecteurs," *Annales* 1 (1929), 1. See the forthcoming study by Georg G. Iggers, "The French *Annales:* An Empirical-Analytical Approach to History."

10. See Lucien Febvre, "Face au vent," *Annales,* 1 (1946), p. 8; "Sur Einstein et sur l'histoire," *Annales,* 10 (1955), pp. 310–311; and his *Un Destin; Martin Luther* (Paris, 1928), p. 365. For a discussion of this aspect of Febvre's critique of academic history in France see Palmer A. Throop, "Lucien Febvre," in S. William Halperin, ed., *Some Twentieth Century Historians* (Chicago: University of Chicago Press, 1961), pp. 284–298.

11. Quoted in *L'Histoire et ses méthodes,* p. 850.

12. Seignobos, who outlived all of his contemporaries in the profession, produced a work from semiretirement that appeared to inter, once and for all, the prewar illusions of creating a science of history based on the conceptions described in this study. In his *Histoire sincère de la nation française* (Paris: Presses universitaires de France, 1946), pp. vi–vii, he observed that while history had succeeded in adopting a more "scientific spirit" that enabled historians to possess "a more exact idea of the past," his discipline was still in a "defective state" and historians were still compelled to admit their "ignorance." In order to be "fully sincere," he decided to avoid using the "conventional and pompous forms" of scholarship in his present work, since they produce a "false impression of reality." He warned his readers that his "explication of the facts" was based on a "personal impression" for which no documents could produce "an indisputable proof," and conceded that his choice of facts was entirely "arbitrary." He unabashedly defended his use of "simple and familiar language" to communicate his ideas, and, in a phrase that would surely have startled his departed colleagues in the scientific school of history, announced his intention to employ a "conversational tone" in his narrative.

13. Clark, "The Structure and Functions of a Research Institute," pp. 89–91; S. C. Humphreys, "The Work of Louis Gernet," *History and Theory,* 10 (1971), 175.

14. Humphreys, "The Work of Louis Gernet," p. 175.

Works Cited

Manuscripts and archival collections

Administration de l'instruction publique (de 1863 à 1869). Ministère de Son Exc. M. Duruy. Paris, Delalain, n.d.

Archives historiques, artistiques, et littéraires. Recueil mensuel de documents curieux et inedits. Paris, Bourlaton, 1889–1914.

Archives Nationales, Files of the Sûreté, Series F7 12721, 12862, 12863, 13206.

Archives Nationales, Files of the Ministry of Public Instruction, Series F17 (hereafter abbreviated as AN, F17), 22600. François Aulard Dossier.

AN, F17 23815. Henri Berr Dossier.

AN, F17 22561. Alfred Croiset Dossier.

AN, F17 20780. Fustel de Coulanges Dossier.

AN, F17 23927. Gustave Lanson Dossier.

AN, F17 21982. Gabriel Monod Dossier.

AN, F17 25874. Gaston Paris Dossier.

AN, F17 25893. Alfred Rambaud Dossier.

AN, F17 23801. Charles Seignobos Dossier.

AN, F17 13051. Distribution of Doctoral Theses, Faculties of Letters, 1897–1892.

AN, F17 13137. General Description of Courses Given at University of Paris, 1886–1897.

AN, F17 13249. Reports on Doctoral Theses, University of Paris, 1890–1901.

Archives de la Préfecture de Police, Département de la Seine. A31950 and A31805.

Bibliothèque Nationale, Manuscript Collection, New French Acquisitions, Correspondance and Private Papers (hereafter abbreviated as BN, MS, N.A.F.) 25166-25172. Papers of Ernest Lavisse.
BN, MS, N.A.F. 24430-24460. Papers of Gaston Paris.
BN, MS, N.A.F. 16006. Papers of Raymond Poincaré.
Circulaires et instructions officielles relatives à l'instruction publique. Ministère de Son Exc. M. Duruy. Paris, Delalain, 1870.
La Commission de l'enseignement. Chambre des deputés, session de 1899. Enquête sur l'enseignement secondaire. 7 vols. Paris, Impr. Nationale, 1899.
Ministère du commerce et l'industrie. Congrès international de l'éducation sociale, 1900. Procès-verbal sommaire. Paris, Impr. Nationale, 1902.
Ministère de l'instruction publique. Direction de l'enseignement supérieur. Règlements des universités. Paris, Impr. Nationale, 1897.
Ministère de l'instruction publique. Enquêtes et documents relatifs à l'enseignement supérieur. Rapports des conseils de l'université. 3 vols. Paris, Impr. Nationale, 1910-1913.
Ministère de l'instruction publique. Statistique de l'enseignement supérieur, 1865-1868. Paris, Impr. Impériale, 1869.
Sénat. Séances des 22 et 23 mai, 1868. Discours prononcés par Son Exc. M. Duruy au sujet d'une pétition relative à l'enseignement supérieur. Paris, Lahure, 1868.
Les Statistiques de l'enseignement primaire, moyen, et supérieur. Paris, Delalain, 1870.

Newspapers and periodicals

Action; L'Action française; L'Anarchie; Annales; Année sociologique; L'Aurore; L'Avant-garde pédagogique; La Dépêche de Toulouse; L'Ecole émancipée; L'Ecole patriote; Ecole Pratique des Hautes Etudes, Annuaire; L'Emancipation de l'instituteur; L'Enseignement public; Le Figaro; La Grande Revue; L'Humanité; International Revue of Social History; Journal des débats; Mercure de France; La Nouvelle Revue; Les Pages libres; La Petite République; Le Radical; La Révolution française; Revue bleue; Revue critique d'histoire et de littérature; Revue de l'enseignement primaire; La Revue générale; Revue d'histoire moderne et contemporaine; Revue historique; Revue internationale de l'enseignement; Revue internationale de sociologie; Revue de Paris; Revue philosophique de la France et de l'étranger; Revue des questions historiques; Revue de synthèse historique; Revue universitaire; Le Siècle; Le Soleil; Le Temps

Books, articles, and dissertations

Albert, François. "La Sorbonne germanisée," *L'Opinion,* July 18 and August 8, 1908.
Alpert, Harry. *Emile Durkheim and His Sociology.* New York, Russell and Russell, 1939.
—— "France's First University Course in Sociology," *American Sociological Review,* 2 (1937), 311-317.
Anderson, E. N. *Nationalism and the Cultural Crisis in Prussia, 1806-1815.* New York, Octagon Books Inc., 1966.
Andler, Charles. *Vie de Lucien Herr.* Paris, Rieder, 1932.

Annales internationales d'histoire. Congrès de la Haye, no. 1, Paris, 1899.
Les Applications sociales de la solidarité. Paris, Alcan, 1904.
Aron, Raymond. *Introduction to the Philosophy of History,* trans. George J. Erwin. Boston, Beacon Press, 1961.
—— *Main Currents in Sociological Thought,* vol. II, trans. R. Howard and H. Weaver. Garden City, N.Y., Anchor, 1970.
Aulard, Alphonse. *Histoire politique de la Revolution française.* Paris, Colin, 1901.
—— "Leçon d'ouverture du cours d'histoire de la Révolution française à la faculté des lettres de Paris," *Etudes et leçons sur la Révolution française,* 1 (Paris 1901).
—— *Les Orateurs de la révolution: l'assemblée constituante.* Paris, E. Cornély, 1905.
—— *Polémique et histoire.* Paris, E. Cornély, 1904.
—— *Taine: historien de la Révolution française.* Paris, Colin, 1907.
Avice, Robert. *Péguy, pélerin d'éspérance.* Bruges, Editions Beyaert, 1947.
Barnes, Harry Elmer. *A History of Historical Writing.* New York, Dover Publications, 1962.
Barrau-Dirigo, L. "Questionnaire sur l'enseignement supérieur de l'histoire," *Revue de synthèse historique,* 8 (April 1904), 164–170.
Barrès, Maurice. *Mes Cahiers,* vols. III and VIII. Paris, Plon, 1930.
—— *Les Déracinés.* Paris, Plon, 1947.
—— "La Querelle des nationalistes et des cosmopolites," *Le Figaro,* 4 July 1892.
Bédier, Joseph. *Hommage à Gaston Paris, leçon d'ouverture du cours de langue et de littérature française du moyen âge, prononcée au Collège de France, le 3 févr. 1904.* Paris, 1904.
—— "Sur l'oeuvre de Gaston Paris," *Cahiers de la Quinzaine,* 5th ser. 14 (1904).
—— and M. Rocques. *Bibliographie des travaux de Gaston Paris.* Paris, 1903.
Belloni, Georges, *Aulard: historien de la Révolution française.* Paris, Presses Universitaires de France, 1949.
Bellesort, André. *Les Intellectuels et l'avènement de la Troisième République.* Paris, Grasset, 1931.
Bémont, Charles. "Gabriel Monod," *Ecole Pratique des Hautes Etudes, section des sciences historiques et philologiques, annuaire,* 1912–1913, pp. 5–27.
—— "Gabriel Monod," *Revue historique,* 110 (May–August 1912).
Ben-David, Joseph. *The Scientist's Role in Society.* Englewood Cliffs, N.J., Prentice-Hall, 1971.
—— and Awraham Zloczower. "Universities and Academic Systems in Modern Societies," *European Journal of Sociology,* 3 (1962), 45–84.
Benrubi, Isaac. *Sources et courants de la philosophie contemporaine en France,* vol. II. Paris, Alcan, 1933.
Bernard, F., and others, *Le Syndicalisme dans l'enseignement.* Avignon, L'Ecole Emancipée, 1924.
Berr, Henri. *L'Avenir de la philosophie: esquisse d'une synthèse des connaissances fondée sur l'histoire.* Paris, Hachette, 1899.
—— *La Synthèse en histoire.* Paris, Colin, 1911.

―――― *Vie et science: lettres d'un vieux philosophe strasbourgeois et d'un étudiant parisien.* Paris, Colin, 1894
Besse, Dom. *Les Religions laïques.* Paris, Nouvelle Librairie Nationale, 1913.
Bierstedt, Robert. *Emile Durkheim.* New York, Dell, 1966.
Bloch, Marc, and Lucien Febvre. "A nos lecteurs," *Annales d'histoire économique et sociale,* 1 (15 January 1929), 1-2.
Bocquillon, Emile. *La Crise du patriotisme à l'école.* Paris, Vuibert et Nony, 1905.
―――― *Pour la patrie.* Paris, Vuibert et Nony, 1907.
Bouglé, Célestin, "L'Année sociologique," *Les Pages libres,* 353 (October 1907), 337-351.
Bourgeois, Léon. *La Solidarité.* 7th ed. Paris, Alcan, 1912.
Bourgin, Hubert. *De Jaurès à Léon Blum: L'Ecole normale et la politique.* Paris, Fayard, 1938.
Bourne, Henry E. *The Teaching of History and Civics in the Elementary and Secondary School.* New York, Longmans, Green & Co., 1902.
Boutroux, Emile. *Etudes d'histoire de la philosophie.* Paris, Alcan, 1897.
―――― "Histoire et synthèse," *Revue de synthèse historique,* 1 (July-December 1900), 9-13.
Brogan, D. W. *The Development of Modern France.* 2 vols. New York, Harper Torchbooks, 1966.
Brunetière, Ferdinand. *Après le procès: réponse à quelques "intellectuels."* Paris, 1898.
―――― *Les Ennemis de l'âme française.* Paris, Hetzel, 1899.
Buisson, Ferdinand. *Nouveau Dictionnaire de pédagogie.* Paris, Hachette, 1911.
―――― and F. E. Farrington, eds. *French Educational Ideals of Today.* Yonkers-on-Hudson, N.Y., World Publishing Co., 1919.
Butterfield, Herbert, *Man on his Past: The Study of the History of Historical Scholarship.* Cambridge, Cambridge University Press, 1955.
―――― *The Whig Interpretation of History.* New York, W. W. Norton and Company, Inc., 1965.
Cahuet, Albert. "La Réaction des historiens contre les manuels d'histoire," *L'Illustration,* 20 May 1933, pp. 110-111.
Cantor, Norman F., and Richard I. Schneider. *How to Study History.* New York, Crowell, 1967.
Caron, Pierre, and Philippe Sagnac. *L'Etat actuel des études d'histoire moderne en France.* Paris, Revue d'histoire moderne et contemporaine, 1902.
Caron, Pierre, "La Société d'histoire moderne," *Revue de synthèse historique,* 8 (April 1904), 245-246.
Chaumeix, André. *Le Lycée Henri Quatre.* Paris, Gallimard, 1936.
Chobaut, H. "L'Oeuvre d'Aulard et l'histoire de la Révolution française," *Annales historiques de la Révolution française,* 6 (1929), 1-4.
Clapp, Margaret, ed., *The Modern University.* Ithaca, Cornell University Press, 1950.
Clark, James M., *Teachers and Politics in France.* Syracuse, Syracuse University Press, 1967.
Clark, Terry N. "Emile Durkheim and the Institutionalization of Sociology in the French University System," *Archives européennes de sociologie,* 9 (1968), 37-71.

—— *Prophets and Patrons: The French University and the Emergence of the Social Sciences.* Cambridge, Mass., Harvard University Press, 1973.
—— "The Structure and Functions of a Research Institute: The *Année sociologique*," *Archives européennes de sociologie,* 9 (1968), 72–91.
Cobban, Alfred. *A History of Modern France.* New York, George Braziller, 1965.
Cohen, Léon. "Alphonse Aulard," *Revue universitaire,* 1 (1929).
Croiset, Alfred. "Les Besoins de la démocratie en matière d'éducation," in Ernest Lavisse and others, *L'Education de la Démocratie.* Paris, Alcan, 1907.
—— "Une Education manquée," *La Suisse universitaire,* May 1903.
—— "L'Unité des principes dans l'enseignement public," *L'Education de la démocratie.* Paris, Alcan, 1907.
—— and others. *Enseignement et démocratie.* Paris, Alcan, n.d.
Croiset, Maurice. "Notice sur la vie et les travaux de M. Gaston Paris," *Bibliothèque de l'Ecole des Chartes,* 65 (1904), 141–173.
Cullivier-Fleury, Mgr. *La Réforme universitaire.* Paris, Claye, 1873.
Delatour, Albert. *Institut de France. Académie des sciences morales et politiques. Notice sur la vie et les travaux de M. Gabriel Monod.* Paris, 1915.
Demartial, Georges. *La Guerre de 1917: comment on mobilisa les consciences.* Paris, Editions des cahiers internationaux, 1922.
Deschamps, Gaston. *La Malaise de la démocratie.* Paris, Colin, 1899.
Desdevises du Dézert, G., and Louis Bréhier, *Le Travail historique.* Paris, Librairie Bloud, 1907.
Digeon, Claude. *La Crise allemande de la pensée française. 1870–1914.* Paris, Presses Universitaires de France, 1959.
Dilthey, Wilhelm. *Einleitung in die Geisteswissenschaften.* Berlin, 1883.
Dimier, Louis. *Les Maîtres de la contre-révolution au dix-neuvième siècle.* Paris, Nouvelle Librairie Nationale, 1907.
—— *Les Préjugés ennemis de l'histoire de France.* Paris, Nouvelle Librairie Nationale, 1917.
Duby, Georges, "Histoire des mentalités," in *L'Histoire et ses méthodes.* Paris, Gallimard, 1961.
Durkheim, Emile. "Cours de science sociale, leçon d'ouverture," *Revue internationale de l'enseignement,* 15 (1888), 23–48.
—— *Education and Sociology,* trans. S. D. Fox. New York, The Free Press, 1956.
—— *L'Evolution pédagogique en France.* Paris, Presses Universitaires de France, 1969.
—— *Moral Education,* trans. E. K. Wilson and H. Schnurer. Glencoe, Ill., The Free Press, 1961.
—— *Sociologie et philosophie.* Paris, Alcan, 1924.
Duruy, Victor. *Notes et souvenirs: 1811–1894,* vol. I. Paris, Hachette, 1902.
Duveau, Georges. *Les Instituteurs.* Paris, Editions du Seuil, 1957.
Ebray, Alcide. *La France qui meurt.* Paris, Société Française d'Imprimerie et de Librairie, 1910.
L'Ecole des Hautes Etudes, 1900–1910. Paris, Alcan, 1911.

L'Education de la démocratie, leçons professées à l'Ecole des Hautes Etudes Sociales par MM, Lavisse, Croiset, Seignobos, Malapert, Lanson, Hadamard. Paris, Alcan, 1907.
Ehrard, Jean, and Guy Palmade, eds. L'Histoire. Paris, Colin, 1964.
Engel-Janosi, Friedrich. Four Studies in French Romantic Historical Writing. Baltimore, Johns Hopkins University Press, 1955.
Enquête de L'Humanité nouvelle sur le militarisme. Paris, Schleicher, 1899.
Enquête sur les livres scolaires d'après-guerre. Conciliation nationale, Bulletin No. 3. La Flèche, Dépôt des Publications de la Conciliation, 1924.
D'Espinay de Briort, C. L. "Une Correspondance inédite: le prince impérial et Ernest Lavisse, 1871-1879," Revue des deux mondes (April 1929), 555-591.
Essertier, Daniel. Psychologie et sociologie. Paris, Alcan, 1927.
Etudes d'histoire du moyen âge. Paris, Cerf & Alcan, 1896.
Etudes romanes, dédiées à Gaston Paris, par ses élèves français et ses élèves étrangers des pays de langue française. Paris, Emile Bouillon, 1891.
Falcucci, Clément. L'Humanisme dans l'enseignement secondaire en France au XIXe siècle. Toulouse, E. Privat, 1939.
Farmer, Paul. France Reviews Its Revolutionary Origins: Social Politics and Historical Opinion in the Third Republic. New York, Octagon Books, 1963.
Febvre, Lucien. "De La Revue de synthèse aux Annales," Annales, 7 (July-September 1952), 289-292.
——— "Face au vent," Annales, 1 (1946), 1-8.
——— "Sur Einstein et sur l'histoire," Annales, 10 (1955), 305-312.
——— "Sur une forme d'histoire qui n'est pas la nôtre," Annales, 3 (1948), 21-24.
——— Un Destin: Martin Luther. Paris, 1928.
——— and Henri Berr. "History," Encyclopedia of the Social Sciences, vol. III. New York, Macmillan, 1935.
Ferré, Max. Histoire du mouvement syndicaliste révolutionnaire chez les instituteurs: des origines à 1922. Paris, Société universitaire d'éditions et de librairie, 1955.
Fischer, David H. Historians' Fallacies, New York, Harper & Row, 1970.
Flint, Robert. History of the Philosophy of History. New York, Scribner, 1894.
Flottes, Pierre. "Aulard professeur," La Revue française, 81 (1928).
Fouillée, Alfred. Education from a National Viewpoint, trans. W. J. Greenstreet. New York, Appleton & Co., 1897.
——— La Morale des idées-forces. Paris, Alcan, 1908.
——— La Réforme de l'enseignement par la philosophie. Paris, Colin, 1901.
——— La Science sociale contemporaine, 2d ed. Paris, Hachette, 1885.
Frary, Raoul. La Question du latin. Paris, Librairie Cerf, 1885.
Frédéricq, Paul. L'Enseignement supérieur de l'histoire: notes et impressions de voyage. Paris, Alcan, 1899.
——— "The Study of History in Germany and France," Johns Hopkins University Studies in History and Political Science, VIII, May-June 1890.
A Gabriel Monod en souvenir de son enseignement, Ecole Pratique des Hautes Etudes, 1868-1904, Ecole Normale Supérieure, 1880-1904, 26 May 1907. Versailles, Impr. Cerf, 1907.

Gautier, Paul. "Le Doctorat de M. Gautier," *La Revue française*, 44 (1903).
Geyl, Pieter. *Napoleon: For and Against*. New Haven, Yale University Press, 1949.
Gide, Charles, and Charles Rist. *A History of Economic Doctrines*. London, Heath and Co., 1909.
Girardet, Raoul, ed. *Le Nationalisme français, 1871-1914*. Paris, Colin, 1966.
Godfrey, James. "Alphonse Aulard," in Bernadotte Schmitt, ed., *Some Historians of Modern Europe*. Port Washington, N.Y., Kennikat Press, Inc., 1966.
Gooch, G. P. *History and Historians in the Nineteenth Century*. London, Longmans, 1952.
Gottschalk, Louis. "Professor Aulard," *Journal of Modern History*, 1 (1929), 85-86.
Goyau, Georges. *L'Idée de patrie et de l'humanitarisme*. Paris, Perrin, 1902.
Grosjean, Georges. *L'Ecole et la patrie*. Paris, Perrin, 1906.
Guerlac, Henry E. "Science and French National Strength," in Edward M. Earle, ed., *Modern France*. Princeton, Princeton University Press, 1951.
Guerlac, Othon. "Ernest Lavisse, French Historian and Educator," *South Atlantic Quarterly*, 22 (January 1923), 23-42.
De Haime, E. *Les Faits acquis de l'histoire*. Paris, D. V. Stock, 1898.
Halévy, Daniel. *Charles Péguy and les Cahiers de la Quinzaine*, trans. Ruth Bethell. London, Dobson, 1946.
Halperin, S. William, ed. *Some Twentieth Century Historians*. Chicago, University of Chicago Press, 1961.
Halphen, Louis. *L'Histoire en France depuis cent ans*. Paris, Colin, 1914.
Harrison, Benjamin. "Gabriel Monod and the Professionalization of History in France, 1844-1912," Ph.D. diss., University of Wisconsin, 1972.
Hauser, Henri. *L'Enseignement des sciences sociales*. Paris, Chevalier-Maresq, 1903.
Hayes, Carlton J. H. *France: A Nation of Patriots*. New York, Columbia University Press, 1930.
Hayward, J. E. S. "Solidarity: The Social History of an Idea in Nineteenth Century France," *International Review of Social History*, 4 (1959), 261-284.
Herrick, Jane. *The Historical Thought of Fustel de Coulanges*. Washington D.C., Catholic University Press, 1954.
Hervé, Gustave. *Patriotism and the Worker*. New Castle, Pa., I. W. W. Publishing House, 1912.
"Histoire de la fédération d'enseignement," unpub. manuscript.
Histoire et historiens depuis cinquante ans: méthodes, organisation et résultats du travail historique de 1876 à 1926. 2 vols. Paris, Alcan, 1927.
L'Histoire et ses méthodes. Paris, Gallimard, 1961.
Hollinger, David A. "T. H. Kuhn's Theory of Science and Its Implications for History," *American Historical Review*, 78 (April 1973), 370-398.
Hughes, H. Stuart. *Consciousness and Society*. New York, Knopf, 1958.
——— *The Obstructed Path: French Social Thought in the Years of Desperation, 1930-1960*. New York, Harper & Row, 1966.
Humphreys, S. C. "The Work of Louis Gernet," *History and Theory*, 10 (1971), 172-196.

Iggers, Georg G. "The Crisis of the Conventional Conception of Scientific History," unpub. manuscript.
—— "The French *Annales:* An Empirical-Analytical Approach to History," forthcoming.
—— *The German Conception of History.* Middletown, Conn., Wesleyan University Press, 1968.
Institut de France, Académie des sciences morales et politiques. *Séances et travaux,* vol. 60. 1900. Speech by Gabriel Monod.
Les Instituteurs syndiqués et la classe ouvrière. Paris, 1907.
Jameson, J. Franklin, "The Expenditures of Foreign Governments in Behalf of History," *American Historical Association Annual Report (1891).* (Washington D.C.: Government Printing Office, 1892.)
De Jubainville, Henri d'Arbois. *Deux manières d'écrire l'histoire.* Paris, E. Bouillon, 1896.
Kahn, Maurice, "Enquête sur le syndicalisme dans l'enseignement primaire," *Les Pages libres,* 337 (15 June 1907), 338 (22 June 1907), 339 (29 June 1907), 340 (6 July 1907), and 341 (15 July 1907).
Kann, Robert A. *The Problem of Restoration.* Berkeley, University of California Press, 1968.
Ker, W. P. *Essays on Medieval Literature.* London, MacMillan, 1905.
Kuhn, Thomas. *The Structure of Scientific Revolutions.* Chicago, University of Chicago Press, 1962.
Lach, Donald F. "Ernest Lavisse," in Bernadotte Schmitt, ed., *Some Historians of Modern Europe.* Port Washington, N.Y., Kennikat Press, 1966.
Lacombe, Paul. *De l'Histoire considérée comme science.* Paris, Hachette, 1894.
—— "La Science de l'histoire d'après Xénopol," *Revue de synthèse historique,* 1 (July-December 1900), 28-51.
Lakatos, Imre, and Alan Musgrave, eds., *Criticism and the Growth of Knowledge.* Cambridge, Mass., Harvard University Press, 1970.
Langlois, Charles Victor. "Ernest Lavisse," *La Revue de France,* 5 (1922).
—— *Les Etudes historiques.* Paris, Larousse, 1915.
—— "L'Histoire au XIXe siècle," *La Revue bleue,* 25 August 1900.
—— *Manuel de bibliographie historique.* Paris, Hachette, 1896, 1901-1904.
—— *Questions d'histoire et d'enseignement.* Paris, Hachette, 1902.
—— "La Tradition de la France," reprinted in *Questions d'histoire et d'enseignement,* 2d ed. Paris, Hachette, 1906.
—— *La Vie en France du moyen age.* Paris, Hachette, 1908.
—— and C. Stein. *Archives de l'histoire de France.* Paris, Picard, 1891.
—— and Charles Seignobos. *Introduction aux études historiques.* Paris, Hachette, 1898.
Lanson, Gustave. "L'Esprit scientifique et la méthode de l'histoire littéraire," *Etudes françaises,* 1 (1 January 1925).
—— *Essais de méthode, de critique, et d'histoire littéraire.* Paris, Hachette, 1965.
—— "Les Etudes modernes dans l'enseignement secondaire," *L'Education de la démocratie.* Paris, Alcan, 1907.
—— "Le Patriotisme et l'école," *Revue bleue,* 16 September 1905, 565-568.
—— *L'Université et la société moderne.* Paris: Colin, 1902.
Lasserre, Pierre. *Alfred Croiset.* Paris, Nouvelle Librairie Nationale, 1909.

―――― *La Doctrine officielle de l'université: critique du haut enseignement de l'état, défense et théorie des humanités classiques.* Paris, Mercure de France, 1912.
Lavisse, Ernest. *A Propos de nos écoles.* Paris, Colin, 1895.
―――― "Le Concours pour l'agrégation d'histoire," *Revue internationale de l'enseignement,* 15 February 1881, pp. 137-151.
―――― La Faculté des Lettres de Paris," *Revue internationale de l'enseignement,* 15 April 1884, pp. 393-406.
―――― *L'Enseignement de l'histoire à l'école primaire.* Paris, Colin, 1912.
―――― *Essais sur L'Allemagne impériale.* Paris, Hachette, 1888.
―――― *Histoire de France: cours élémentaire.* Paris, Colin, 1875.
―――― *La Fondation de l'Université de Berlin à propos de la réforme de l'enseignement supérieur en France.* Paris, Hachette, 1876.
―――― *La Marche de Brandenbourg sous la dynastie ascanienne: étude sur l'une des origines de la monarchie prussienne.* Paris, Hachette, 1875.
―――― *Questions d'enseignement national.* Paris, Librairie Classique, Armand Colin et Cie, 1885.
―――― "La Société de L'Enseignement Supérieur. Actes de la Société, *Revue internationale de l'enseignement,* 1 (15 January 1881), 105.
―――― *Souvenirs.* Paris, C. Lévy, 1912.
―――― "Souvenirs d'une éducation manquée," *L'Education de la démocratie.* Paris, Alcan, 1907.
―――― *Un Ministre: Victor Duruy.* Paris, Colin, 1895.
―――― and Alfred Rambaud, eds. *Histoire générale du IVe siècle à nos jours.* 12 vols. Paris, Colin, 1892-1901.
Lefebvre, Georges. "L'Oeuvre historique d'Albert Mathiez," *Annales historiques de la Révolution française,* 9 (1932), 98-102.
Lefranc, Abel. *La Fondation et les commencements du Collège de France, 1530-1542.* Paris, Presses Universitaires de France, 1932.
Legrand, Louis. *L'Idée de patrie.* Paris, Hachette, 1897.
Leguay, Pierre. "M. Seignobos et l'histoire," *Mercure de France,* 88 (1910), 36-52.
―――― *La Sorbonne.* Paris, Grasset, 1910.
―――― *Universitaires d'aujourd'hui.* Paris, Grasset, 1912.
Leland, Waldo J. "L'Organisation internationale des études historiques," in *Histoire et historiens depuis cinquante ans,* (Paris, Alcan, 1927), II.
Lemaître, Jules. *Première Conférence.* Paris, Bureau de la Patrie Française, 1899.
Lexis, Wilhelm. *Die deutschen Universitäten.* Berlin, A. Asher, 1893.
―――― *A General View of the History and Organisation of Public Education in the German Empire,* trans. G. J. Tamson. Berlin, A. Asher, 1904.
Liard, Louis. *L'Enseignement supérieur en France, 1789-1893,* vol. II. Paris, Colin, 1894.
Lot, Ferdinand. *Diplômes d'études et dissertations inaugurales. Etude de statistique comparée.* Paris, Champion, 1910.
―――― "L'Enseignement de l'histoire et de l'histoire de l'art dans les universités d'Allemagne et de France. Etudes statistiques," *Bulletin de la Société d'Histoire Moderne,* 21 (February 1904), 114-121.
―――― *La Faculté de philosophie en Allemagne et les facultés des lettres et des sciences en France. Recherches statistiques.* Paris, Colin, 1896.

MacSay, Stephen. *Vers l'Education humaine: la laïque contre l'enfant.* Mons, Impr. Générale, 1911.
Madelin, Louis. "Le Mouvement historique en France depuis 1871," *Revue des études historiques* (May-June 1933), 267-282.
Maîtron, J. *Histoire du mouvement anarchiste en France.* Paris, Sudel, 1951.
Marcuse, Herbert. *Reason and Revolution.* Boston, Beacon Press, 1964.
Marrou, Henri Irenée. *De la Connaissance historique.* Paris, Editions de Seuil, 1959.
Massis, Henri. *Evocations.* Paris, Plon, 1931.
—— *La Guerre de trente ans.* Paris, Plon, 1940.
—— and Alfred de Tarde [Agathon]. *L'Esprit de la Nouvelle Sorbonne: la crise de la culture classique, la crise du français.* Paris, Mercure de France, 1911.
—— *Les Jeunes Gens d'aujourd'hui.* Paris, Plon-Nourrit, 1913.
Maurras, Charles. *Avenir de l'intelligence.* Paris, Nouvelle Librairie Nationale, 1909.
—— *Quand les français ne s'aimaient pas,* 2d ed. Paris, Nouvelle Librairie Nationale, 1926.
Maurice, Gaston. *Le Parti radical.* Paris, 1929.
Mayer, Arno J. *Dynamics of Counterrevolution in Europe.* New York, Harper Torchbooks, 1971.
McNeil, G. H. "Charles Seignobos," in Bernadotte Schmitt, ed., *Some Historians of Modern Europe.* Port Washington, N.Y., Kennikat Press, Inc., 1966.
Mellon, Stanley. *The Political Uses of History: A Study of Historians in the French Restoration.* Stanford, Stanford University Press, 1958.
Mitard, M. "Le Rôle de l'enseignement historique," *L'Enseignement public,* 10 (November 1927), 370-388.
Mitchell, Allan. "German History in France after 1870," *Journal of Contemporary History,* 2 (July 1967).
Monod, Gabriel. *Allemands et Français.* Paris, Sandoz et Fischbacher, 1872.
—— *La Chaire de l'histoire au Collège de France.* Paris, Editions de la Revue politique et littéraire et de la Revue scientifique, 1906.
—— [Pierre Molé]. *Exposé impartial de l'Affaire Dreyfus.* Paris, 1898.
—— "M. Fustel de Coulanges et son ouvrage sur les institutions de l'ancienne France," *La Revue politique et littéraire,* 43 (May 1875), 1037-1042.
—— *Gaston Paris.* Nogent-le-Rotron, Impr. de Daupeley-Gouverneur, 1903.
—— *A la Mémoire de M. le Professeur Georges Waitz.* Nogent-le-Rotron: Impr. de Daupeley-Gouverneur, 1886.
—— *Les Maîtres de l'histoire: Renan, Taine, Michelet.* Paris, Lévy, 1894.
—— *La Méthode en histoire.* Evreux, Charles Herissey et Fils, n.d.
—— *Michelet à l'Ecole normale.* Paris, Hachette, 1895.
—— *Portraits et souvenirs.* Paris, C. Lévy, 1897.
—— *De la Possibilité d'une réforme de l'enseignement supérieur.* Paris, Ernest Leroux, 1876.
—— *La Vie et la pensée de Jules Michelet: cours professé au Collège de France.* Paris, Champion, 1923.

Moreau, Pierre. *La Critique littéraire en France*. Paris, Colin, 1960.
Nietzsche, Friedrich. *The Use and Abuse of History*. Trans. Adrian Collins. New York, Liberal Arts Press, 1957.
Nisbet, Robert A., ed. *Emile Durkheim*. Englewood Cliffs, N.J., Prentice-Hall, 1965.
Nora, Pierre. "Ernest Lavisse: son rôle dans la formation du sentiment national," *Revue historique*, 228 (July 1962), 73-106.
D'Ocagne, Mortimer. *Les Grandes Ecoles de France*. Paris, Hetzel, 1887.
Péguy, Charles. "A nos amis, à nos abonnés," in *Oeuvres complètes*, vol. III. Paris, Editions de la Nouvelle Revue Française, 1927.
────── "L'Argent suite," in *Oeuvres complètes*, vol. XIV. Paris, Editions de la Nouvelle Revue Française, 1932.
────── "Clio I," in *Temporal and Eternal*, trans. Alexander Dru. New York, Harper & Brothers, 1958.
────── "Langlois tel qu'on le parle," in *Oeuvres complètes*, vol. XIII. Paris, Editions de la Nouvelle Revue Française, 1931.
────── "Un Nouveau Théologien, M. Fernand Laudet," in *Oeuvres complètes*, vol. XIII. Paris, Editions de la Nouvelle Revue Française, 1931.
────── "De la Situation faite à l'histoire et à la sociologie dans les temps modernes," *Cahiers de la quinzaine*, 8th ser. 3 (1906).
────── "De la Situation faite au parti intellectuel dans le monde moderne," Cahier of December 2, 1906, in *Oeuvres complètes*, vol. III. Paris, Editions de la Nouvelle Revue Française, 1927.
────── "De la Situation faite au parti intellectuel devant les accidents de gloire temporelle," in *Oeuvres complètes*, vol. III. Paris, Editions de la Nouvelle Revue Française, 1927.
────── "Zangwill," in *Oeuvres complètes*, vol. II. Paris, Editions de la Nouvelle Revue Française, 1922.
Peyre, Henri. "Durkheim: The Man, His Time, and His Intellectual Background," in Kurt H. Wolff, ed., *Essays on Sociology and Philosophy*. New York, Harper & Row, 1964.
Pfister, Christian. "Le Cinquantenaire de la Revue historique," in *Histoire et historiens depuis cinquante ans*. Paris, Alcan, 1927.
Pilant, Paul. *Le Patriotisme en France et à l'étranger*. Paris, Perrin, 1912.
Piobetta, J. B. *Les Institutions universitaires*. Paris, Presses Universitaires de France, 1951.
Prost, Antoine. *Histoire de l'enseignement en France, 1800-1967*. Paris, Colin, 1968.
Prou, Maurice. *L'Ecole des Chartes*. Paris, Picard, 1921.
Puaux, Frank. *Vers la Justice*. Paris, Fischbacher, 1906.
Ranke, Leopold von. *The Theory and Practice of History*. Ed. Georg G. Iggers and Konrad von Moltke. New York, Bobbs-Merrill, 1973.
Renan, Ernest. "L'Instruction supérieure en France," *Revue des deux mondes*, 1 May 1864.
────── *La Réforme intellectuelle et morale*. Paris, Calmann-Lévy, 1872.
Ribot, Alexandre. *La Réforme de l'enseignement secondaire*. Paris, Colin, 1900.
Ringer, Fritz K. *The Decline of the German Mandarins: The German Academic Community, 1890-1933*. Cambridge, Mass., Harvard University Press, 1969.

Roche, Alphonse. *Les Idées traditionalistes en France de Rivarol à Charles Maurras.* Urbana, Ill., University of Illinois Press, 1937.
Sagnac, Philippe. "Le Doctorat de M. Sagnac," *La Revue française,* 36 (1899).
Sartre, Jean-Paul. *What Is Literature?* trans. Bernard Frechtman. New York, Harper & Row, 1965.
Schmitt, Bernadotte, ed. *Some Historians of Modern Europe,* Port Washington, N.Y., Kennikat Press, Inc., 1966.
Schmitt, Hans A. *Charles Péguy: The Decline of an Idealist.* Baton Rouge, La., Louisiana State University Press, 1967.
Scott, John A. *Republican Ideas and the Liberal Tradition in France, 1870-1914.* New York, Columbia University Press, 1951.
Séailles, Gabriel. "Patrie et patriotisme," *La Grande Revue,* 25 July 1910.
Seignobos, Charles. "Les Conditions psychologiques de la connaissance en histoire," *Revue philosophique de la France et de l'étranger,* 24 (July-December 1887), 1-29.
——— "L'Enseignement de l'histoire comme instrument d'éducation politique," *Conférences du musée pédagogique.* Paris, Imprimerie Nationale, 1907.
——— L'Enseignement de l'histoire dans les facultés," *Revue internationale de l'enseignement,* 10 (October 1883), 1076-1088; 7 (July 1884), 35-60; 8 (August 1884), 97-111.
——— "L'Enseignement de l'histoire dans les universités allemandes," *Revue internationale de l'enseignement,* 1 (15 June 1881), 563-600.
——— "Ernest Lavisse," *La Revue universitaire,* 9 (1922), 257-264.
——— *Histoire sincère de la nation française.* Paris, Presses Universitaires de France, 1946.
——— *L'Histoire dans l'enseignement secondaire.* Paris, Colin, 1906.
——— *La Méthode historique appliquée aux sciences sociales.* Paris, Alcan, 1901.
——— *Le Régime de l'enseignement des lettres.* Paris, Impr. Nationale, 1904.
——— and others. *L'Education de la démocratie: leçons professées à l'Ecole des Hautes Etudes Sociales.* Paris, Alcan, 1907.
Shotwell, J. T. *At the Paris Peace Conference.* New York, Macmillan, 1927.
Siegel, Martin. "Henri Berr's *Revue de synthèse historique,*" *History and Theory,* 9 (1970), 322-334.
——— "Science and the Historical Imagination: Patterns of French Historiographical Thought, 1866-1914," Ph.D. diss., Columbia University, 1965.
Simiand, François, "Méthode historique et science sociale," *Revue de synthèse historique,* 2 (1903), 1-57.
Simon, W. M. *European Positivism in the Nineteenth Century.* Ithaca, N.Y., Cornell University Press, 1963.
Smith, Robert. "L'Atmosphère politique à l'Ecole normale supérieure à la fin du XIXe siècle," *Revue d'histoire moderne et contemporaine,* 20 (April-June 1973), 248-268.
La Société Amicale Gaston Paris, Bulletin, 1903-1904, 1905.
La Société d'histoire moderne. Statuts, liste de membres, communications. Paris, Société d'histoire moderne, 1904.
La Solidarité. Paris, Alcan, 1902.
Sorel, Georges. *Reflections on Violence,* trans. T. E. Hulme and J. Roth. Glencoe, Ill., The Free Press, 1950.

―――― *Le Système historique de Renan.* Paris, G. Jacques, 1905.
Soucy, Robert. *Fascism in France: The Case of Maurice Barrès.* Berkeley, University of California Press, 1972.
Stadler, Peter. *Geschichtschreibung und historisches Denken in Frankreich, 1789-1870.* Zurich, Berichthaus, 1958.
Steed, Henry Wickham. *Through Thirty Years, 1892-1922.* Garden City, N.J., Doubleday, Page & Co., 1924.
Stern, Fritz. *The Politics of Cultural Despair: A Study in the Rise of the Germanic Ideology,* Berkeley, University of California Press, 1961.
―――― , ed. *The Varieties of History.* Cleveland, World Publishing Co., 1965.
Sternhell, Zeev. *Maurice Barrès et le nationalisme français.* Paris, Colin, 1972.
Stock, Phyllis H. "New Quarrel of Ancients and Moderns: The French University and Its Opponents, 1899-1914," Ph.D. diss., Yale University, 1965.
"Sur les thèses en Sorbonne de Péguy," *Amitié Charles Péguy,* no. 76 (1960).
Throop, Palmer A. "Lucien Febvre," in S. William Halperin, ed., *Some Twentieth Century Historians.* Chicago, University of Chicago Press, 1961.
Tint, Herbert. *The Decline of French Patriotism: 1870-1914.* London, Weidenfeld & Nicolson, 1964.
Tiryakian, Edward. "A Problem for the Sociology of Knowledge: The Mutual Unawareness of Emile Durkheim and Max Weber," *Archives européennes de sociologie,* 7 (1966), 330-336.
Turner, Brian. "Emile Durkheim: The Social Functions of Social Science," unpub. paper, Columbia University, Department of Anthropology.
Worms, René. "Sur la définition de la sociologie," *Revue internationale de sociologie,* 1 (1893), 1-13.
La Vérité historique. Paris, 1900.
Vidal de la Blache, Paul. "Notice sur la vie et les oeuvres de M. Alfred Rambaud," *Mémoires de l'académie des sciences morales et politiques de l'Institut de France,* vol. XXVII. Paris, Firmin-Didot, 1910.
La Vie universitaire à Paris. Paris, Colin, 1918.
Weber, Eugen. *Action Française.* Stanford, Calif., Stanford University Press, 1962.
―――― *The Nationalist Revival in France, 1905-1914.* Berkeley, University of California Press, 1959.
Williams, Roger L. *The World of Napoleon III, 1851-1870.* New York, Collier Books, 1962.
Wilson, Edmund. *To the Finland Station: A Study in the Writing and Acting of History.* Garden City, N.Y., Doubleday and Co., Inc., 1953.
Xénopol, A.-D. *La Notion de "valeur" en histoire.* Versailles, Impr. Cerf, 1906.
―――― *Les Principes fondamentaux de l'histoire.* Paris, Leroux, 1899.

Index

Académie Française, 30, 107, 152, 173
Académie des Inscriptions et Belles Lettres, 28–29, 32. *See also* Benedictines
Action Française, 145, 204–205, 206–207. *See also* Right, French
Administration, Educational, historians role in, 60–62, 67, 239n17
Agrégation, 63, 64, 72, 84, 239n23. *See also* Examinations and degrees, university
Alcan, Félix, 167, 169
American historical profession, 4–5
Amicales, 148–151, 158. *See also* Unionism, French school teachers and
Analogy, use of in historical writing, 76, 86, 182, 185
Anarchism, 155–156, 162, 165
Andler, Charles, 115, 143
Annales d'histoire économique et sociale, 139, 211
Année sociologique, 114, 133, 136, 167, 170, 213–214. *See also* Durkheim, Emile; Sociology and sociologists
Antimilitarism, academic historians and, 100, 145–150, 154–157
Anti-Semitism, 141, 143, 164. *See also* Dreyfus Affair

Aron, Raymond, 87, 139, 251n51, 261n97
Aulard, Alphonse: named to Sorbonne chair, 68–69; criticizes Taine, 68, 175; founds new school of history, 69; role in Dreyfus Affair, 143; defends internationalism, 159–160; viewed as model of objective historian, 172–173, 199; conflict with Albert Sorel, 68, 174; training in rhetoric and literature, 69, 197; jingoism of during First World War, 209
Aumale, Duc d', 95

Baccalauréat, 56, 84, 188. *See also* Examinations and degrees, university
Bainville, Jacques, 210
Barrès, Maurice, 93, 143, 150, 158, 159, 162, 206
Basch, Victor, 143
Ben-David, Joseph, 13, 15, 232n15
Benedictines, 28, 29, 33, 71. See also Académie des Inscriptions et Belles Lettres
Bergson, Henri, 138, 249n11, 259n73
Bernard, Claude, 129
Berr, Henri: disenchantment with university training, 125–127; criticism of scholarly specialization, 128–129, 210;

intellectual influences on, 128–130; as advocate of synthetic history, 129–135; view of sociology, 130–131, 132, 135; relationship to academic historians, 132–133, 135, 137–138, 250n47; influence of on young generation, 139, 210–211
Bert, Paul, 157
Bertrand, Louis, 210
Bibliographies, historical, 102, 179
Biology, function of as model for historical knowledge, 124
Blanc, Louis, 68
Bloch, Marc, 139, 211, 213
Bocquillon, Emile, 152
Bouglé, Célestin, 143, 166–167, 169, 184, 246n1, 257n24, 259n72
Boulanger, Georges-Ernest, 53, 142, 163, 164
Bourgeois, Léon, 165–167, 261n98
Bourget, Paul, 143, 150, 206
Bourses d'études, see Scholarships, university
Boutroux, Emile, 11, 112, 128, 134–135, 184
Brière, Georges, 102
Broglie, Albert, Duc de, 105
Brunetière, Ferdinand, 176, 206, 258n43
Buisson, Ferdinand, 139, 143, 167, 243n6

Cahiers de la quinzaine, 202. See also Péguy, Charles
Cambridge Modern History, 105. See also Collaborative histories
Cantor, Norman, 9
Carnegie Endowment for International Peace, 99
Caron, Pierre, 69, 102, 171–175, 178–179
Cartesianism, 45, 112, 184, 187, 194
Catholic historians, 32–33
Chairs, professorial, in French universities: prior to academic reorganization, 22, 23, 27, 56; after academic reorganization, 60, 61, 63; in history, 59, 60, 63, 65–68, 138–139, 184; in literature, 60; in philosophy, 60, 184; in sociology, 114, 139, 167; in the science of education, 164, 167
Civic instruction, see Patriotism, academic historians' role in promoting
Clark, Terry N., 13, 15, 65, 232n18, 247n10
Classical languages (Greek and Latin), 7, 23, 189, 197–198, 205, 260n89
Classicism and the classical view of man, 191–194, 197–198
Clemenceau, Georges, 153, 155

Colin, Armand, publishing house of, 95
Collaborative histories, 104–106
Collège de France, 24, 65, 138, 139
Combes, Emile, 149
Comité des Travaux Historiques, 102
Comte, Auguste, 9, 57, 111, 256n20
Confédération Générale du Travail, 148, 150–151, 152–153, 158, 165. See also Syndicalism, revolutionary; Unionism, French school teachers and
Conférences, 26, 37, 46, 50, 56, 72
Conseil Supérieur de l'Instruction Publique, 61–62
Conseils de l'Université, 61–62
Conservatism, see Right, French
Counterrevolutionary tradition, See Right, French
Cours fermé, 62, 70, 72
Cousin, Victor, 80
Croce, Benedetto, 136
Croiset, Alfred: as dean of Sorbonne, 61, 67; named to Sorbonne chair, 67; role in Dreyfus Affair, 143; presidency of Ecole des Hautes Etudes Sociales, 169; views on educational reform, 67, 191, 194–196; intellectual influences on, 197, 198; rightist attacks on, 144, 204
La Culture générale, 23–24, 45, 63, 190–191

Democracy, relevance of historical instruction to, 58–59, 200
Deroulède, Paul, 143, 147, 150, 159, 162, 164
Desdevises du Dézert, Georges, 137
Diez, Friedrich, 38
Dilthey, Wilhelm, 87, 121, 139, 248n35
Dimier, Louis, 205
Diplomatics, 24, 26
Diplôme d'archiviste, 172. See also Examinations and degrees, university
Diplôme d'études supérieures, 84, 172. See also Examinations and degrees, university
Dissertations, doctoral, 63, 84, 103, 173
Division of labor in society, 164, 166, 177
Dreyfus Affair: threat to republican consensus posed by, 89, 141, 162–163, 166; academic historians' role in, 89, 142–145; antimilitarism as outgrowth of, 145–147, 150; as basis for cooperation between historians and sociologists, 168–170; literary intelligentsia's role in, 207, 251n6. See also Anti-Semitism
Drumont, Edouard, 164
Durkheim, Emile: training in philosophy, 10–11, 111–112, 183–184; career at

University of Bordeaux, 65, 112, 114; views toward history, 112–113, 168–169; Boutroux's influence on, 112, 128; Fustel de Coulanges's influence on, 112; Renouvier's influence on, 119, 184; and *L'Année sociologique*, 114–115; and the *Revue de synthese historique*, 135; named to Sorbonne chair, 139–140, 167, 188; role in Dreyfus Affair, 143; and solidarism, 166–167, 184; and educational reform, 190–191, 192–193, 197. *See also* Sociology and sociologists
Duruy, Albert, 37, 39
Duruy, Victor: accession to Ministry of Public Instruction, 20; concern about French educational decadence, 20–23, 46–47; failure to reform existing academic system, 23–24, 27, 44; and foundation of Ecole Pratique des Hautes Etudes, 25–27, 34; dismissal of, 35; and Gabriel Monod, 37; and Ernest Lavisse, 39; influence of on later educational reformers, 65

Ebray, Alcide, 158
Ecole alsacienne, 41
Ecole d'Athènes, 47
Ecole des Chartes: origins and character of, 24, 29, 47, 64, 84; prejudice against modern history at, 24, 171–172; criticism of, 52, 81; absorption of by Sorbonne, 64; graduates of, 27, 82, 83; lack of interest in methodology at, 137
Ecole des Hautes Etudes Sociales, 166–167, 169–171
Ecole Libre des Sciences Politiques, 12, 257n37
Ecole Normale Supérieure: intellectual influences on historians at, 5, 24, 36, 38, 69, 82–83; origins and character of before academic reorganization, 23–24, 36, 52, 64, 72, 113, 188; historians' criticism of, 38, 197–198; reform of, 61, 64, 188; historians' careers at, 65, 66–67, 72–73, 95–96, 128; sociologists' training at, 111–112
Ecole Pratique des Hautes Etudes. Fourth Section: foundation and character of, 25–27, 33, 37–38, 47, 72–73, 84; historians' teaching at, 26–27, 33, 37–38, 62, 65; function of as model for university reform, 44, 50, 55; relationship of to rest of university, 64; lack of interest in methodology at, 137; prejudice against modern history at, 171–172

Ecole Pratique des Hautes Etudes. Sixth Section, 214–215
Ecole de Rome, 47
Economic and social history, academic historians and, 103, 212–213
Emancipation de l'Instituteur, 150–151
Epigraphy, 26
Examinations and degrees, university, 63–64, 84

Faculties of letters (degree granting faculties), 21, 26, 33, 63, 64
Faculty of Letters of Paris, *see* Sorbonne
Fagniez, Gustave, 51, 144
Faguet, Emile, 105, 206, 258n43
Fayard, Arthème, 210
Febvre, Lucien, 9, 139, 211–213, 214
Ferry, Jules, 63, 66, 91, 96, 147
Fouillée, Alfred, 164, 166, 185–187
Francis I (King of France), 25
Franco-Prussian War, 40–44, 45–46
Frédéricq, Paul, 21, 72
Free-lance historical tradition, 27–28, 34, 44, 52, 173–176, 188, 201, 210
French Academy, *see* Académie Française
French Revolution, *see* Revolution, French
Funck-Brentano, Franz, 174, 175, 210, 257n37
Fustel de Coulanges, Numa Denis: greatness of, 12, 232n12; isolation from historical reform movement of, 12, 232n12; academic historians' criticism of, 12, 30–31, 198, 262n121; as director of the Ecole Normale, 66, 239n17; as tutor of the Prince Imperial, 91; and Ernest Lavisse, 95–96; influence on Durkheim of, 112; influence on Berr of, 128, 249n11; French right's praise of, 105, 206

Gaxotte, Pierre, 210
General culture, *see* La Culture générale
Generalizations in historical writing, 44, 54, 76–77, 81, 132–133, 181, 186
Germany: academic historical tradition of, 8, 27, 31–32, 36–37, 42–45, 51, 92, 106; universities of, 21–22, 25, 37–39, 56, 60, 73–74; French students' preparation in, 26–27, 36–37, 75–76, 112; Monod and, 36–37, 43–45, 51, 54; Lavisse and, 39, 41–42; Seignobos and, 75–77; neo-Kantianism in, 87; sociologists and, 112, 118, 120–121
Gide, Charles, 165–166
Girardet, Raoul, 96, 100

Grosjean, Georges, 158
Guild, function of as metaphor for academic historical profession, 25, 70
Guizot, François, 4, 28, 45, 48–49, 62, 102

Hague Peace Conference (1899), 146, 159
Halbwachs, Maurice, 166, 246n1
Hanotaux, Gabriel, 72, 143
Hauser, Henri, 143, 213
Havet, Louis, 143
Hayes, Carlton J. H., 99
Hegel, Georg Wilhelm Friedrich, 80, 130
Herr, Lucien, 115
Hervé, Gustave, 100, 154–155, 159
Historicism, 8–9, 120
Historische Zeitschrift, 30, 34
Hollinger, David A., 14
Hughes, H. Stuart, 210–211

Iggers, Georg G., 8, 9, 43
Imagination, use of in historical understanding, 52, 76, 78, 119
Instituteurs: as agents of republican patriotism, 92–93, 96–98, 147–148; influence of internationalism on, 146–147, 151, 154–157; unionization of, 148–155; influence of antimilitarism on, 150, 154–157; rightist criticism of, 152, 158; academic historians' support of, 159
International Center for Synthesis, 132
International Congress of Social Education, 166
Internationalism, 94, 146, 151, 154–156, 158–161

Jaffé, Philipp, 36
Jaurès, Jean, 103, 213
Journal des débats, 30

Kantianism and neo-Kantianism, 87, 121, 124, 164, 184
Kuhn, Thomas H., 14–15, 88, 232n17, 242n20

Labrousse, Ernest, 213
Lacombe, Paul, 116–120, 121, 123, 124, 135, 140
Lamartine, Alphonse de, 28, 68
Lamprecht, Karl, 136
Langlois, Charles Victor: Sorbonne historiography course of, 77, 82–83; training and career of, 82–83, 98, 107, 142; conception of scientific history of, 83–85, 99, 107, 136, 178–180; methodological writings of, 102, 179–181, 183; internationalism of, 160

Lanson, Gustave: role in Dreyfus Affair, 143; criticism of internationalist teachers, 157; role in Ecole des Hautes Etudes Sociales, 169; training and career of, 176, 197, 198–199; conception of scientific history of literature, 176–177, 188, 194–195, 198–199, 262n122; views on education, 197
Lasserre, Pierre, 204–206, 209
Lavisse, Ernest: relationship to Duruy, 37, 39; disenchantment with training, 38, 197–198; career before Franco-Prussian War, 39, 197; view of Germany, 39, 41–42; and patriotic uses of history, 41, 92–93, 93–97, 97–98, 143, 156, 168; and educational reform, 59–61, 70–71, 178, 188, 189–190; career after Franco-Prussian War, 66, 95–96; as author of textbooks and general histories, 66–67, 83, 97–98, 104, 105, 156; as patron of Langlois and Seignobos, 75, 82, 107; evolution of political views of, 94–95, 142; concern about excessive specialization, 105–106, 127; role in Dreyfus Affair, 144; role in Ecole des Hautes Etudes Sociales, 169; jingoism of during First World War, 209
Laws of development, historical, 11, 86, 118, 122–123, 129–130, 136, 183
League for the Defense of the Rights of Man, see Ligue pour la Défense des Droits de l'Homme
League of the French Fatherland, see Ligue de la Patrie Française
League of Patriots, 147
Lefebvre, Georges, 69
Leguay, Pierre, 59, 145
Lemaître, Jules, 206, 258n43
Levasseur, Emile, 213
Leygues, Georges, 149
Liard, Louis, 21, 26, 112, 138, 139
Licence, 56, 62–63, 63–64, 72. *See also* Examinations and degrees, university
Ligue de la Patrie Française, 144, 159, 251n6
Ligue pour la Défense des Droits de l'Homme, 143
Literary conception of history: prevalence of before academic reorganization, 6–7, 27–28, 34, 44–46, 81; Ecole Normale and, 23–24, 82, 83, 188; Aulard and, 68–69, 199; Faguet and, 105, 206; Durkheim and, 113; persistence of, 173–176, 188, 200
Literary intelligentsia, 30, 173–175, 188, 201, 205–207, 251n6
Literature, history of, 176–177, 188, 198–199

Literature, position in university curriculum of 7, 24, 60, 198
Littré, Emile, 57
Lot, Ferdinand, 58, 172
Louis-Philippe, 49
Lycées, 62-63, 97-98, 127, 188-191

Macaulay, Thomas Babington, 4
MacMahon, Marie-Edmé-Patrice-Maurice, 53, 95, 163
Madelin, Louis, 174, 175
Maître de conférences, 62, 66-67, 70
Marion, Henri, 164, 166
Maritain, Jacques, 183
Marrou, Henri Irenée, 139, 212
Marxism, see Socialism, international
Massis, Henri, 206
Mathiez, Albert, 69, 210
Maurras, Charles, 95, 143, 162, 205. See also Action Française
Mauss, Marcel, 143, 257n24, 259n69
Methods and methodology, historical: vain quest for a definition of, 19, 74; Seignobos's conception of, 75-82, 136, 181-182; Langlois's conception of, 83-84, 136, 178; Monod's conception of, 36-38, 44-45, 51-54, 86-87; academic historians' hesitancy to examine, 87-88, 137; Durkheim's conception of, 112-113; Lacombe's conception of, 116-121, 124; Xénopol's conception of, 121-124; Berr's conception of, 129-136; Lanson's conception of, 177-178; Fouillée's conception of, 185-187; *littérateurs'* criticism of, 201-207
Meyer, Paul, 82, 234n36
Michelet, Jules: as "literary" historian, 28-29; and the political uses of history, 49; and the history of the French Revolution, 68; as tutor of royal princesses, 91; academic historians' criticism of, 138, 195, 198, 262n121; twentieth century historians' return to, 210
Mignet François Auguste, 28, 45
Millerand, Alexandre, 167
Ministry of Public Instruction: powers of, 3, 59-60, 61, 97; Duruy's tenure at, 20-27, 34-35; historians' connection with, 62-63, 138; and unionization of school teachers, 148-149, 151; attitude toward "internationalism" in education of, 154
Modern and contemporary history: French university's prejudice against, 24, 87-88, 171-172; creation of Borbonne chair in, 66; problem of value judgments in, 87-88, 96-97, 173; increased interest in, 171-172
Monod, Gabriel: relations with Michelet and Fustel de Coulanges of, 36, 138, 198, 262n121; intellectual training of, 36-37, 197; and Germany, 36-37, 43, 44, 51, 54, 235n8; and Duruy, 37; at Ecole Pratique des Hautes Etudes, 37-38, 40; and Lavisse, 37, 39; and history as source of patriotism, 41-43, 126; criticism of French historical tradition of, 44-45, 51, 54, 198; and *Revue historique*, 51-54; and scientific conception of history, 52-54; and educational reform, 56, 71; professional advancement of after 1870, 67, 138; scholarly achievements of, 83, 98, 102; writings on historical method of, 36-38, 44-45, 51-54, 86-87; and Henri Berr, 132, 138, 250n47; role in Dreyfus Affair, 143, 170
Monographic historical writing, see Specialization, scholarly
Morel, Charles, 30-31, 234n36

Napoleon I, 64
Napoleon III, 25, 35, 47
Neo-idealism, 80, 120
Niebuhr, Barthold Georg, 43
Nietzsche, Friedrich, 115, 185

Objectivity in historical writing: Seignobos's view of, 79; Monod's view of, 86; neo-Kantians' view of, 87; faith in, 88-89, 90, 98-99, 174-175, 178, 209, 212; Lavisse's view of, 93; collective works and, 104-105; Caron's and Sagnac's view of, 174-175; Langlois's view of, 178; Croiset's view of, 196

Pacifism, 100, 146, 159, 160, 162
Paleography, 26, 66, 76
Panama scandal, 164
Paris, Gaston: at Ecole Pratique des Hautes Etudes, 27, 38, 39, 65-66; and philology, 27, 38, 65-66; at *Revue critique*, 34, 234n36; at Collège de France, 65; and German historical methods, 27, 38, 106
Patriotism, academic historians' role in promoting: after 1870, 43-44, 46, 54, 142-143, 146-147, 168; Duruy's view of, 20; Lavisse's view of, 42; Monod's view of, 43; as civic instruction in primary schools, 90-99, 150; reaction against after 1900, 146, 150, 156, 162; French Right and, 143, 150; Aulard's view of, 159-160; Langlois's view of, 160; and republican defense after

Dreyfus Affair, 170, 187; reaction against after First World War, 215
Péguy, Charles, 202–204, 208, 249n11
Periodicals, professional, 30–34, 47, 51–53, 67, 103, 132–139, 161, 173, 210–213
Petit-Dutaillis, Charles, 137
Philology, 26, 38, 65–66, 76
Philosophy: dominant position in *lycée* curriculum of, 23; university chairs in, 24, 60; academic historians' relationship to, 44, 80, 137, 183, 198; sociologists' relationship to, 112, 133, 136, 183–184; Henri Berr and, 128, 133, 135, 137; psychologists' relationship to, 183–184, 187; Fouillée's defense of, 185–187
Philosophy of history: academic historians' criticism of, 80–81, 130, 136, 212; social scientists' revival of interest in, 124–125, 130–131, 139, 212
Political approach to history, 89, 212
Political uses of history: under Second Empire, 23; general discussion of, 47–50, 98; early nineteenth century examples of, 48–49; in Third Republic (1871–1900), 49–50, 53, 92–96, 99–100, 142; in Third Republic (1900–1914), 145, 160–163, 167–168, 170, 187, 193–197, 212; in Third Republic (1919–1939), 210
Popularization in historical writing, 81–82, 85, 210, 211–212. *See also* Public, general, and history writing and teaching
Positivism: definitions of, 8–10; as paradigm of new school of history, 65, 139; neo-Kantian criticism of, 87; neo-idealist criticism of, 120–121, 135–136; Berr's criticism of, 138–139; Fouillée's criticism of, 186; Sorel's criticism of, 206; interwar reaction against, 210
Primary schools, historical instruction in, 3, 68, 90–93, 97–99, 156
Prince Imperial (pretender to Bonapartist throne), 39, 91, 94–95
Privatdozenten, 56, 62
Professionalism in historical writing: common formative experiences of academic historians as contribution to, 5; roadblocks to, 21, 52; and the Ecole Pratique des Hautes Etudes, 29, 34; and the *Revue critique,* 29, 31, 34; and the *Revue historique,* 52, 54; and the reformed university, 70–71; and the problem of public appeal, 85, 107, 127
Psychology, 118, 120, 124, 182, 183, 187, 259n74
Public, general, and history writing and teaching, 56, 70–72, 81, 105–106, 107, 127, 180, 212. *See also* Popularization in historical writing
Public courses (in French universities), 21–22, 55–56, 62, 71–73

Quinet, Edgar, 28, 45, 69

Rambaud, Alfred: as student at Ecole Normale with Monod and Lavisse, 38; at Ecole Pratique des Hautes Etudes, 38, 39–40; as adviser to Ferry, 63; as Minister of Public Instruction during academic reorganization, 64–65; named to Sorbonne chair, 66, 172; as co-editor with Lavisse, 66, 104; role in Dreyfus Affair, 144
Ranke, Leopold von, 8, 36, 234n32
Reform Act of 1902 (Secondary Education), 188–189, 205, 261n92
Renan, Ernest, 115, 129, 183, 206, 248n38
Renouvier, Charles, 119, 164, 166, 184, 247n5
Répétiteur (seminar leader), 26–27, 37, 38, 50
La Révolution française (periodical), 103, 173
Revolution, French: university course in history of, 68–69, 102–103; role in civic instruction of, 92, 96–97, 100; and doctrines of internationalism, 146, 159–160; and social solidarity, 163–164, 165–166, 191, 210
Revue critique d'histoire et de littérature, 30–32, 34, 47, 51
Revue des deux mondes, 30
Revue de l'enseignement primaire, 147, 155
Revue d'histoire économique, 213
Revue d'histoire moderne et contemporaine, 172
Revue historique, 51–54, 67, 103, 133, 161
Revue internationale de l'enseignement, 60–61, 75–76
Revue internationale de sociologie, 114
Revue des questions historiques, 32–33, 47, 53
Revue de synthèse historique, 11, 132–137, 139, 210–211
Revue universitaire, 115
Rhetoric, position in educational curriculum of, 7, 23, 128, 132, 188, 197
Rickert, Heinrich, 87, 124, 139
Right, French: failure in 1870s, 95, 161–162; revival of during Dreyfus Affair, 141, 162; new nationalism of, 143, 150; noted *littérateurs'* support of, 173–174, 177; attacks on academic historians by, 204–207; historians of during interwar period, 210

Ringer, Fritz K., 9-10
Romanticism, 28, 46, 195

Sagnac, Philippe, 69, 103, 171-175, 178-179
Schneider, Richard, 9
Scholarships, university, 56, 62-63
School teachers, French, *see* Instituteurs
Scientific conception of history: in pre-1870 France, 26, 30, 33, 51-52, 53-54; German origins of, 2, 8, 27, 31, 36-37, 44-46, 51-52; and reform of Sorbonne, 56-58, 71; Seignobos and Langlois and, 78-85, 99, 136, 179-182, 200; other academic historians and, 83, 86, 121-124, 172-174, 195-196, 198-199; philosophers' criticism of, 87, 128-136, 138-139, 185-187; and conflict with ideological function of historical instruction, 93-94, 98-100, 157; *littérateurs*, sociologists, and, 113f, 203f
Seignobos, Charles: early career of, 75-76, 107, 142; criticism of German historical methods of, 76-77; methodological writings of, 76-82, 89, 99, 107, 119, 181-182, 200; Sorbonne historiography course of, 77; scholarly achievements of, 83, 98, 105; role in Dreyfus Affair, 144; support for internationalism, 159; participation in Ecole des Hautes Etudes Sociales, 169, 171; and educational reform, 171, 181, 190, 200; later criticism of political approach to history of, 212, 265n12
Siegel, Martin, 232n12, 249n11
Simiand, François, 135
Social History, *see* Economic and social history
Socialism, international, 146, 147, 151, 159, 162, 164-165
Société de l'Enseignement Supérieur, 60-62
Société d'Histoire Contemporaine, 174
Société d'Histoire Moderne, 172, 174
Société de l'Histoire de la Révolution Française, 103
Societies, professional, 60-62, 103, 132, 172, 174
Sociology and sociologists: competition and disputes with historians, 108-114; relationship to philosophy, 112, 133, 135, 183-184, 187; foundations of as academic discipline, 111-115, 139-140, 167; Lacombe's analysis of, 116, 120; Berr's view of, 130-132; and synthetic history, 133-134, 135; role in Dreyfus Affair, 143; and solidarism, 166-167; later cooperation with historians, 169-170; decline of during interwar period, 213-214
Solidarity and solidarism, 164-167, 169, 184, 191
Sombart, Werner, 213
Sorbonne: defects of historical study at before reforms, 21, 23, 38-39, 52, 55-56; reform of, 55-72, 181, 183; professorial chairs at, 56, 60, 63, 65-66, 66-69; absorption of Ecole Pratique, Ecole des Chartes, and Ecole Normale by, 64-65; course in history of the French Revolution at, 68-69; historiography course at, 77-78; Langlois and scientific historical tradition at, 82-83; doctoral dissertations and theses in history at, 84, 172; sociology as academic discipline at, 112, 139-140, 167; scientific history of literature at, 188
Sorel, Albert, 12, 68, 105, 174, 175, 240n42, 257n37
Sorel, Georges, 153, 206
Specialization, scholarly: at Ecole des Chartes, 52; in professional historians' training, 63-64, 84; as division of labor in scholarship, 82, 103, 113, 177, 179; Langlois as foremost defender of, 84, 180-181; academic historians' second thoughts about, 106; sociologists' criticism of, 113, 114-115; Berr's criticism of, 128-130; Fouillée's criticism of, 186-187; Febvre's criticism of, 211
Spuller, Eugène, 148
Steed, Henry Wickham, 73
Stern, Fritz R., 127
Students (in French universities), 21, 26, 56, 65, 71, 74
Subjectivity in historical writing, *see* Objectivity in historical writing
Sybel, Heinrich von, 34, 43
Syndicalism, revolutionary, 100, 146, 152-157, 162, 165. *See also* Confédération Générale du Travail; Unionism, French school teachers and
Syndicat des Instituteurs et Institutrices, 148
Synthesis in history: Seignobos's early concern about, 76-77, 79, 81, 181; Lavisse, Rambaud, and collaborative approach to, 104; Durkheim criticism of history's neglect of, 114f; Boutroux and, 128; Renan's defense of, 129; Berr's advocacy of, 131-133, 138-139
Syveton, Gabriel, 159

Taine, Hippolyte, 12, 68, 123, 129, 174-176, 206, 237n49, 257n37

Textbooks, history: as vehicles for historians' influence, 3; Duruy sponsorship of, 20-21; poor quality of, 20, 91; Lavisse authorship of, 66-67, 97-98; academic historians' authorship of, 97-98; as source of political and patriotic education, 98-99; Hervé attacks on patriotic biases of, 154; anarchists' attacks on patriotic biases of, 156
Thalamas, François, 154
Theology, position of in university curriculum, 183
Thierry, Augustin, 28, 45, 48-49, 68
Thiers, Adolphe, 28, 62
Thureau-Dangin, Paul, 105
Treitschke, Heinrich von, 4, 43
Troeltsch, Ernst, 213

Union des Instituteurs Patriotes, 152
Unionism, French school teachers and, 148-158. *See also* Confédération Générale du Travail; Syndicalism, revolutionary

Value judgments in historical writing, *see* Objectivity in historical writing
Vandal, Albert, 174-175, 257n37
Vico, Giambattista, 130

Waddington, William, 62, 65
Waitz, Georg, 36-37
Wallon, Henri, 51, 66, 239n17
Weber, Max, 87, 121, 139, 201, 213
Windelband, Wilhelm, 87, 124
Worms, René, 114

Xénopol, Alexandre, 121-124, 248n43

Zola, Emile, 141, 143

Augsburg College
George Sverdrup Library
Minneapolis, Minnesota 55404